# General Responsibility Assignment Software Patterns (GRASP)

| Pattern | Description |
|---|---|
| **Expert** | Who, in the general case, is responsible?<br><br>Assign a responsibility to the information expert—the class that has the information necessary to fulfill the responsibility. |
| **Creator** | Who creates?<br><br>Assign class B the responsibility to create an instance of class A if one of the following is true:<br>1. B contains A 4. B records A<br>2. B aggregates A 5. B closely uses A<br>3. B has the initializing data for A |
| **Controller** | Who handles a system event?<br><br>Assign the responsibility for handling a system event message to a class representing one of these choices:<br>1. The business or overall organization (a façade controller).<br>2. The overall "system" (a façade controller).<br>3. An animate thing in the domain that would perform the work (a role controller).<br>4. An artificial class (Pure Fabrication) representing the use case (a use case controller). |
| **Low Coupling (evaluative)** | How to support low dependency and increased reuse ?<br><br>Assign responsibilities so that coupling remains low. |
| **High Cohesion (evaluative)** | How to keep complexity manageable?<br><br>Assign responsibilities so that cohesion remains high. |
| **Polymorphism** | Who, when behavior varies by type?<br><br>When related alternatives or behaviors vary by type (class), assign responsibility for the behavior–using polymorphic operations–to the types for which the behavior varies. |
| **Pure Fabrication** | Who, when you are desperate, and do not want to violate High Cohesion and Low Coupling?<br><br>Assign a highly cohesive set of responsibilities to an artificial class that does not represent anything in the problem domain, in order to support high cohesion, low coupling, and reuse. |
| **Indirection** | Who, to avoid direct coupling?<br><br>Assign the responsibility to an intermediate object to mediate between other components or services, so that they are not directly coupled. |
| **Don't Talk to Strangers (Law of Demeter)** | Who, to avoid knowing about the structure of indirect objects?<br><br>Assign the responsibility to a client's direct object to collaborate with an indirect object, so that the client does not need to know about the indirect object. Within a method, messages can only be sent to the following objects:<br>· The *this* object (or *self*).<br>· A parameter of the method.<br>· An attribute of self.<br>· An element of a collection which is an attribute of self.<br>· An object created within the method. |

# APPLYING UML
# AND PATTERNS

## AN INTRODUCTION TO
## OBJECT-ORIENTED ANALYSIS AND DESIGN

### CRAIG LARMAN

To join a Prentice Hall PTR Internet
mailing list, point to:
http://www.prenhall.com/mail_lists/

**Prentice Hall PTR**
**Upper Saddle River, New Jersey 07458**

ISBN 0-13-748880-7

9 780137 488803

90000

**Library of Congress Cataloging-in-Publication Data**

Larman, Craig.

    Applying UML and patterns : an introduction to object-oriented
analysis and design / Craig Larman
       p.     cm.
    Includes index.
    ISBN 0-13-748880-7
    1. Object-oriented methods (Computer science)  2. UML (Computer
science) 3. System analysis. 4. System design. I. Title.
QA76.9.035L37  1997
005.1'17--DC21                       97-33977
                                 CIP

Editorial/production supervision: *Dawn Speth White*
Art design director: *Jerry Votta*
Cover designer: *Bruce Kenselaar*
Manufacturing manager: *Alexis R. Heydt*
Marketing manager: *Stephen Solomon*
Acquisitions editor: *Paul Becker*
Editorial assistant: *Bart Blanken*

Published by Prentice Hall PTR
Prentice-Hall, Inc.
A Simon & Schuster Company
Upper Saddle River, NJ 07458

Prentice Hall books are widely used by corporations and government agencies
for training, marketing, and resale.

The publisher offers discounts on this book when ordered in bulk quantities.
For more information, contact: Corporate Sales Department, Phone: 800-382-3419;
Fax: 201-236-7141; E-mail: corpsales@prenhall.com; or write: Prentice Hall PTR,
Corp. Sales Dept., One Lake Street, Upper Saddle River, NJ 07458.

Printed in the United States of America
10 9 8 7 6 5 4 3 2 1

**ISBN   0-13-748880-7**

Prentice-Hall International (UK) Limited, *London*
Prentice-Hall of Australia Pty. Limited, *Sydney*
Prentice-Hall Canada Inc., *Toronto*
Prentice-Hall Hispanoamericana, S.A., *Mexico*
Prentice-Hall of India Private Limited, *New Delhi*
Prentice-Hall of Japan, Inc., *Tokyo*
Simon & Schuster Asia Pte. Ltd., *Singapore*
Editora Prentice-Hall do Brasil, Ltda., *Rio de Janeiro*

*For Julie*

*Without your support, this would not have been possible.*

*For Haley and  Hannah*

*Thanks for putting up with a distracted Daddy.*

# CONTENTS—SHORT

# CONTENTS—EXPANDED

# PART IV DESIGN PHASE (1) 159

# PREFACE

Congratulations and thank you for reading this book! You hold in your hands a practical guide and roadmap through the landscape of object-oriented analysis and design. Here is how it will benefit you.

*Design robust and maintainable object systems.*

First, the use of object technology is proliferating in the development of software—even more so with the widespread adoption of Java—and mastery of object-oriented analysis and design is critical for you to create robust and maintainable object-oriented systems. It also opens up new opportunities for you as an architect, analyst, and designer.

*Follow a roadmap through requirements, analysis, design and coding.*

Second, if you are new to object-oriented analysis and design, you are understandably challenged about how to proceed through this complex subject; this book presents a well-defined activity roadmap so that you can move in a step-by-step process from requirements to code.

*Use the UML to illustrate analysis and design models.*

Third, the Unified Modeling Language (UML) has emerged as the standard notation for modeling; so it is useful for you to be conversant in it. This book teaches the skills of object-oriented analysis and design using the UML notation.

*Improve designs by applying the "gang-of-four" and GRASP design patterns.*

Fourth, design patterns communicate the "best practice" idioms and solutions that object-oriented design experts apply in order to create systems. In this book you will learn to apply design patterns, including the popular "gang-of-four" patterns, and most importantly the GRASP patterns which communicate very fundamental principles of responsibility assignment in object-oriented design. Learning and applying patterns will accelerate your mastery of analysis and design.

*Learn efficiently by following a refined presentation.*

Fifth, the structure and emphasis in this book is based on years of experience in training and mentoring people in the art of object-oriented analysis and design. It reflects that experience by providing a refined, proven, and efficient approach to learning the subject so your investment in reading and learning is optimized.

| | |
|---|---|
| *Learn from a realistic exercise.* | Sixth, it exhaustively examines a single case study—to realistically illustrate the entire object-oriented analysis and design process, and goes deeply into thorny details of the problem; it is a realistic exercise. |
| *Translate to code.* | Seventh, it shows how to map object-oriented design artifacts to code in Java. |
| *Design a layered architecture.* | Eighth, it explains how to design a layered architecture and relate the graphical user interface layer to domain and system services layers. This is a matter of practical importance that is often overlooked. |
| *Design a framework.* | Finally, it shows you how to design an object-oriented framework and specifically applies this to the creation of a framework for persistent storage in a database. |

## Objectives

The overarching objective is this:

> Help students and developers create better object-oriented designs through the application of a set of explainable principles and heuristics.

By studying and applying the information and techniques presented here, you will become more adept at understanding a problem in terms of its processes and concepts, and designing a solid solution using objects.

## Intended Audience

This book is for the following audience:

- Developers with experience in an object-oriented programming language, but who are new—or relatively new—to object-oriented analysis and design.

- Students in computer science or software engineering courses studying object technology.

- Those with some familiarity in object-oriented analysis and design who want to learn the Unified Modeling Language notation, apply patterns, or who want to sharpen and deepen their analysis and design skills.

## Prerequisites

Some prerequisite knowledge is assumed—and necessary—to benefit from this book:

- Knowledge and experience in an object-oriented programming language such as C++, Java, or Smalltalk.

- Knowledge of fundamental object technology concepts, such as class, instance, interface, polymorphism, encapsulation, and inheritance.

Fundamental object technology concepts are not defined.

## Book Organization

The overall strategy in the organization of this book is that object-oriented analysis and design topics are introduced in an order similar to that of a software development project running across two iterative development cycles. The first development cycle introduces analysis and design. In the second development cycle, new analysis and design topics are presented and existing ones are explored more deeply.

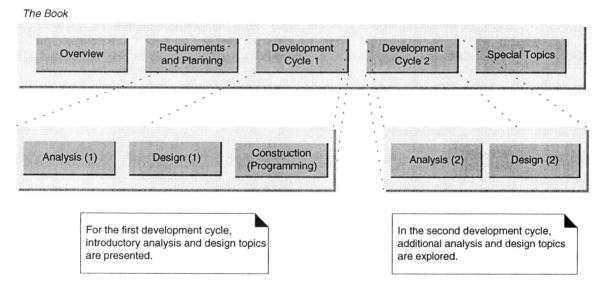

**Figure 1.** The organization of the book follows that of a development project.

# Motivation for this Book

Object technology holds great promise, but its potential will not be fully realized without the appropriate skills. It is my goal to promote the successful adoption of object technology through the skillful activity of object-oriented analysis and design, and to promote the acquisition of related abilities, because I observe these are critical for the successful creation and maintenance of significant systems.

# Acknowledgments

Thanks to all the users and students of the UML and object-oriented analysis and design who I have tried to assist; they are my best teachers.

Special thanks to the reviewers of this book (or portions), including Kent Beck, Jens Coldewey, Clay Davis, Tom Heruska, Luke Hohmann, David Norris, David Nunn, Brett Schuchert, and the entire Mercury team. Thanks to Grady Booch for reviewing a tutorial related to this work, and to Jim Rumbaugh for some feedback related to the relationship between the UML and process.

For insightful feedback on process and models, thanks to Todd Girvin, John Hebley, Tom Heruska, David Norris, David Nunn, Charles Rego, and Raj Wall.

Many thanks to Grady Booch, Ivar Jacobson, and Jim Rumbaugh for the development of the Unified Modeling Language; creating an open, standard notation in the current Tower of Babel environment is most welcome. In addition, I have learned much from their teachings.

Thanks to my colleague Jef Newsom for providing the case study Java solution.

Thanks to my publisher at Prentice-Hall, Paul Becker, for believing that this would be a worthwhile project.

Finally, a special thanks to Graham Glass for opening a door.

# About the Author

Craig Larman has a B.Sc. and M.Sc. in computing science and since 1978 has been developing large and small software systems on platforms ranging from mainframes to microcomputers, using software technologies ranging from 4GLs to logic programming to object-oriented programming.

In the early 1980s he fell in love with artificial intelligence and knowledge systems programming techniques, from which he received his first exposure to object-oriented programming (in Lisp). He has taught and worked with object-oriented programming in Lisp since 1984, Smalltalk since 1986, C++ since 1991, and recently Java, in conjunction with teaching a variety of object-oriented analysis and design methods. He has assisted over 2,000 students in learning object technology topics.

He is currently Principal Instructor at ObjectSpace, a company specializing in distributed computing, agents, and object technology.

Craig may be reached at clarman@acm.org

## Typographical Conventions

This is a **new term** in a sentence.

This is a *Class* or *method* name in a sentence.

This is an author reference [Bob67].

A language independent scope resolution operator "--" is used to indicate a method and its associated class as follows: *ClassName--methodName()*.

## Production Notes

The manuscript of this book was created with Adobe FrameMaker. All drawings were done with Visio. The body font is New Century Schoolbook.

# PART I INTRODUCTION

# OBJECT-ORIENTED ANALYSIS AND DESIGN

```
┌─────────────────────────────────────────────────────────────┐
│                                                               │
│                         Objectives                            │
│                                                               │
│   ■  Compare and contrast analysis and design.                │
│                                                               │
│   ■  Define object-oriented analysis and design.              │
│                                                               │
│   ■  Relate by analogy object-oriented analysis and design    │
│      to organizing a business.                                │
│                                                               │
└─────────────────────────────────────────────────────────────┘
```

## 1.1 Applying UML, Patterns, and Object-Oriented Analysis and Design

*Develop skills in OOA/D*

What does it mean to have a well-designed object-oriented system? This book assists developers and students in the application and development of practical skills in object-oriented analysis and design. These skills are essential for the creation of well-designed, robust, and maintainable software systems using object technology and object-oriented programming languages such as C++, Java, or Smalltalk.

The proverb "owning a hammer doesn't make one an architect" is especially true with respect to object technology. Knowing an object-oriented language (such as Java) and access to a rich library (such as the Java library) is a necessary but insufficient first step in creating object systems. Analyzing and designing a system from an object perspective is also critical.

The practice of object-oriented analysis and design is illustrated in a relatively thorough single case study that is followed throughout the book, going deep enough into the analysis and design so that many of the gory details of what must be considered and solved in a realistic problem are considered, and solved.

"UML" stands for **Unified Modeling Language**, a notation (mainly diagrammatic) for modeling systems using object-oriented concepts. This book helps developers learn the UML notation, and applies it to a case study.

How should responsibilities be allocated to classes of objects? How should objects interact? What classes should do what? These are critical questions in the design of a system. Certain tried-and-true solutions to design problems can be (and have been) expressed as a set of principles, heuristics or **patterns**—named problem-solution formulas that codify exemplary design principles. This book, by teaching patterns, supports quick learning and skillful use of these fundamental object-oriented design idioms.

Given many possible activities from requirements through to implementation, how should a developer or teams of developers proceed? This book presents a *sample* **development process** which describes a possible order of activities and a development life-cycle. It does not, however, prescribe a definitive process or method; it provides a sample of common steps.

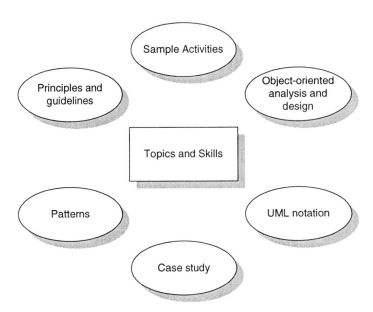

**Figure 1.1** Topics and skills covered

> In conclusion, this book helps a developer:
>
> ■ Apply principles and patterns to learn how to create better designs.
>
> ■ Follow a set of common activities in analysis and design.
>
> ■ Create useful artifacts in the UML notation.
>
> It illustrates this in the context of a single case study.

## 1.2 Assigning Responsibilities

*Assigning responsibilities to components is the most critical design skill.*

There are many possible activities and artifacts in analysis and design, and a wealth of principles and guidelines. Suppose we must choose a single practical skill from all the topics discussed here—a "desert island" skill. What would it be?

> The most single important ability in object-oriented analysis and design is to skillfully assign responsibilities to software components.

Why? Because it is the one activity which must be performed (it is inescapable) and it has the most profound effect on the robustness, maintainability, and reusability of software components.

Next to assigning responsibilities, a close second in terms of importance is finding suitable objects or abstractions. Both are critical; responsibility assignment is emphasized because it tends to be the more challenging skill to master.

On a real project, a developer might not have the opportunity to perform any other analysis or design activities—the "rush to code" development process. Even in this situation, assigning responsibilities is inevitable.

Consequently, the design phase of this book emphasizes principles in responsibility assignment, and provides tools to help a developer master this skill.

> Nine fundamental responsibility assignment principles, codified in the GRASP patterns, are presented and applied to help master how to assign responsibilities.

This is not to suggest that other activities are unimportant. For example, it is essential to create a conceptual model which identifies concepts (objects) in the problem domain. However, as a "desert island" skill, knowing how to assign responsibilities is what ultimately makes or breaks a system.

## 1.3    What is Analysis and Design?

*Analysis—investigation*

*Design—solution*

To create a software application, a description of the problem and requirements is required—what the problem is about and what a system must do. **Analysis** emphasizes an *investigation* of the problem rather than how a solution is defined. For example, if a new computerized library information system is desired, what are the business processes related to its use?

To develop an application, it is also necessary to have high level and detailed descriptions of the logical solution and how it fulfills requirements and constraints. **Design** emphasizes a *logical solution*, how the system fulfills the requirements. To illustrate, how exactly will the library information system software capture and record book loans? Ultimately, designs can be implemented in software and hardware.

## 1.4    What is Object-Oriented Analysis and Design?

*OO analysis—concepts?*

*OO design—software objects?*

The essence of **object-oriented analysis and design** is to emphasize considering a problem domain and logical solution from the perspective of objects (things, concepts, or entities) as shown in Figure 1.2.

During **object-oriented analysis**, there is an emphasis on finding and describing the objects—or concepts—in the problem domain. For example, in the case of the library information system, some of the concepts include *Book, Library* and *Patron*.

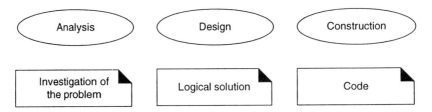

**Figure 1.2** Meaning of development activities.

During **object-oriented design**, there is an emphasis on defining logical software objects that will ultimately be implemented in an object-oriented programming language. These software objects have attributes and methods. To illustrate, in the library system, a *Book* software object may have a *title* attribute and a *print* method (see Figure 1.3).

Finally, during **construction** or **object-oriented programming**, design components are implemented, such as a *Book* class in C++, Java, Smalltalk, or Visual Basic.

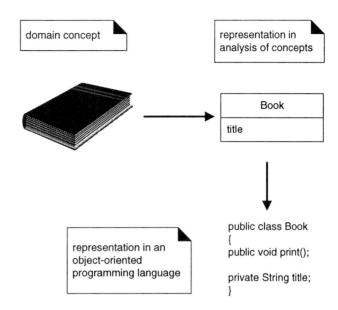

**Figure 1.3** Object-orientation emphasizes representation of objects.

# 1.5     An Analogy—Organizing the MicroChaos Business

*Organizing a busi-*
*ness and OOA/D*
*are analogous*

Some of the major steps in object-oriented analysis and design can be illustrated by analogy to how to organize a business.

## 1.5.1     *MicroChaos is growing fast...*

Imagine you are the founder and chief executive officer of MicroChaos, a recent start-up company specializing in software that applies the mathematical models of chaos theory to stock market analysis (it has really been done). Your flagship product is *MicroButterfly*.

As a booming startup, everyone shared the work: answering phones, handling orders, writing the software. Business has been unpredictably successful, there are many new employees, and everyone is getting unfocused, doing too many different tasks. So now it is time to add some organization to the business. So how do you, as chief executive officer, proceed in organizing people and tasks?

## 1.5.2 What are the business processes?

Step one is to consider what the business must do—its business processes—in order to keep running: making sales, paying employees and creditors, developing software.

In object-oriented analysis and design method terms, this is analogous to **requirements analysis**, in which business processes and requirements are discovered and expressed in use cases. **Use cases** are textual narrative descriptions of the processes in an enterprise or system, as shown here.

| | |
|---|---|
| Use case: | Place an Order |
| Description: | This use case begins when the a customer phones a sales representative to request a purchase of MicroButterfly. The sales representative records the customer and product information in a new order. |

Identifying processes and recording them in use cases is not actually an object-oriented analysis activity; there is nothing object-centric about it.

However, it is an important and widely practiced early step in what are termed object-oriented analysis and design methods. Also, use cases are part of the UML. Here is our analogy so far.

| Business Analogy | Object-oriented Analysis & Design | Associated Documents |
|---|---|---|
| What are the business processes? | Requirements analysis | Use cases |

## 1.5.3 What are the roles in the organization?

The next step is to identify the roles of people who will be involved in the processes: customer, sales representative, software engineer, and so on.

In object-oriented analysis and design terms, this is analogous to **object-oriented domain analysis** expressed with a conceptual model. A **conceptual model** illustrates the different categories of things in the domain; not just the roles of people, but all things of interest, as shown in Figure 1.4.

| Customer | Order | Sales Representative |
| --- | --- | --- |

**Figure 1.4** Concepts in the business.

| Business Analogy | Object-oriented Analysis & Design | Associated Documents |
| --- | --- | --- |
| What are the business processes? | Requirements analysis | Use cases |
| What are the employee roles? | Domain analysis | Conceptual model |

## 1.5.4 Who does what? How do they collaborate?

Having identified your business processes and people, it is time to determine how to fulfill the processes. This is a design—or solution-oriented—activity. Working with your employees, you define their responsibilities in order to complete the tasks needed to fulfill a process. You  also need to define how people will collaborate, or share the work.

In object-oriented analysis and design terms, this activity is analogous to **object-oriented design** emphasizing responsibility assignment. **Responsibility assignment** means to allocate tasks and responsibilities to the various software objects in the application, just as responsibilities and tasks are allocated to the roles of people. Software objects usually collaborate or interact in order to fulfill their responsibilities, as do people.

The illustration of responsibility assignment and object interactions is often expressed with **design class diagrams** and **collaboration diagrams**—diagrams which show the definition of classes and the flow of messages between software objects.

| Business Analogy | Object-oriented Analysis & Design | Associated Documents |
|---|---|---|
| What are the business processes? | Requirements analysis | Use cases |
| What are the employee roles? | Domain analysis | Conceptual model |
| Who is responsible for what? How do they interact? | Responsibility assignment, interaction design | Design class diagrams, collaboration diagrams |

## 1.6    An Example of Object-Oriented Analysis and Design

*A simple example to see the big picture*

A significant amount of information is required to fully explain object-oriented analysis and design. Before getting lost in a forest of details, here is a bird's eye view of some of the steps and diagrams using a simple example—a "dice game" in which a player rolls two die. If the total is seven, they win; otherwise, they lose.

The notations used are part of the **UML**.

Please note that not all possible steps and diagrams are presented in this example; only the most essential and commonly used steps are shown.

### 1.6.1    Defining Use Cases

Understanding the requirements includes, in part, understanding the domain processes and the external environment—external actors who participate in processes. These domain processes can be expressed in **use cases**—narrative descriptions of domain processes in a structured prose format.

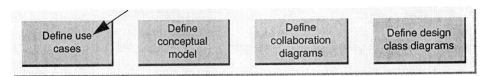

Use cases are not actually an object-oriented analysis artifact, they simply describe processes, and can be equally effective in a non-object technology project. However, they are a useful preliminary step in describing the requirements of a system.

For example, in the dice game, here is the *Play a Game* use case.

| | |
|---|---|
| Use case: | Play a Game |
| Actors: | Player |
| Description: | This use case begins when then the player picks up and rolls the dice. If the dice total seven, they win; otherwise, they lose. |

## 1.6.2    Defining a Conceptual Mode

Object-oriented analysis is concerned with creating a specification of the problem domain and the requirements from the perspective of classification by objects, and from the perspective of understanding the terms used in the problem domain. A decomposition of the problem domain involves an identification of the concepts, attributes, and associations in the domain that are considered important. The result can be expressed in a **conceptual model**, which is illustrated in a set of diagrams that depict concepts (objects). l

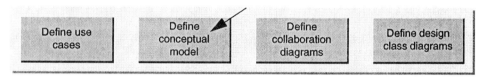

For example, as shown in Figure 1.5, in the domain of the dice game, a portion of the conceptual model shows the concepts *Player*, *Die* and *DiceGame*, their associations, and attributes:

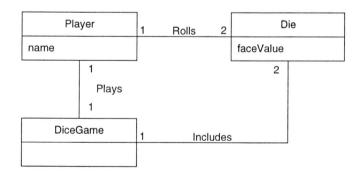

**Figure 1.5** Conceptual model of the dice game.

The conceptual model is not a description of software components; it represents concepts in the real-world problem domain.

## 1.6.3    Defining Collaboration Diagrams

Object-oriented design is concerned with defining logical software specifications that fulfill the functional requirements based on decomposition by classes of objects. An essential step in this phase is the allocation of responsibilities to objects and illustrating how they interact via messages, expressed in **collaboration diagrams**. Collaboration diagrams show the flow of messages between instances and the invocation of methods.

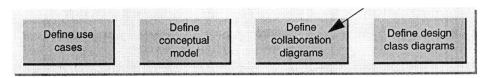

For example, assume that a simulation in software of the dice game is desired. This collaboration diagram in Figure 1.6 illustrates the essential step of playing by sending messages to instances of the *Player* and *Die* classes.

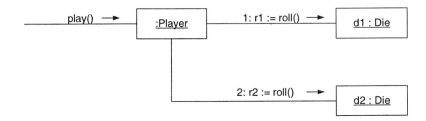

**Figure 1.6** Collaboration diagram illustrating messages between software objects.

## 1.6.4    Defining Design Class Diagrams

In order to define a class, several questions must be answered:

- How do objects connect to other objects?

- What are the methods of a class?

To answer these questions, inspect the collaboration diagrams, which suggests the necessary connections between objects, and the methods that each software class must define. A diagram expressing these design details is the **design class diagram**. These illustrate class definitions that are to be implemented in software.

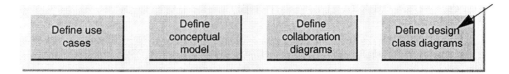

For example, in the dice game, an inspection of the collaboration diagram leads to the following design class diagram. Since a *play* message is sent to a *Player* instance, *Player* requires a *play* method, while *Die* requires a *roll* method.

In contrast to the conceptual model, this diagram does not illustrate real-world concepts; it describes software components.

To illustrate how objects connect to each other via attributes, a line with an arrow at the end may suggest an attribute. For example, *DiceGame* has an attribute that points to an instance of a *Player.*

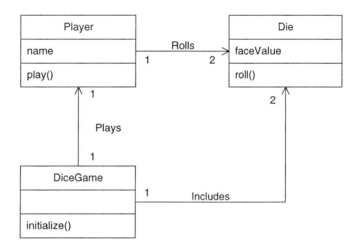

**Figure 1.7** Design class diagram of software components.

The design class diagram in Figure 1.7 is not complete; it represents only the start of the software specifications needed to fully define each class.

## 1.6.5   Summary of the Dice Game Example

The dice game is a very simple problem, presented in order to focus on some of the steps and artifacts in object-oriented analysis and design rather than on the problem domain. Future chapters explore analysis and design and these artifacts in closer detail, with a more complex and realistic problem.

## 1.7      Object Versus Function-Oriented Analysis and Design

Software projects are complex, and decomposition (divide-and-conquer) is the primary strategy to deal with this complexity—breaking a problem up into manageable units. Prior to object-oriented analysis and design, the most popular approach to decomposing a problem was **structured analysis and design**, whose dimension of decomposition is primarily by function or process, resulting in a hierarchical breakdown of processes composed of sub-processes.

However, other dimensions of decomposition are possible; object-oriented analysis and design emphasizes decomposing a problem space by objects rather than by functions, as shown in Figure 1.8.

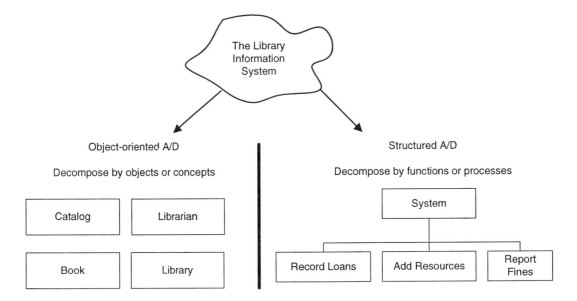

**Figure 1.8** Object-oriented versus function-oriented decomposition.

## 1.8      Warning: "Analysis" and "Design" Can Lead to Terminology Wars

The division between analysis and design is fuzzy; analysis and design work exists on a continuum (see Figure 1.9), and different practitioners of "analysis and design" methods classify an activity at varying points on the continuum. Therefore, it is not helpful being rigid about what constitutes an analysis versus a design step.

More analysis-oriented

More design-oriented

- what
- requirements
- investigation
  of domain

- how
- logical solution

**Figure 1.9** Analysis and design activities exist on a continuum.

Since different people and methods mean a variety of things by these terms, debating the definition is not particularly constructive; what is important is understanding how to solve the problem of creating and maintaining software better, faster, and cheaper.

Nevertheless, some consistent distinction is useful in practice between *investigation* (analysis) and *solution* (design) because it is advantageous to have a well-defined step that emphasizes an inquiry of what the problem is before diving in to how to create a solution. It is also sets an expectation of suitable behavior among the teams members; for example, during analysis members expect to emphasize *understanding* the problem while deferring issues related to the solution, performance, and so on.

# 1.9   The Unified Modeling Language

The UML is a "a language for specifying, visualizing and constructing the artifacts of software systems..." [BJR97]. It is a notational system (including semantics for its notations) aimed at modeling systems using object-oriented concepts.

The UML is an emerging industry standard for object-oriented modeling. It started as an effort by Grady Booch and Jim Rumbaugh in 1994 to combine their two popular methods—the Booch and OMT (Object Modeling Technique) methods. Later they were joined by Ivar Jacobson, the creator of the OOSE (Object-Oriented Software Engineering) method. In response to an OMG (Object Management Group, an industry standards body) request to define a standard modeling language and notation, the UML was submitted in 1997 as a candidate.

Regardless of OMG acceptance or not, the UML has received *de facto* approval in industry, since its creators represent very popular first-generation object-oriented analysis and design methods. Many software development organizations and CASE tool vendors have adopted the UML, and it is very probable that it will become a worldwide standard used by developers, authors, and CASE tool vendors.

This book does not cover every minute aspect of the UML, which is a relatively large body of notation. It focuses on diagrams which will be used frequently, and the most commonly used features within those diagrams.

For a thorough treatment of raw UML notation, the complete specification is available at Rational Corporation's webset: www.rational.com

There are at least ten different notations available for object-oriented analysis and design artifacts; this situation hinders effective and consistent communication, the ability to learn, and CASE tools. The UML authors—Booch, Jacobson and Rumbaugh—have done a great service to the object technology community by creating a standardized modeling language which is elegant, expressive, and flexible.

The UML is a language for modeling; it does not guide a developer in how to *do* object-oriented analysis and design, or what development process to follow.

Consequently, methodologists will continue to define methods, models, and development processes for the effective creation of software systems; only now they can do so in a common language—the UML.

# INTRODUCTION TO A DEVELOPMENT PROCESS

## Objectives

- Motivate the order of the subsequent chapters, which follow the process steps discussed in this chapter.

- Follow a simple development process from requirements through to implementation.

## 2.1    Introduction

A **software development process** is a method to organize the activities related to creation, delivery, and maintenance of software systems.

This chapter provides a very brief introduction to fundamental activities in a process, laying out a sample roadmap for major steps. The motivation for this discussion at this point is:

- The coming chapters introduce object-oriented analysis and design by following these activities.

- Following a process similar to the one presented here provides a foundation for creating a manageable, repeatable, and successful development project.

For additional process-related topics, please see Chapter 37.

## 2.1.1    Recommended Process and Models—RPM

The UML does not define a standard process. The UML authors recognize that a robust modeling language and process are both important. They will offer their advice on what constitutes a suitable process in separate publications from the UML, because process standardization was outside the scope of the UML definition.

Neither does this book prescribe a standard or new process.

> More important than following an official process or method is that a developer acquire skill in how to create a good design, and that organizations foster this kind of skill development. This comes from mastering a set of principles and heuristics related to identifying and abstracting suitable objects and to assigning responsibilities to them.

This book presents a fairly typical view of best practices, basic activities and models in a development process for object-oriented systems based on an iterative and incremental, use case driven approach. The suggested steps and models are a *tour* through the landscape of software development using object technology, rather than a formula. These sample activities are offered as a starting point for discussion, experimentation, and the creation of a custom development process suitable for your organization's needs.

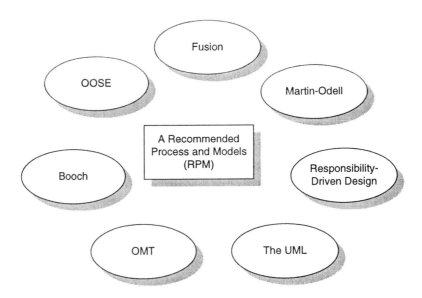

**Figure 2.1** Influences on the RPM described here.

This is not a new method, but a description of fairly common recommended process and models (RPM) applied by practitioners and presented in other object-oriented analysis and design methods under varying names and with slight shifts in emphasis [Rumbaugh97]. For convenience, the name *RPM* will occasionally be used to suggest common recommended process and models, and also to suggest the cyclical nature of iterative development.

The primary influences on the RPM described here (see Figure 2.1) include the author's development experience, development work at ObjectSpace, the UML itself, Fusion [Coleman94], Martin-Odell [MO95], Responsibility-Driven Design [Wirfs-Brock90], OOSE (Objectory) [Jacobson92], OMT [Rumbaugh91], and Booch [Booch94].

## 2.1.2   Scope

Fundamentally, a process description includes the activities from requirements through to delivery. Additionally, a complete process addresses broader issues related to the industrialization of software development, such as the long-term life-cycle of a product, documentation, support and training, parallel work and coordination between parties.[1] This introduction emphasizes only basic activities, with minimal elaboration.

Several essential process steps and issues will be ignored in this exploration, such as: conception, planning, parallel team interaction, project management, documentation, and testing.

These steps are bypassed because they are outside of the core purpose of this book—learning and applying skills in object-oriented analysis and design—or because the scope of the topic is too large to adequately investigate.

# 2.2   The UML and Development Processes

The UML standardizes artifacts and notation, but it does not define a standard development process. Reasons include:

1.   To increase the likelihood of widespread acceptance of a standard modeling *notation* without having to commit to a standard process.

2.   There is significant variability in what constitutes an appropriate process, depending on staff skills, research-development ratio, nature of the problem, tools, and so on.

---

1. Jacobson distinguishes between a *method*, which covers the individual and sequential steps in development, and a *process*, which scales up a method to larger-scale team development and industrialization issues [Jacobson92]. Although this is a relevant distinction, for simplicity in what is already a terminology-laden domain, I will not stress the difference.

That said, general principles and typical steps that guide a successful process can be explained.

# 2.3    Macro-level Steps

At a high level, major steps in delivering an application include the following (shown in Figure 2.2):

1. **Plan and Elaborate**—planning, defining requirements, building prototypes, and so on.

2. **Build**—the construction of the system.

3. **Deploy**—the implementation of the system into use.

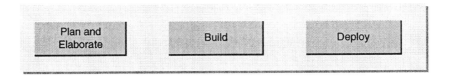

**Figure 2.2** Macro-level steps in development.

# 2.4    Iterative Development

An iterative life-cycle is based on successive enlargement and refinement of a system through *multiple* development cycles of analysis, design, implementation, and testing.

The system grows by adding new functions within each development cycle. After a preliminary Plan and Elaborate" phase, development proceeds in a Build phase through a series of development cycles.

Each cycle tackles a relatively small set of requirements, proceeding through analysis, design, construction, and testing (see Figure 2.3). The system grows incrementally as each cycle is completed.

This is in contrast to a classic waterfall life-cycle in which each activity (analysis, design, and so on) is done once for the entire set of system requirements.

Advantages of iterative development include:

■ The complexity is never overwhelming.

■ Early feedback is generated, because implementation occurs rapidly for a small subset of the system.

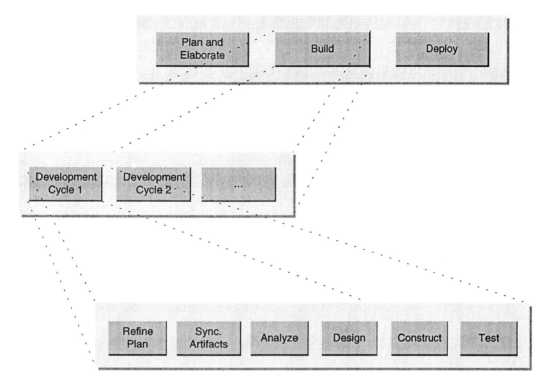

**Figure 2.3** Iterative development cycles.

## 2.4.1    *Time-boxing a Development Cycle*

A useful strategy within each development cycle is to bound it within a time-box—a rigidly fixed time, such as four weeks. All work must be accomplished in that time frame. A range between two weeks and two months is suitable. Any less, and it is difficult to complete tasks; any more, and the complexity becomes overwhelming, and feedback is delayed (see Figure 2.4).

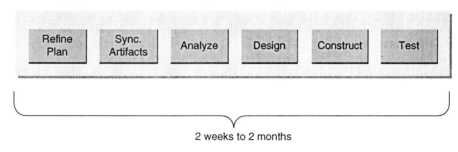

**Figure 2.4** Time-boxing a development cycle.

To succeed with a time-box schedule, it is necessary to choose the requirements carefully, and to have the development team be responsible for the choice—they are the ones responsible for meeting the deadline.

## 2.4.2   Use Cases and Iterative Development Cycles

A use case is a narrative description of a domain process, such as *Borrow Books from a Library*.

> Iterative development cycles are organized by use case requirements.

That is to say, a development cycle is assigned to implement one or more use cases, or simplified versions of use cases (which is quite common when the complete use case is too complex to tackle in one cycle). See Figure 2.5.

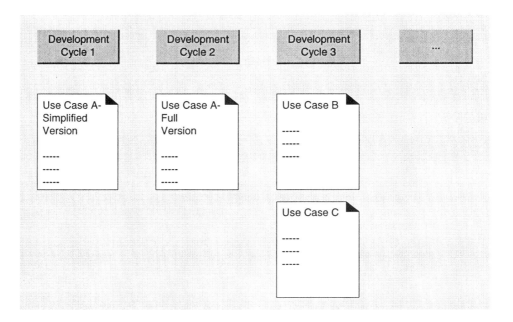

**Figure 2.5**  Use case driven development cycles.

In addition to the relatively evident use case requirements that need to be tackled, some development cycles—especially early ones—must focus on non-evident requirements, such as the creation of supporting services (persistence, security, and so on).

## 2.4.3 Ranking Use Cases

Use cases should be ranked, and high ranking use cases should be tackled in early development cycles. The overarching strategy is to first pick use cases that significantly influence the core architecture by fleshing out the domain and high-level services layers, or which are critical high-risk use cases.

# 2.5 The Plan and Elaborate Phase

The Plan and Elaborate phase of a project includes the initial conception, investigation of alternatives, planning, specification of requirements, and so on.

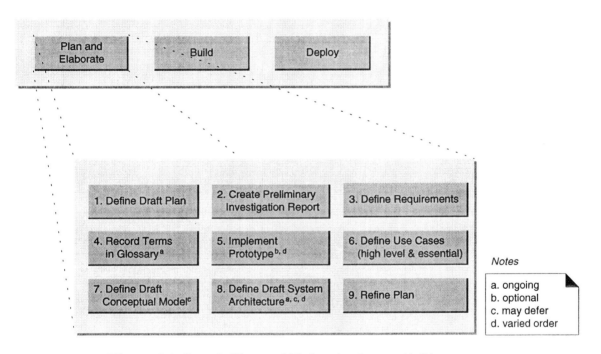

**Figure 2.6** Sample Plan and Elaborate phase activities.

Figure 2.6 illustrates sample activities in this phase. Artifacts generated here may include the following:

- *Plan*—schedule, resources, budget, and so on.

- *Preliminary Investigation Report*—motivation, alternatives, business needs.

- *Requirements Specification*—declarative statement of requirements.

- *Glossary*—a dictionary of terms (concept names, and so on) and any associated information, such as constraints and rules.

- *Prototype*—a prototype system created to aid understanding of the problem, high risk problems, and requirements.

- *Use Cases*—prose descriptions of domain processes.

- *Use Case Diagrams*—illustration of all use cases and their relationships.

- *Draft Conceptual Model*—a rough preliminary conceptual model as an aid in understanding the vocabulary of the domain, especially as it relates to the use cases and requirement specification.

## 2.5.1   Order of Artifact Creation

Although the road map in Figure 2.6 may suggest a linear order of artifact creation, that is not strictly the case. Some artifacts may be made in parallel, for example. This is especially true of the conceptual model, glossary, use cases, and use case diagram. While the use cases are explored, the other artifacts are developed to reflect the information arising from the use cases. In subsequent chapters, these artifacts are introduced in a linear order to keep the presentation straightforward. But in practice there is much more interplay.

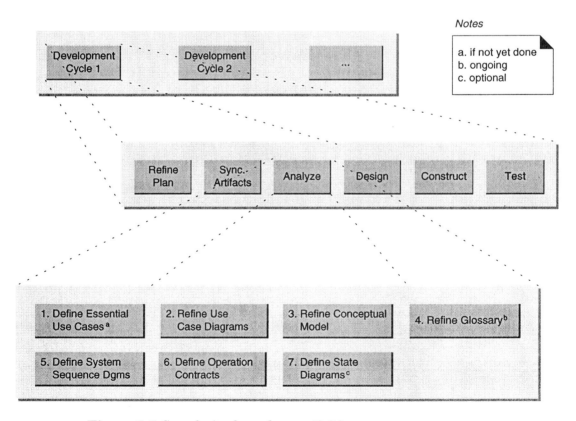

**Figure 2.7** Sample Analyze phase activities.

## 2.6    Build Phase—Development Cycles

The Build phase of a project involves repeated development cycles (probably time-boxed) within which the system is extended. The final objective is a working software system that correctly meets the requirements.

Within a single development cycle, the major steps are to analyze and design, which are shown in Figure 2.7 and Figure 2.8. The details of these steps are elaborated in the following chapters and in Chapter 37, which explores some other process issues.

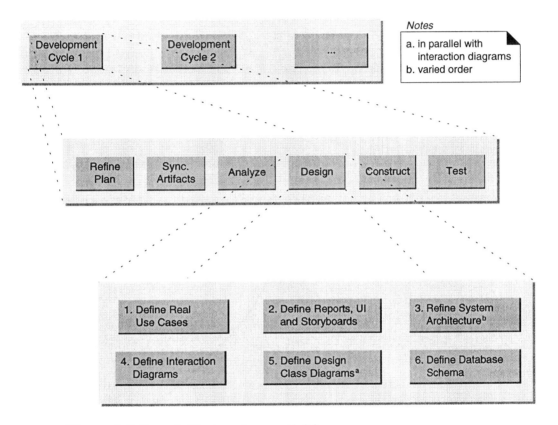

**Figure 2.8** Sample Design phase activities.

### 2.6.1    Order of Development Cycle Artifact Creation

As with the requirements phase artifacts, the linear order that may be inferred from Figure 2.7 is not strictly the case. Some artifacts may be made in parallel, such as:

- Create conceptual model and glossary in parallel.

- Create interaction diagrams and design class diagrams in parallel.

# 2.7    Choosing When to Create Artifacts

Certain artifacts, such as a draft conceptual model (a model of real-world concepts) and expanded use cases (detailed narrative descriptions of processes), may be created during the early Plan and Elaborate phase. This section discusses the timing of their creation.

## 2.7.1    When to Create the Conceptual Model?

A **conceptual model** is a representation of concepts or objects in the problem domain, such as *Book* and *Library*. The amount of effort applied to the creation of a draft conceptual model during the Plan and Elaborate phase needs to be tempered. The goal is to obtain a basic understanding of the vocabulary and concepts used in the requirements. Therefore, a fine-grained investigation is not called for, and runs the very real risk of front-loading the investigation of too much—complexity overload. In large problem domains, such as a system for airline reservations, a thorough conceptual model is overwhelmingly complex.

> The recommended middle-ground strategy is to quickly create a rough conceptual model where the emphasis is on finding obvious concepts expressed in the requirements while deferring a deep investigation. Later, within each development cycle, the conceptual model is incrementally refined and extended for the requirements under consideration within that cycle.

Another strategy is to completely defer creation of the conceptual model until each development cycle; starting from a blank slate in development cycle one, and then growing it over each cycle. This has the advantage of deferring complexity, but the disadvantage of less up-front information, which may have been useful for general comprehension, the glossary, and while scoping and estimating. The major case study takes this deferred approach to creating the conceptual model, not because it is preferred, but because it supports a gradual explanation of how to create them

## 2.7.2    When to Create the Expanded Use Cases?

**High-level use cases** are very brief, usually two or three sentence descriptions of a process. **Expanded use cases** are long narratives that may contain hundreds of sentences describing the process.

> During the Plan and Elaborate phase, create all the high-level use cases, but only rewrite the most critical and important use cases in an expanded (long) format, deferring the rest until the development cycle in which they are tackled.

As with the conceptual model, there are trade-offs in terms of the benefit of the early acquisition of information versus tackling too much complexity. The advantage of investigating and writing all the detailed expanded use cases during the Plan and Elaborate phase is more information; this can help with comprehension, risk management, scope, and estimating. However, the disadvantage is early complexity overload—this investigation will spawn myriad detailed issues. Furthermore, the expanded use cases may not be very reliable because of incomplete or misinformation and because the requirements may be a changing target.

> Therefore, the recommended middle-ground strategy is to expend effort investigating only the most important use cases in detail during the Plan and Elaborate phase.

# DEFINING MODELS AND ARTIFACTS

## Objectives

- Define analysis and design models.
- Illustrate the dependencies between analysis and design artifacts.

## 3.1    Introduction

This chapter introduces sample models in object-oriented analysis and design, and illustrates the dependent relationship between the artifacts within the models.

The purpose is to introduce the overall picture; subsequent chapters elaborate on the details of these models and artifacts.

## 3.2    Modeling Systems

A system (in the real world or software) is usually overwhelmingly complex, so it is necessary to decompose it into understandable chunks in order to comprehend and manage the complexity. These chunks may be represented as **models** which describe and abstract essential aspects of the system [Rumbaugh97].

Therefore, a useful step in building a software system is to first create models which organize and communicate the important details of the real world problem it is related to and of the system to be built. These models should contain cohesive, strongly related elements.

UML stands for Unified *Modeling* Language because it is a language intended to describe models of systems—real world and software—based on object concepts.

Models are composed of other models or **artifacts**—diagrams and documents which describe things. The UML specifies a variety of diagrams, such as a use case diagram and interaction diagram, which are the concrete artifacts from which models are composed. Models are visualized with **views**—visual projections of the model and the UML diagrams, such as interaction diagrams, comprise the views of a model.

Models can be characterized emphasizing **static** or **dynamic** information about a system. A **static model** describes structural properties, while a **dynamic model** describes behavioral properties of a system.

## 3.3    Sample Models

The UML is a flexible modeling language that allows the definition of arbitrary models. This section presents sample analysis and design models which illustrate the membership of concrete artifacts within models.

---

These are *sample* models; they are not meant to be definitive.

---

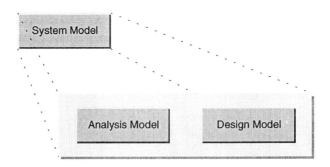

**Figure 3.1** The System Model.

### 3.3.1    The System Model

In this example the overall System Model (shown in Figure 3.1) is composed of the:

- **Analysis Model**—models related to an investigation of the domain and problem space, but not of the solution.

- **Design Model**—models related to the logical solution.

Subsequent chapters explore these models (shown in Figure 3.1) in greater detail.

## 3.4 Relationship Between Artifacts

Independent of how artifacts are organized into models, there are influential dependencies between artifacts. For example, a use case diagram which illustrates all the use cases is dependent on the use case definitions themselves. It is useful to understand the dependency and influence between the artifacts so that consistency checks and traceability can be achieved, and so that dependent artifacts are effectively used as input to creating later artifacts.[1]

For example, Figure 3.2 illustrates dependencies between artifacts created during the Plan and Elaborate phase. The following chapters elaborate on the meaning of these artifacts and their dependencies.

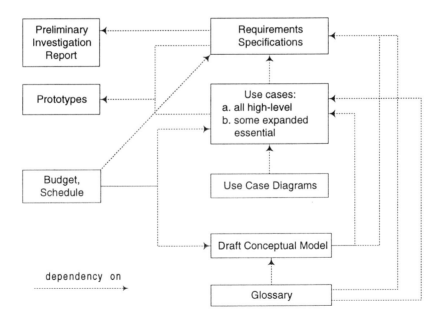

**Figure 3.2** Plan and Elaborate phase artifact influence.

---

1. If an artifact is created which has no dependents, and is not used as input to anything else, we should seriously question the value of that artifact and the time spent in its creation!

# PART I PLAN AND ELABORATE PHASE

# 4 CASE STUDY: POINT-OF-SALE

## 4.1 The Point-of-Sale System

Our main case study is a point-of-sale terminal (POST) system.[1] A point-of-sale terminal is a computerized system used to record sales and handle payments; it is typically used in a retail store. It includes hardware components such as a computer and bar code scanner, and software to run the system.

Assume that we have been requested to create the software to run a point-of-sale terminal. Using an iterative-incremental development strategy, we are going to proceed through requirements, object-oriented analysis, design, and implementation.

**Figure 4.1** A point-of-sale terminal.

---

1. A problem also explored in [Coad95], although this work was developed independently, and largely prior to that.

Why this problem? It is representative of many information systems and touches upon common problems that a developer may encounter. The analysis and design will be taken far enough so that it will be seen how to tackle such problems with sufficient detail to apply this method to new projects.

## 4.2    Architectural Layers and Case Study Emphasis

A typical information system that includes a graphical user interface and database access is usually architecturally designed in terms of several layers (see Figure 4.2), such as:

- **Presentation**—graphical interface; windows.

- **Application Logic - Problem Domain Objects**—objects representing domain concepts (for example, Sale objects) that fulfill application requirements.

- **Application Logic - Service Objects**—non-problem domain objects that provide supporting services, such as interfacing with a database.

- **Storage**—a persistent storage mechanism, such as an object-oriented or relational database.

> Object-oriented analysis and design is generally most relevant for modeling the application logic layers.

The topic of a layered architecture is explored in Chapter 22.

The point-of-sale case study primarily emphasizes the problem domain objects, allocating responsibilities to them to fulfill the requirements of the application. In Chapter 38 we apply object-oriented design to create a set of service layer objects for interfacing with a database.

In this design approach, the presentation layer has very little responsibility; it is said to be *thin*. Windows do *not* contain code that handles application logic or processing. Rather, task requests are forwarded on to the problem domain and service layers.

## 4.3    Our Strategy: Iterative Learning and Development

This book is organized to follow an iterative development strategy. Object-oriented analysis and design is applied to the point-of-sale system in two iterative development cycles in which the first development cycle is for a simple core-functions application. The second development cycle expands the functionality of the system (see Figure 4.3).

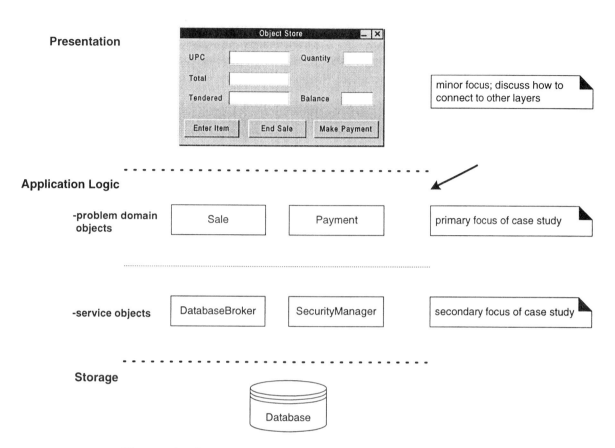

**Figure 4.2** Layers in a typical object-oriented information system.

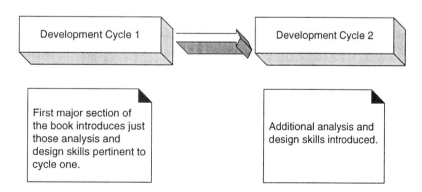

**Figure 4.3** Learning path follows development cycles.

In conjunction with iterative development, the *presentation* of object-oriented analysis and design topics, UML notation, and patterns is introduced iteratively. In development cycle one of the point-of-sale system, a core set of analysis and design topics and notation is presented. The second development cycle expands into new ideas, UML notation, and patterns.

The intention of this strategy is a "just-in-time" learning model. This emphasizes presenting frequently used ideas first, hopefully close to when you perceive the need to learn them in order to carry on. The book focuses on fundamental ideas and skills first without overloading you with new information that is not immediately applicable. Less frequently used skills and ideas are presented later.

# UNDERSTANDING REQUIREMENTS

## Objectives

- Create requirement phase artifacts, such as function specifications.
- Identify and categorize system functions.
- Identify and categorize system attributes and relate them to functions.

## 5.1    Introduction

Correct and thorough requirements specifications is essential to a successful project. It involves a host of skills, a careful examination of which are outside the scope of this work, since the objective here is acquiring skill in object-oriented analysis and design. However, an introduction to the requirements for the point-of-sale application is presented, since in real practice it is a critical step, and pointers to additional requirements phase artifacts are suggested. For a good treatment that focuses on the skills necessary to elucidate meaningful requirements, *Exploring Requirements: Quality Before Design* [GW89] is highly recommended.

The objective of this chapter is to be able to express requirements, rather than become experts in the domain of stores and point-of-sale terminal systems. Therefore, the list of system functions and attributes is representative rather than exhaustive.

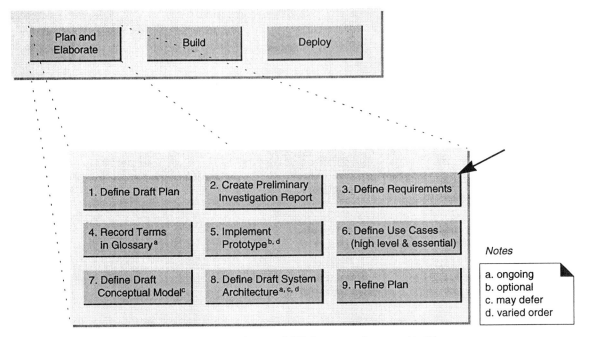

Plan and Elaborate phase activities.

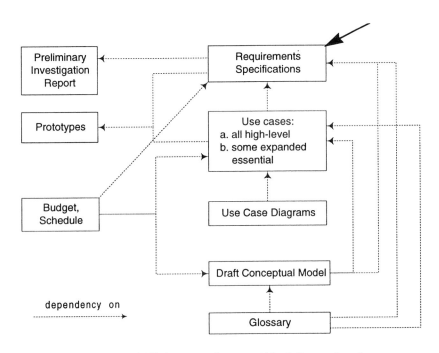

Plan and Elaborate phase artifact dependencies.

None of the artifacts introduced in this section are UML-specific; they are simply common requirements phase documents.

# 5.2    Requirements

**Requirements** are a description of needs or desires for a product. The primary goal of the requirements phase is to identify and document what is really needed, in a form that clearly communicates to the client and to development team members. The challenge is to define the requirements unambiguously, so that the risks are identified and there are no surprises when the product is finally delivered.

The following sample artifacts are recommended in the requirements phase:

- overview statement
- customers
- goals
- system functions
- system attributes

Other relevant documents, outside the scope of this discussion, are mentioned at the end of this chapter.

## 5.2.1    Pulling Together the Pieces

In this case study the definition of requirements appears tidy—the reality is anything but! It typically involves gathering and digesting varied paper and electronic documents, interview results, group requirements definition meetings, and so on.

# 5.3    Overview Statement

The purpose of this project is to create a point-of-sale terminal system to be used in retail sales.

# 5.4    Customers

ObjectStore, Inc., a multinational object retailer.

## 5.5    Goals

In general, the goal is increased checkout automation, to support faster, better and cheaper services and business processes. More specifically, these include:

- Quick checkout for the customer.

- Fast and accurate sales analysis.

- Automatic inventory control.

## 5.6    System Functions

**System functions** are what a system is supposed to *do*, such as authorize credit payments. They should be identified and listed in logical cohesive groupings.

> To verify that some X is indeed a system function, it should make sense in the following sentence:
>
> The system should do <X>.

For example, *The system should do credit payment authorization.*

In contrast, **system attributes** are nonfunctional system qualities—such as ease-of-use—that are often confused with functions. Note that "ease-of-use" does not fit in the verification sentence, *The system should do ease-of-use.* System attributes should not be part of the functional specification document, but rather part of a separate system attribute specification document.

### 5.6.1    Function Categories

Functions, such as *authorize credit payments*, should be categorized in order to prioritize them and identify those that might otherwise be taken for granted (but which consume time and other resources). Categories include:

| Function Category | Meaning |
|---|---|
| Evident | Should perform, and user should be cognizant that it is performed. |
| Hidden | Should perform, but not be visible to users. This is true of many underlying technical services, such as *save information in a persistent storage mechanism*. Hidden functions are often (incorrectly) missed during the requirements gathering process. |
| Frill | Optional; adding it does not significantly affect cost or other functions. |

## 5.6.2    Basic Functions

The following system functions for the point-of-sale terminal application are a representative sample, rather than a complete list. Our goal is to understand the details of analysis and design, not the business of a store.

| Ref # | Function | Category |
|---|---|---|
| R1.1 | Record the underway (current) sale—the items purchased. | evident |
| R1.2 | Calculate current sale total, including tax and coupon calculations. | evident |
| R1.3 | Capture purchase item information from a bar code using a bar code scanner, or manual entry of a product code, such as a universal product code (UPC). | evident |
| R1.4 | Reduce inventory quantities when a sale is committed. | hidden |
| R1.5 | Log completed sales. | hidden |
| R1.6 | Cashier must log in with an ID and password in order to use the system. | evident |
| R1.7 | Provide a persistent storage mechanism. | hidden |

| Ref # | Function | Category |
|-------|----------|----------|
| R1.8 | Provide inter-process and inter-system communication mechanisms. | hidden |
| R1.9 | Display description and price of item recorded. | evident |

## 5.6.3    Payment Functions

| Ref # | Function | Category |
|-------|----------|----------|
| R2.1 | Handle cash payments, capturing amount tendered and calculating balance due. | evident |
| R2.2 | Handle credit payments, capturing credit information from a card reader or by manual entry, and authorizing payment with the store's (external) credit authorization service via a modem connection. | evident |
| R2.3 | Handle check payments, capturing drivers license by manual entry, and authorizing payment with the store's (external) check authorization service via a modem connection. | evident |
| R2.4 | Log credit payments to the accounts receivable system, since the credit authorization service owes the store the payment amount. | hidden |

# 5.7    System Attributes

System attributes are characteristics or dimensions of the system; they are not functions. For example

| | | |
|---|---|---|
| ease of use | fault tolerance | response time |
| interface metaphor | retail cost | platforms |

System attributes may cut across all functions (such as the operating system platform) or be specific to a particular function or group of functions.

System attributes have a possible set of **attribute details**, which tend to be discrete, fuzzy, symbolic values of the attribute, such as

response time = (psychologically appropriate)

interface metaphor = (graphical, colorful, forms-based)

Some system attributes may also have **attribute boundary constraints**, which are mandatory boundary conditions, usually on a numeric range of values of an attribute, such as

response time = (five seconds maximum)

Here are some other examples

| Attribute | Details and Boundary Constraints |
|---|---|
| response time | *(boundary constraint)* When recording a sold item, the description and price will appear within 5 seconds. |
| interface metaphor | *(detail)* Forms-metaphor windows and dialog boxes<br><br>*(detail)* maximize for easy keyboard navigation rather than pointer navigation |
| fault tolerance | *(boundary constraint)* must log authorized credit payments to accounts receivable within 24 hours, even if power or device failure |
| operating system platforms | *(detail)* Microsoft Windows 95 and NT |

## 5.7.1    System Attributes in Function Specifications

It is useful to describe all the system attributes that are clearly related to functions *within* the function specification list. Additionally, attribute details and boundary constraints may be categorized as *must* versus *want*.[1]

---

1. A boundary constraint is usually a *must*, otherwise it suggests it wasn't a solid constraint.

| Ref # | Function | Cat. | Attribute | Details and Constraints | Cat. |
|---|---|---|---|---|---|
| R1.9 | Display description and price of item recorded. | evident | response time | 5 seconds max | must |
| | | | interface metaphor | forms based output<br>colorful | must<br>want |
| R2.4 | Log credit payments to the accounts receivable system, since the credit authorization service owes the store the payment amount. | hidden | fault tolerance | must log to accounts receivable within 24 hours, even if power or device failure | must |
| | | | response time | 10 seconds max | must |

# 5.8     Other Requirements Phase Artifacts

This is a very sparse introduction to requirements; it is properly the subject of entire books. System functions and attributes are the absolute minimum requirements documents, but additional important artifacts necessary to reduce risk and understand the problem include:

- *Requirements and Liaison Teams*—List of parties that should be involved in specifying the functions and system attributes, and performing reviews, testing, negotiations, and so on.

- *Affected Groups*—Those impacted by either the development or deployment of the system.

- *Assumptions*—Things we assume will be true.

- *Risks*—Things which can lead to failure or delay.

- *Dependencies*—Other parties, systems and products that this project depends upon for completion.

- *Glossary*—Definition of all relevant terms; explored in subsequent chapters.

- *Use cases*—Narrative descriptions of the domain processes; explored in subsequent chapters.

- *Draft Conceptual Model*—A model of important concepts and their relationships; explored in subsequent chapters.

# USE CASES: DESCRIBING PROCESSES

---

### Objectives

- Identify and write use cases.

- Draw use case diagrams.

- Contrast high-level and expanded use cases.

- Contrast essential and real use cases.

---

## 6.1    Introduction

An excellent technique to improve understanding of requirements is the creation of use cases—narrative descriptions of domain processes. This chapter explores some introductory use case concepts and illustrates use cases for the point-of-sale terminal application.

In the next chapter, we rank the use cases and choose what ones to tackle in the first development cycle.

The UML formally includes the notion of use cases and use case diagrams.

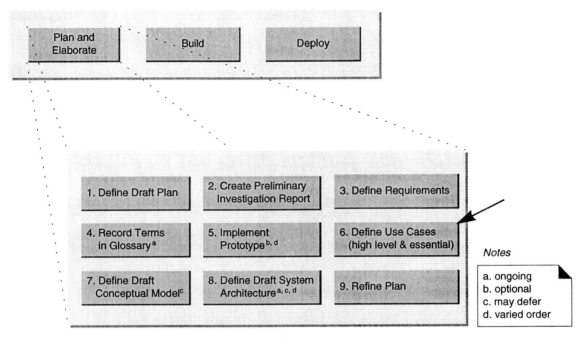

Plan and Elaborate phase activities.

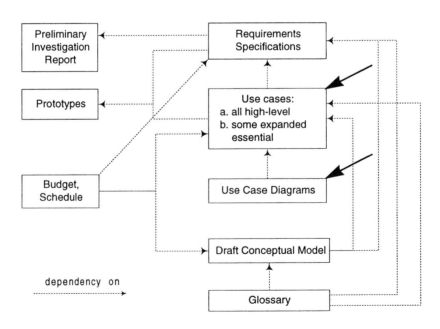

Plan and Elaborate phase artifact dependencies.

## 6.2 Activities and Dependencies

Uses cases are dependent on having at least partial understanding of the requirements of the system, ideally expressed in a requirements specifications document.

## 6.3 Use Cases

A **use case** is a narrative document that describes the sequence of events of an actor (an external agent) using a system to complete a process [Jacobson92]. They are stories or cases of using a system. Use case are not exactly requirements or functional specifications, but they illustrate and imply requirements in the stories they tell.

**Figure 6.1** The UML icon for a use case.

### 6.3.1 Example of a High-level Use Case: Buy Items

The following high-level use case tersely describes the process of buying things at a store when a point-of-sale terminal is used.

| | |
|---|---|
| Use case: | **Buy Items** |
| Actors: | Customer, Cashier |
| Type: | primary (to be discussed) |
| Description: | A Customer arrives at a checkout with items to purchase. The Cashier records the purchase items and collects payment. On completion, the Customer leaves with the items. |

The headings and structure of the use case are typical. Nevertheless, UML does not specify a rigid format; it may be altered to meet the needs and spirit of documentation—clarity of communication.

It is useful to start with high-level use cases to quickly obtain some understanding of the overall major processes.

## 6.3.2 Example of an Expanded Use Case: Buy Items with Cash

An **expanded use case** shows more detail than a high level one; they are useful in order to obtain a deeper understanding of the processes and requirements. They are often done in a "conversational" style between the actors and the system [Wirfs-Brock93]. Here is an example of an expanded use case for *Buy Items* that has been simplified to handle cash payments only and ignore inventory management (for simplicity, in this first example).

| | |
|---|---|
| Use case: | **Buy Items with Cash** |
| Actors: | Customer (initiator), Cashier |
| Purpose: | Capture a sale and its cash payment. |
| Overview: | A Customer arrives at a checkout with items to purchase. The Cashier records the purchase items and collects a cash payment. On completion, the Customer leaves with the items. |
| Type | primary and essential |
| Cross References: | *Functions*: R1.1, R1.2, R1.3, R1.7, R1.9, R2.1, |

**Typical Course of Events**

| Actor Action | System Response |
|---|---|
| 1. This use case begins when a Customer arrives at a POST checkout with items to purchase. | |
| 2. The Cashier records the identifier from each item.<br><br>If there is more than one of the same item, the Cashier can enter the quantity as well. | 3. Determines the item price and adds the item information to the running sales transaction.<br><br>The description and price of the current item are presented. |
| 4. On completion of item entry, the Cashier indicates to the POST that item entry is complete. | 5. Calculates and presents the sale total. |
| 6. The Cashier tells the Customer the total. | |

**Typical Course of Events**

| Actor Action | System Response |
|---|---|
| 7. The Customer gives a cash payment—the "cash tendered"—possibly greater than the sale total. | |
| 8. The Cashier records the cash received amount. | 9. Shows the balance due back to the Customer. |
| | Generates a receipt. |
| 10. The Cashier deposits the cash received and extracts the balance owing. | 11. Logs the completed sale. |
| The Cashier gives the balance owing and the printed receipt to the Customer. | |
| 12. The Customer leaves with the items purchased. | |

Alternative Courses

■ Line 2: Invalid identifier entered. Indicate error.

■ Line 7: Customer didn't have enough cash. Cancel sales transaction.

## 6.3.3   Explaining the Expanded Format

The top portion of the expanded form is summary information.

| Use case: | **Name of use case.** |
|---|---|
| Actors: | List of actors (external agents), indicating who initiates the use case. |
| Purpose: | Intention of the use case. |
| Overview: | Repetition of the high-level use case, or some similar summary. |
| Type: | 1. primary, secondary or optional (to be discussed) |
| | 2. essential or real (to be discussed) |
| Cross References: | Related use cases and system functions. |

The middle section, the *typical course of events*, is the heart of the expanded format; it describes in detail the conversation of interaction between the actors and the system. A critical aspect of this section is that it describes the most common, or typical, sequence of events—the average story of activities and successful completion of a process. Alternative situations are *not* included in the typical course.

**Typical Course of Events**

| **Actor Action** | **System Response** |
| --- | --- |
| Numbered actions of the actors. | Numbered descriptions of system responses. |

The final section, the *alternative course of events*, describes important alternatives or exceptions that may arise with respect to the typical course. If complex, these alternatives may themselves by expanded into their own use cases.

Alternative Courses

- Alternatives that may arise at line number. Description of exception.

# 6.4    Actors

An actor is an entity external to the system who in some way participates in the story of the use case. An actor typically stimulates the system with input events, or receives something from it. Actors are represented by the role they play in the use case, such as Customer, Cashier, and so on. It is desirable to capitalize actors in the use case prose for ease of identification.

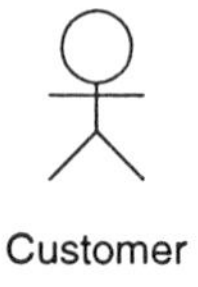

Customer

**Figure 6.2** The UML icon for a use case actor.[1]

For a use case, there is one **initiator actor** who generates the starting stimu-

---

1. Although the standard icon is a stick figure, some prefer to use a computer-like icon for actors which are other computer systems rather than humans.

lus, and possibly several other **participating actors**; it may be useful to indicate who the initiator is.

Actors are usually the roles that humans play, but may be any kind of system, such as an external computerized banking system. Kinds of actors include:

- roles that people play
- computer systems
- electrical or mechanical devices

# 6.5  A Common Mistake with Use Cases

A common error in identifying use cases is to represent individual steps, operations, or transactions as use cases. For example, in the point-of-sale terminal domain, one may (inappropriately) define a use case called "Printing the Receipt" when in fact the printing operation is merely a step in the much larger use case process *Buy Items*.

> A use case is a relatively large end-to-end process description that typically includes many steps or transactions; it is not normally an individual step or activity in a process.

It *is* possible to break down activities or portions of a use case into sub-use cases (called **abstract use cases**)—even down to individual steps—but this is not the norm, and will not be discussed until Chapter 26.

# 6.6  Identifying Use Cases

Each of following steps for identifying use cases involves brainstorming and reviewing existing requirement specification documents.

One method used to identify use cases is actor-based.

1.  Identify the actors related to a system or organization.

2.  For each actor, identify the processes they initiate or participate in.

A second method to identify use cases is event-based.

1.  Identify the external events that a system must respond to.

2.  Relate the events to actors and use cases.

For the point-of-sale application some possibly relevant actors and the processes they initiate include

| | |
|---|---|
| Cashier | Log In |
| | Cash Out |
| Customer | Buy Items |
| | Refund Items |

# 6.7    Use Case and Domain Processes

A use case describes a process, such as a business process. A **process** describes, from start to finish, a sequence of events, actions, and transactions required to produce or complete something of value to an organization or actor.

The following are some example processes:

■   Withdraw cash from an ATM

■   Order a product

■   Register for courses at a school

■   Check the spelling of a document in a word processor

■   Handle a telephone call

## 6.8    Use Cases, System Functions, and Traceability

The system functions identified during the prior requirements specifications should all be allocated to use cases. In addition, it should be possible, via the *Cross References* section of the use case, to verify that all functions have been allocated. This provides a important link in terms of traceability between the artifacts. Ultimately, all system functions and use cases should be traceable through to implementation and testing.

## 6.9    Use Case Diagrams

A sample use case diagram for the point-of-sale system is shown in Figure 6.3.

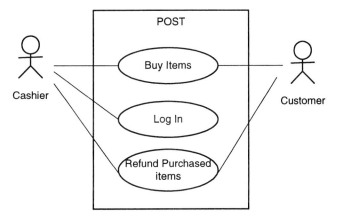

**Figure 6.3** Partial use case diagram.

A **use case diagram** illustrates a set of use cases for a system, the actors, and the relation between the actors and use cases. Use cases are illustrated in ovals, actors are stick figures. There are lines of communication between the use cases and actors; arrows can indicate flow of information or stimulus.

The purpose of the diagram is to present a kind of context diagram by which one can quickly understand the external actors of a system and the key ways in which they use it.

## 6.10    Use Case Formats

In practice, use cases may be expressed with varying degrees of detail and commitment to design decisions. That is to say, the same use case may be written in different formats, with different levels of detail. Later we will explore other ways to format and categorize them, but for now we will focus on a basic division: **high-level** versus **expanded** format use cases.

### 6.10.1  High-Level Format

A **high-level use case** describes a process very briefly, usually in two or three sentences. It is useful to create this type of use case during the initial requirements and project scoping in order to quickly understand the degree of complexity and functionality in a system. High level use cases are very terse, and vague on design decisions.

### 6.10.2  Expanded Format

An **expanded use case** describes a process in more detail than a high-level one. The primary difference from a high-level use case is that it has a *Typical Course of Events* section, which describes the step-by-step events. During the requirements phase, it is useful to write the most important and influential use cases in the expanded format, but less important ones can be deferred until the development cycle in which they are being tackled.

## 6.11  Systems and their Boundaries

A use case describes interaction with a "system". Typical system boundaries include:

- hardware/software boundary of a device or computer system

- department of an organization

- entire organization

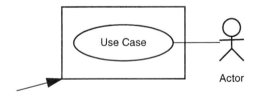

**Figure 6.4**  Use case boundary.

Defining the system boundary is important in order to identify what is external versus internal, and what the responsibilities of the system are. The external environment is represented only by actors.

As an example of the influence of choosing the system boundary, consider the point-of-sale terminal checkouts and the store. If we choose the entire store or business as "the system" (see Figure 6.5), then only the customer is an actor, not the cashier, because the cashier is a resource within the business system that carries out the tasks. However, if we choose the point-of-sale terminal hardware and software as the system (see Figure 6.6), then both the customer and cashier may be treated as actors.

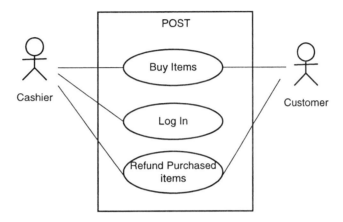

**Figure 6.5** Use cases and actors when the **POST** system is the boundary.

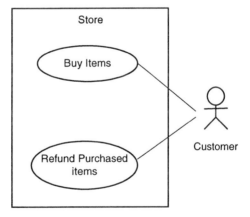

**Figure 6.6** Use cases and actors when the **store** is the boundary.

The choice of the system boundary is influenced by the needs of the investigation. If we are engaged in development for a software application or device, then setting the system boundary at the hardware and software boundary usually makes sense—for example, the point-of-sale terminal and its software constitute "the system" and the customer and cashier are external actors.

If we are engaged in **business process re-engineering**—reorganizing processes or the organization to increase competitiveness or quality—then choosing the entire business or store as the system is relevant. For the POST system, we will define "the system" as the point-of-sale terminal and its software.

# 6.12    Primary, Secondary, and Optional Use Cases

Use cases should be categorized as either primary, secondary, or optional. Later, based on these designations, we will rank our set of use cases to prioritize their development.

**Primary use cases** represent major common processes, such as *Buy Items*.

**Secondary use cases** represent minor or rare processes, such as *Request for Stocking New Product*.

**Optional use cases** represent processes that may not be tackled.

# 6.13    Essential versus Real Use Cases

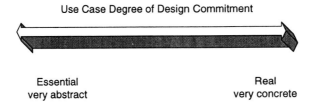

**Figure 6.7** Essential versus real use cases exist on a continuum.

## 6.13.1    *Essential Use Cases*

**Essential use cases** [Constantine97] are expanded use cases that are expressed in an ideal form that remains relatively free of technology and implementation details; design decisions are deferred and abstracted, especially those related to the user interface. An essential use case describes the process in terms of its essential activities and motivation. The degree of abstraction by which one is described exists on a continuum; use cases may be more or less essential in their description.

High-level use cases are always essential in nature, due to their brevity and abstraction.

Following is an example of an ATM *Withdraw Cash* use case expressed in a relatively essential form.

**Essential**

| Actor Action | System Response |
|---|---|
| 1. The Customer identifies them-selves. | 2. Presents options. |
| 3. and so on. | 4. and so on. |

*How* a customer identifies themselves changes over time—it is a design deci-sion—but it is part of the essential process that identification occurs, somehow.

It is desirable to create essential use cases during early requirements elicitation in order to more fully understand the scope of the problem and the functions required. They are advantageous because you can see the essence of the process and its fundamental motivation without being overwhelmed with design details. They also tend to be correct for a long period of time, since they exclude design decisions, and so their creation is an investment in understanding and recording the fundamental forces behind business processes. An organization can retrieve and reread essential use cases in the distant future, making them useful to a new development project.

## 6.13.2   Real Use Cases

In contrast, a **real use case** concretely describes the process in terms of its real current design, committed to specific input and output technologies, and so on. When a user interface is involved, they often show screen shots and discuss interaction with the widgets. Here is the *Withdraw Cash* use case expressed in a relatively *real* form.

**Real**

| Actor Action | System Response |
|---|---|
| 1. The Customer inserts their card. | 2. Prompts for PIN. |
| 3. Enters PIN on keypad. | 4. Displays options menu. |
| 5. and so on. | 6. and so on. |

Note that the essential action of "Customer identifies themselves" from the essential use case is now concretely realized in the series of actions starting with "The Customer inserts their card."

Ideally, real use cases are created during the design phase of a development cycle, since they are a design artifact. In some projects, early design decisions regarding the user interface are expected, so real use cases must be created during the early elaboration phase. It is undesirable to create real use cases in the Plan and Elaborate phase because of the premature commitment to a design and overwhelming complexity involved. However, some organizations commit to a development contract on the basis of the user interface specifications.

Chapter 19 examines the real use cases for the point-of-sale application.

## 6.13.3  Essential Buy Items Use Case

The expanded *Buy Items* use case already shown tends towards being an essential use case. Note that the description is very non-committal with respect to the technical realization. This use case is written in a way that one can almost imagine it being true of this process one hundred years in the past and future, which is indicative of its essential nature.

**Essential**

| Actor Action | System Response |
|---|---|
| **1.** The Cashier records the identifier from each item.<br><br>If there is more than one of the same item, the Cashier can enter the quantity as well. | **2.** Determines the item price and adds the item information to the running sales transaction.<br><br>The description and price of the current item are presented. |
| **3.** and so on. | **4.** and so on. |

## 6.13.4  Real Buy Items Use Case

In contrast to an essential version of the use case, a real version makes design commitments; a full version of the real version will be discussed in a later chapter. Note, in the following real version example, the decision to use a UPC for the item identifier[1] and a graphical user interface for the interface.

---

1. It is not unacceptable to commit to some choices such as the use of a UPC in the essential use case, and in the early analysis phase. Essential, real, analysis, and design are terms on a continuum of abstraction, rather than polar opposites. What is valuable is to appreciate that whenever a commitment is made during the analysis phase, there is the possibility of premature design creep, information overload, and less flexibility.

**Real**

| Actor Action | System Response |
|---|---|
| **1.** For each item, the Cashier types in the Universal Product Code (UPC) in the UPC input field of Window1. They then press the "Enter Item" button with the mouse or by pressing the <Enter> key. | **2.** Displays the item price and adds the item information to the running sales transaction.<br><br>The description and price of the current item are displayed in Textbox 2 of Window1. |
| **3.** etc. | **4.** etc. |

# 6.14    Notational Points

## 6.14.1    *Naming Use Cases*

Name a use case starting with a verb in order to emphasize that it is a process. For example:

■   Buy Items

■   Enter an Order

## 6.14.2    *Starting off an Expanded Use Case*

Start an expanded use case with the following schema:

**1.**   This use case begins when <Actor> <initiates an event>

For example

**1.**   This use case begins when a Customer arrives at a POST with items to purchase.

This encourages a clear identification of the initiating actor and event.

## 6.14.3    *Notating Decision Points and Branching*

A use case may contain decision points. For example, in *Buy Items*, the customer may choose to pay via cash, credit, or check at payment time. If one of these decision paths represents the overwhelming typical case, and the other alternatives are rare, unusual or exceptional, then the typical case should be the only one written about in the *Typical Course of Events*, and the alternatives should be written in the *Alternatives* section.

However, sometimes the decision point represents alternatives which are all relatively equal and normal in their likelihood; this is true of the payment types cash, credit and check. In this case, use the following notational structure:

1. Within the main section *Typical Course of Events*, indicate branches to subsections.

2. Write a subsection for each branch, again using a Typical Course of Events. Start the event numbering at one for each section.

3. If subsections have alternatives, write them in an Alternatives section for each subsection.

## Section: Main

### Typical Course of Events

| Actor Action | System Response |
|---|---|
| 1. This use case begins when a Customer arrives at the POST checkout with items to purchase. | |
| 2. (intermediate steps excluded)... | |
| 3. Customer chooses payment type: | |
|    a. If cash payment, see section *Pay by Cash*. | |
|    b. If credit payment, see section *Pay by Credit*. | |
|    c. If check payment, see section *Pay by Check*. | |
| | 4. Logs the completed sale. |
| | 5. Prints a receipt. |
| 6. The Cashier gives the receipt to the Customer. | |
| 7. The Customer leaves with the items purchased. | |

### Section: Pay by Cash

**Typical Course of Events**

| Actor Action | System Response |
|---|---|
| 1. The Customer gives a cash payment—the "cash tendered"—possibly greater than the sale total. | |
| 2. The Cashier records the cash tendered. | 3. Shows the balance due back to the Customer. |
| 4. The Cashier deposits the cash received and extracts the balance owing. | |
| The Cashier gives the balance owing to the Customer. | |

Alternative Courses

■ Line 4: Insufficient cash in drawer to pay balance. Ask for cash from supervisor, or ask Customer for a payment closer to sale total.

### Section: Pay by Credit

Typical and alterative courses for credit payment story.

### Section: Pay by Check

Typical and alterative courses for check payment story.

# 6.15    Use Cases Within a Development Process

## 6.15.1    Plan and Elaborate Phase Steps

1. After system functions have been listed, define the system boundary and then identify actors and use cases.

2.  Write all use cases in the *high-level* format. Categorize them as primary, secondary or optional.

3.  Draw a use case diagram.

4.  Relate use cases and illustrate relationships in the use case diagram (use case relationships are discussed later in the book).

5.  Write the most critical, influential and risky use cases in the *expanded essential* format to better understand and estimate the nature and size of the problem. Defer writing the expanded essential form of less critical use cases until the development cycles in which they will be tackled, in order to delay complex analysis.

6.  Ideally, *real* use cases should be deferred until the design phase of a development cycle, since their creation involves design decisions. However, it is sometimes necessary to create some real use cases during the early requirements phase if:

    ❑  Concrete descriptions significantly aid comprehension.

    ❑  Clients demand specifying their processes in this fashion.

7.  Rank use cases (discussed in the next chapter).

## 6.15.2  Iterative Development Cycle Phase Steps

1.  Analyze phase—Write expanded essential use cases for those currently being tackled, if not already done.

2.  Design phase—Write real use cases for those currently being tackled, if not already done.

# 6.16  Process Steps for the Point-of-Sale System

Some of the following activities will be deferred until later chapters, as they require significant discussion or can be deferred to avoid information overload. Since our goal is to acquire skill in applying use cases rather than becoming store experts, not all use cases will be written in detail.

## 6.16.1  Identify Actors and Use Cases

For the point-of-sale application, define the system boundary to be the hardware/software system—the usual case. A sample list of relevant actors and the processes they initiate—not intended to be exhaustive—includes:

| Cashier | Log In |
| | Cash Out |
| Customer | Buy Items |
| | Refund Items |
| Manager | Start Up |
| | Shut Down |
| System Administrator | Add New Users |

## 6.16.2   Write Use Cases in the High-level Format

A sample of high-level use cases includes:

| | |
|---|---|
| Use case: | **Buy Items** |
| Actors: | Customer (initiator), Cashier |
| Type: | primary |
| Description: | A Customer arrives at a checkout with items to purchase. The Cashier records the purchase items and collects a payment. On completion, the Customer leaves with the items. |

| | |
|---|---|
| Use case: | **Start Up** |
| Actors: | Manager |
| Type: | primary |
| Description: | A Manager powers on a POST in order to prepare it for use by Cashiers. The Manager validates that the date and time are correct, after which the system is ready for Cashier use. |

## 6.16.3   Draw a Use Case Diagram

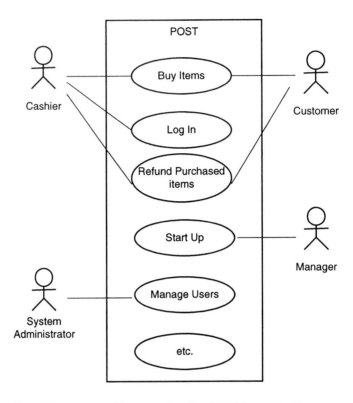

**Figure 6.8** Partial use case diagram for the POST application.

## 6.16.4   Relate use cases

To be explored in a subsequent chapter.

## 6.16.5   Write Some Expanded Essential Use Cases

Really significant primary use cases include:

■   Buy Items

■   Refund Purchased Items

Writing these in an expanded essential form will provide more information and clarification regarding the requirements. Here is the *Buy Items* use case, in its full-blown essential expanded form:

# Use Case: Buy Items

## Section: Main

| | |
|---|---|
| Use case: | **Buy Items** |
| Actors: | Customer (initiator), Cashier |
| Purpose: | Capture a sale and its payment. |
| Overview: | A Customer arrives at a checkout with items to purchase. The Cashier records the purchase items and collects a payment, which may be authorized. On completion, the Customer leaves with the items. |
| Type | primary and essential |
| Cross References: | *Functions*: R1.1, R1.2, R1.3, R1.7, R1.9, R2.1, R2.2, R2.3, R2.4 |

*Use Cases*: Cashier must have completed the *Log In* use case.

### Typical Course of Events

| Actor Action | System Response |
|---|---|
| 1. This use case begins when a Customer arrives at the POST checkout with items to purchase. | |
| 2. The Cashier records each item.<br><br>If there is more than one of an item, the Cashier can enter the quantity as well. | 3. Determines the item price and adds the item information to the running sales transaction.<br><br>The description and price of the current item are presented. |
| 4. On completion of item entry, the Cashier indicates to the POST that item entry is complete. | 5. Calculates and presents the sale total. |
| 6. The Cashier tells the Customer the total. | |

**Typical Course of Events**

| Actor Action | System Response |
|---|---|
| 7. Customer chooses payment type: | |
|    a. If cash payment, see section *Pay by Cash*. | |
|    b. If credit payment, see section *Pay by Credit*. | |
|    c. If check payment, see section *Pay by Check*. | |
| | 8. Logs the completed sale. |
| | 9. Updates inventory levels. |
| | 10. Generates a receipt. |
| 11. The Cashier gives the receipt to the Customer. | |
| 12. The Customer leaves with the items purchased. | |

Alternative Courses

■ Line 2: Invalid item identifier entered. Indicate error.

■ Line 7: Customer could not pay. Cancel sales transaction.

## Section: Pay by Cash

**Typical Course of Events**

| Actor Action | System Response |
|---|---|
| 1. The Customer gives a cash payment—the "cash tendered"—possibly greater than the sale total. | |

**Typical Course of Events**

| Actor Action | System Response |
|---|---|
| **2.** The Cashier records the cash tendered. | **3.** Presents the balance due back to the Customer. |
| **4.** The Cashier deposits the cash received and extracts the balance owing. | |
| The Cashier gives the balance owing to the Customer. | |

Alternative Courses

- Line 1: Customer does not have sufficient cash. May cancel sale or initiate another payment method.

- Line 4: Cash drawer does not contain sufficient cash to pay balance. Cashier requests additional cash from supervisor or asks Customer for different payment amount or method.

## Section: Pay by Credit

**Typical Course of Events**

| Actor Action | System Response |
|---|---|
| **1.** The Customer communicates their credit information for the credit payment. | **2.** Generates a credit payment request and sends it to an external Credit Authorization Service. |
| **3.** Credit Authorization Service authorizes the payment. | **4.** Receives a credit approval reply from the Credit Authorization Service (CAS). |
| | **5.** Posts (records) the credit payment and approval reply information to the Accounts Receivable system. (The CAS owes money to the Store, hence A/R must track it). |
| | **6.** Displays authorization success message. |

Alternative Courses

■ Line 3: Credit request denied by Credit Authorization Service. Suggest different payment method.

**Section: Pay by Check**

**Typical Course of Events**

| Actor Action | System Response |
|---|---|
| 1. The Customer writes a check and identifies self. | |
| 2. Cashier records identification information and requests check payment authorization. | 3. Generates a check payment request and sends it to an external Check Authorization Service. |
| 4. Check Authorization Service authorizes the payment. | 5. Receives a check approval reply from the Check Authorization Service. |
| | 6. Indicates authorization success. |

Alternative Courses

■ Line 4: Check request denied by Check Authorization Service. Suggest different payment method.

## 6.16.6 *If Necessary, Write Some Real Use Cases*

It is not desirable or necessary to create any real use cases at this time; this work will be deferred until the development cycles.

## 6.16.7 *Rank Use Cases*

To be explored in the next chapter.

# 6.17    Sample Models

High-level and essential use cases and use case diagrams are members of the Analysis Use Case Model (see Figure 6.9).

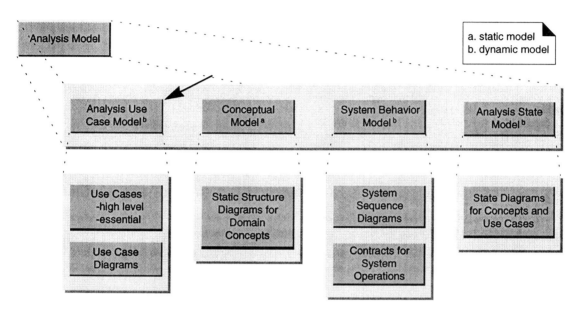

**Figure 6.9** The Analysis Model.

# 7

# RANKING AND SCHEDULING USE CASES

---

### Objectives

- Rank use cases.

- Where necessary, create simplified versions of use cases.

- Allocate use cases to development cycles.

---

## 7.1　Introduction

In the Plan and Elaborate Phase requirement specifications and use cases are defined. Additionally, it is optionally possible to create a draft Conceptual Model and design a draft system architecture, although those activities will be deferred in this case study in order to present a more graduated introduction of topics.

Assuming all desired artifacts have been generated (for example, requirements specifications and use cases), the next step is to transition to the iterative development cycle Build phase and start implementing the system. In an iterative development life-cycle, the work to fulfill use cases is distributed over multiple development cycles.

This chapter explores the ranking and scheduling of use cases. Once complete, we are ready to proceed to development cycle one, and explore object-oriented analysis and design in detail.

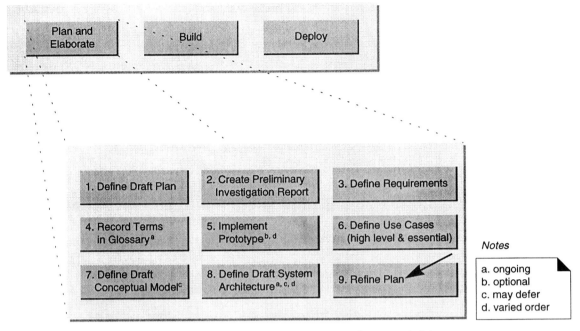

Plan and Elaborate phase activities.

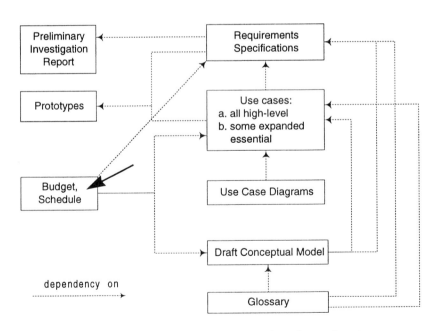

Plan and Elaborate phase artifact dependencies.

## 7.2    Scheduling Use Cases to Development Cycles

### 7.2.1    Use Cases and Development Cycles

Development cycles are organized around use case requirements. That is to say, a development cycle is assigned to implement one or more use cases, or simplified versions of use cases, when the complete use case is too complex to tackle in one cycle (see Figure 7.1).

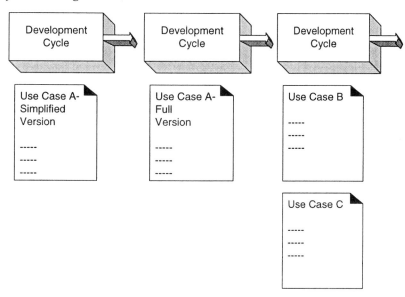

**Figure 7.1** Allocating use cases to development cycles.

### 7.2.2    Ranking Use Cases

Use cases need to be ranked, and high ranking use cases need to be tackled in early development cycles. The overarching strategy is to first pick use cases that significantly influence the core architecture. Qualities that increase the ranking of a use case include:

a.  Significant impact on the architectural design, such as adding many classes to the domain layer or requiring persistence services.

b.  Significant information and insight regarding the design is obtained with relatively little effort.

c.  Include risky, time-critical, or complex functions.

d.  Involve significant research, or new and risky technology.

e.  Represent primary line-of-business processes.

f.  Directly support increased revenue or decreased costs.

The ranking scheme may use a simple fuzzy classification such as high-medium-low.

Alternatively, the scheme can apply scores (possibly augmented with weighting), based on the qualities affecting the rank, such as[1]

| Use Case | a | b | c | d | e | f | Sum |
|----------|---|---|---|---|---|---|-----|
| Buy Items | 5 | 3 | 2 | 0 | 5 | 3 | 18 |
| and so on | | | | | | | |

## 7.3 Ranking the Point-of-Sale Application Use Cases

Based on the prior ranking criteria, here is an informal fuzzy ranking of the sample point-of-sale application use cases. This list is not meant to be exhaustive.

| Rank | Use Case | Justification |
|------|----------|---------------|
| High | Buy Items | Scores on most increased ranking criteria. |
| Medium | Add New Users | Affects security subdomain. |
| | Log In | Affects security subdomain. |
| | Refund Items | Important process; affects accounting. |
| Low | Cash Out | Minimal effect on architecture. |
| | Start Up | Definition is dependent on other use cases. |
| | Shut Down | Minimal effect on architecture. |

## 7.4 The "Start Up" Use Case

Virtually all systems have a *Start Up* use case. Although it may not rank high by other criteria, it is necessary to tackle at least some simplified version of *Start Up* in the very first development cycle so that the initialization assumed by other cases is provided. Within each development cycle, the *Start Up* use case

---

1. The scheme is suggestive rather than complete.

is incrementally developed to satisfy the start up needs of the other use cases. We will ignore explicitly showing the scheduling of this use case, and assume that it is always implicitly developed as needed.

# 7.5    Scheduling the Point-of-Sale Application Use Cases

Based on the ranking, *Buy Items* should be tackled in the first development cycle. As discussed, some simple version of *Start Up* will also be tackled to support the other use cases.

## 7.5.1    Creating Multiple Versions of Complex Use Cases

Whenever a use case is assigned, it is necessary to estimate if the entire use case can be tackled within the limited time-box of a cycle (for example, four weeks), or if the work of the use case needs to be distributed across multiple cycles. In this case, *Buy Items* is an extremely complex use case that may very well require five or more development cycles, assuming each cycle is fixed to exactly four weeks long. A **time-box** scheduling strategy is assumed, in which a development cycle is set to a fixed time limit.

In this situation, the use case is redefined in terms of several use case versions, each of which encompasses more and more of the complete use case requirements. Each use case version is limited to cover what is estimated to be a reasonable amount of work within the confines of the development cycle time-box (say, four weeks). For example:

- Buy Items—version 1 (cash payments, no inventory updates, ...)
- Buy Items—version 2 (allow all payment types)
- Buy Items—version 3 (complete version including inventory updates, ...)

These versions are then distributed over a series of development cycles, along with other use cases.

## 7.5.2    Use Case Allocation

Based on the ranking of use cases and multiple versions of the *Buy Items* use case, some of the use cases might be allocated to development cycle as shown in Figure 7.2.

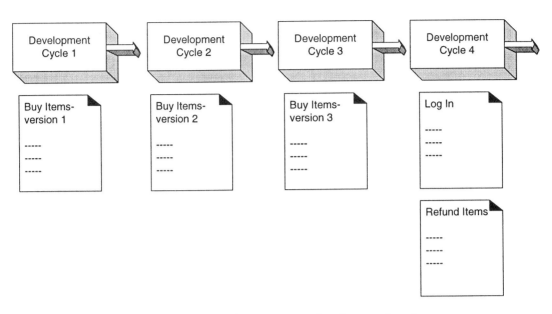

**Figure 7.2** Allocation of use cases to development cycles.

# 7.6 Use Case Versions of "Buy Items"

Once it has been decided to simplify a use case and express it, several increasingly complex versions must be written. It must also be stated what simplifications, goals, and assumptions each version makes. The following sections provide hints.

## 7.6.1 Buy Items-Version 1

### Simplifications, Goals, and Assumptions

■ Cash payments only.

■ No inventory maintenance.

■ It is a stand-alone store, not part of a larger organization.

■ Manual entry of UPCs; no bar code reader.

■ No tax calculations.

■ No coupons.

■ Cashier does not have to log in; no access control.

■ There is no record maintained of the individual customers and their buying habits.

- There is no control of the cash drawer.

- Name and address of store, and date and time of sale, are shown on the receipt.

- Cashier ID and POST ID are not shown on receipt.

- Completed sales are recorded in an historical log.

| | |
|---|---|
| Use case: | **Buy Items-version 1** |
| Actors: | Customer (initiator), Cashier |
| Purpose: | Capture a sale and its cash payment. |
| Overview: | A Customer arrives at a checkout with items to purchase. The Cashier records the purchase items and collects a cash payment. On completion, the Customer leaves with the items. |
| Type | primary and essential |
| Cross References: | *Functions*: R1.1, R1.2, R1.3, R1.5, R1.7, R1.9, R2.1 |

### Typical Course of Events

| Actor Action | System Response |
|---|---|
| 1. This use case begins when a Customer arrives at a POST checkout with items to purchase. | |
| 2. The Cashier records the universal product code (UPC) from each item.<br>If there is more than one of the same item, the Cashier can enter the quantity as well. | 3. Determines the item price and adds the item information to the running sales transaction.<br><br>The description and price of the current item are presented. |
| 4. On completion of item entry, the Cashier indicates to the POST that item entry is complete. | 5. Calculates and presents the sale total. |
| 6. The Cashier tells the Customer the total. | |
| 7. The Customer gives a cash payment—the "cash tendered"—possibly greater than the sale total. | |

### Typical Course of Events

| Actor Action | System Response |
|---|---|
| 8. The Cashier records the cash received amount. | 9. Shows the balance due back to the Customer. |
| | Generates a receipt. |
| 10. The Cashier deposits the cash received and extracts the balance owing.<br>The Cashier gives the balance owing and the printed receipt to the Customer. | 11. Logs completed sale. |
| 12. The Customer leaves with the items purchased. | |

## 7.6.2   Buy Items-Version 2

### Simplifications, Goals, and Assumptions

All simplifications in version 1 apply, except that payment may be by cash, credit, and check. Credit and check payments are authorized.

| | |
|---|---|
| Use case: | **Buy Items-version 2** |
| Actors: | Customer (initiator), Cashier |
| Purpose: | Capture a sale and its payment. |
| Overview: | A Customer arrives at a checkout with items to purchase. The Cashier records the purchase items and collects a payment, which may be authorized. On completion, the Customer leaves with the items. |
| | and so on ... |

# 7.7   Summary

We are now prepared to transition to the iterative development phase. In the first development cycle the use case *Buy Items—version 1* will be tackled.

# STARTING A DEVELOPMENT CYCLE

```
+--------------------------------------------------------------+
|                        Objectives                            |
|                                                              |
|  ■  Summarize the transition from the Plan and Elaborate     |
|     phase to the iterative Build phase.                      |
|                                                              |
+--------------------------------------------------------------+
```

## 8.1    Starting a Development Cycle

Assume that the Plan and Elaborate phase has completed, and that the use cases have been identified, ranked, and scheduled—at least for the first couple of development cycles. A major transition now occurs—the Build phase starts, within which iterative development cycles occur (see Figure 8.1). In the first development cycle it has been decided to tackle a simplified version of *Buy Items* that includes cash-only payments and no inventory control.

The initial activities within the cycle are project management related. In the general case, this is followed by (or more likely, occurring in parallel) a synchronization of documentation (for example, diagrams) from the last cycle with the actual state of the code, because during the coding phase of the last cycle the design artifacts and the code invariably diverge.

Then an analyze phase (or analysis phase) is entered, within which the problems of the current cycle are closely investigated. Within the analysis phase, one of the early activities is the development of a conceptual model, the subject of the next chapter.

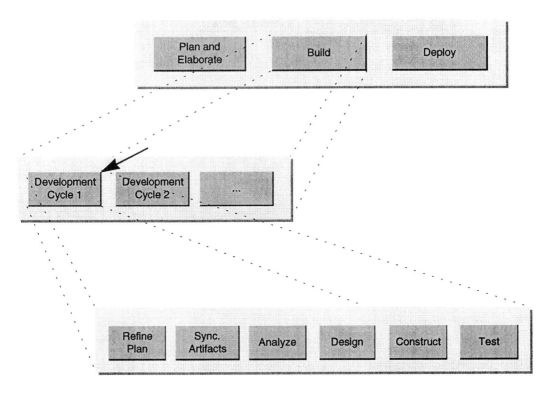

**Figure 8.1** A development cycle.

# PART II ANALYZE PHASE (1)

# BUILDING A CONCEPTUAL MODEL

## Objectives

- Identify concepts related to the current development cycle requirements.

- Create an initial conceptual model.

- Distinguish between correct and incorrect attributes.

- Add *specification* concepts, when appropriate.

- Compare and contrast the terms concept, type, interface and class.

## 9.1    Introduction

A conceptual model illustrates meaningful (to the modelers) concepts in a problem domain; it is the most important artifact to create during object-oriented analysis.[1] This chapter explores introductory skills in creating conceptual models. The following two chapters expand on conceptual modeling skills—looking at attributes and associations.

Identifying a rich set of objects or concepts is at the heart of object-oriented analysis, and well worth the effort in terms of payoff during the design and

---

1. Use cases are an important requirements analysis artifact, but are not really *object*-oriented. They emphasize a process view of the domain.

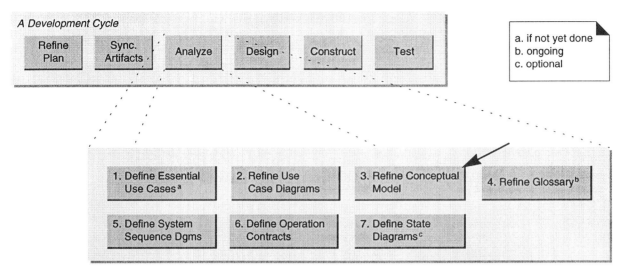

Analyze phase activities within a development cycle

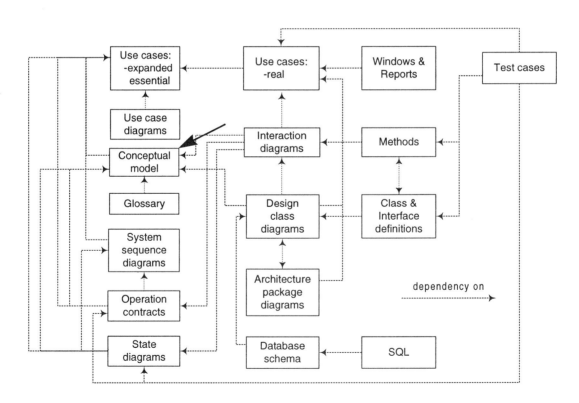

Build phase artifact dependencies.

implementation phase.

The identification of concepts is part of an investigation of the problem domain. The UML contains notation in the form of static structure diagrams to illustrate conceptual models.

---

A critical quality to appreciate about a conceptual model is that it is a representation of real-world things, not of software components.

---

## 9.2     Activities and Dependencies

One of the early major activities within a development cycle is the creation a conceptual model for the use cases of the current cycle. Its creation is dependent on having use cases and other documents from which concepts (objects) can be identified. The creation may not be linear; for example, the conceptual model may be made in parallel to the development of the use cases.

## 9.3     Conceptual Models

The quintessential *object*-oriented step in analysis or investigation is the decomposition of the problem into individual concepts or objects—the things we are aware of. A **conceptual model** is a representation of concepts in a problem domain [MO95, Fowler96]. In the UML, a conceptual model is illustrated with a set of **static structure diagrams** in which no operations are defined. The term *conceptual model* has the advantage of strongly emphasizing a focus on domain concepts, not software entities.

It may show:

■    concepts

■    associations between concepts

■    attributes of concepts

For example, Figure 9.1 shows a partial conceptual model in the domain of the store and sales. It illustrates that the concept of *Payment* and *Sale* are significant in this problem domain, that a *Payment* is related to a *Sale* in a way that is meaningful to note, and that a *Sale* has a date and time. The details of the notation are not important at this time.

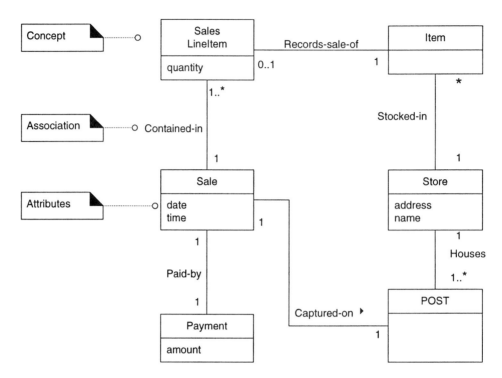

**Figure 9.1** Partial conceptual model. The numbers at each end of the line indicate multiplicity, which is described in a subsequent chapter.

## 9.3.1 Understanding Domain Vocabulary

In addition to decomposing the problem space into comprehensible units (concepts), creating a conceptual model aids in clarifying the terminology or vocabulary of the domain. It can be viewed as a model that communicates (to interested parties such as developers) what the important terms are, and how they are related.

## 9.3.2 Conceptual Models are not Models of Software Designs

A conceptual model, as shown in Figure 9.2, is a description of things in the real world problem domain, *not* of the software design, such as a Java or C++ class (see Figure 9.3). Therefore, the following elements are not suitable in a conceptual model:

■ No software artifacts, such as a window or a database, unless the domain being modeled is of software concepts, such as a model of graphical user interfaces.

■ No responsibilities or methods.[1]

**Figure 9.2** A conceptual model shows real-world concepts.

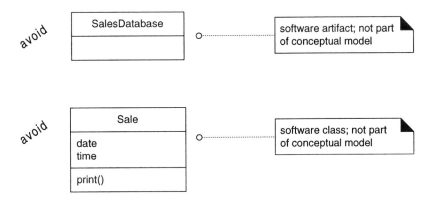

**Figure 9.3** A conceptual model does not show software artifacts or classes.

## 9.3.3 Concepts

Informally, a concept is an idea, thing, or object. More formally, a concept may be considered in terms of its symbol, intension, and extension [MO95] (see Figure 9.4).

■ **Symbol**—words or images representing a concept.

■ **Intension**—the definition of a concept.

■ **Extension**—the set of examples to which the concept applies.

For example, consider the concept of the event of a purchase transaction. I may choose to name it by the symbol *Sale*. The intension of a *Sale* may state that it "represents the event of a purchase transaction, and has a date and time." The extension of *Sale* is all the examples of sales; in other words, the set of all sales.

---

1. Responsibilities are usually related to software entities, and methods always are, but the conceptual model describes real-world concepts, not software entities. Considering responsibilities during the *design* phase is very important; it is just not part of this model.

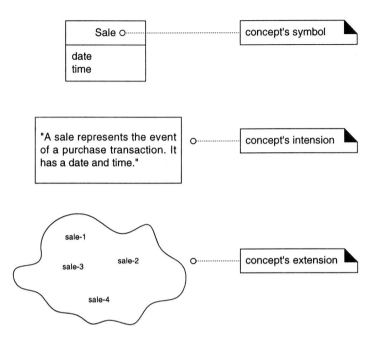

**Figure 9.4** A concept has a symbol, intension, and extension.

When creating a conceptual model, it is usually the symbol and intensional view of a concept that is of most practical interest.

## 9.3.4   Conceptual Models and Decomposition

Software problems can be complex; decomposition—divide-and-conquer—is a common strategy to deal with this complexity by division of the problem space into comprehensible units. In **structured analysis** the dimension of decomposition is by processes or *functions*. However, in object-oriented analysis the dimension of decomposition is fundamentally by concepts.

> A central distinction between object-oriented and structured analysis: division by concepts (objects) rather than division by functions.

Therefore a primary task of the analysis phase is to identify different concepts in the problem domain and document the results in a conceptual model.

## 9.3.5    Concepts in the Point-of-Sale Domain

For example, in the real-world problem domain of buying items in a store at a point-of-sale terminal, there are the concepts of a *Store*, *POST,* and a *Sale*. Therefore, our conceptual model, shown in Figure 9.5, may include a *Store*, *POST,* and *Sale*.

**Figure 9.5** Partial conceptual model in the domain of the store.

# 9.4    Strategies to Identify Concepts

Our goal is to create a conceptual model of interesting or meaningful concepts in the domain under consideration. In this case, that means concepts related to the use case *Buy Items—version 1*. The central task is therefore to identify concepts; two strategies are presented.

The following is an useful guideline in identifying concepts:

> It is better to overspecify a conceptual model with lots of fine-grained concepts, than to underspecify it.

Do not think that a conceptual model is better if it has fewer concepts; quite the opposite tends to be true.

It is common to miss concepts during the initial identification phase, and to discover them later during the consideration of attributes or associations, or during the design phase. When found, they are added to the conceptual model.

Do not exclude a concept simply because the requirements do not indicate any obvious need to remember information about it (a criterion common in data modeling for relational database design, but not relevant to conceptual modeling), or because the concept has no attributes. It is perfectly valid to have attributeless concepts, or concepts which have a purely behavioral role in the domain instead of an information role.

## 9.4.1    Finding Concepts with the Concept Category List

Start the creation of a conceptual model by making a list of candidate concepts from the following list. It contains many common categories that are usually worth considering, though not in any particular order of importance. Examples are drawn from the store and airline reservation domains.

| Concept Category | Examples |
|---|---|
| physical or tangible objects | *POST* <br> *Airplane* |
| specifications, designs, or descriptions of things | *ProductSpecification* <br> *FlightDescription* |
| places | *Store* <br> *Airport* |
| transactions | *Sale, Payment* <br> *Reservation* |
| transaction line items | *SalesLineItem* |
| roles of people | *Cashier* <br> *Pilot* |
| containers of other things | *Store, Bin* <br> *Airplane* |
| things in a container | *Item* <br> *Passenger* |
| other computer or electro-mechanical systems external to our system | *CreditCardAuthorizationSystem* <br> *AirTrafficControl* |
| abstract noun concepts | *Hunger* <br> *Acrophobia* |
| organizations | *SalesDepartment* <br> *ObjectAirline* |
| events | *Sale, Robbery, Meeting* <br> *Flight, Crash, Landing* |
| processes <br> (often *not* represented as a concept, but may be) | *SellingAProduct* <br> *BookingASeat* |

| Concept Category | Examples |
|---|---|
| rules and policies | *RefundPolicy* <br> *CancellationPolicy* |
| catalogs | ProductCatalog <br> PartsCatalog |
| records of finance, work, contracts, legal matters | *Receipt, Ledger, EmploymentContract* <br> *MaintenanceLog* |
| financial instruments and services | *LineOfCredit* <br> *Stock* |
| manuals, books | *EmployeeManual* <br> *RepairManual* |

## 9.4.2   *Finding Concepts with Noun Phrase Identification*

Another useful technique (because of its simplicity) proposed in [Abbot83] is to identify the noun and noun phrases in textual descriptions of a problem domain, and consider them as candidate concepts or attributes.

> Care must be applied with this method; a mechanical noun-to-concept mapping isn't possible, and words in natural languages are ambiguous (especially English).

Nevertheless, it is another source of inspiration. The expanded use cases are an excellent description to draw from for this analysis. For example, the *Buy Items-version 1* use case can be used.

|  | **Actor Action** | | **System Response** |
|---|---|---|---|
| **1.** | This use case begins when a **Customer** arrives at a **POST checkout** with **items** to purchase. | | |
| **2.** | The **Cashier** records the **universal product code** (UPC) from each **item**. | **3.** | Determines the **item price** and adds the item information to the running **sales transaction**. |
|  | If there is more than one of the same **item**, the **Cashier** can enter the **quantity** as well. | | The **description** and **price** of the current **item** are displayed. |

Some of these noun phrases are candidate concepts; some may be attributes of concepts. Please see the subsequent section and chapter on attributes for advice on distinguishing between the two.

A weakness of this approach is the imprecision of natural language; different noun phrases may represent the same concept or attribute, among other ambiguities. Nevertheless, it is recommended in combination with the *Concept Category List* technique.

# 9.5   Candidate Concepts for the Point-of-Sale Domain

From the *Concept Category List* and noun-phrase analysis, we generate a list of candidate concepts for the point-of-sale application. The list is constrained to the requirements and simplifications currently under consideration—the simplified use cases *Buying Items-version 1*.

| | |
|---|---|
| *POST* | *ProductSpecification* |
| *Item* | *SalesLineItem* |
| *Store* | *Cashier* |
| *Sale* | *Customer* |
| *Payment* | *Manager* |
| *ProductCatalog* | |

## 9.5.1    Report Objects—Include Receipt in the Model?

A receipt is a record of a sale and payment and a relatively prominent concept in the domain of sales, so should it be shown in the model? Here are some factors to consider:

- A receipt is a report of a sale. In general, showing a report in a conceptual model is not useful since all its information is derived from other sources. This is one reason to exclude it.

- A receipt has a special role in terms of the business rules: it usually confers the right to the bearer of the receipt to return their bought items. This is a reason to show it in the model.

Since item returns are not being considered in this development cycle, *Receipt* will be excluded. During the development cycle that tackles the *Return Items* use case, it would be justified to include.

## 9.5.2    The Point-of-Sale Conceptual Model (concepts only)

The previous list of concept names may be represented graphical (see Figure 9.6) in the UML static structure diagram notation to show the genesis of the conceptual model.

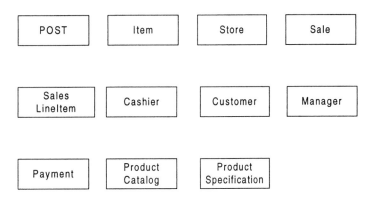

**Figure 9.6** Initial conceptual model for the point-of-sale domain.

Consideration of the attributes and associations for the conceptual model will be deferred to the subsequent chapters.

# 9.6    Conceptual Modeling Guidelines

## 9.6.1    How to Make a Conceptual Model

Apply the following steps to create a conceptual model.

---

To make a conceptual model:

1. List the candidate concepts using the *Concept Category List* and noun phrase identification related to the current requirements under consideration.

2. Draw them in a conceptual model.

3. Add the associations necessary to record relationships for which there is a need to preserve some memory (discussed in a subsequent chapter).

4. Add the attributes necessary to fulfill the information requirements (discussed in a subsequent chapter).

---

## 9.6.2    On Naming and Modeling Things: The Mapmaker

The mapmaker strategy applies to both maps and conceptual models.

---

Make a conceptual model in the spirit of how a cartographer or mapmaker works:

■    Use the existing names in the territory.

■    Exclude irrelevant features.

■    Do not add things that are not there.

---

A conceptual model is a kind of map of concepts or things in a domain. This spirit emphasizes the analytical role of a conceptual model, and suggests the following:

■    Mapmakers uses the names of the territory—they do not change the names of cities on a map. For a conceptual model, this means to *use the vocabulary of the domain when naming concepts and attributes*. For example, if developing a model for a library, name the customer a *"Borrower"* or *"Patron"*—the terms used by the library staff.

- A mapmaker deletes things from a map if they are not considered relevant to the purpose of the map; for example, topography or populations need not be shown. Similarly, a conceptual model may exclude concepts in the problem domain not pertinent to the requirements. For example, we may exclude *Pen* and *PaperBag* from our conceptual model (for the current set of requirements) since they do not have any obvious noteworthy role.

- A mapmaker does not show things that are not there, such as a mountain that does not exist. Similarly, the conceptual model should exclude things *not* in the problem domain under consideration.

### 9.6.3 A Common Mistake in Identifying Concepts

Perhaps the most common mistake when creating a conceptual model is to represent something as an attribute when it should have been a concept. A rule of thumb to help prevent this mistake is:

> If we do not think of some concept X as a number or text in the real world, X is probably a concept, not an attribute.

For example, consider the domain of airline reservations. Should *destination* be an attribute of *Flight*, or a separate concept *Airport*?

In the real world, a destination airport is not considered a number or text—it is a massive thing that occupies space. Therefore, *Airport* should be a concept.

> If in doubt, make it a separate concept.

## 9.7 Resolving Similar Concepts—POST versus Register

In earlier times, long before point-of-sale terminals, a store maintained a *register*—a book that logged sales and payments. Eventually this was automated in a mechanical cash register. Today, a point-of-sale terminal fulfills the role of the register (see Figure 9.7).

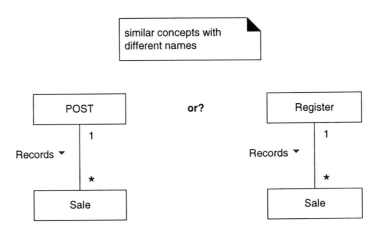

**Figure 9.7** POST and register are similar concepts.

A register is a thing which records sales and payments, but so is a point-of-sale terminal. However, the term *register* seems somewhat more abstract and less implementation oriented than *POST*. So, in the conceptual model, should the symbol *Register* be used instead of *POST*?

> First, as a rule of thumb, a conceptual model is not absolutely correct or wrong, but more or less useful; it is a tool of communication.

By the mapmaker principle, *POST* is a term familiar in the territory, so it is a useful symbol from the point of view of familiarity and communication. By the goal of creating models which represent abstractions and are implementation independent, *Register* is appealing and useful.[1]

Both choices have merits; *POST* has been chosen in this case study somewhat arbitrarily, *Register* would also have been suitable.

# 9.8    Modeling the *Unreal* World

Some software systems are for domains that find very little analog in natural or business domains; software for telecommunications is an example. It is still possible to create a conceptual model in these domains, but it requires a high degree of abstraction and stepping back from familiar designs.

---

1. Note that in earlier times a *register* was just one possible implementation of how to record sales. The term has acquired a generalized meaning over time.

For example, here are some candidate concepts related to a telecommunication switch: *Message, Connection, Dialog, Route, Protocol*.

# 9.9 Specification or Description Concepts

Assume the following:

- An *Item* instance represents a physical item in a store; as such, it may even have a serial number.

- An *Item* has a description, price, and UPC which are not recorded anywhere else.

- Everyone working in the store has amnesia.

- Every time a real physical item is sold, a corresponding software instance of *Item* is deleted from "software land."

With these assumptions, what happens in the following scenario?

There is strong demand for the popular new vegetarian burger—ObjectBurger. The store sells out, implying that all *Item* instances of ObjectBurgers are deleted from computer memory.

Now, here is the heart of the problem: if someone asks, "How much do Object-Burgers cost?", no one can answer, because the memory of their price was attached to inventoried instances, which were deleted as they were sold.

Notice also that the current model, if implemented in software as described, has duplicate data and is space inefficient, because the description, price, and UPC are duplicated for every *Item* instance of the same product.

## 9.9.1 The Need for Specifications

The preceding problem illustrates the need for a concept of objects that are specifications or descriptions of other things. To solve the *Item* problem, what is needed is a *ProductSpecification* (or *ItemSpecification, ProductDescription*, ...) concept that records information about items. A *ProductSpecification* does not represent an *Item*, it represents a description of information *about* items. Note that even if all inventoried items are sold and their corresponding *Item* software instances are deleted, the *ProductSpecifications* still remain.

Description or specification objects are strongly related to the things they describe. In a conceptual model, it is common to state that an *XSpecification Describes an X*.

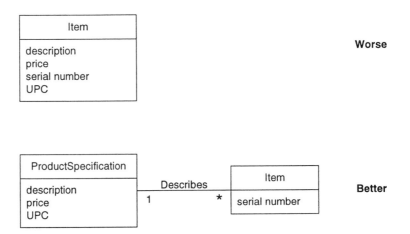

**Figure 9.8** Specifications about other things. The "*" means a multiplicity of "many". It indicates that one *ProductSpecification* may describe many (*) *Items*.

The need for specification concepts is common in sales and product domains. It is also common in manufacturing, where a *description* of a manufactured thing is required that is distinct from the thing itself. Time and space have been taken in motivating specification concepts because they are very common; it is not a rare modeling concept.

## 9.9.2 When are Specification Concepts Required?

The following guideline suggests when to use specifications.

> Add a specification or description concept (for example, *ProductSpecification*) when:
>
> ■ Deleting instances of things they describe (for example, *Item*) results in a loss of information that needs to be maintained, due to the incorrect association of information with the deleted thing.
>
> ■ It reduces redundant or duplicated information.

## 9.9.3 Another Specification Example

As a final example, consider an airline company which suffers a fatal crash of one of their planes. Assume that all their flights are cancelled for six months pending completion of an investigation. Also assume that when flights are cancelled, their corresponding *Flight* software objects are deleted from computer memory. Therefore, after the crash, all *Flight* objects are deleted.

If the only record of what airport a flight goes to is in the *Flight* instances, which represent specific flights for a particular date and time, then there is no longer a record of what flight routes the airline has.

To solve this problem, a *FlightDescription* (or *FlightSpecification*) is required that describes a flight and its route, even when a particular flight is not scheduled (see Figure 9.9).

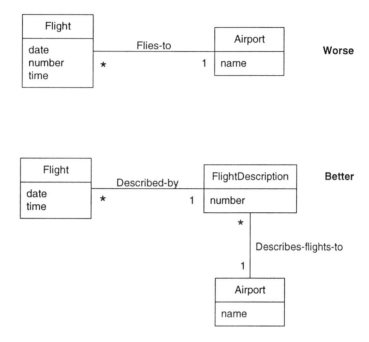

**Figure 9.9** Specifications about other things.

# 9.10 Defining Terms in the UML

In the UML, the terms "class" and "type" are used, but not "concept". There is no universal agreement on the meaning of class and type, so to avoid ambiguity the UML precisely defines these terms as used in its metamodel (the model of the UML itself), although alternative and contradictory definitions are used by other authors and practioners.

Regardless of the definition, the bottom line is that it is useful to distinguish between the perspective of a domain analyst looking at real-world concepts such as a sale, and software designers specifying software entities such as a *Sale* class in Java. The UML can be used to illustrate both perspectives with very similar notation and terminology, so it is important to bear in mind which perspective is being taken (an analysis, design, or implementation view).

> To keep things simple, in this book the term "concept" will be used to refer to real-world things, and "class" will be used to refer to software specifications and implementations.

The UML definition of a **class** is "a description of a set of objects that share the same attributes, operations, methods, relationships, and semantics" [BJR97]. Some authors restrict the definition of a class to being a concrete software implementation, such as a Java class [Fowler96]. However, in the UML, the term is treated more broadly, encompassing specifications that precede implementation. In the UML, an implemented software class is called more specifically an **implementation class**.

In the UML, an **operation** is "a service that can requested from an object to effect behavior" [BJR97], and a **method** is the implementation of an operation, specifying the operation's algorithm or procedure.

The UML definition of a **type** is similar to a class—it describes a set of like objects with attributes and operations—but it may not include any methods. The implication is that a type is a *specification* of a software entity, rather than an implementation. This also implies that a UML type is language independent.

Although not strictly accurate in the context of the UML, this book sometimes uses the terms "concept" and "type" interchangeably, because in popular usage the term "type" is often defined as a synonym for a real-world concept [MO95].

The term **interface** is defined as a set of externally visible operations. In terms of the UML, they may be associated with types and classes (and with packages—which group elements). Although real-world concepts may have an interface (for example, the interface to a phone), the term is typically used in the context of an interface for software entities, such as the Java *Runnable* interface.

# 9.11    Sample Models

The Conceptual Model is composed of UML static structure diagrams illustrating concepts in the domain, as shown in Figure 9.10.

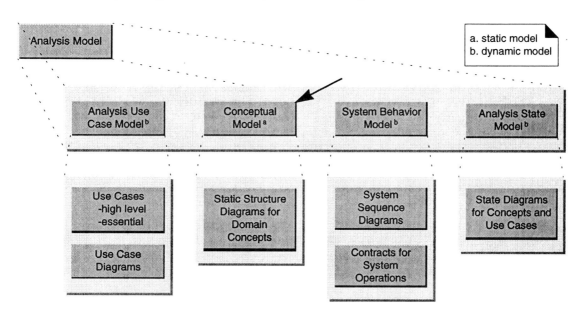

**Figure 9.10**  The Analysis Model.

# CONCEPTUAL MODEL— ADDING ASSOCIATIONS

## 10.1    Introduction

It is necessary to identify those associations of concepts that are needed to satisfy the information requirements of the current use cases under development, and which aid in comprehension of the conceptual model. This chapter explores the identification of suitable associations, and adds associations to the conceptual model for the point-of-sale system.

## 10.2    Associations

An **association** is a relationship between concepts that indicates some meaningful and interesting connection (see Figure 10.1).

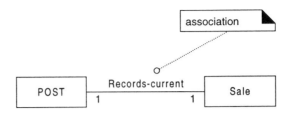

**Figure 10.1** Associations.

In the UML they are described as "structural relationships between objects of different types."

### 10.2.1 Criteria for Useful Associations

Associations worth noting usually imply knowledge of a relationship that needs to be preserved for some duration—it could be milliseconds or years, depending on context. In other words, between what objects do we need to have some memory of a relationship? For example, do we need to remember what *SalesLineItem* instances are associated with a *Sale* instance? Definitely, otherwise it would not be possible to reconstruct the sale, print a receipt, or calculate a sale total.

---

Consider including the following associations in a conceptual model:

- Associations for which knowledge of the relationship needs to be preserved for some duration ("need-to-know" associations).

- Associations derived from the *Common Associations List*.

---

In contrast, do we need to have memory of a relationship between a current *Sale* and a *Manager*? No, the requirements do not suggest that any such relationship is needed. It may not be incorrect to show a relationship between a *Sale* and *Manager*, but it is not compelling or useful in the context of our requirements.

## 10.3 The UML Association Notation

An association is represented as a line between concepts with an association name. The association is inherently bidirectional, meaning that from objects of either type logical traversal to the other is possible. This traversal is purely abstract; it is *not* a statement about connections between software entities.

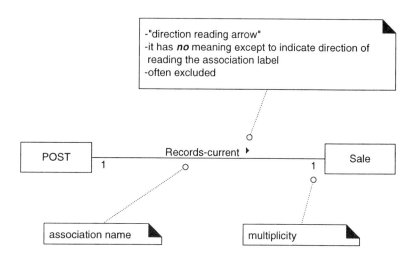

**Figure 10.2** The UML notation for associations.

The ends of an association may contain a multiplicity expression indicating the numerical relationship between instances of the concepts.

An optional reading direction arrow (or "name-direction arrow") indicates the direction to read the association name; it does not indicate direction of visibility or navigation. If not present, it is conventional to read the association from left to right or top to bottom, although the UML does not make this a rule (see Figure 10.2).

> The reading direction arrow has no semantic meaning; it is only an aid to the reader of the diagram.

## 10.4 Finding Associations—Common Associations List

Start the addition of associations by using the following list. It contains common categories that are usually worth considering. Examples are drawn from the store and airline reservation domains.

| Category | Examples |
|---|---|
| A is a physical part of B | *Drawer—POST*<br>*Wing—Airplane* |
| A is a logical part of B | *SalesLineItem—Sale*<br>*FlightLeg—FlightRoute* |
| A is physically contained in/on B | *POST—Store, Item—Shelf*<br>*Passenger—Airplane* |
| A is logically contained in B | *ItemDescription—Catalog*<br>*Flight—FlightSchedule* |
| A is a description for B | *ItemDescription—Item*<br>*FlightDescription—Flight* |
| A is a line item of a transaction or report B | *SalesLineItem—Sale*<br>*MaintenanceJob—Maintenance-Log* |
| A is known/logged/recorded/reported/captured in B | *Sale—POST*<br>*Reservation—FlightManifest* |
| A is a member of B | *Cashier—Store*<br>*Pilot—Airline* |
| A is an organizational subunit of B | *Department—Store*<br>*Maintenance—Airline* |
| A uses or manages B | *Cashier—POST*<br>*Pilot—Airplane* |
| A communicates with B | *Customer—Cashier*<br>*ReservationAgent—Passenger* |
| A is related to a transaction B | *Customer—Payment*<br>*Passenger—Ticket* |

| Category | Examples |
|---|---|
| A is a transaction related to another transaction B | *Payment—Sale*<br>*Reservation—Cancellation* |
| A is next to B | *POST—POST*<br>*City—City* |
| A is owned by B | *POST—Store*<br>*Plane—Airline* |

### 10.4.1  High Priority Associations

Here are some high priority association categories that are invariably useful to include in a conceptual model:

- A is a *physical or logical part* of B.

- A is *physically or logically contained* in/on B.

- A is *recorded in* B.

## 10.5  How Detailed Should Associations Be?

Associations are important, but a common pitfall in creating conceptual models is to spend too much time during investigation trying to discover them. It is critical to appreciate the following:

> Finding *concepts* is much more important than finding associations. The majority of time spent in conceptual model creation should be devoted to identifying concepts, not associations.

## 10.6    Association Guidelines

> Association Guidelines:
>
> ■  Focus on those associations for which knowledge of the relationship needs to be preserved for some duration ("need-to-know" associations).
>
> ■  It is more important to identify *concepts* than to identify associations.
>
> ■  Too many associations tend to confuse a conceptual model rather than illuminate it. Their discovery can be time-consuming, with marginal benefit.
>
> ■  Avoid showing redundant or derivable associations.

## 10.7    Roles

Each end of an association is called a **role**. Roles may optionally have:

■  name

■  multiplicity expression

■  navigability

Multiplicity is investigated now, but the other two features are discussed in later chapters.

### 10.7.1   Multiplicity

**Multiplicity** defines how many instances of a type *A* can be associated with one instance of a type *B*, at a particular moment in time (see Figure 10.3).

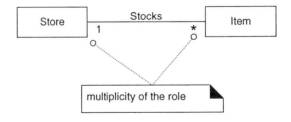

**Figure 10.3** Multiplicity on an association.

For example, a single instance of a *Store* can be associated with "many" (zero or more, indicated by the * ) *Item* instances.

Some examples of multiplicity expressions are shown in Figure 10.4.

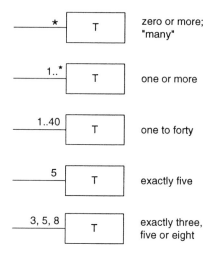

**Figure 10.4** Multiplicity values.

In the UML, the multiplicity value is context dependent. Rumbaugh [Rumbaugh91] gives the excellent example of *Person* and *Company* in the *Works-for* association. Indicating if a *Person* instance works for one or many *Company* instances is dependent on the context of the model; the tax department is interested in *many*; a union probably only *one*.

# 10.8    Naming Associations

> Name an association based on a *TypeName-VerbPhrase-TypeName* format where the verb phrase creates a sequence that is readable and meaningful in the model context.

Association names should start with a capital letter. A verb phrase should be constructed with hyphens.

In Figure 10.5, the default direction to read an association name is left to right or top to bottom. This is not a UML default, but it is a relatively common conventio

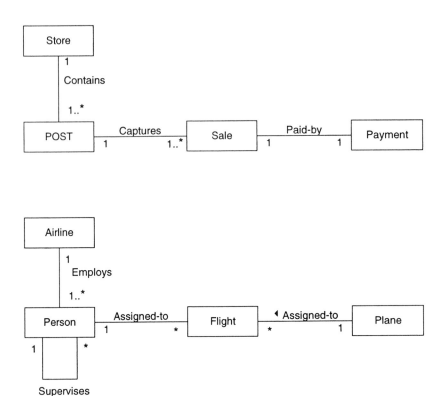

**Figure 10.5** Association names.

# 10.9 Multiple Associations Between Two Types

Two types may have multiple associations between them; this is not uncommon. There is no outstanding example in our POST system, but an example from the domain of the airline is the relationships between a *Flight* and an *Airport* (see Figure 10.6); the flying-to and flying-from associations are distinctly different relationships which should be shown separately. Note also that not every flight is guaranteed to land at an airport!

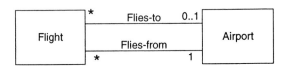

**Figure 10.6** Multiple associations.

## 10.10    Associations and Implementation

During the analysis phase, an association is *not* a statement about data flows, instance variables, or object connections in a software solution; it is a statement that a relationship is meaningful in a purely analytical sense—in the real world. Practically speaking, many of these relationships will typically be implemented in software as paths of navigation and visibility, but their presence in an investigative or analytical view of a conceptual model does not require their implementation.

When creating a conceptual model, we may define associations that are not necessary during construction. Conversely, we may discover associations that needed to be implemented but were missed during the analysis phase. In that case, the conceptual model should be updated to reflect these discoveries.

Later on we will discuss ways to implement associations in an object-oriented programming language (the most common is to use an attribute that points to an instance of the associated class), but for now it is valuable to think of them as purely analytical expressions; *not* statements about a database or software solution. As always, deferring design considerations frees us from extraneous information and decisions within the analysis model and maximizes our options later on.

## 10.11    Point-of-Sale Domain Associations

We can now add associations to our point-of-sale system conceptual model. We should add those associations which the requirements (for example, use cases) suggest or imply a need to remember, or which otherwise are strongly suggested in our perception of the problem domain. When tackling a new problem, the common categories of associations presented earlier should be reviewed and considered, as they represent many of the relevant associations that typically need to be recorded.

### 10.11.1  Unforgettable Relationships in the Store

The following sample of associations are justified in terms of a need-to-know. It is based on the use cases currently under consideration.

| *POST Captures Sale* | In order to know the current sale, generate a total, print a receipt. |
|---|---|

| *Sale Paid-by Payment* | In order to know if the sale has been paid, relate the amount tendered to the sale total, and print a receipt. |
| *ProductCatalog Records Item-Specification* | In order to retrieve an *ItemSpecification*, given a UPC. |

## 10.11.2 Applying the Category of Associations Checklist

We will run through the checklist, based on previously identified types, considering the current use case requirements.

| **Category** | **POST System** |
|---|---|
| A is a physical part of B | *not applicable* |
| A is a logical part of B | *SalesLineItem—Sale* |
| A is physically contained in/on B | *POST—Store*<br>*Item—Store* |
| A is logically contained in B | *ProductSpecification—ProductCatalog*<br>*ProductCatalog—Store* |
| A is a description for B | *ProductSpecification—Item* |
| A is a line item of a transaction or report B | *SalesLineItem—Sale* |
| A is logged/recorded/reported/captured in B | *(completed) Sales—Store*<br>*(current) Sale—POST* |
| A is a member of B | *Cashier—Store* |
| A is an organizational subunit of B | *not applicable* |
| A uses or manages B | *Cashier—POST*<br>*Manager—POST*<br>*Manager—Cashier, but probably not applicable.* |
| A communicates with B | *Customer—Cashier* |

| Category | POST System |
|---|---|
| A is related to a transaction B | *Customer—Payment*<br>*Cashier—Payment* |
| A is a transaction related to another transaction B | *Payment—Sale* |
| A is next to B | *POST—POST, but probably not applicable* |
| A is owned by B | *POST—Store* |

# 10.12 Point-of-Sale Conceptual Model

The conceptual model in Figure 10.7 shows a set of concepts and associations that are candidates for our point-of-sale application. The associations were primarily derived from the candidate association checklist.

## 10.12.1 Preserve Only Need-to-Know Associations?

The set of associations shown in the conceptual model of Figure 10.7 were fairly mechanically derived from the association checklist. However, it may be desirable to be more choosy in the associations included in our conceptual model. Viewed as a tool of communication, it is undesirable to overwhelm the conceptual model with associations that are not strongly required and which do not illuminate our understanding. Too many uncompelling associations obscure rather than clarify.

As previously suggested, the following criteria for showing associations is recommended:

> - Focus on those associations for which knowledge of the relationship needs to be preserved for some duration ("need-to-know" associations).
> - Avoid showing redundant or derivable associations.

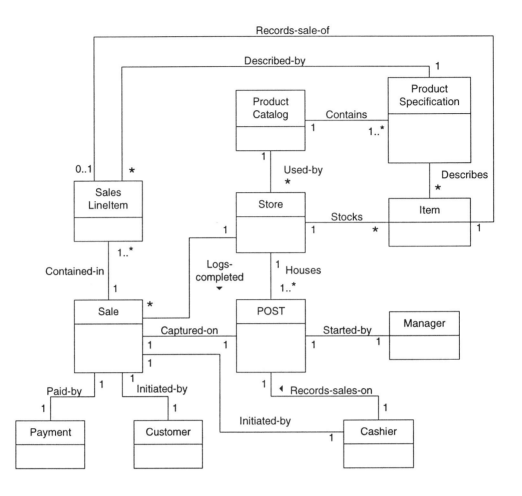

**Figure 10.7** A point-of-sale conceptual model.

Based on this advice, not every association currently shown is compelling. Consider the following:

| Association | Discussion |
|---|---|
| *Sale Entered-by Cashier* | The requirements do not indicate a need-to-know or record the current cashier. Also, it is derivable if the *POST Used-by Cashier* association is present. |
| *POST Used-by Cashier* | The requirements do not indicate a need-to-know or record the current cashier. |

| Association | Discussion |
|---|---|
| *POST Started-by Manager* | The requirements do not indicate a need-to-know or record the manager who starts up a *POST*. |
| *Sale Initiated-by Customer* | The requirements do not indicate a need-to-know or record the current customer who initiates a sale. |
| *Store Stocks Item* | The requirements do not indicate a need-to-know or maintain inventory information. |
| *SalesLineItem Records-sale-of Item* | The requirements do not indicate a need-to-know or maintain inventory information. |

Note that the ability to justify an association in terms of need-to-know is dependent on the requirements; obviously a change in these—such as requiring that the cashier's ID show on a receipt—changes the need to remember a relationship.

Based on the above analysis, it *may* be justifiable to delete the associations in question.

## 10.12.2 Associations For Need-to-Know versus Comprehension

A strict need-to-know criterion for maintaining associations will generate a minimal "information model" of what is needed to model the problem domain—bounded by the current requirements under consideration. However, this approach may create a model which does not convey (to ourselves or another person) a full understanding of the domain.

Sometimes we view the conceptual model not as a strict information model but as a tool of communication in which we are trying to understand the important concepts and their relationships. From this viewpoint, deleting some associations that are not strictly demanded on a need-to-know basis can create a model which misses the point; it does not communicate key ideas and relationships.

For example, in the point-of-sale application: although on a strict need-to-know basis it might not be necessary to record *Sale Initiated-by Customer*, its absence leaves out an important aspect in understanding the domain—that a customer generates sales.

In terms of associations, a good model is constructed somewhere in the middle between a minimal need-to-know model and one which illustrates every conceivable relationship. The basic criterion for judging its value?—Does it satisfy all need-to-know requirements and additionally clearly communicate an essential understanding of the important concepts in the problem domain?

> Emphasize need-to-know associations, but add choice comprehension-only associations to enrich critical understanding of the domain.

# CONCEPTUAL MODEL—
# ADDING ATTRIBUTES

---

### Objectives

- Identify attributes in a conceptual model.

- Distinguish between correct and incorrect attributes.

---

## 11.1    Introduction

It is necessary to identify those attributes of concepts that are needed to satisfy the information requirements of the current use cases under development. This chapter explores the identification of suitable attributes, and adds attributes to the conceptual model for the point-of-sale domain.

---

Recall that the conceptual model is a representation of real-world things, not of software components. Any statements regarding attributes should be interpreted in the context of real-world entities.

---

## 11.2    Attributes

An **attribute** is a logical data value of an object.

> Include the following attributes in a conceptual model:
>
> Those for which the requirements (for example, use cases) suggest or imply a need to remember information.

For example, a sales receipt normally includes a date and time. Consequently, the *Sale* concept needs a *date* and *time* attribute.

## 11.3    UML Attribute Notation

Attributes are shown in the second section of the concept box (see Figure 11.1). Their type may optionally be shown.

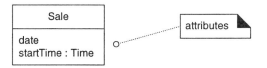

**Figure 11.1** Concept and attributes.

## 11.4    Valid Attribute Types

There are some things that should not be represented as attributes, but rather as associations. This section explores valid attributes.

### 11.4.1    *Keep Attributes Simple*

Intuitively, most simple attribute types are what are often thought of as primitive data types. The type of an attribute should not normally be a complex domain concept, such as a *Sale* or *Airport*. For example, the following *current-POST* attribute in the *Cashier* type in Figure 11.2 is undesirable because its type is meant to be a *POST*, which is not a simple attribute type (such as *Number* or *String*). The most useful way to express that a *Cashier* uses a *POST* is with an association, not with an attribute.

The attributes in a conceptual model should preferably be **simple attributes** or **pure data values**.

Very common simple attribute types include:

*Boolean, Date, Number, String (Text), Time*

Other common types include:

*Address, Color, Geometrics (Point, Rectangle, ...), Phone Number, Social Security Number, Universal Product Code (UPC), SKU, ZIP or postal codes, enumerated types*

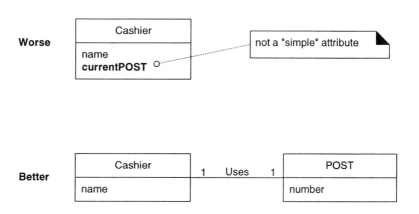

**Figure 11.2** Relate with associations, not attributes.

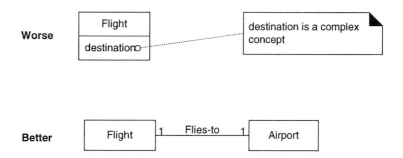

**Figure 11.3** Avoid representing complex domain concepts as attributes; use associations.

To repeat an earlier example, a common confusion is modeling a complex domain concept as an attribute. To illustrate, a destination airport is not really a string; it is a complex thing that occupies many square kilometers of space. Therefore, *Flight* should be related to *Airport* via an association, not with an attribute, as shown in Figure 11.3.

> Relate concepts with an association, not with an attribute.

## 11.4.2  Analysis versus Design: What About Attributes in Code?

The restriction that attributes in the conceptual model be only of simple data types does *not* imply that C++, Java, or Smalltalk attributes (data members, instance variables) must only be of simple, primitive data types. The conceptual model focuses on pure analytical statements about a problem domain, not software entities.

Later, during the design and construction phases it will be seen that the associations between objects expressed in the conceptual model will often be implemented as attributes that point to other complex types. However, this is but one of a number of possible design solutions to implement an association, and so the decision should be deferred during the analysis phase. During analysis is not the time to prematurely make design decisions.

## 11.4.3  Pure Data Values

More generally, attributes should be **pure data values** (or **DataTypes** in UML terms)—those for which unique identity is not meaningful (in the context of our model or system) [Rumbaugh91]. For example, it is not (usually) meaningful to distinguish between:

- Separate instances of the *Number* 5.

- Separate instances of the *String* 'cat'.

- Separate instances of *PhoneNumber* that contain the same number.

- Separate instances of *Address* that contain the same address.

In contrast, it *is* meaningful to distinguish (by identity) between two separate instances of a *Person* whose names are both "Jill Smith" because the two instances can represent separate individuals with the same name.

In terms of software, there are few situations where one would compare the memory address of instances of *Number, String, PhoneNumber,* or *Address*; only value-based comparisons are relevant. In contrast, it is conceivable to compare the memory addresses of *Person* instances, and to distinguish them, even if they had the same attribute values, because their unique identity is important.

> An element of a pure data value type may be illustrated in the attribute box section of another concept, although it is also acceptable to model it as a distinct concept.

Pure data values are also known as **value objects**.

The notion of pure data values is subtle. As a rule of thumb, stick to the basic test of "simple" attribute types: make it an attribute if it is naturally thought of as number, string, boolean, date, or time (and so on); otherwise represent it as a separate concept.

> If in doubt, define something as a separate concept rather than as an attribute.

## 11.4.4   Design Creep: No Attributes as Foreign Keys

Attributes should not be used to relate concepts in the conceptual model. The most common violation of this principle is to add a kind of **foreign key attribute**, as is typically done in relational database designs, in order to associate two types. For example, in Figure 11.4 the *currentPOSTNumber* attribute in the *Cashier* type is undesirable because its purpose is to relate the *Cashier* to a *POST* object. The better way to express that a *Cashier* uses a *POST* is with an association, not with a foreign key attribute. Once again, relate types with an association, not with an attribute.

There are many ways to relate objects—foreign keys being but one—and we should defer how we are going to implement the relation until the design phase, in order to avoid **design creep**.

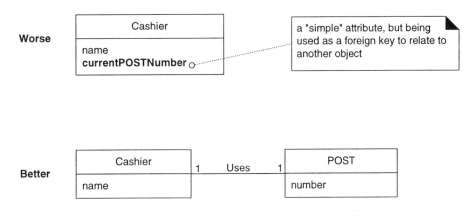

**Figure 11.4** Do not use attributes as foreign keys.

## 11.5    Non-primitive Attribute Types

The type of an attribute may be expressed as a non-primitive type in its own right in the conceptual model. For example, in the point-of-sale system there is a UPC (Universal Product Code). It is typically viewed as just a number. So should it be represented as a non-primitive type? Apply this guideline:

Represent what may initially be considered a primitive data type (such as a number or string) as a non-primitive type if:

■ It is composed of separate sections.

   ❏ phone number, name of person

■ There are operations usually associated with it, such as parsing or validation.

   ❏ social security number

■ It has other attributes.

   ❏ promotional price could have a start and end date

■ It is a quantity with a unit.

   ❏ payment amount has a unit of currency

Applying these guidelines to the point-of-sale conceptual model attributes yields the following analysis:

■ The *upc* should be a non-primitive *UPC* type, because it can be check-sum validated and may have other attributes (such as the manufacturer who assigned it).

■ The *price* and *amount* attributes should be non-primitive *Quantity* types, because they are quantities in a unit of currency.

■ The *address* attribute should be a non-primitive *Address* type because it has separate sections.

The types *UPC, Address,* and *Quantity* are pure data values (unique identity is not meaningful), so they may be shown in the attribute box section rather than related with an association line.

### 11.5.1   *Where to Illustrate Non-primitive Attribute Types and Pure Data Values?*

Should the *UPC* type be shown as a separate concept in a conceptual model? It depends on what you want to emphasize in the diagram. Since UPC is a *pure data value* (unique identity is not important), it may be shown in the attribute section of the concept box, as shown in Figure 11.5. But since it is a non-primitive type, with its own attributes and associations, it may be interesting to show it as a concept in its own box. There is no correct answer; it depends on how the conceptual model is being used as a tool of communication, and the significance of the concept in the domain.

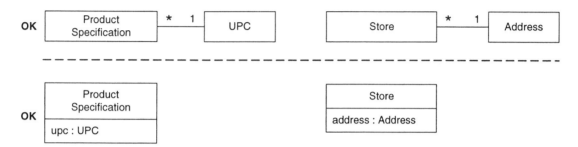

**Figure 11.5** If the attribute type is a pure data value, it may be shown in the attribute box.

> A conceptual model is a tool of communication; choices about what is shown should be made with that consideration.

# 11.6    Modeling Attribute Quantities and Units

Informally, the amount of a *Payment* may be represented as a *Number*. However, in the general case, this is not a robust or flexible scheme, because the *units* of a number are often important. Consider:

■   currency

■   velocity

For example, it is a common requirement that units need to be converted (for example, imperial to metric conversions). Assuming the point-of-sale software is for the international market, it would be necessary to know the currency unit of payments.

The solution is to represent *Quantity* as a distinct concept, with an associated *Unit*. Since quantities are considered pure data values (unique identity is not important), it is acceptable to collapse their illustration into the attribute section of the type box (see Figure 11.6).

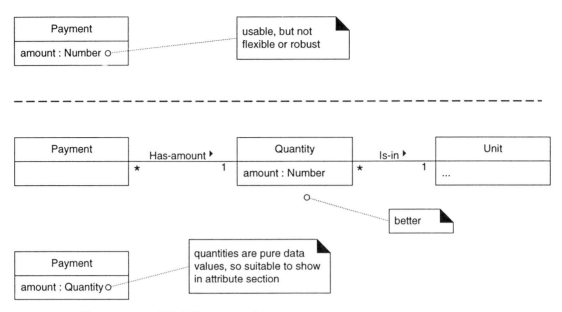

**Figure 11.6** Modeling quantities.

# 11.7    Attributes for the Point-of-Sale System

It is necessary to generate a list of attributes for the concepts of the point-of-sale domain. The list should primarily be constrained to the requirements and simplifications currently under consideration—the simplified use cases *Buy Items-version 1*.

Some attributes are clearly called for by reading:

■   requirements specifications

■   current use cases under consideration

■   simplification, clarification, and assumption documents

For example, it is ordinarily necessary to record the date and time of a sale. Therefore, the *Sale* concept requires a *date* and *time* attribute.

Other attributes are not obvious and may not be identified during analysis. This is acceptable; during the design and construction phases the remaining attributes will be discovered and added.

The next section summarizes the attribute choices suggested by the current use cases.

# 11.8    Attributes in the Point-of-Sale Model

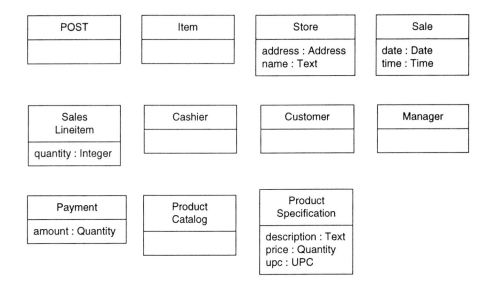

**Figure 11.7** Conceptual model showing attributes.

## 11.8.1   Discussion of POST Attributes

| | |
|---|---|
| *Payment* | *amount*—In order to determine if sufficient payment was provided, and to calculate change, an amount (also known as "amount tendered") must be captured. |
| *ProductSpecification* | *description*—In order to show the description on a display or receipt. |
| | *UPC*—In order to look up ItemSpecification, given an entered UPC, it is necessary to relate them to a *UPC*. |
| | *price*—In order to calculate the sales total, and show the line item price. |
| *Sale* | *date, time*—A receipt is a paper report of a sale. It normally shows date and time of sale. |

| | |
|---|---|
| *SalesLineItem* | *quantity*—In order to record the quantity entered, when there is more than one item in a line item sale (for example, *five* packages of tofu). |
| *Store* | *address, name*—The receipt requires the name and address of the store. |

## 11.9    Multiplicity From SalesLineItem to Item

It is possible for a cashier to receive a group of like items (for example, six tofu packages), enter the UPC once, and then enter a quantity (for example, six). Consequently, an individual *SalesLineItem* can be associated with more than one instance of an item. The quantity that is entered by the cashier may be recorded as a attribute of the *SalesLineItem* (Figure 11.8). However, the quantity can be calculated from the actual multiplicity value of the relationship, so it may be characterized as a **derived attribute**—one that may be derived from other information. In the UML, a derived attribute is indicated with a "⁄" symbol.

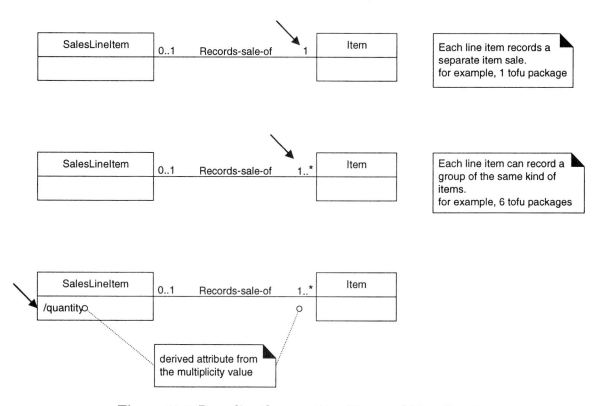

**Figure 11.8** Recording the quantity of items sold in a line item.

## 11.10  Point-of-Sale Conceptual Model

Combining the concepts, associations, and attributes discovered in the previous investigation yields the model illustrated in Figure 11.9.

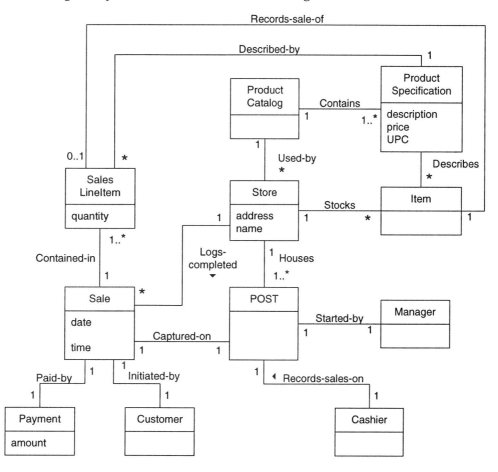

**Figure 11.9** A conceptual model for the point-of-sale domain.

## 11.11  Conclusion

A relatively useful conceptual model for the domain of the point-of-sale application has been created. There is no such thing as a single correct model. All models are approximations of the domain we are attempting to understand. A good conceptual model captures the essential abstractions and information required to understand the domain in the context of the current requirements, and aids people in understanding the domain—its concepts, terminology, and relationships.

# RECORDING TERMS IN THE GLOSSARY

---

### Objectives

■ Express terms in a glossary.

---

## 12.1 Introduction

A glossary is a simple document that defines terms. This chapter provides an example for the point-of-sale domain.

## 12.2 Glossary

At the very least, a **glossary** or **model dictionary** (similar to a data dictionary) lists and defines all the terms that require clarification in order to improve communication and reduce the risk of misunderstanding.

Consistent meaning and a shared understanding of terms is extremely important during application development, especially when many team members are involved.

## 12.3    Activities and Dependencies

The glossary is originally created during the Plan and Elaborate phase as terms are generated, and is continually refined within each development cycle as new terms are encountered. It is usually made in parallel with the requirements specifications, use cases, and conceptual model. Maintaining the glossary is an ongoing activity throughout the project.

### 12.3.1    Domain Rules and Constraints

The glossary is a useful document within which to record domain or business rules, constraints, and so on, although this approach will not be explored here. Other artifacts within which to record this kind of information include the use cases, contracts (to be discussed in a later chapter), and attaching constraint notes to elements (such as concepts) to which the rule or constraint applies.

## 12.4    Sample Point-of-Sale System Glossary

There is no official format for a glossary. Here is a sample:

| Term | Category | Comments |
|------|----------|----------|
| Buy Items | use case | Description of the process of a customer buying items in a store. |
| ProductSpecification.description : Text | attribute | A short description of an item in a sale, and its associated *ProductSpecification*. |
| Item | type | An item for sale in a *Store*. |
| Payment | type | A cash payment. |
| ProductSpecification.price : Quantity | attribute | The price of an item in a sale, and its associated *ProductSpecification*. |
| SalesLineItem.quantity : Integer | attribute | The quantity of one kind of Item bought. |
| Sale | type | A sales transaction. |
| SalesLineItem | type | A line item for a particular item bought within a *Sale*. |

| Term | Category | Comments |
|---|---|---|
| Store | type | The place where sales of items occur. |
| Sale.total : Quantity | attribute | The grand total of the *Sale*. |
| Payment.amount : Quantity | attribute | The amount of cash tendered, or presented, from the customer for payment. |
| ProductSpecification.upc : UPC | attribute | The universal product code of the Item and its *ProductSpecification*. |

# System Behavior— System Sequence Diagrams

## Objectives

- Identify system events and system operations.
- Create system sequence diagram for use cases.

## 13.1 Introduction

A system sequence diagram illustrates events from actors to systems. This chapter discusses how to create them.

The creation of a system sequence diagrams is considered part of the investigation into what system to build; it is therefore included within the Analysis Model.

The UML contains notation in the form of sequence diagrams to illustrate events from actors to a system.

## 13.2 Activities and Dependencies

The creation of system sequence diagrams occurs during the analysis phase of a development cycle. Their creation is dependent on the prior development of the use cases.

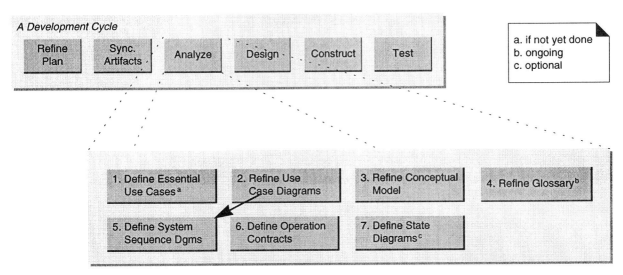

Analyze phase activities within a development cycle.

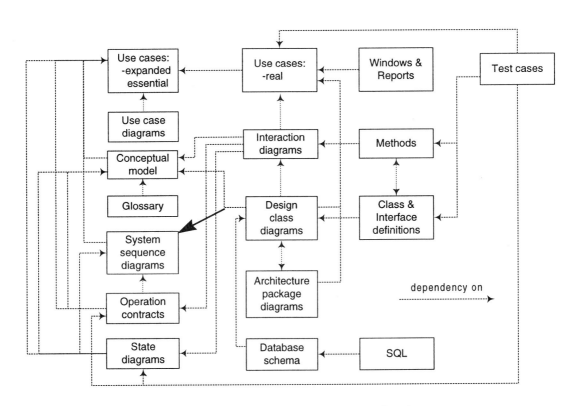

Build phase artifact dependencies.

## 13.3    System Behavior

Before proceeding to a logical design of how a software application will work, it is necessary to investigate and define its behavior as a "black box." **System behavior** is a description of *what* a system does, without explaining how it does it. One part of that description is a system sequence diagram.

## 13.4    System Sequence Diagrams

The use cases suggest how actors interact with the software system we are ultimately interested in creating. During this interaction an actor generates events to a system, requesting some operation in response. For example, when a cashier enters an item's UPC, the cashier requests the POST system to record that item purchase. That request event initiates an operation upon the system.

It is desirable to isolate and illustrate the operations that an actor requests of a system, because they are an important part of understanding system behavior. The UML includes **sequence diagrams** as a notation that can illustrate actor interactions and the operations initiated by them.

A **system sequence diagram** is a picture that shows, for a particular scenario of a use case[1], the events that external actors generate, their order, and inter-system events. All systems are treated as a black box; the emphasis of the diagram is events that cross the system boundary from actors to systems.

A system sequence diagram should be done for the typical course of events of the use case, and possibly others, for the most interesting alternative courses.

## 13.5    Example of a System Sequence Diagram

A **system sequence diagram** shows, for a particular course of events within a use case, the external actors that interact directly with the system, the system (as a black box), and the system events that the actors generate (see Figure 13.1). Time proceeds downwards, and the ordering of events should follow their order in the use case.

---

1. A scenario of a use case is a particular instance or realized path through the use—a real example of its enactment.

System events may include parameters.

This example is for the typical course of events in the *Buy Items* use case. It indicates that the cashier is the only actor for the POST system, and that the cashier generates *enterItem, endSale,* and *makePayment* system events.

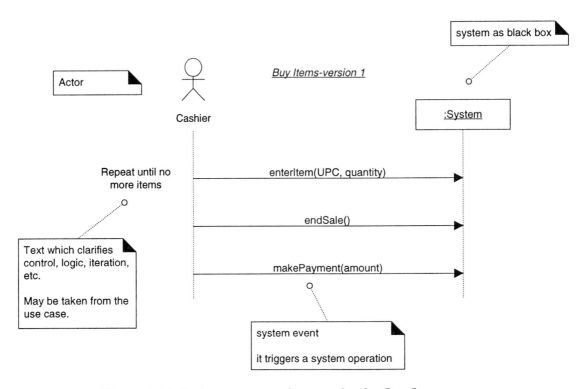

**Figure 13.1** System sequence diagram for the *Buy Items* use case.

## 13.6    System Events and System Operations

A **system event** is an external input event generated by an actor to a system. An event initiates a responding operation. A **system operation** is an operation of the system that executes in response to a system event (see Figure 13.2). For example, when the cashier generates the *enterItem* system event, it causes the execution of the *enterItem* system operation; the name of the event and operation are identical; the distinction is that the event is the named stimulus, the operation is the response.[1]

---

1. The same is true with messages and methods.

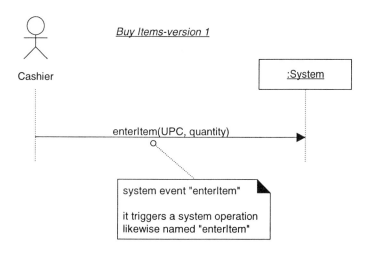

**Figure 13.2** System events initiate system operations.

## 13.6.1   Recording System Operations

The set of all required system operations is determined by identifying the system events. With parameters, they are:

- *enterItem(UPC, quantity)*
- *endSale()*
- *makePayment(amount)*

Where should these operations be recorded? The UML includes notation to record operations of a type, as shown in Figure 13.3.

**Figure 13.3** The UML notation for operations.

With this notation, the system operations can be grouped as operations of a type named *System* (shown in Figure 13.4). The parameters may optionally be ignored.

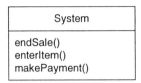

**Figure 13.4** System operations recorded in a type named *System*.

This scheme also works well when recording the system operations of multiple systems or processes in a distributed application; each system is given a unique name (*System1*, *System2*, ...), and assigned its own system operations.

Observe that the representation of the *System* type is very different than what was expressed in the conceptual model. Whereas elements of the conceptual model represent real-world concepts, the *System* type is a somewhat artificial construct. In addition, it shows operations—something new. This is because—in contrast to the conceptual model, which shows static information—we are describing the behavior of the system, which is dynamic information.

## 13.7 How to Make a System Sequence Diagram

> To make system sequence diagrams for the typical course of events for a use case:
>
> 1. Draw a line representing the system as a black box.
>
> 2. Identify each actor that directly operates on the system. Draw a line for each such actor.
>
> 3. From the use case typical course of events text, identify the system (external) events that each actor generates. Illustrate them on the diagram.
>
> 4. Optionally, include the use case text to the left of the diagram.

## 13.8 System Sequence Diagrams and other Artifacts

The identification and ordering of the system events to show in system sequence diagrams (see Figure 13.5) comes from inspection of the use cases.

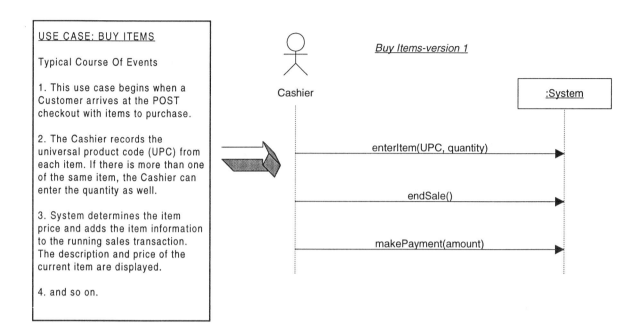

USE CASE: BUY ITEMS

Typical Course Of Events

1. This use case begins when a Customer arrives at the POST checkout with items to purchase.

2. The Cashier records the universal product code (UPC) from each item. If there is more than one of the same item, the Cashier can enter the quantity as well.

3. System determines the item price and adds the item information to the running sales transaction. The description and price of the current item are displayed.

4. and so on.

*Buy Items-version 1*

Cashier

:System

enterItem(UPC, quantity)

endSale()

makePayment(amount)

**Figure 13.5** System sequence diagrams are derived from use cases.

# 13.9    System Events and the System Boundary

In order to identify system events it is necessary to be clear on the choice of system boundary, as discussed in the previous chapter on use cases. For the purposes of software development, the system boundary is usually chosen to be the software (and possibly hardware) system itself; in this context, a system event is an external event that directly stimulates the software (see Figure 13.6). For business re-engineering, the system boundary—and hence system events—could be widened to include manual processes, but that is outside the scope of our discussion.

Let us consider the *Buy Items* use case in order to identify system events. First we must determine the actors that directly interact with the software system. The customer interacts with the cashier, but does not directly interact with the POST software—only the cashier does. Therefore, the customer is not a generator of system events; only the cashier is.

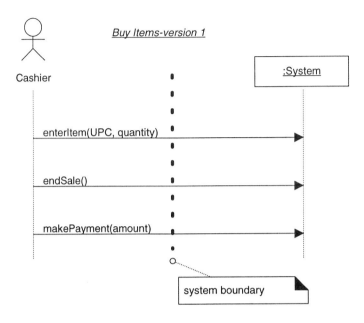

**Figure 13.6** Defining the system boundary.

## 13.10 Naming System Events and Operations

System events (and their associated system operations) should be expressed at the level of intent rather than in terms of the physical input medium or interface widget level.

It also improves clarity to start the name of a system event with a verb (add..., enter..., end..., make...), as in Figure 13.7, since it emphasizes the command orientation of these events.

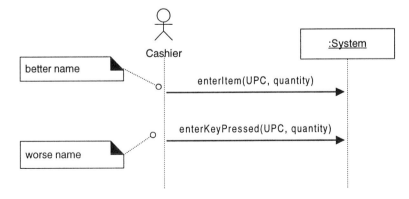

**Figure 13.7** Choose event and operation names at an abstract level.

Thus "endSale" is better than "enterKeyPressed" because it captures the intent of the operation while remaining abstract and noncommittal with respect to design choices about what interface is used to capture the system event.

In terms of expressing operations at the level of intent, strive for the highest level or ultimate goal in naming the operation. For example, with respect to the operation that captures the payment:

| | |
|---|---|
| *enterAmountTendered(amount)* | poor |
| *enterPayment(amount)* | better |
| *makePayment(amount)* | perhaps even better |

# 13.11   Showing Use Case Text

It is sometimes desirable to show at least fragments of the use case text in the sequence diagram, in order to illustrate its strong relationship to the use case (see Figure 13.8).

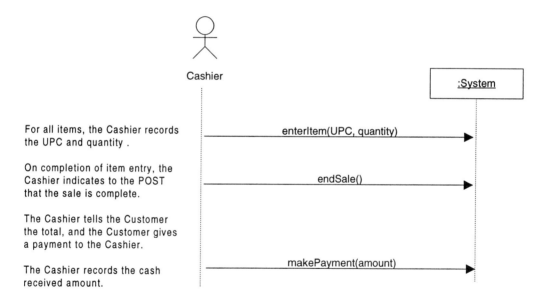

**Figure 13.8** System sequence diagram with use case text.

# 13.12   Sample Models

System sequence diagrams are part of the System Behavior Model, as shown in Figure 13.9, which specifies what system events a system responds to, and what responsibilities and post-conditions the corresponding system operations have.

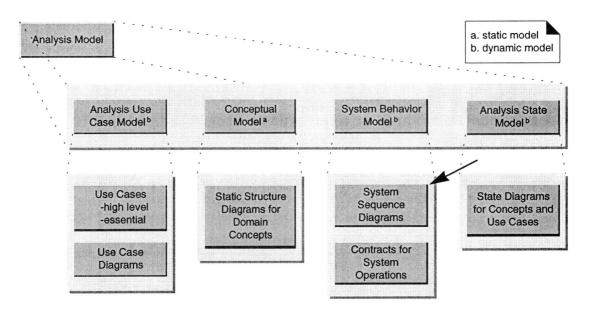

**Figure 13.9** The Analysis Model.

# SYSTEM BEHAVIOR— CONTRACTS

## Objectives

■ Create contracts for system operations.

## 14.1 Introduction

Contracts help define system behavior; they describe the effect of operations upon the system. This chapter explores their use.

The UML contains support for defining contracts by allowing the definition of pre- and post-conditions of operations.[1]

## 14.2 Activities and Dependencies

The creation of system operation contracts occurs during the analysis phase, within a development cycle. Their creation is dependent on the prior development of the conceptual model, system sequence diagrams, and the identification of system operations.

---

1. In the UML formal definition—or metamodel— operations have a set of predefined properties that include their pre- and post-conditions.

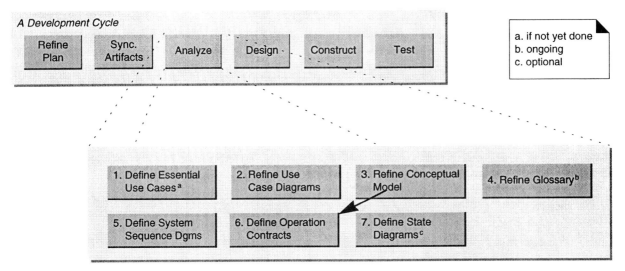

Analyze phase activities within a development cycle.

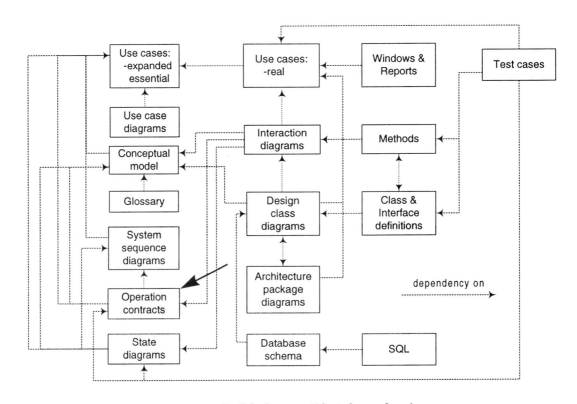

Build phase artifact dependencies.

## 14.3    System Behavior

Before proceeding to a logical design of how a software application will work, it is necessary to investigate and define its behavior as a "black box." **System behavior** is a description of *what* a system does, without explaining how it does it. Contracts are useful documents that describe system behavior in terms of what a system's state changes are when a system operation is invoked.

## 14.4    Contracts

The system sequence diagram in Figure 14.1 shows the system events that an external actor generates, but it does not elaborate on the details of the functionality associated with the system operations invoked. It is missing the details necessary to understand the system response—the system behavior.

In general, a **contract**[1] is a document that describes what an operation commits to achieve. It is usually declarative in style, emphasizing *what* will happen, rather than *how* it will be achieved. It is common for contracts to be expressed in terms of pre- and post-conditions state changes. A contract can be written for an individual method of a software class, or for a more sweeping system operation.

A **system operation contract** describes changes in the state of the overall system when a system operation is invoked.

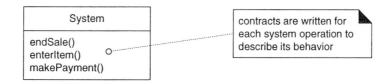

**Figure 14.1**  System operations need contract descriptions.

To reiterate, a contract can be used for a high-level system operation applied to an entire system, or for a low-level method of a particular class. At this point, we will only emphasize their use for system operations.

## 14.5    Example contract—enterItem

The following example describes a contract for the *enterItem* system operation.

---

1. The term was first popularized by Betrand Meyer.

## Contract

| | |
|---|---|
| **Name:** | enterItem<br>(upc : number,<br>quantity : integer) |
| **Responsibilities:** | Enter (record) sale of an item and add it to the sale. Display the item description and price. |
| **Type:** | System |
| **Cross References:** | System Functions: R1.1, R1.3, R1.9<br>Use Cases: Buy Items |
| **Notes:** | Use superfast database access. |
| **Exceptions:** | If the UPC is not valid, indicate that it was an error. |
| **Output:** | |
| **Pre-conditions:** | UPC is known to the system |
| **Post-conditions:** | |

- If a new sale, a *Sale* was created (*instance creation*).

- If a new sale, the new *Sale* was associated with the *POST* (*association formed*).

- A *SalesLineItem* was created (*instance creation*).

- The *SalesLineItem* was associated with the *Sale* (*association formed*).

- *SalesLineItem.quantity* was set to *quantity* (*attribute modification*).

- The *SalesLineItem* was associated with a *ProductSpecification*, based on *UPC* match (*association formed*).

## 14.6    Contract Sections

A description of each section in a contract is shown in the following schema. Not all sections are necessary, although the *Responsibilities* and *Post-conditions* sections are recommended.

## Contract

| | |
|---|---|
| **Name:** | Name of operation, and parameters |
| **Responsibilities:** | An informal description of the responsibilities this operation must fulfill. |
| **Type:** | Name of type (concept, software class, interface) |

| | |
|---|---|
| **Cross References:** | System function reference numbers, use cases, etc. |
| **Notes:** | Design notes, algorithms, and so on. |
| **Exceptions:** | Exceptional cases. |
| **Output:** | Non-UI outputs, such as messages or records that are sent outside of the system. |
| **Pre-conditions:** | Assumptions about the state of the system before execution of the operation. |
| **Post-conditions:** | |

- The state of the system after completion of the operation. Discussed in detail in a following section.

# 14.7    How to Make A Contract

Apply the following advice to create contracts.

To make contracts for each use case:

1. Identify the system operations from the system sequence diagrams.

2. For each system operation, construct an contract.

3. Start by writing the *Responsibilities* section, informally describing the purpose of the operation.

4. Then complete the *Post-conditions* section, declaratively describing the state changes that occur to objects in the conceptual model.

5. To describe the post-conditions, use the following categories:

   - Instance creation and deletion.

   - Attribute modification.

   - Associations formed and broken.

## 14.7.1    Contracts and other Artifacts

- The use cases suggests the system events and system sequence diagrams.

- The system operations can then be identified.

■ The effect of the system operations is described in contracts.

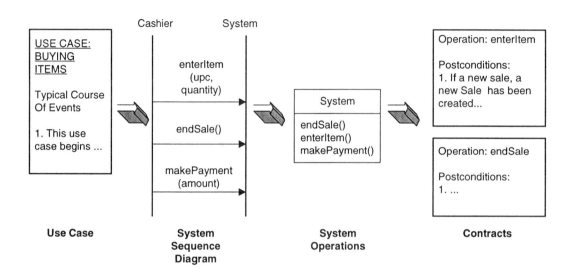

**Figure 14.2** Contracts and other artifacts.

# 14.8   Post-conditions

Notice that each of the post-conditions in the *enterItem* example included a categorization such as *instance creation* or *association formed*. Next to the *Responsibilities* section, the most important part of the contract are these post-conditions, which state how the system has changed as a result of this operation. The post-conditions are not actions to be performed during the operation, rather they are declarations about the system state that are true when the operation has finished—*after the smoke has cleared*.

The UML does not constrain how the post-conditions should be expressed, but the following categories of state changes have been found to be useful in practice, and you are encouraged to express your post-conditions in a similar fashion.

Useful contract post-condition categories:

■ Instance creation and deletion.

■ Attribute modification.

■ Associations formed and broken.

The UML does not define how to express post-conditions, you may choose any format that appeals to you. The important factor is to be declarative and state-change oriented rather than action-oriented, since post-conditions should be declarations about states or outcomes rather than a description of actions to execute.

### 14.8.1   Post-conditions are Related to the Conceptual Model

These post-conditions are expressed in the context of the conceptual model. What instances can be created? Those from the conceptual model. What associations can be formed? Those in the conceptual model. And so on.

It is common during the creation of the contracts that you will discover the need to record new concepts, attributes, or associations in the conceptual model. Do not be limited to the prior definition of the conceptual model; enhance it as you make new discoveries while thinking through the operation contracts.

### 14.8.2   The Advantage of Post-conditions

Expressed in a declarative state-change fashion, the contract is an excellent tool of investigation to describe the state changes required of a system operation without having to describe *how* they are to be achieved. In other words, the software design and solution can be deferred, and you can focus analytically on *what* must happen, rather than how it is to be accomplished.

## 14.9   The Spirit of Post-conditions: the *Stage and Curtain*

Post-conditions should describe the state of a system; they should not be actions to perform. Express post-conditions in the past tense, in order to emphasize they are declarations about a past state change. For example:

■   (better) A *SalesLineItem* **was** created.

rather than

■   (worse) Create a *SalesLineItem*.

Think about post-conditions using the following image:

> *The system and its objects are presented on a theatre stage.*

1. Before the operation, take a picture of the stage.

2. Close the curtains on the stage, and apply the system operation (*background noise of clanging, screams, and screeches...*).

3. Open the curtains and take a second picture.

4. Compare the before and after picture, and express as post-conditions the

changes in the state of the stage (*A SalesLineItem was created...*).

# 14.10   Discussion—*enterItem* Post-conditions

The following section dissects the motivation for the post-conditions of the *enterItem* system operation.

## 14.10.1  Instance Creation and Deletion

After the UPC and quantity of an item have been entered by the cashier, what new objects should have been created? If it is a new sale, a *Sale* should have been instantiated. A *SalesLineItem* should have unconditionally been created. Thus:

- If a new sale, a *Sale* was created (instance creation).

- A *SalesLineItem* was created (instance creation).

## 14.10.2  Attribute Modification

After the UPC and quantity of an item have been entered by the cashier, what attributes of new or existing objects should have been modified? The quantity of the *SalesLineItem* should have been set. Thus:

- *SalesLineItem.quantity* was set to *quantity* (attribute modification)

## 14.10.3  Associations Formed and Broken

After the UPC and quantity of an item have been entered by the cashier, what associations between new or existing objects should have been formed or broken? The new SalesLineItem should have been related to its Sales, and related to its Item. If it was a new sale, the Sale should have been related to the POST within which it is recorded. Thus:

- If a new sale, the new *Sale* was associated with the *POST* (association formed).

- The *SalesLineItem* was associated with the *Sale* (association formed).

- The *SalesLineItem* was associated with an *ProductSpecification*, based on *UPC* match (association formed).

## 14.11   How Complete Should Post-conditions Be?

Generating a complete and accurate set of post-conditions for a system operation is not likely—or even necessary—during the analysis phase. Treat their creation as an initial best guess, with the understanding that the contracts will not be complete. Their early creation—even if incomplete—is certainly better than deferring this investigation until the design phase, when developers should be concerned with the design of a solution, rather than investigating *what* should be done.

Some of the fine details—and perhaps even larger ones—will be discovered during the design phase. That is not necessarily a bad thing; there is a diminishing return on effort expended during the investigation phase if it is drawn out too long. Some discovery naturally arises during the design phase, which can then inform the investigation phase of a later iterative cycle. This is one of the advantages of iterative development: discoveries generated during the design phase of one cycle can enhance the investigation and analysis work of the following cycle.

## 14.12   Describing Design Details and Algorithms—Notes

The Notes section of the contract is a place where design statements may be made regarding the operation. For example, if it is known that a particular algorithm is preferred to handle an operation, the Notes section is a suitable location for its documentation.

## 14.13   Pre-conditions

The pre-conditions define assumptions about the state of the system at the beginning of the operation. There are many possible pre-conditions we can declare for an operation, but experience suggests that the following pre-conditions are worth noting:

- Things that are important to test in software at some point during execution of the operation.

- Things that will not be tested, but upon which the success of the operation hinges. We wish to communicate this assumption to future readers of the contract, in order to highlight their importance and to raise their awareness in the mind of the readers.

# 14.14   Advice on Writing Contracts

■ After filling in the operation name, fill in the *Responsibilities* section first, *Post-conditions* section next, *Pre-conditions* last. These are the most important sections in terms of likely use later in the project. Of course, if a developer finds no use in filling in a particular section, don't bother.

■ Use the *Notes* section to discuss any design details, such as algorithms or the high-level sequential steps.

■ Use the *Exceptions* section to discuss the reaction to exceptional situations.

■ Use these categories of state changes in the post-conditions:

  ❏ Instance creation and deletion.

  ❏ Attribute modification.

  ❏ Associations formed and broken.

■ State the post-conditions in a declarative, passive past tense form (*was* …) to emphasize the declaration of a state change rather than a design of how it is going to be achieved. For example:

(better) A *SalesLineItem* **was** created.

rather than

(worse) Create a *SalesLineItem*.

  ❏ The difference between these two statements may seem academic and superficial, but if the active tense is used instead of the passive past, experience has shown that developers quickly slip into a frame of mind designing how they are going to solve the operation in software. The spirit of the contract is to emphasize a declaration of state changes while eschewing the means of solution.

■ Remember to establish a memory between existing objects or those newly created by defining the forming of an association. For example, it is not enough that a new *SalesLineItem* instance is created when the *EnterItem* operation occurs. After the operation is complete, it should also be true that the newly created instance was associated with *Sale*; thus:

  ❏ The *SalesLineItem* was associated with the *Sale* (association formed)

## 14.14.1  The Most Common Mistake in Creating Contracts

The most common problem is forgetting to include the *forming of associations*. Particularly when new instances were created, it is very likely that associations to several objects needs to have been established. Don't forget!

# 14.15   Contracts for the *Buy Items* Use Case

## 14.15.1  *Contract for enterItem*

Contract

| | |
|---|---|
| **Name:** | enterItem<br>(upc : number,<br>quantity : integer) |
| **Responsibilities:** | Enter (record) sale of an item and add it to the sale. Display the item description and price. |
| **Type:** | System |
| **Cross References:** | System Functions: R1.1, R1.3, R1.9<br>Use Cases: Buy Items |
| **Notes:** | Use superfast database access. |
| **Exceptions:** | If the UPC is not valid, indicate that it was an error. |
| **Output:** | |
| **Pre-conditions:** | UPC is known to the system |
| **Post-conditions:** | |

- If a new sale, a *Sale* was created (*instance creation*).

- If a new sale, the new *Sale* was associated with the *POST* (*association formed*).

- A *SalesLineItem* was created (*instance creation*).

- The *SalesLineItem* was associated with the *Sale* (*association formed*).

- *SalesLineItem.quantity* was set to *quantity* (*attribute modification*).

- The *SalesLineItem* was associated with a *ProductSpecification*, based on *UPC* match (*association formed*).

## 14.15.2  Contract for endSale

|  | **Contract** |
|---|---|
| **Name:** | endSale() |
| **Responsibilities:** | Record that it is the end of entry of sale items, and display sale total. |
| **Type:** | System |
| **Cross References:** | System Functions: R1.2 |
|  | Use Cases: Buy Items |
| **Notes:** |  |
| **Exceptions:** | If a sale is not underway, indicate that it was an error. |
| **Output:** |  |
| **Pre-conditions:** | UPC is known to the system. |
| **Post-conditions:** |  |

- *Sale.isComplete* was set to *true* (attribute modification).

## 14.15.3  Contract for makePayment

|  | **Contract** |
|---|---|
| **Name:** | makePayment . (amount : Number or Quantity) |
| **Responsibilities:** | Record the payment, calculate balance and print receipt. |
| **Type:** | System |
| **Cross References:** | System Functions: R2.1 |
|  | Use Cases: Buy Items |
| **Notes:** |  |
| **Exceptions:** | If the sale is not complete, indicate an error. |
|  | If the amount is less than the sale total, indicate an error. |
| **Output:** |  |
| **Pre-conditions:** |  |
| **Post-conditions:** |  |

- A *Payment* was created (instance creation).

- *Payment.amountTendered* was set to *amount* (attribute modification).

- The *Payment* was associated with the *Sale* (relationship formed).

- The *Sale* was associated with the *Store*, to add it to the historical log of completed sales (relationship formed).

# 14.16   Contracts for the *StartUp* Use Case

## 14.16.1  Contract for StartUp

|  | **Contract** |
| --- | --- |
| **Name:** | startUp() |
| **Responsibilities:** | Initialize the system. |
| **Type:** | System |
| **Cross References:** | |
| **Notes:** | |
| **Exceptions:** | |
| **Output:** | |
| **Pre-conditions:** | |
| **Post-conditions:** | |

- A *Store, POST, ProductCatalog and ProductSpecifications* have been created (*instance creation*).

- *ProductCatalog* was associated with *ProductSpecifications* (*association formed*).

- *Store* was associated with *ProductCatalog* (*association formed*).

- *Store* was associated with *POST* (*association formed*).

- *POST* was associated with *ProductCatalog* (*association formed*).

## 14.17   Changes to the Conceptual Model

There is one datum suggested by these contracts that is not yet represented in the conceptual: completion of item entry to the sale. The *endSale* specification modifies it, and the *makePayment* specification tests it as a precondition.

One way to represent this information is as an *isComplete* (or *entryIsComplete*) attribute of the *Sale*, as a boolean value:

There are alternative solutions to represent the changing state of the system. One technique is called the **State Pattern**, which is explored in a later chapter.

## 14.18   Sample Models

Contracts for system operations are part of the System Behavior Model—describing the external interface and behavior of the overall system (see Figure 14.3).

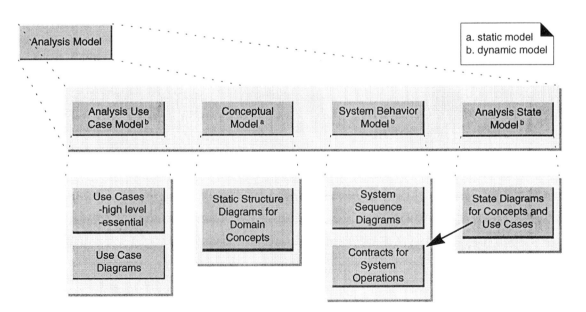

**Figure 14.3** The Analysis Model.

# PART III DESIGN PHASE (1)

# FROM ANALYSIS TO DESIGN

---

**Objectives**

■  Motivate the transition from analysis to design.

---

## 15.1  Analysis Phase Conclusion

The analysis phase of development emphasizes an understanding of the requirements, concepts, and operations related to a system. Investigation and analysis are often characterized as focussing on questions of *what*—what are the processes, concepts, and so on.

There are other artifacts in UML that can be used to capture the results of an investigation, but the following—which have been explored in prior chapters—are a useful minimal set:

| Analysis Artifact | Questions Answered |
|---|---|
| Use cases | What are the domain processes? |
| Conceptual Model | What are the concepts, terms? |
| System sequence diagrams | What are the system events and operations? |
| Contracts | What do the system operations do? |

## 15.2    Design Phase Initiation

During an iterative development cycle it is possible to move to a design phase, once these analysis documents are complete. During this step a logical solution based upon the object-oriented paradigm is developed. The heart of this solution is the creation of **interaction diagrams**, which illustrate how objects will communicate in order to fulfill the requirements.

Following the generation of interaction diagrams, **design class diagrams** can be drawn which summarize the definition of the classes (and interfaces) that are to be implemented in software.

The following chapters explore the creation of these artifacts. Of the two, interactions diagrams are the most important (from the point of view of developing a god design), and require the greatest degree of creative effort. The creation of interaction diagrams requires the application of principles for assigning **responsibilities** and the use of **design patterns**. Therefore the emphasis of the following chapters is on these principles and patterns in object-oriented design.

---

The creation of interaction diagrams requires knowledge of:

■ Principles of responsibility assignment.

■ Design patterns.

---

# DESCRIBING REAL USE CASES

## 16.1    Introduction

Real use cases show a concrete design of how the use case will be realized. This chapter explores their creation.

## 16.2    Activities and Dependencies

The definition of real use cases is one of the first design phase activities within a development cycle. Their creation is dependent upon the prior creation of the associated essential use cases.

## 16.3    Real Use Cases

A **real use case** describes the real or actual design of the use case in terms of concrete input and output technology and its overall implementation. For example, if a graphical user interface is involved, the real use case will include dia-

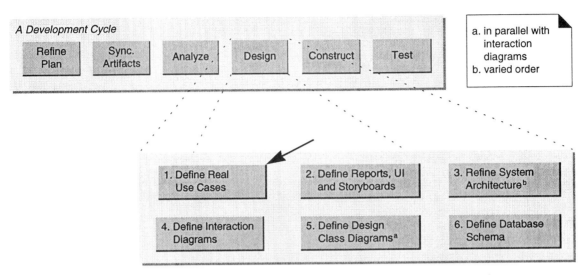

Design phase activities within a development cycle.

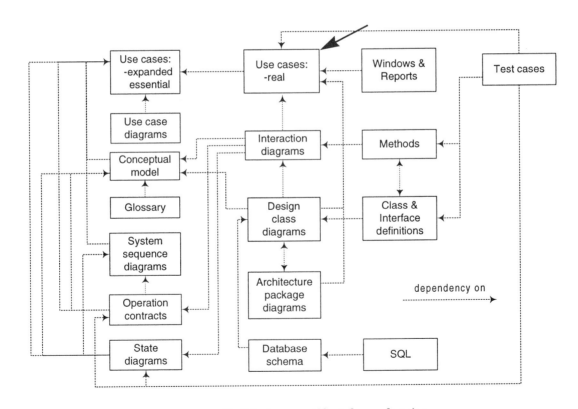

Build phase artifact dependencies.

grams of the windows involved, and discussion of the low-level interaction with the interface widgets.

They may not be necessary to create. As an alternative, the designer may create rough user interface storyboards, and nail down the details during the implementation.

They are useful if the developers or client require excruciatingly detailed interface descriptions prior to implementation.

# 16.4    Example—Buy Items-Version 1

In the following example and Figure 16.1, note the use of a coding scheme for the window widgets to keep the description terse.

| | |
|---|---|
| **Use case:** | **Buy Items-version 1 (Cash only)** |
| Actors: | Customer (initiator), Cashier |
| Purpose: | Capture a sale and its cash payment. |
| Overview: | A Customer arrives at a checkout with items to purchase. The Cashier records the purchase items and collects a cash payment. On completion, the Customer leaves with the items. |
| Type | primary and real |
| Cross References: | *Functions*: R1.1, R1.2, R1.3, R1.7, R1.9, R2.1, |

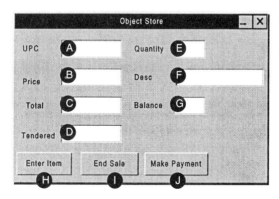

**Figure 16.1** Window-1.

**Typical Course of Events**

| Actor Action | System Response |
|---|---|
| 1. This use case begins when a Customer arrives at the POST checkout with items to purchase. | |
| 2. For each item, the Cashier types in the Universal Product Code (UPC) in A of Window-1. If there is more than one of an item, the quantity may optionally be entered in E. They press B after each item entry. | 3. Adds the item information to the running sales transaction. The description and price of the current item are displayed in B and F of Window1. |
| 4. On completion of item entry, the Cashier indicates to the POST that item entry is complete by pressing widget I. | 5. Calculates and displays the sale total in C. 6. ... |

## 16.5   Sample Models

Real use cases are members of the Design Use Case Model.

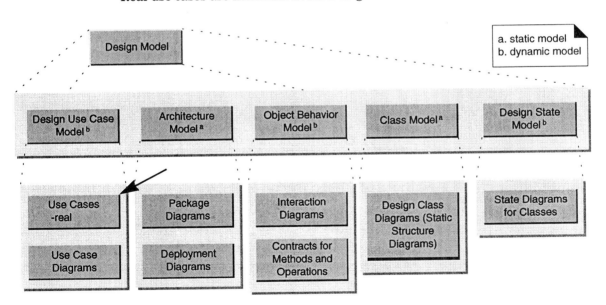

**Figure 16.2** The Design Model.

# COLLABORATION DIAGRAMS

## Objectives

- Read the UML collaboration diagram notation.

## 17.1 Introduction

A preliminary best guess at post-conditions for the system operations *startup, enterItem, endSale,* and *makePayment* is shown in the operation contracts. However, the contracts do not show a solution of how software objects are going to fulfill the post-conditions.

The UML includes **interaction diagrams** to illustrate how objects interact via messages to fulfill tasks. We will explore their creation for the point-of-sale application.

## 17.2 Activities and Dependencies

The creation of interaction diagrams occurs within the design phase of a development cycle. Their creation is dependent upon the prior creation of the following artifacts:

- Conceptual model—from this, the designer may choose to define software classes corresponding to concepts. Objects of these classes participate in interactions illustrated in the interaction diagrams.

- System operation contracts—from these, the designer identifies the responsibilities and post-conditions that the interaction diagrams must fulfill.

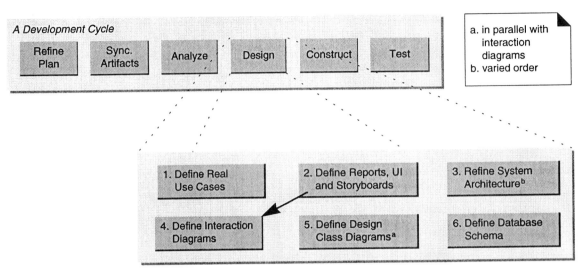

Design phase activities within a development cycle.

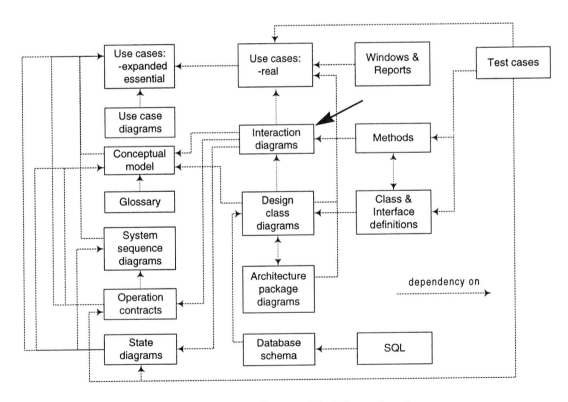

Build phase artifact dependencies.

■ Real (or essential) use cases—from these, the designer may glean information about what tasks the interaction diagrams fulfill, in addition to what is in the contracts.

# 17.3    Interaction Diagrams

An **interaction diagram** illustrates the message interactions between instances (and classes) in the class model. The starting point for these interactions is the fulfillment of the post-conditions of the operation contracts.

The UML defines two kinds of interaction diagrams, either of which can be used to express similar or identical message interactions:

1. collaboration diagrams

2. sequence diagrams

**Collaboration diagrams** illustrate object interactions in a graph or network format, as shown in Figure 17.1.

**Figure 17.1** Collaboration diagram.

**Sequence diagrams** illustrate interactions in a kind of fence format as shown in Figure 17.2.

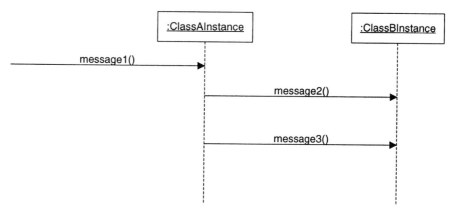

**Figure 17.2** Sequence diagram.

In this chapter and throughout the book, collaboration diagrams will be emphasized over sequence diagrams, because of their exceptional expressiveness, ability to convey more contextual information, and their relative spatial economy.[1] However, either notation can express similar constructs.

## 17.4    Example Collaboration Diagram: makePayment

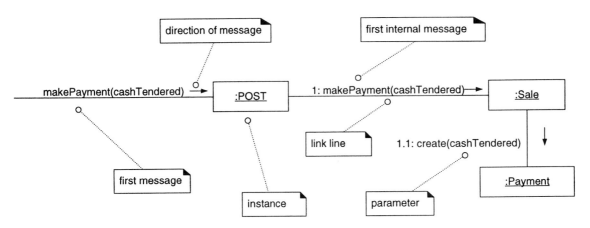

**Figure 17.3** Collaboration diagram.

The collaboration diagram shown in Figure 17.3 is read as follows:

1. The message *makePayment* is sent to an instance of a *POST*. It corresponds to the *makePayment* system operation message.

2. The *POST* object sends the *makePayment* message to a *Sale* instance.

3. The *Sale* object creates an instance of a *Payment*.

## 17.5    Interaction Diagrams are a Valuable Artifact

At common problem in object technology projects is a lack of appreciation for how valuable is the creation of interaction diagrams, the careful consideration of responsibility assignment, and the underlying skills required. The assignment of responsibilities and design of object collaborations is very important.

A significant percentage of project effort should be spent in the phase of interaction diagramming and responsibility assignment. Furthermore, it is primarily during this step that the application of design skill is required, in terms of patterns, idioms, and principles.

---

1. It is possible to say more in a given space with collaboration diagrams, than with sequence diagrams, and to express more contextual information, such as the kind of visibility between objects. It is also easier to express conditional logic and concurrency.

Relatively speaking, the creation of use cases, conceptual models, and other artifacts is easier than the assignment of responsibilities and the creation of well-designed interaction diagrams. This is because there is a larger number of subtle design principles which underlie a well-designed interaction diagram than any other object-oriented analysis and design artifact.

> Interaction diagrams are one of the most important artifacts created in object-oriented analysis and design.
>
> The amount of time and effort spent on their generation should absorb a significant percentage of the overall project effort.
>
> Codified patterns, principles, and idioms can be applied to improve the quality of their design.

The design principles necessary for the successful construction of interaction diagrams *can* be codified, explained, and applied in a methodical fashion. This approach to understanding and using design principles is based on **patterns**—structured guidelines and principles. Therefore, after introducing the syntax of interaction diagrams, attention (in subsequent chapters) will turn to design patterns and their application in interaction diagrams.

## 17.6 This is a Notation-Only Chapter

The purpose of this chapter is to introduce and summarize the UML notation for a particular kind of interaction diagram called a collaboration diagram. It does not explain the principles and guidelines of how to create a well-designed collaboration diagram.

It is not essential to know every notational feature in this chapter before proceeding. Nevertheless, it is advisable to skim the examples and get some familiarity with the notation before moving on to the following chapters.

## 17.7 Read the Following Chapters for Design Guidelines

In order to create well-designed interaction diagrams there are several design principles that must be understood. After acquiring some familiarity with the notation of interaction diagrams, it is valuable to read the following chapters on these principles and how they can be applied.

# 17.8    How to Make Collaboration Diagrams

Apply the following guidelines when creating collaboration diagrams.

To make collaboration diagrams:

1.  Create a separate diagram for each system operation under development in the current development cycle.

    ❑   For each system operation message, make a diagram with it as the starting message.

2.  If the diagram gets complex (for example, does not easily fit on an 8.5 x 11 sheet of paper), split it into smaller diagrams.

3.  Using the operation contract responsibilities and post-conditions, and use case description as a starting point, design a system of interacting objects to fulfill the tasks. Apply the GRASP and other patterns to develop a good design.

## 17.8.1   *Collaboration Diagrams and other Artifacts*

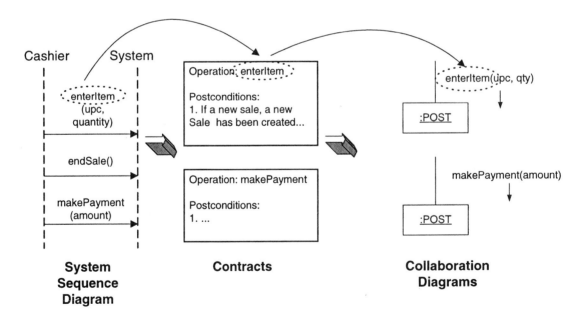

**Figure 17.4** Relationship between artifacts.

As shown in Figure 17.4, the relationship between artifacts includes:

■ The use cases suggests the system events, which are explicitly shown in system sequence diagrams.

■ An initial best guess at the effect of the system operations is described in contracts.

■ The system operations represent messages that initiate interaction diagrams, which illustrate how objects interact to fulfill the required tasks.

# 17.9 Basic Collaboration Diagram Notation

## 17.9.1 Illustrating Classes and Instances

The UML has adopted a simple and consistent approach to illustrate instances versus types (see Figure 17.5):

■ For any kind of UML element (class, actor, ...) an instance uses the same graphic symbol as the type, but the designator string is <u>underlined</u>.

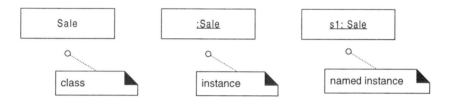

**Figure 17.5** Class and instances.

Therefore, to show an instance of a class in an interaction diagram, the regular class box graphic symbol is used, but the name is underlined. Additionally, in a collaboration diagram, the class name should always be preceded by a colon.

Finally, an instance name can be used to uniquely identify the instance.

## 17.9.2 Illustrating Links

A **link** is a connection path between two instances; it indicates some form of navigation and visibility between the instances is possible (see Figure 17.6). More formally, a link is an instance of an association. Viewing two instances in a client/server relationship, a path of navigation from the client to server means that messages may be sent from the client to the server. For example, there is a link—or path of navigation—from a *POST* to a *Sale*, along which messages may flow, such as the *addPayment* message.

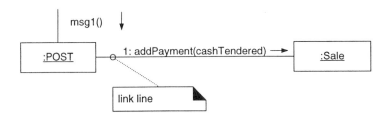

**Figure 17.6** Link lines.

## 17.9.3 Illustrating Messages

Messages between objects are represented via a labeled arrow on a link line. Any number of messages may flow along this link (Figure 17.7). A sequence number is added to show the sequential order of messages in the current thread of control.

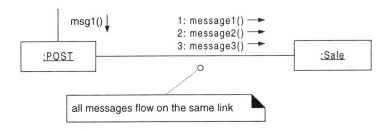

**Figure 17.7** Messages.

## 17.9.4 Illustrating Parameters

Parameters of a message may be shown within parentheses following the message name (Figure 17.8). The type of the parameter may optionally be shown.

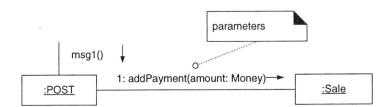

**Figure 17.8** Parameters.

## 17.9.5   Illustrating a Return Value

A return value may be shown by preceding the message with a return value variable name and an assignment operator (':=') (see Figure 17.9). The type of the return value may optionally be shown.

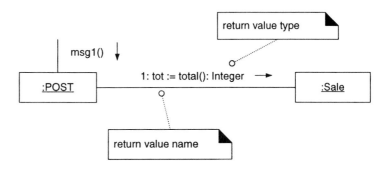

**Figure 17.9**  Return values.

## 17.9.6   Message Syntax

The UML has a standard syntax for messages:

```
return := message(parameter : parameterType) : returnType
```

However, as shown in Figure 17.10, it is legal to use another syntax, such as Java or Smalltalk. Using standard UML syntax is recommended in order to keep the collaboration diagrams relatively language independent.

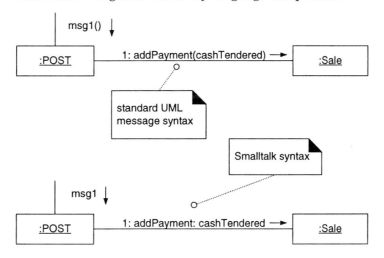

**Figure 17.10**  Messages may be expressed in different syntax.

### 17.9.7 Illustrating Messages to "self" or "this"

A message can be sent from an object to itself (Figure 17.11).

This is illustrated by a link to itself, with messages flowing along the link.

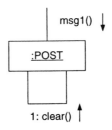

**Figure 17.11** Messages to "this."

### 17.9.8 Illustrating Iteration

Iteration is indicated by following the sequence number with a star ("*").

This expresses that the message is being sent repeatedly, in a loop, to the receiver (see Figure 17.12).

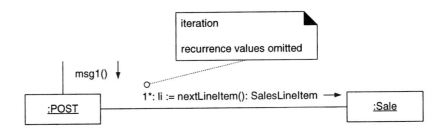

**Figure 17.12** Iteration.

It is also possible to include an iteration clause indicating the recurrence values (Figure 17.13).

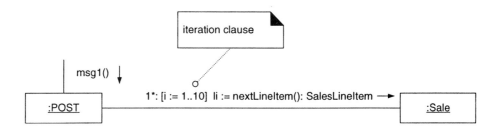

**Figure 17.13** Iteration clause.

To express more than one message happening within the same iteration clause (for example, a set of messages within a *for* loop), repeat the iteration clause on each message (see Figure 17.14).

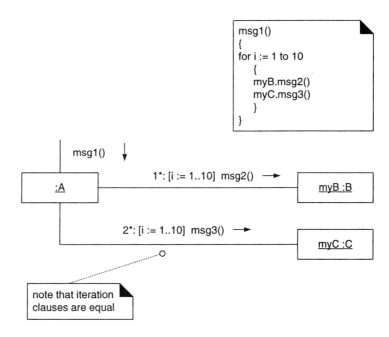

**Figure 17.14** Multiple messages within the same iteration clause.

## 17.9.9 Illustrating Creation of Instances

The language independent creation message is *create*, shown being sent to the instance being created (see Figure 17.15).

Although in most object-oriented languages creation of instances is usually done by using a *new* message (or operator) with the class and not to an instance, this notation is economical, if not exactly accurate.

Optionally, the new instance may include a «*new*» symbol[1].

The *create* message may include parameters, indicating the passing of initial values. This indicates, for example, constructor parameters in Java.

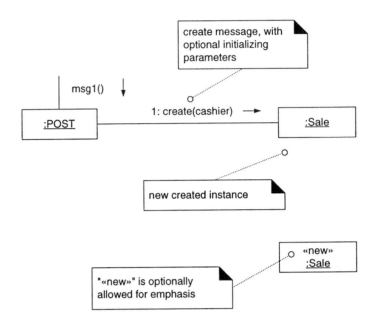

**Figure 17.15** Instance creation.

The *create* message is translated as follows, in various languages:

| Language | Meaning of *create()* |
| --- | --- |
| C++ | Automatic allocation, or *new* operator followed by constructor call. |
| Java | *new* operator followed by constructor call. |
| Smalltalk | *new* message or a variation of *new:* followed by *initialize* message. |

---

1. A UML **stereotype**, discussed later.

## 17.9.10 Illustrating Message Number Sequencing

The order of messages is illustrated with **sequence numbers**, as shown in Figure 17.16. The numbering scheme is:

1. The first message is not numbered. Thus, *msg1()* is unnumbered.

2. The order and nesting of subsequent messages is shown with a legal numbering scheme in which nested messages have appended to them a number. Nesting is denoted by prepending the incoming message number to the outgoing message number.

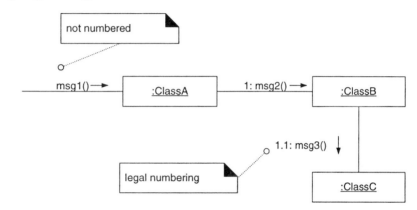

**Figure 17.16** Sequence numbering.

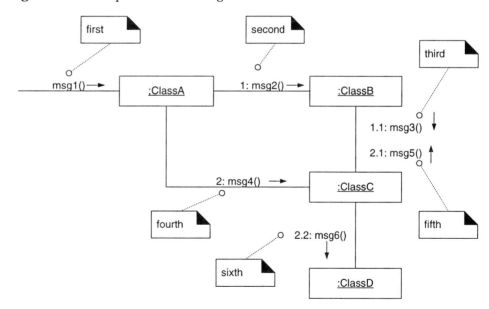

**Figure 17.17** Complex sequence numbering.

## 17.9.11 Illustrating Conditional Messages

A conditional message (Figure 17.18) is shown by following a sequence number with a conditional clause in square brackets, similar to an iteration clause. The message is only sent if the clause evaluates to *true*.

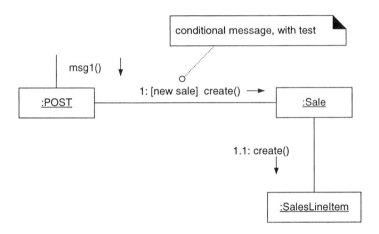

**Figure 17.18** Conditional message.

## 17.9.12 Illustrating Mutually Exclusive Conditional Paths

The example in Figure 17.19 illustrates the sequence numbers with mutually exclusive conditional paths.

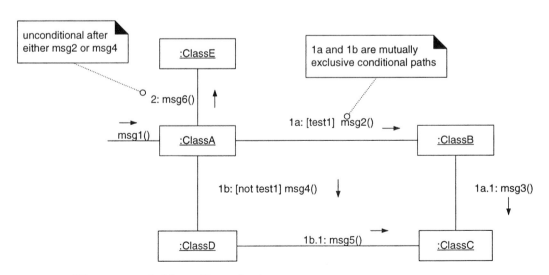

**Figure 17.19** Mutually exclusive messages.

In this case it is necessary to modify the sequence expressions with a conditional path letter. The first letter used is **a** by convention. Figure 17.19 states that either *1a* or *1b* could execute after *msg1()*. Both are sequence number 1 since either could be the first internal message.

Note that subsequent nested messages are still consistently prepended with their outer message sequence. Thus *1b.1* is nested message within *1b*.

## 17.9.13 *Illustrating Collections*

A **multiobject**, or set of instances, may be shown with a stack icon as illustrated in Figure 17.20.

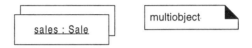

**Figure 17.20** A multiobject.

A multiobject is usually implemented as a group of instances stored in a container or collection object, such as a C++ STL *vector*, Java *Vector* or a Smalltalk *OrderedCollection*. However, it does not have to; it merely represents a logical set of instances.

## 17.9.14 *Illustrating Messages to Multiobjects*

A message to a multiobject icon indicates that it is sent to the collection object itself. For example, in Figure 17.21 the *size* message is being sent to a *java.util.Vector* instance in order to query the number of elements in the *Vector*.

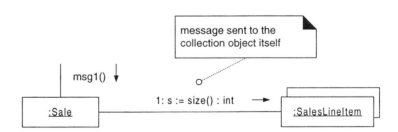

**Figure 17.21** Message to multiobject.

In the UML 1.1, messages to a multiobject are *not* broadcast to each element (as was the case in prior versions of the UML).

Figure 17.22 illustrates messages to a multiobject and an element.

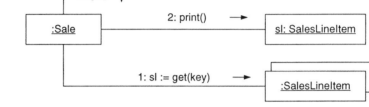

**Figure 17.22** Messages to a multiobject and an element.

## 17.9.15 Illustrating Messages to a Class Object

Messages may be sent to a class itself, rather than an instance, in order to invoke class methods. For example, in Java these are implemented as static methods; in Smalltalk they are class methods.

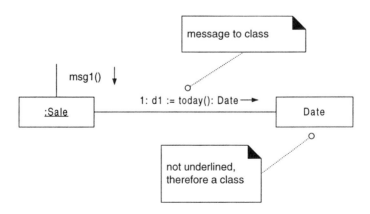

**Figure 17.23** Messages to a class object (static method invocation).

Quite simply, a message is shown to a class box whose name is not underlined, indicating the message is being sent to a class rather than an instance (see Figure 17.23).

> Consequently, it is important to be consistent in underlining your instance names when an instance is intended, otherwise messages to instances versus classes may be incorrectly interpreted.

# 17.10   Sample Models

Interaction diagrams are members of the Object Behavior Model because they describe the behavior of software objects.

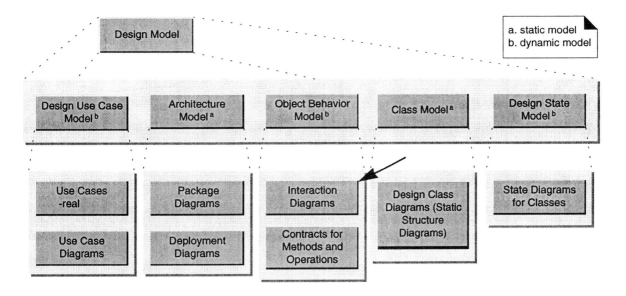

**Figure 17.24** The Design Model.

# GRASP: Patterns for Assigning Responsibilities

**Objectives**

■ Define patterns.

■ Learn to apply five of the GRASP patterns.

## 18.1    Introduction

An object-oriented system is composed of objects sending messages to other objects to complete operations. A preliminary best guess at responsibilities and postconditions for the system operations *startup, enterItem, endSale,* and *makePayment* is shown in the contracts. Interaction diagrams illustrate the solution—in terms of interacting objects—that satisfy these responsibilities and postconditions.

There is great variability in the potential quality of object interaction design and responsibility assignment. Poor choices lead to systems and components which are fragile and hard to maintain, understand, reuse, or extend. A skillful implementation is founded on the cardinal principles of good object-oriented design. Some of these principles, applied during the creation of interaction diagrams and/or responsibility assignment, are codified in the GRASP patterns.

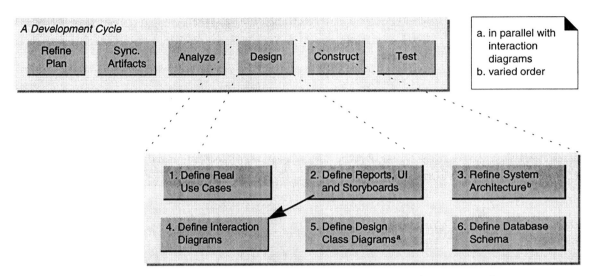

Design phase activities within a development cycle.

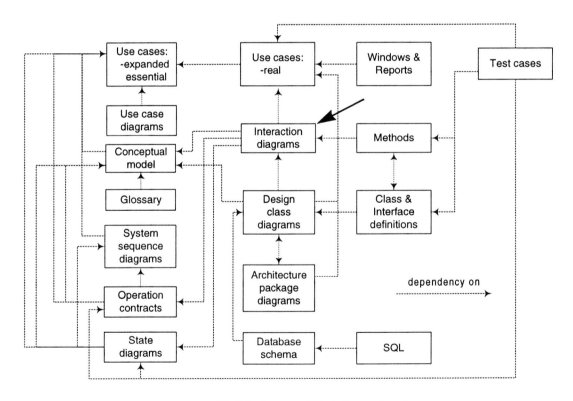

Build phase artifact dependencies.

## 18.2 Activities and Dependencies

These patterns are applied during the creation of interaction diagrams when assigning responsibilities to objects and designing object collaborations.

## 18.3 Well-Designed Interaction Diagrams are Valuable

To reiterate some points made in the previous chapter on collaboration diagram notation:

- Interaction diagrams are one of the most important artifacts created in object-oriented analysis and design.

- The skillful assignment of responsibilities that occurs while creating interaction diagrams is very important.

- The amount of time and effort spent on their generation, and the careful consideration of responsibility assignment, should absorb a significant percentage of the design phase of a project.

- Codified patterns, principles, and idioms can be applied to improve the quality of their design.

The design principles necessary for the successful construction of interaction diagrams can be codified, explained, and applied in a methodical fashion. This approach to understanding and using design principles is based on *patterns of assigning responsibilities*.

## 18.4 Responsibilities and Methods

Booch and Rumbaugh define **responsibility** as "a contract or obligation of a type or class"[BJR97]. Responsibilities are related to the obligations of an object in terms of its behavior. Basically, these responsibilities are of the following two types:

1. knowing
2. doing

**Doing** responsibilities of an object include:

- doing something itself
- initiating action in other objects

❏ controlling and coordinating activities in other objects

**Knowing** responsibilities of an object include:

❏ knowing about private encapsulated data

❏ knowing about related objects

❏ knowing about things it can derive or calculate

Responsibilities are assigned to objects during object-oriented design. For example, I may declare that "a *Sale* is responsible for printing itself" (a doing), or "a *Sale* is responsible for knowing its date" (a knowing). Responsibilities related to "knowing" are often inferable from the conceptual model, because of the attributes and associations it illustrates.

The translation of responsibilities into classes and methods is influenced by the granularity of the responsibility. The responsibility to "provide access to relational databases" may involve dozens of classes and hundreds of methods. In contrast, the responsibility to "print a sale" may involve only a single or few methods.

A responsibility is not the same thing as a method, but methods are implemented to fulfill responsibilities. Responsibilities are implemented using methods which either act alone or collaborate with other methods and objects. For example, the *Sale* class might define one or more methods that perform printing of a *Sale* instance; say, a method named *print*. To fulfill that responsibility, the *Sale* may collaborate with other objects, such as sending a message to *SalesLineItem* objects asking them to print themselves.

# 18.5    Responsibilities and Interaction Diagrams

The purpose of this chapter is to help you apply fundamental principles for assigning responsibilities to objects. Within the UML artifacts, a common context where these responsibilities (implemented as methods) are considered is during the creation of interaction diagrams, whose notation we examined in the prior chapter.

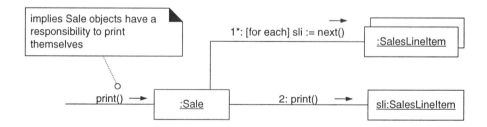

**Figure 18.1** Responsibilities and methods are related.

Figure 18.1 indicates that *Sale* objects have been given a responsibility to print themselves, which is invoked with a *print* message and handled with a corresponding *print* method. Furthermore, the fulfillment of this responsibility requires collaboration with *SalesLineItem* objects asking them to print.

In summary, interaction diagrams show choices in assigning responsibilities to objects. When created, decisions in responsibility assignment are made which are reflected in what messages are sent to different classes of objects. This chapter emphasizes fundamental principles—expressed in the GRASP patterns—to guide choices in where to assign responsibilities. These choices are reflected in interaction diagrams.

# 18.6    Patterns

Experienced object-oriented developers (and other software developers) build up a repertoire of both general principles and idiomatic solutions that guide them in the creation of software. These principles and idioms, if codified in a structured format describing the problem and solution, and given a name, may be called **patterns**. For example, here is a sample pattern:

| | |
|---|---|
| Pattern Name: | Expert |
| Solution: | Assign a responsibility to the class that has the information needed to fulfill it. |
| Problem it Solves: | What is the most basic principle by which to assign responsibilities to objects? |

In object technology, a **pattern** is a named description of a problem and solution that can be applied to new contexts; ideally, it provides advice in how to apply it in varying circumstances.[1] Many patterns provide guidance for how responsibilities should be assigned to objects, given a specific category of problem.

> Most simply, a **pattern** is a named problem/solution pair that can be applied in new contexts, with advice on how to apply it in novel situations.

"One person's pattern is another person's primitive building block" is an object technology adage illustrating the vagueness of what can be called a pattern [GHJV94]. This treatment of patterns will bypass the issue of what is appropriate to label a pattern, and focus on the pragmatic value of using the pattern style as a vehicle for presenting and remembering useful software engineering principles.

---

1. The formal notion of patterns originated with the architectural patterns of Christopher Alexander [AIS77]. Their application to software originated in the 1980s from Kent Beck and Ward Cunningham [Beck94, Coplien95].

## 18.6.1   Patterns Do Not Usually Contain New Ideas

The point of patterns is not to discover and express new software engineering principles. Quite the opposite is true—patterns attempt to codify *existing* knowledge, idioms and principles; the more honed and widely used, the better. Consequently, the GRASP patterns—which will soon be introduced—do not state any new ideas; they are a codification of widely used basic principles.

## 18.6.2   Patterns Have Names

All patterns ideally have suggestive names. Naming a pattern, technique, or principle has the following advantages:

- It supports chunking and incorporating that concept into our understanding and memory.
- It facilitates communication.

Naming a complex idea such as a pattern is an example of the power of abstraction—reducing a complex form to a simple one by eliminating detail.Therefore, the GRASP patterns have concise names such as *Expert, Creator, Controller*.

## 18.6.3   Naming Patterns Improves Communication

When a pattern is named, we can discuss with others an entire principle with a simple name. Consider the following discussion between two software designers, using a common vocabulary of patterns (*Expert*, *Model-View Separation*, and so on) to decide upon a design:

**Fred**: "Where do you think we should place the responsibility for printing a *Sale*? I think *Model-View Separation* would work well—how about a *SaleReportView*?"

**Wilma**: "I think *Expert* is a better choice since it is a simple print and the Sales has all the data required in the printout—let the *Sale* do it."

**Fred**: "OK, I agree."

Chunking design idioms and principles with commonly understood names facilitates communication and raises the level of inquiry to a higher degree of abstraction.

# 18.7  GRASP: Patterns of General Principles in Assigning Responsibilities

To summarize the proceeding introduction:

■ The skillful assignment of responsibilities is extremely important in object-oriented design.

■ Determining the assignment of responsibilities often occurs during the creation of interaction diagrams.

■ Patterns are named problem/solution pairs that codify good advice and principles often related to the assignment of responsibilities.

We are ready to explore the GRASP patterns.

| | |
|---|---|
| **Question**: | What are the GRASP patterns? |
| **Answer**: | The GRASP patterns describe fundamental principles of assigning responsibilities to objects, expressed as patterns. |

Understanding and being able to apply these principles during the creation of interaction diagrams is important because a software developer new to object technology needs to master these basic principles as quickly as possible; they form the foundation of how a system will be designed.

GRASP is an acronym that stands for **G**eneral **R**esponsibility **A**ssignment **S**oftware **P**atterns.[1] The name was chosen to suggest the importance of *grasping* these principles in order to successfully design object-oriented software.

## 18.7.1  How to Apply the GRASP Patterns

The following sections present the first five GRASP patterns:

■ Expert

■ Creator

■ High Cohesion

■ Low Coupling

■ Controller

There are others, introduced in a later chapter, but it is worthwhile mastering

---

1. Technically, one should write "GRAS Patterns" rather than "GRASP Patterns," but the latter sounds better.

these five first because they address very basic, common questions and fundamental design issues.

Please study the following patterns, note how they are used in the example interaction diagrams, and then apply them during the creation of new interaction diagrams. Start by mastering *Expert, Creator, Controller, High Cohesion* and *Low Coupling*. Later, learn the remaining patterns.

## 18.8    The UML Class Diagram Notation

The UML class diagrams illustrate software classes as opposed to domain concepts. The class box has three sections; the third illustrates the methods of the class, as shown in Figure 18.2

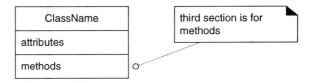

**Figure 18.2**  Software classes illustrate method names.

The details of this notation are explored in a subsequent chapter. In the following discussion on patterns, this form of class box will occasionally be used.

# 18.9    Expert

**Solution**    **Assign a responsibility to the information expert—the class that has the *information* necessary to fulfill the responsibility.**

**Problem**    What is the most basic principle by which responsibilities are assigned in object-oriented design?

A class model may define dozens or hundreds of software classes, and an application may require hundreds or thousands of responsibilities to be fulfilled. During object-oriented design, when the interactions between objects are defined, we make choices about the assignment of responsibilities to classes. Done well, systems tend to be easier to understand, maintain, and extend, and there is an opportunity to reuse components in future applications.

**Example**    In the point-of-sale application, some class needs to know the grand total of a sale.

> Start assigning responsibilities by clearly stating the responsibility.

By this advice, the statement is:

> Who should be responsible for knowing the grand total of the sale?

By Expert, we should look for that class of objects that has the information needed to determine the total. Consider the partial conceptual model in Figure 18.3.

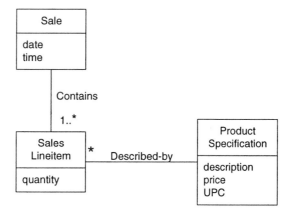

**Figure 18.3** Associations of the Sale.

What information is needed to determine the grand total? It is necessary to know about all the *SalesLineItem* instances of a sale and the sum of their subtotals. Only a *Sale* instance knows this; therefore, by Expert, *Sale* is the correct class of object for this responsibility; it is the *information expert*.

As mentioned, it is in the context of the creation of interaction diagrams (such as collaboration diagrams) that these questions of responsibility often arise. Imagine we are starting to work through the drawing of diagrams in order to assign responsibilities to objects. The partial collaboration diagram and class diagram in Figure 18.4 illustrate our decisions so far.

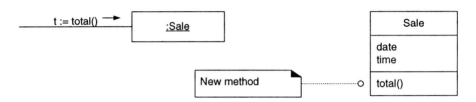

**Figure 18.4** Partial collaboration diagram.

We are not done yet. What information is needed to determine the line item subtotal? *SalesLineItem.quantity* and *ProductSpecification.price* are needed. The *SalesLineItem* knows its quantity and its associated *ProductSpecification*; therefore, by Expert, *SalesLineItem* should determine the subtotal; it is the *information expert*.

In terms of a collaboration diagram, this means that the *Sale* needs to send *subtotal* messages to each of the *SalesLineItems* and sum the results; the design is shown in Figure 18.5

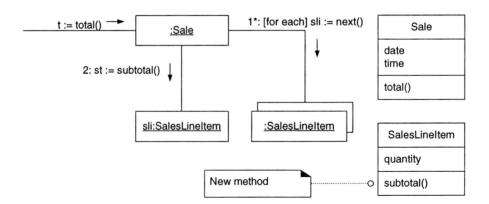

**Figure 18.5** Calculating the Sale total.

In order to fulfill the responsibility of knowing and answering its subtotal, a *SalesLineItem* needs to know the product price. The *ProductSpecification* is an information Expert on answering its price; therefore, a message must be sent to it asking for its price. The design is shown in Figure 18.6.

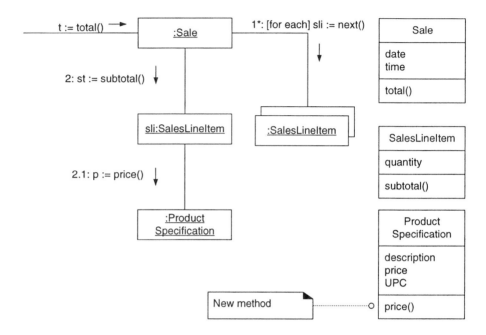

**Figure 18.6** Calculating the Sale total.

In conclusion, in order to fulfill the responsibility of knowing and answering the sale's total, three responsibilities were assigned to three classes of objects as follows:

| Class | Responsibility |
|---|---|
| Sale | knows sale total |
| SalesLineItem | knows line item subtotal |
| ProductSpecification | knows product price |

The context in which these responsibilities were considered and decided upon was while drawing a collaboration diagram. The method section of a class diagram can then summarize the methods.

The principle by which each responsibility was assigned was Expert—placing it with the object that had the information needed to fulfill it.

**Discussion**    Expert is used more than any other pattern in the assignment of responsibilities; it is a basic guiding principle used continuously in object-oriented design. Expert is not meant to be an obscure or fancy idea; it expresses the common "intuition" that objects do things related to the information they have.

Notice that the fulfillment of a responsibility often requires information that is spread across different classes of objects. This implies that there are many "partial" experts who will collaborate in the task. For example, the sales total problem ultimately required the collaboration of three classes. Whenever information is spread across different objects, they will need to interact via messages in order to share the work.

Expert leads to designs where a software object does those operations which are normally done to the real-world thing it represents; Peter Coad calls this the "Do it Myself" strategy [Coad95]. For example, in the real world, without the use of electro-mechanical aids, a sale does not tell you its total; it is an inanimate concept. Someone calculates the total of the sale. But in object-oriented software land, all software objects are "alive" or "animate", and they can take on responsibilities and do things. Fundamentally, they do things related to the information they know. I call this the "Animation" principle in object-oriented design; it is like being in a cartoon where everything is alive.

The Expert pattern—like many things in object technology—has a real-world analogy. We commonly give responsibility to individuals who have the information necessary to fulfill the task. For example, in a business, who should be responsible for creating a profit-and-loss statement? The person who has access to all the information necessary to create it—perhaps the chief financial officer. And just as software objects collaborate because the information is spread around, so it is with people. The company's chief financial officer may ask accountants in accounts receivable and accounts payable to generate separate reports on credits and debits.

**Benefits**    ■ Encapsulation is maintained, since objects use their own information to fulfill tasks. This supports **low coupling**, which leads to more robust and maintainable systems. (Low Coupling is a GRASP pattern that is discussed ahead).

■ Behavior is distributed across the classes that have the required information, thus encouraging more cohesive "lightweight" class definitions that are easier to understand and maintain. **High cohesion** is supported (a pattern discussed ahead).

**Also Known As;**    "Place responsibilities with data," "That which knows, does," "Animation," "Do it
**Similar To**    Myself," "Put Services with the Attributes They Work On."

# 18.10  Creator

**Solution**  Assign class B the responsibility to create an instance of class A if one of the following is true:

- B *aggregates* A objects.

- B *contains* A objects.

- B *records* instances of A objects.

- B *closely uses* A objects.

- B *has the initializing data* that will be passed to A when it is created (thus B is an Expert with respect to creating A).

B is a *creator* of A objects.

If more than one option applies, prefer a class B which *aggregates* or *contains* class A.

**Problem**  Who should be responsibility for creating a new instance of some class?

The creation of objects is one of the most common activities in an object-oriented system. Consequently, it is useful to have a general principle for the assignment of creation responsibilities. Assigned well, the design can support low coupling, increased clarity, encapsulation, and reusability.

**Example**  In the point-of-sale application, who should be responsible for creating a *SalesLineItem* instance? By Creator, we should look for a class that aggregates, contains, and so on, *SalesLineItem* instances. Consider the partial conceptual model in Figure 18.7.

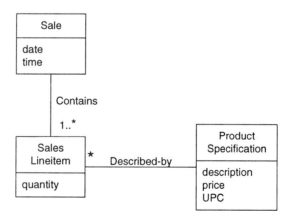

**Figure 18.7**  Partial conceptual model.

Since a *Sale* contains (in fact, aggregates) many *SalesLineItem* objects, the Creator pattern suggests *Sale* is a good candidate to have the responsibility of creating SalesLineItem instances.

This leads to a design of object interactions in a collaboration diagram, as shown in Figure 18.8.

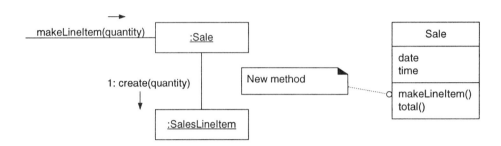

**Figure 18.8** Creating a SalesLineItem.

This assignment of responsibilities requires that a *makeLineItem* method be defined in *Sale*.

Once again, the context in which these responsibilities were considered and decided upon was while drawing a collaboration diagram. The method section of a class diagram can then summarize the responsibility assignment results, concretely realized as methods.

**Discussion**   Creator guides assigning responsibilities related to the creation of objects, a very common task in object-oriented systems. The basic intent of the Creator pattern is to find a creator which needs to be connected to the created object in any event. Choosing it as the creator supports low coupling.

Aggregate *aggregates* Part, Container *contains* Content, Recorder *records* Recorded are all very common relationships between classes in a class diagram. Creator suggests that the enclosing container or recorder class is a good candidate for the responsibility of creating the thing contained or recorded. Of course, this is only a guideline.

Note that the concept of **aggregation** has been used in considering the Creator pattern. Aggregation will be fully discussed later in the book, but a brief definition is that aggregation involves things that are in a strong whole-part or assembly-part relationship, such as Body aggregates Leg, or Paragraph aggregates Sentence.

Sometimes a creator is found by looking for the class that has the initializing data that will be passed in during creation. This is actually an example of the Expert pattern. Initializing data is passed in during creation via some kind of initialization method, such as a Java constructor that has parameters.

For example, assume that a *Payment* instance needs to be initialized, when created, with the *Sale* total. Since *Sale* knows the total, *Sale* is a candidate creator of the *Payment*.

**Benefits** ■ **Low Coupling** (described ahead) is supported, which implies lower maintenance dependencies and higher opportunities for reuse. Coupling is probably not increased because the *created* class is likely already visible to the *creator* class, due to the existing associations that motivated its choice as creator.

**Related Patterns** ■ Low Coupling

■ Whole-Part [BMRSS96] describes a pattern to define aggregate objects that supports encapsulation of its components.

# 18.11   Low Coupling

**Solution**   **Assign a responsibility so that coupling remains low.**

**Problem**   How to support low dependency and increased reuse?

**Coupling** is a measure of how strongly one class is connected to, has knowledge of, or relies upon other classes. A class with low (or weak) coupling is not dependent on too many other classes; "too many" is context dependent but will be examined.

A class with high (or strong) coupling relies upon many other classes. Such classes are undesirable; they suffer from the following problems:

■  Changes in related classes force local changes.

■  Harder to understand in isolation.

■  Harder to reuse because its use requires the additional presence of the classes it is dependent upon.

**Example**   Consider the following partial class diagram from a point-of-sale terminal application:

Assume we have a need to create a *Payment* instance and associate it with the *Sale*. What class should be responsible for this? Since a *POST* "records" a *Payment* in the real-world domain, the Creator pattern suggests *POST* as a candidate for creating the *Payment*. The *Post* instance could then send an *addPayment* message to the *Sale*, passing along the new *Payment* as a parameter. A possible partial collaboration diagram reflecting this is shown in Figure 18.9.

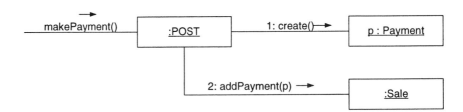

**Figure 18.9**  POST creates Payment.

This assignment of responsibilities couples the *POST* class to knowledge of the *Payment* class. An alternative solution to creating the *Payment* and associating it with the *Sale* is shown in Figure 18.10.

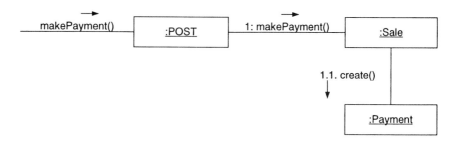

**Figure 18.10** Sale creates Payment.

Which design, based on assignment of responsibilities, supports Low Coupling? In both cases we will assume the *Sale* must eventually be coupled to knowledge of a *Payment*. Design One, in which the *Post* creates the *Payment*, adds coupling of *POST* to *Payment*, while Design Two, in which the *Sale* does the creation of a *Payment*, does not increase the coupling. Purely from the point of view of coupling, Design Two is preferable because overall lower coupling is maintained. This an example where two patterns—Low Coupling and Creator—may suggest different solutions. In practice, the level of coupling alone can not be considered in isolation from other principles such as Expert and High Cohesion. Nevertheless, it is one factor to consider in improving a design.

**Discussion**  Low Coupling is a principle to keep in mind during all design decisions; it is an underlying goal to continually consider. It is an *evaluative pattern* which a designer applies while evaluating all design decisions.

In object-oriented languages such as C++, Java, and Smalltalk, common forms of coupling from *TypeX* to *TypeY* include:

■  *TypeX* has an attribute (data member or instance variable) that refers to a *TypeY* instance, or *TypeY* itself.

■  *TypeX* has a method which references an instance of *TypeY*, or *TypeY* itself, by any means. These typically include a parameter or local variable of type *TypeY*, or the object returned from a message being an instance of *TypeY*.

■  *TypeX* is a direct or indirect subclass of *TypeY*.

■  *TypeY* is an interface, and *TypeX* implements that interface.

Low Coupling encourages assigning a responsibility so that its placement does not increase the coupling to such a level that it leads to the negative results that high coupling can produce.

Low Coupling supports the design of classes that are more independent, which reduces the impact of changes, and more reusable, which improves the opportunity for higher productivity. It can not be considered in isolation from other patterns such as Expert and High Cohesion, but rather needs to be included as one of several design principles that influence a choice in assigning a responsibility.

Coupling may not be that important if reuse is not a goal. As a support to improve reuse of components by making them more independent, the entire context of reuse goals must be taken into consideration before an effort is made to minimize coupling. For example, excessive time is sometimes spent on trying to achieve reusable components for future "mythical" projects, even though there is no clear indication there is a need for reuse of the component. This is not to say trying to achieve reuse is wasted effort, but the effort should be tempered by cost-benefit considerations.

A subclass is strongly coupled to its superclass. The decision to derive from a superclass needs to be carefully considered since it is such a strong form of coupling. For example, suppose that objects need to be stored persistently in a relational or object database. In this case, it is a relatively common, but somewhat undesirable, design to create an abstract superclass called *PersistentObject* from which other classes derive. The disadvantage of this subclassing is that it highly couples domain objects to a particular service, whereas the advantage is automatic inheritance of persistence behavior, a "marriage of convenience"—seldom a wise choice in relationships!

There is no absolute measure of when coupling is too high. What is important is that a developer can gauge the current degree of coupling, and assess if increasing it will lead to problems. In general, classes which are inherently very generic in nature, and with a high probability for reuse, should have especially low coupling.

The extreme case of Low Coupling is when there is very little or no coupling between classes. This is not desirable because a central metaphor of object technology is a system of connected objects that communicate via messages. If Low Coupling is taken to excess, it yields a poor design because it leads to a few incohesive, bloated, and complex active objects that do all the work, with many very passive zero-coupled objects that act as simple data repositories. Some moderate degree of coupling between classes is normal and necessary in order to create an object-oriented system in which tasks are fulfilled by a collaboration between connected objects.

**Benefits**
- not effected by changes in other components
- simple to understand in isolation
- convenient to reuse

# 18.12   High Cohesion

**Solution**   **Assign a responsibility so that cohesion remains high.**

**Problem**   How to keep complexity manageable?

In terms of object-oriented design, **cohesion** (or more specifically, functional cohesion) is a measure of how strongly related and focused the responsibilities of a class are. A class with highly related responsibilities, and which does not do a tremendous amount of work, has high cohesion.

A class with low cohesion does many unrelated things or does too much work. Such classes are undesirable; they suffer from the following problems:

- hard to comprehend

- hard to reuse

- hard to maintain

- delicate; constantly effected by change

Low cohesion classes often represent a very "large-grain" of abstraction, or have taken on responsibilities that should have been delegated to other objects.

**Example**   The same example problem used in the Low Coupling pattern can be analyzed for High Cohesion.

Assume we have a need to create a (cash) *Payment* instance and associate it with the *Sale*. What class should be responsible for this? Since *POST* records a *Payment* in the real-world domain, the Creator pattern suggests *POST* as a candidate for creating the *Payment*. The *Post* instance could then send an *addPayment* message to the *Sale*, passing along the new *Payment* as a parameter, as shown in Figure 18.11.

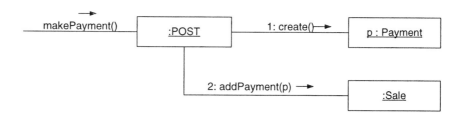

**Figure 18.11**  POST creates Payment.

This assignment of responsibilities places the responsibility for making a payment in the *POST*. The *POST* is taking on part of the responsibility for fulfilling the *makePayment* system operation.

In this isolated example, this is acceptable, but if we continue to make the *POST* class responsibility for doing some or all of the work related to more and more system operations, it will become increasingly burdened with tasks and become incohesive.

Imagine that there were fifty system operations, all received by *POST*. If it did the work related to each, it would become a "bloated" incohesive object. The point is not that this single *Payment* creation task in itself makes the *POST* incohesive, but as part of a larger picture of overall responsibility assignment, it may suggest a trend toward low cohesion.

In contrast, as shown in Figure 18.12, the second design delegates the payment creation responsibility to the *Sale*, which supports higher cohesion in the POST. Since the second design supports both high cohesion and low coupling, it is desirable.

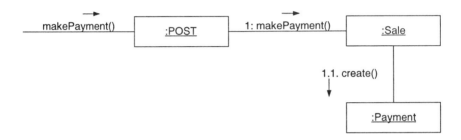

**Figure 18.12** Sale creates Payment.

In practice, the level of cohesion alone can not be considered in isolation from other responsibilities and other principles such as Expert and Low Coupling.

**Discussion**  Like Low Coupling, High Cohesion is a principle to keep in mind during all design decisions; it is an underlying goal to continually consider. It is an evaluative pattern which a designer applies while evaluating all design decisions.

Grady Booch describes high functional cohesion as existing when the elements of a component (such as a class) "all work together to provide some well-bounded behavior" [Booch94].

Here are some scenarios that illustrate varying degrees of functional cohesion:

1.  *Very low cohesion.* A class is solely responsible for many things in very different functional areas.

    ❑   Assume a class exists called *RDB-RPC-Interface* which is completely responsible for interacting with relational databases and for handling remote procedure calls. These are two vastly different functional areas, and each requires lots of supporting code. The responsibilities should be split into a family of classes related to RDB access and a family related to RPC support.

2.  *Low cohesion.* A class has sole responsibility for a complex task in one functional area.

     ❏   Assume a class exists called *RDBInterface* which is completely responsible for interacting with relational databases. The methods of the class are all related, but there are lots of them, and a tremendous amount of supporting code; there may be hundreds or thousands of methods. The class should split into a family of lightweight classes sharing the work to provide RDB access.

3. *High cohesion.* A class has moderate responsibilities in one functional area and collaborates with other classes to fulfill tasks.

     ❏   Assume a class exists called *RDBInterface* which is only partially responsible for interacting with relational databases. It interacts with a dozen other classes related to RDB access in order to retrieve and save objects.

4. *Moderate cohesion.* A class has lightweight and sole responsibilities in a few different areas that are logically related to the class concept, but not to each other.

     ❏   Assume a class exists called *Company* which is completely responsible for (a) knowing its employees and (b) knowing its financial information. These two areas are not strongly related to each other, although both are logically related to the concept of a company. In addition, the total number of public methods is small, as is the amount of supporting code.

As a rule of thumb, a class with high cohesion has a relatively small number of methods, with highly related functionality, and does not do too much work. It collaborates with other objects to share the effort if the task is large.

A class with high cohesion is advantageous because it is relatively easy to maintain, understand, and reuse. The high degree of related functionality, combined with a small number of operations, also simplifies maintenance and enhancements. The fine grain of highly related functionality also supports increased reuse potential.

The High Cohesion pattern—like many things in object technology—has a real-world analogy. It is a common observation that if a person takes on too many unrelated responsibilities—especially ones that should properly be delegated to others—then the person is not effective. This is observed in some managers who have not learned how to delegate. These people suffer from low cohesion; they are ready to become "unglued".

**Benefits** ■ Clarity and ease of comprehension of the design is increased.

    ■ Maintenance and enhancements are simplified.

    ■ Low coupling is often supported.

    ■ The fine grain of highly related functionality supports increased reuse potential because a highly cohesive class can be used for a very specific purpose.

# 18.13 Controller

**Solution**  Assign the responsibility for handling a system event message to a class representing one of the following choices:

- Represents the overall "system" (*facade controller*).

- Represents the overall business or organization (*facade controller*).

- Represents something in the real-world that is active (for example, the role of a person) that might be involved in the task (*role controller*).

- Represents an artificial handler of all system events of a use case, usually named "\<UseCaseName\>Handler" (*use-case controller*).

Use the same controller class for all the system events in the same use case.

*Corollary*: Note that "window," "applet," "application," "view," and "document" classes are not on this list. Such classes should *not* fulfill the tasks associated with system events, they typically receive these events and delegate them to a controller.

**Problem**  Who should be responsible for handling a system event?

A **system event** is a high level system event generated by an external actor; it is an external input event. They are associated with **system operations**—operations of the system in response to system events. For example, when a cashier using a point-of-sale terminal system presses the "End Sale" button, he is generating a system event indicating "the sale has ended". Similarly, when a writer using a word processor presses the "spell check" button, he is generating a system event indicating "perform a spell check."

A **Controller** is a non-user interface object responsible for handling a system event. A Controller defines the method for the system operation.

**Example**  In the point-of-sale application, there are several system operations, as illustrated in Figure 18.13.

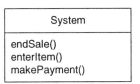

**Figure 18.13** System operations associated with the system events.

During system behavior analysis, system operations are assigned to the type *System*, to indicate they are system operations. However, this does *not* mean that a class named *System* fulfills them during design.

Rather, during design, a Controller class is assigned the responsibility for system operations (see Figure 18.14).

Who should be the controller for the system events such as *enterItem* and *endSale*?

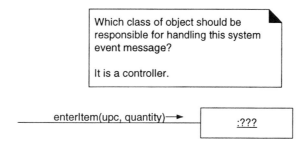

Which class of object should be responsible for handling this system event message?

It is a controller.

enterItem(upc, quantity)→      :???

**Figure 18.14** Controller for enterItem?

By the Controller pattern, here are the choices:

| | |
|---|---|
| represents the overall "system" | *POST* |
| represents the overall business or organization | *Store* |
| represents something in the real-world that is active (for example, the role of a person) that might be involved in the task | *Cashier* |
| represents an artificial handler of all system operations of a use case. | *BuyItemsHandler* |

In terms of collaboration diagrams, it means that one of the examples in Figure 18.15 will be used.

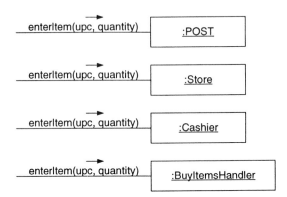

**Figure 18.15** Controller choices.

The choice of which of these four classes is the most appropriate controller is influenced by other factors, such as cohesion and coupling. The discussion section elaborates on this.

During design the system operations identified during system behavior analysis are assigned to one or more controller classes, such as *POST*, as shown in Figure 18.16.

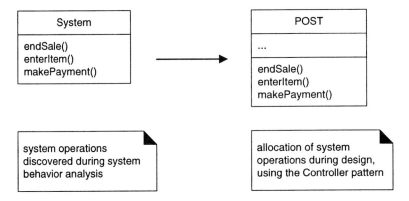

**Figure 18.16** Allocation of system operations.

**Discussion**  Most systems receive external input events, typically involving a graphical user interface (GUI) operated by a person. Other mediums of input include external messages such as in a call processing telecommunications switch, or signals from sensors such as in process control systems.

In all cases, if an object-oriented design is used, controllers must be chosen to handle these incoming events. The Controller pattern provides guidance for generally accepted suitable choices.

The same controller class should be used for all the system events of one use case so that it is possible to maintain information about the state of the use case. Such information is useful, for example, to identify out-of-sequence system events (for example, a *makePayment* operation before an *endSale* operation). Different controllers may be used for different use cases.

A common defect in the design of controllers is to give them too much responsibility. Normally, a controller should delegate to other objects the work that needs to be done while coordinating the activity. Please see the *Issues and Solutions* section later for elaboration.

The first category of controller is a facade controller representing the overall "system".That is a class representing, in some way, what the designer may consider to represent the entire system. It could be a physical unit, such as a *POST, TelecommSwitch,* or *Robot*; a class representing the entire software system, such as *RetailInformationSystem, MessageHandlingSystem,* or *RobotController*; or any other concept which the designer chooses to represent the overall system.

Facade controllers are suitable when there are only a few system events, or it is not possible to redirect system event messages to alternating controllers, such as in a message processing system.

If the fourth category of controller—an artificial "use case handler"—is applied, then there is a different controller for each use case. Note that this is not a domain object; it is an artificial construct to support the system (a *Pure Fabrication* in terms of the GRASP patterns). For example, if the point-of-sale application contains use cases such as "Buy Items" and "Return Items," then there will be a *BuyItemsHandler* and a *ReturnItemsHandler* class.

When should you choose a use case controller? It is an alternative to consider when placing the responsibilities in any of the other choices of controller leads to designs with low cohesion or high coupling, typically when an existing controller is becoming "bloated" with excessive responsibilities. A use case controller is a good choice when there are many system events across different processes; it factors their handling into manageable separate classes, and also provides a basis for reasoning about the state of the current process.

A important corollary of the Controller pattern is that external interfacing objects (for example, window objects, applets) and the presentation layer should not have responsibility for fulfilling system events.

In other words, system operations—which reflect business or domain processes—should be handled in the domain layer of objects rather than in the interface, presentation, or application layers of a system. See the following *Issues and Solutions* section for an example.

**Benefits**  ■ *Increased potential for reusable components.* It ensures that business or domain processes are handled by the layer of domain objects rather than by the interface layer. The responsibilities of a controller could technically be handled in an interface object, but the implication of such a design is that program code and logic related the fulfillment of pure domain processes would be embedded in interface or window objects. An interface-as-controller design reduces the opportunity to reuse domain process logic in future applications, since it is bound to a particular interface (for example, window-like object) that is seldom applicable in other applications. In contrast, delegating a system operation responsibility to a controller among the domain classes supports the reuse of the logic for handling the related business process in future applications.

■ *Reason about the state of the use case.* It is sometimes necessary to ensure that system operations occur in a legal sequence, or to be able to reason about the current state of activity and operations within the use case that is underway. For example, it may be necessary to guarantee that the *MakePayment* operation can not occur until the *EndSale* operation has occurred. If so, this state information needs to be captured somewhere; the controller is one reasonable choice, especially if the same controller is used throughout the use case (which is recommended).

**Issues and Solutions**

## Bloated Controllers

Poorly designed, a controller class will have low cohesion—unfocused and handling too many areas of responsibility; this is called a **bloated controller**. Signs of bloating include:

■ There is only a *single* controller class receiving *all* system events in the system, and there are many of them. This sometimes happens if a role controller or facade controller is chosen.

■ The controller itself performs many of the tasks necessary to fulfill the system event, without delegating the work. This usually involves a violation of the Expert and High Cohesion patterns.

■ A controller has many attributes, and maintains significant information about the system or domain, which should have been distributed to other objects, or duplicates information found elsewhere.

There are several cures to a bloated controller, including:

1. Add more controllers—a system does not have to have only one. In addition to facade-controllers, use role-controllers or use-case-controllers. For example, consider an application with many system events, such as an airline res-

ervation system. It may contain the following controllers:

| Role-controllers | Use-case-controllers |
|---|---|
| ReservationAgent | MakeAReservationHandler |
| Scheduler | ManageSchedulesHandler |
| FareAnalyst | ManageFaresHandler |

2.  Design the controller so that it primarily delegates the fulfillment of each system operation responsibility on to other objects.

## Warning: Role Controllers May Lead to Poor Designs

Assigning a responsibility to a human-role object in a way that mimics what that role does in the real world (for example, *Cashier* software object handing *makePayment*) is acceptable if the designer is cognizant of the potential hazards, and avoids these. In particular, there is the danger of creating an incohesive role controller that does not delegate. A good object-oriented design "brings objects to life" by giving them responsibilities, even though they represent inanimate things in the real world. If a role controller is chosen, avoid the trap of designing person-like objects to do all the work; instead, delegate.

In general, role controllers should be used sparingly.

## Presentation Layer Does Not Handle System Events

To reiterate: an important corollary of the Controller pattern is that interface objects (for example, window objects, applets) and the presentation layer should not have responsibility for handling system events. In other words, system operations—which reflect business or domain processes—should be handled in the domain layer of objects rather than in the interface, presentation, or application layers of a system.

As an example, consider a design in Java which uses an applet to display the information.

Assume the point-of-sale application has a window that displays sale information and captures cashier operations. Using the Controller pattern, Figure 18.17 illustrates an acceptable relationship between the applet and Controller and other objects in a portion of the point-of-sale system (with simplifications).

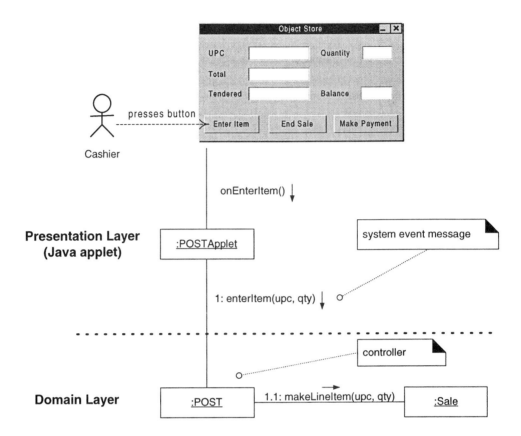

**Figure 18.17** Desirable coupling of presentation to domain layer.

Notice that the *POSTApplet* class—part of the presentation layer—passes on the *enterItem* message to the *POST* object. It did not get involved in processing the operation or deciding how to handle it, the applet only delegated it to the domain layer.

Assigning the responsibility for system operations to objects in the domain layer—using the Controller pattern—rather than the presentation layer supports increased reuse potential. If an interface layer object (like the *POSTApplet*) handled a system operation—which represents part of a business process—then business process logic would be contained in an interface (for example, window-like) object, which has low opportunity for reuse because of its coupling to a particular interface and application.

Consequently, the design in Figure 18.18 is undesirable.

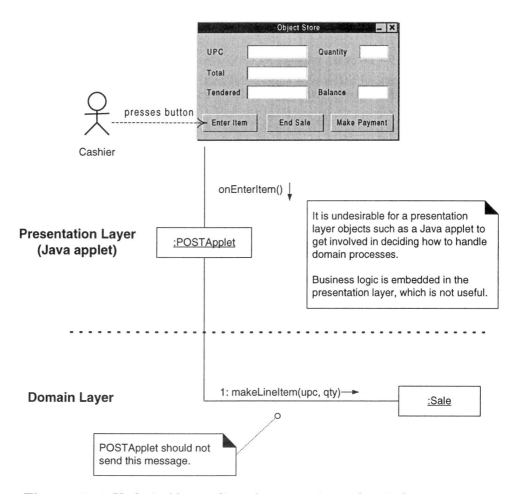

**Figure 18.18** Undesirable coupling of presentation to domain layer.

Placing system operation responsibility in a domain object controller makes it easier to reuse the program logic supporting the associated business process in future applications. It also makes it easier to unplug the interface layer and use a different interface framework or technology, or to run the system in an off-line "batch" mode.

## Message Handling Systems and the Command Pattern

Many applications do not have a user interface, but instead receive messages from some other external system; they are message-handling systems. A telecommunications switch is a common example. The message may be encoded in a record or raw stream of bytes, or if an object-oriented interprocess communication mechanism such as CORBA is used, as a "real" message to an object.

In an application with a user interface (for example, a window), the window may choose who the controller object will be. Different windows may collaborate with different controllers, especially if a use-case controller is used.

In contrast, in a message-handling application, the design of the interface and controller is different. For a simple case, the following design is suggested. For a more elaborate and feature-rich design, see the Forwarder-Receiver pattern in [BMRSS96].

To handle system event messages in a message-handling system:

1. Define a single controller for all system event messages; it may be a facade controller, or a single use-case type controller named something like *MessageHandler*.

2. Use the Command pattern [GHJV95] to handle the request.

The **Command** pattern specifies the definition of a class for each message or command, each with an *execute* method. The controller will create a Command instance corresponding to the system event message, and send it an *execute* message. Each Command class has a unique *execute* method which specifies the actions for that command, as shown in Figure 18.19.[1]

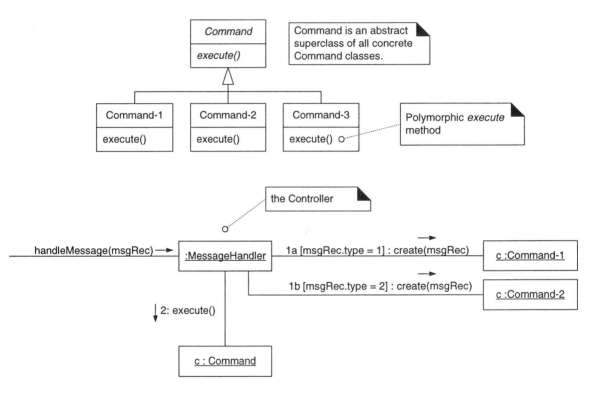

**Figure 18.19** The controller and use of the Command pattern.

---

1. An abstract Command *interface*, as opposed to abstract superclass, is also possible.

**Related Patterns** ■ **Command**—In a message-handling system, each message may be represented and handled by a separate Command object [GHJV95].

■ **Facade**—Choosing an object representing the entire system or organization to be a controller is a kind of Facade [GHJV95].

■ **Forwarder-Recover**—This is a Siemens pattern [BMRSS96] useful for message-handling systems.

■ **Layers**—This is a Siemens pattern [BMRSS96]. Placing domain logic in the domain layer rather than the presentation layer is part of the Layers pattern.

■ **Pure Fabrication**—This is another GRASP pattern. A Pure Fabrication is an artificial class, not a domain concept. A use-case controller is a kind of Pure Fabrication.

# 18.14   Responsibilities, Role Playing and CRC Cards

Although not formally part of the UML, another device sometimes used to help assign responsibilities and indicate collaboration with other objects are **CRC cards** (Class-Responsibility-Collaborator cards) [BC89]. These were pioneered by Kent Beck and Ward Cunningham, who are largely responsible for encouraging objects designers to think more abstractly in terms of responsibility assignment and collaborations.

CRC cards are index cards, one for each class, upon which the responsibilities of the class are briefly written, and a list of objects collaborated with to fulfill those responsibilities. They are usually developed in a small group session where people **role play** being the various classes. Each person holds onto the CRC cards for the classes that they are playing the role of.

To learn how to think in terms of objects and responsibilities, role playing is both helpful and fun. However, text-based CRC cards are limited in their ability to record collaborations in a comprehensive way. Graphical collaboration diagrams and class diagrams better illustrate the connections between objects and the overall context.

Group design efforts with responsibility assignment and role playing is useful and recommended; the results can be recorded in CRC cards and/or graphical diagrams. CRC cards are one approach to recording the results of responsibility assignment and collaborations. The recording can be enhanced with the use of collaboration and class diagrams. The real value is not the cards, but the consideration of responsibility assignment and the activity of role playing.

# DESIGNING A SOLUTION WITH OBJECTS AND PATTERNS

---

### Objectives

- Apply the GRASP patterns to assign responsibilities to classes.

- Use the UML collaboration diagram notation to illustrate the design of object interaction.

---

## 19.1    Introduction

This chapter explores how to create interaction diagrams (in this case, collaboration diagrams) for the point-of-sale application. Their relationship to prior artifacts such as contracts and the conceptual model is investigated. Particular attention is given to the application of the GRASP patterns to develop a well-designed solution.

This chapter communicate the principles, using the point-of-sale example, by which an object-oriented designer assigns responsibilities and establishes object interactions—a core skill in object-oriented development.

In practice, developers find that the creation of interaction diagrams is one of the most time-consuming (and worthwhile) steps. Also note:

---

The assignment of responsibilities and development of interaction diagrams is the most significant creative step during the design phase.

---

The material is intentionally detailed; it attempts to exhaustively illustrate that there is no "magic" or unjustifiable decisions in object-oriented design; alternative assignments of responsibilities and the choice of object interactions can be rationally explained and learned.

To review the steps in creating interaction diagrams:

---

To make interaction diagrams:

1. Create a separate diagram for each system operation under development in the current iterative step.

   ◻ For each system event, make a diagram with it as the starting message.

2. If the diagram gets complex, split it into smaller diagrams.

3. Using the contract responsibilities and post-conditions, and use case description as a starting point, design a system of interacting objects to fulfill the tasks. Apply the GRASP and other patterns to develop a good design.

---

# 19.2    Interaction Diagrams and Other Artifacts

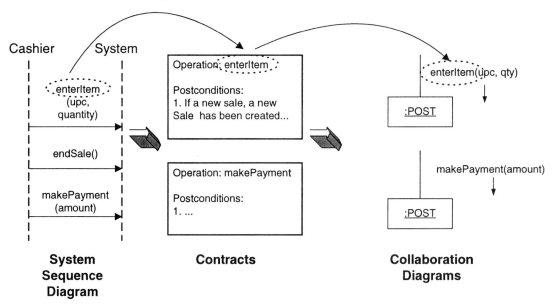

**Figure 19.1** Relationship between artifacts in terms of system events.

Figure 19.1 illustrates the relationship between the artifacts.

- The use cases suggests the system events which are explicitly shown in system sequence diagrams.

- An initial best guess at the effect of the system events is described in system operation contracts.

- The system events represent messages that initiate interaction diagrams, which illustrate how objects interact to fulfill the required tasks.

- The interaction diagrams involve message interaction between objects defined in the conceptual model, plus other classes of objects.

## 19.2.1   Interaction Diagrams and System Events

In the current iteration of the point-of-sale application we are considering two use cases and their associated system events:

- Buy Items

    - enterItem

    - endSale

    - makePayment

- Start Up

    - startUp

> For each system event, create a collaboration diagram whose starting message is the system event message.

Therefore there will be at least four interaction diagrams; one for each system event. Using the Controller pattern, the *POST* class could be chosen as the controller for handling the events (Figure 19.2).

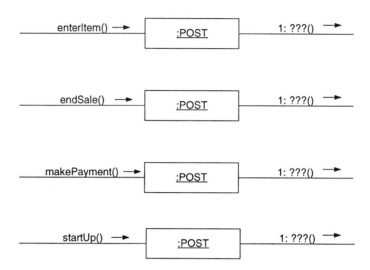

**Figure 19.2** System events.

## 19.2.2 Interaction Diagrams and Contracts

> Using the contract responsibilities and post-conditions, and use cases as a starting point, design a system of interacting objects to fulfill the tasks.

For each system operation a contract exists which elaborates on what the operation must achieve. For example:

Contract

Name:             enterItem
                     (upc : number,
                      quantity : integer)

Responsibilities:   Enter (record) sale of an item and add it to the sale. Display the item description and price.

Post-conditions:

- If a new sale, a *Sale* was created (*instance creation*).

- If a new sale, the new *Sale* was associated with the *POST* (*association formed*).

- and so on...

For each contract, we work through the responsibilities and post-condition state changes, and design message interactions—illustrated in the collaboration diagram—to satisfy the requirements. Note that if we bypassed the contract creation we could still construct the interaction diagrams by returning to the use cases and thinking through what must be achieved. However, the contracts organize and isolate the information in a workable format, and encourage investigative work during the analysis phase rather than the design phase.

For example, given this partial *enterItem* system operation, a partial collaboration diagram is shown in Figure 19.3 that satisfies the state change of *Sale* creation.

**Figure 19.3** Partial collaboration diagram.

### 19.2.3   The Post-conditions are Only an Estimate

Interaction diagrams may be created with the motivation of fulfilling the post-conditions of the contracts. However, it is essential to recognize that the previously defined post-conditions are merely an initial best guess or estimate of what must be achieved. They may not be accurate. This is also true of the conceptual model—it is a starting point that will contain errors and omissions. Treat contracts as a starting point for determining what must be done, but do not be bound by them. It is very likely that some existing post-conditions will not be necessary, and that there are as-yet-undiscovered tasks to complete. An advantage of iterative development is that it naturally supports the discovery of new analysis and design results during the solution and construction phases.

The spirit of iterative development is to capture a "reasonable" degree of information during the analysis phase, filling in details during the design phase. Similarly, it is in the spirit of this process to capture a "reasonable" degree of design results during the design phase, filling in details during the implementation (coding) phase. The definition of "reasonable" is, of course, a matter of judgment; this book attempts to present a reasonable degree of effort for each step.

### 19.2.4   Collaboration Diagrams and the Conceptual Model

Some of the objects that interact via messages in the collaboration diagrams are drawn from the conceptual model. The choice of appropriate responsibility placement using the GRASP patterns relies, in part, upon information in the conceptual model. As mentioned, the existing conceptual model is not likely to be perfect; errors and omissions are to be expected. You will discover new concepts that were previously missed, ignore concepts that were previously identified, and do likewise with associations and attributes.

## 19.3    Point-of-Sale Conceptual Model

As a reminder, Figure 19.4 shows a conceptual model for the point-of-sale application. These are objects that may participate in the object interactions. Must the set of interacting objects be limited to this model? Not at all; it is appropriate to discover new types during this design phase that were missed during the earlier analysis. At that time, newly discovered types are added to the model.

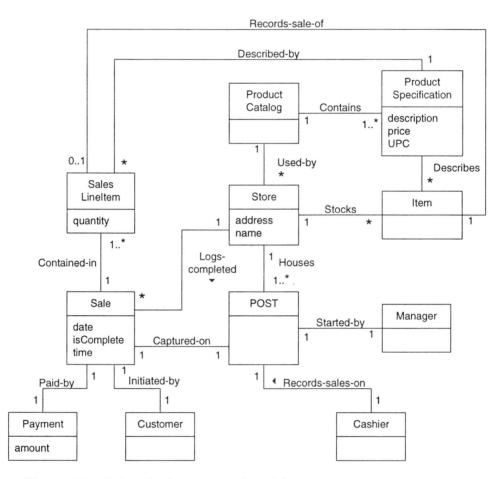

**Figure 19.4**  Point-of-sale conceptual model.

## 19.4    Collaboration Diagrams for the POST Application

This section explores the choices and decisions made while creating a collaboration diagram, based on the GRASP patterns. The explanations are intentionally detailed, in an attempt to illustrate that there does not have be any "hand waving" in the creation of well-designed collaboration diagrams; their construction is based on justifiable principles.

# 19.5    Collaboration Diagram: enterItem

The *enterItem* system operation occurs when a cashier enters the UPC and quantity of an item to be purchased. Here is the complete contract; bear in mind that it is an initial estimate and may not be complete:

Contract

| | |
|---|---|
| Name: | enterItem<br>(upc : number,<br>quantity : integer) |
| Responsibilities: | Enter (record) sale of an item and add it to the sale. Display the item description and price. |
| Type: | System |
| Cross References: | System Functions: R1.1, R1.3, R1.9 |
| | Use Cases: Buy Items |
| Notes: | Use superfast database access. |
| Exceptions: | If the UPC is not valid, indicate that it was an error. |
| Output: | |
| Preconditions: | UPC is known to the system |
| Post-conditions: | |

- If a new sale, a *Sale* was created (*instance creation*)

- If a new sale, the new *Sale* was associated with the *POST* (*association formed*)

- A *SalesLineItem* was created (*instance creation*)

- The *SalesLineItem* was associated with the *Sale* (*association formed*)

- *SalesLineItem.quantity* was set to *quantity* (*attribute modification*)

- The *SalesLineItem* was associated with a *ProductSpecification*, based on *UPC* match (*association formed*)

A collaboration diagram will be constructed to satisfy the post-conditions of *enterItem*. As stressed in the GRASP patterns chapter, each choice of message implies the assignment of a responsibility, and the GRASP patterns will be used to choose and justify each message sent to a class of objects.

## 19.5.1    *Choosing the Controller Class*

Our first choice involves choosing the controller for the system operation message *enterItem*. By the Controller pattern, here are the choices:

| | |
|---|---|
| represents the entire system (facade-controller) | *POST,* or a new class such as *RetailSystem* |
| represents the overall business or organization (facade-controller) | *Store* |
| represents something in the real-world that is active (for example, the role of a person) that might be involved in the task (role-controller) | *Cashier* |
| represents an artificial handler of all system operations of a use case (use-case-controller). | *BuyItemsHandler* |

Choosing a facade-controller like *POST* is satisfactory if there are only a few system operations and the facade-controller is not taking on too many responsibilities (in other words, if it is becoming incohesive). Choosing a role-controller or use-case-controller are suitable when there are many system operations and we wish to distribute responsibilities in order to keep each controller class lightweight and focused (in other words, cohesive). In this case, *POST* will suffice, since there are only a few system operations.

> It is important to appreciate that this *POST* instance in an object in "software land". It is not a real physical point-of-sale terminal; but a software abstraction that represents the register.

Thus, the collaboration diagram shown in Figure 19.5 begins by sending the *enterItem* message, with a UPC and quantity parameter, to a *POST* instance.

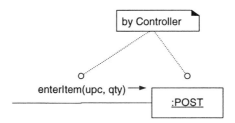

**Figure 19.5** Applying the GRASP Controller pattern.

## 19.5.2   Displaying the Item Description and Price

Because of a design principle called **Model-View Separation**, it is not the responsibility of domain objects (such as a *POST* or *Sale*) to communicate with the user interface layer (for example, graphical windows). Therefore, the display of the item description and price will be ignored at this time.

All that is required with respect to responsibilities for the display of information is that the data is known, which it is in this case.

## 19.5.3 Making a New Sale

It is necessary to consider those requirements, as expressed in the contracts, that need to be satisfied in software in order to make the system execute correctly. Two of the contract post-conditions state:

- If a new sale, a *Sale* was created (*instance creation*).

- If a new sale, the new *Sale* was associated with the *POST* (*association formed*).

This indicates a responsibility in creation, and the GRASP Creator pattern suggests assigning the responsibility for creation to a class that aggregates, contains or records the class to be created.

Analyzing the conceptual model, or reflection on the domain objects, reveals that a *POST* may be thought of as recording a *Sale*[1]; thus, *POST* is a reasonable candidate for creating a *Sale*. And by having the *POST* create the *Sale*, the *POST* can easily be associated with it over time, so that during future operations, the *POST* will have a reference to the current *Sale* instance.

In addition to the above, when the *Sale* is created, it must create an empty collection (container, such as a Java *Vector*) to record all the future *SalesLineItem* instances that will be added. This collection will be maintained by the *Sale* instance, which implies by Creator that the *Sale* is a good candidate for creating it.

Therefore, the *POST* creates the *Sale*, and the *Sale* creates an empty collection, represented by a multiobject in the collaboration diagram.

---

1. Note that *POST* is roughly synonymous with a *register*—a recorder of sales.

Hence, the collaboration diagram in Figure 19.6 illustrates the design.

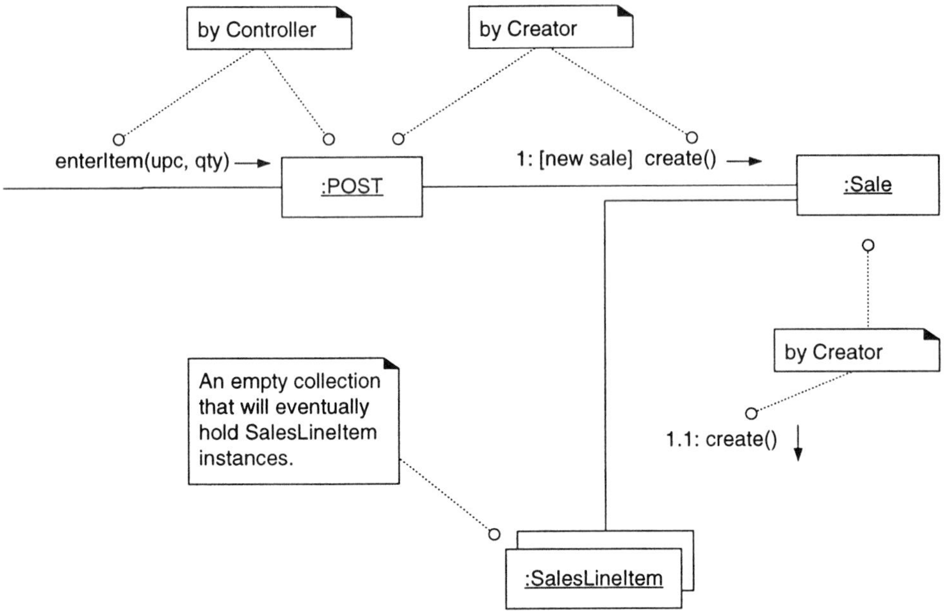

**Figure 19.6** Sale creation.

## 19.5.4 Creating a New SalesLineItem

Some other *enterItem* contract post-conditions state:

■ A *SalesLineItem* was created (*instance creation*).

■ The *SalesLineItem* was associated with the *Sale* (*association formed*).

■ *SalesLineItem.quantity* was set to *quantity* (*attribute modification*).

■ The *SalesLineItem* was associated with a *ProductSpecification*, based on *UPC* match (*association formed*).

This indicates a responsibility to create a *SalesLineItem* instance. Analyzing the class diagram reveals that a *Sale* contains *SalesLineItem* objects; hence, by Creator it is an appropriate candidate for creating line items. And by having the *Sale* create the *SalesLineItem*, the *Sale* can be associated with it over time by storing the new instance in its collection of line items. The post-conditions indicate that the new *SalesLineItem* needs a quantity, when created, therefore, the *POST* must pass it along to the *Sale*, which must pass it along as a parameter in the *create* message.

Therefore, by Creator, a *makeLineItem* message is sent to a *Sale* in order for it to create a *SalesLineItem*. The *Sale* creates a *SalesLineItem*, and then stores the new instance in its permanent collection.

The parameters to the *makeLineItem* message include the *quantity*, so that the *SalesLineItem* can record it, and likewise the *ProductSpecification* which matches the UPC.

## 19.5.5    Finding a ProductSpecification

The *SalesLineItem* needs to be associated with the *ProductSpecification* that matches the incoming UPC. This implies it is necessary to retrieve a *ProductSpecification,* based on a UPC match.

Before considering *how* to achieve the look up, it is very important to consider *who* should be responsible for it. A useful first step is:

> Start assigning responsibilities by clearly stating the responsibility.

To restate the problem:

Who should be responsibility for knowing a *ProductSpecification*, based on a UPC match?

This is neither a creation problem nor one of choosing a controller. In most cases, the Expert GRASP pattern is the principle one to apply. Expert suggests that the object that has the information required to fulfill the responsibility should do it. Who knows about all the *ProductSpecification*? Analyzing the class diagram reveals that the *ProductCatalog* logically contains all the *ProductSpecifications*, and thus, by Expert, *ProductCatalog* is a good candidate for this look up responsibility.

## 19.5.6    Visibility to a ProductCatalog

Who should send the *specification* message to the *ProductCatalog* to ask for a *ProductSpecification*?

It is reasonable to assume that a *POST* and *ProductCatalog* instance were created during the initial *Start Up* use case, and that there is a permanent connection from the *POST* object to the *ProductCatalog* object. With that assumption, then it is possible for the *POST* to send the *specification* message to the *ProductCatalog*.

This implies another concept in object-oriented design: visibility. **Visibility** is the ability of one object to "see" or have a reference to another object.

> In order for an object to send a message to another object it must have visibility to it.

Since we will assume that the *POST* has a permanent connection—or reference—to the *ProductCatalog*, it has visibility to it, and, henc,e can send it messages such as *specification*.

The following chapter will explore the question of visibility more closely.

### 19.5.7  Retrieving ProductSpecifications from a Database

In the final version of a real point-of-sale application it is unlikely that all the *ProductSpecifications* will actually be in memory. They will most likely be stored in a relational or object database and retrieved on demand. However, the issues surrounding retrieval from a database will be deferred for now in the interest of simplicity. It will be assumed that all the *ProductSpecifications* are in memory. Chapter 38 explores the topic of database access of persistent objects.

### 19.5.8  The enterItem Collaboration Diagram

Given the above discussion concerning who should create the *SalesLineItem*, retrieve a *ProductSpecification*, and so on, the collaboration diagram in Figure 19.7 reflects the decisions regarding the assignment of responsibilities and how objects should interact. Observe that considerable reflection was made to arrive at this design, based on the GRASP patterns; the design of object interactions and responsibility assignment require deliberation.

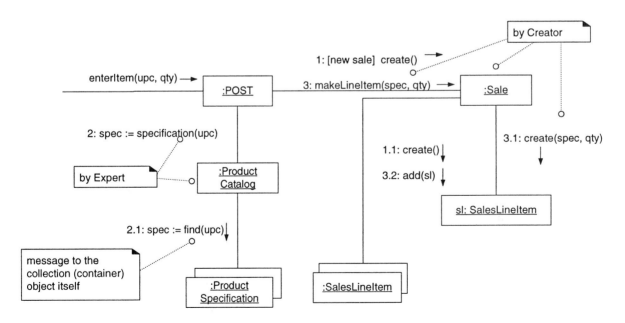

**Figure 19.7** The enterItem collaboration diagram.

## 19.5.9   Messages to Multiobjects

Notice that although the default interpretation of a message sent to a multiobject is that it is implicitly sent to all elements of the collection/container, it may alternatively be interpreted as a message to the collection object itself. This is especially true for generic collection operations such as *find*, and *add*. For example, in the *enterItem* collaboration diagram:

- The *find* message (2.1) sent to the *ProductSpecification* multiobject is a message being sent once to the collection data structure represented by the multiobject (such as a Java *Vector*).

- The *create* message (1.1) sent to the *SalesLineItem* multiobject is for the creation of the collection data structure represented by the multiobject (such as a Java *Vector*), it is not the creation of an instance of class *SalesLineItem*.

- The *add* message (3.2) sent to the *SalesLineItem* multiobject is to add an element to the collection data structure represented by the multiobject.

# 19.6   Collaboration Diagram: endSale

The *endSale* system operation occurs when a cashier presses a button indicating the end of a sale. Here is the complete contract:

### Contract

| | |
|---|---|
| Name: | endSale() |
| Responsibilities: | Record that it is the end of entry of sale items, and display sale total. |
| Type: | System |
| Cross References: | System Functions: R1.2 |
| | Use Cases: Buy Items |
| Notes: | |
| Exceptions: | If a sale is not underway, indicate that it was an error. |
| Output: | |
| Preconditions: | UPC is known to the system. |
| Post-conditions: | |

- *Sale.isComplete* was set to *true* (attribute modification).

A collaboration diagram will be constructed to satisfy the post-conditions of *endSale*. As stressed in the GRASP patterns chapter, each choice of message implies the assignment of a responsibility, and the GRASP patterns will be used to choose and justify the messages.

## 19.6.1 Choosing the Controller Class

Our first choice involves handling the responsibility for the system operation message *endSale*. Based on the Controller GRASP pattern, as for *enterItem*, we will continue to use *POST* as a controller.

## 19.6.2 Setting the Sale.isComplete Attribute

The contract post-conditions state:

■ *Sale.isComplete* has been set to *true* (attribute modification).

As always, Expert should be the first pattern considered unless it is a controller or creation problem (which it is not).

Who should be responsible for setting the *isComplete* attribute of the *Sale* to true?

By Expert, it should be the *Sale* itself, since it owns and maintains the *isComplete* attribute. Thus the *POST* will send a *becomeComplete* message to the *Sale* in order to set it to *true*. Note in Figure 19.8 the use of a constraint note containing pseudo-code to clarify the purpose of the makeComplete operation; this is recommended when you need to explain the details of an operation.

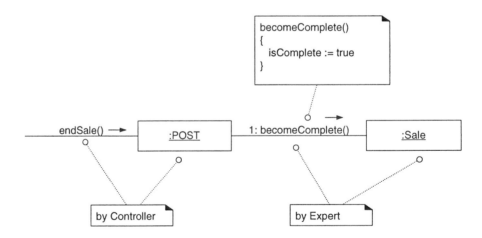

**Figure 19.8** Completion of item entry.

## 19.6.3 The Display of Information

It states in the responsibilities of the *endSale* contract that the sale total must be displayed. Let us clear up the issue of who should be responsible for the display of information, such as on a graphical window. In brief, the layer of domain objects, such as *Sale, Store,* and so on, should have *no* knowledge of or direct communication with windows or a presentation layer. This is the essence of the *Model-View Separation* pattern, which is discussed in Chapter 22.

During the creation of collaboration diagrams, do not be concerned with the display of information, except insofar as the required information is known.

Therefore, ignore any requirements that involve the display of information, with the following exception:

Ensure that all information that must be displayed is known and available from the domain objects.

For example, the above requirement indicates that the sale total must be known by some object.

## 19.6.4   Calculating the Sale Total

Because of the Model-View Separation pattern, we should not concern ourselves with how the sale total will be displayed, but it is necessary to ensure that the total is known. Note that no class currently knows the sale total, so we need to create a design of object interactions, using a collaboration diagram, that satisfies this requirement.

As always, Expert should be the first pattern considered unless it is a controller or creation problem (which it is not).

It is probably obvious the *Sale* itself should be responsible for knowing its total, but just to make the reasoning process to find an Expert crystal clear—with a simple example—please consider the following analysis.

1. State the responsibility:

   ❏   Who should be responsible for knowing the sale total?

2. Summarize the information required:

   ❏   The sale total is the sum of the subtotals of all the sales line-items.

   ❏   sales line-item subtotal := line-item quantity * product description price

3. List the information required to fulfill this responsibility and the classes that know this information.

| Information Required for Sale Total | Expert Class |
|---|---|
| *ProductSpecification.price* | *ProductSpecification* |
| *SalesLineItem.quantity* | *SalesLineItem* |
| all the *SalesLineItems* in the current Sale | *Sale* |

A detailed analysis follows:

■ Who should be responsible for calculating the *Sale* total? By Expert, it should be the *Sale* itself, since it knows about all the *SalesLineItem* instances whose subtotals must be summed to calculate the sale total. Therefore, *Sale* will have the responsibility of knowing its total, implemented as a *total* operation.

■ For a *Sale* to calculate its total, it needs the subtotal for each *SalesLineItem*. Who should be responsible for calculating the *SalesLineItem* subtotal? By Expert, it should be the *SalesLineItem* itself, since it knows the quantity and the *ProductSpecification* it is associated with. Therefore, *SalesLineItem* will have the responsibility of knowing its subtotal, implemented as a *subtotal* operation.

■ For the *SalesLineItem* to calculate its subtotal, it needs the price of the *ProductSpecification*. Who should be responsible for providing the *ProductSpecification* price? By Expert, it should be the *ProductSpecification* itself, since it encapsulates the price as an attribute. Therefore, *ProductSpecification* will have the responsibility of knowing its price, implemented as a *price* operation.

> Although the above analysis is trivial in this case, and the degree of excruciating elaboration presented is uncalled for, the same reasoning strategy to find an Expert can and should be applied in more difficult situations. You will find that once you learn the GRASP patterns you can quickly perform this kind of reasoning mentally.

## 19.6.5 The Sale Total Collaboration Diagram

Given the above discussion, it is now desirable to construct a collaboration diagram that illustrates what happens when a *Sale* is sent a *total* message. The first message in this diagram is *total*, but observe that the *total* message in not a system event. This leads to the following observation:

Not every collaboration diagram starts with a system event message; they can start with any message for which the designer wishes to show the interactions for.

The collaboration diagram required is shown in Figure 19.9. First, the *total* message is sent to a *Sale* instance. The *Sale* will then send a *subtotal* message to each related *SalesLineItem* instance. The *SalesLineItem* will in turn send a *price* message to its associated *ProductSpecifications*.

Since arithmetic is not (usually) illustrated via messages, the details of the calculations can be illustrated by attaching constraints to the diagram that define the calculations.

Who will send the *total* message to the *Sale*? Most likely it will be an object in the presentation layer, such as a Java applet.

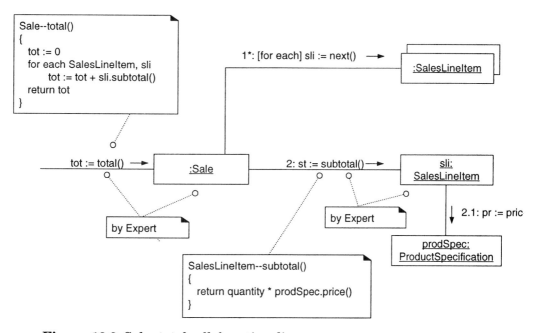

**Figure 19.9** Sale--total collaboration diagram.

# 19.7  Collaboration Diagram: makePayment

The *makePayment* system operation occurs when a cashier enters the amount of cash tendered for payment. Here is the complete contract:

Contract

| | |
|---|---|
| Name: | makePayment<br>. (amount : Number or Quantity) |
| Responsibilities: | Record the payment, calculate balance and print receipt. |
| Type: | System |
| Cross References: | System Functions: R2.1 |
| | Use Cases: Buy Items |

Notes:

| | |
|---|---|
| Exceptions: | If the sale is not complete, indicate an error. |
| | If the amount is less than the sale total, indicate an error. |

Output:

Preconditions:

Post-conditions:

■ A *Payment* was created (instance creation).

■ *Payment.amountTendered* was set to *amount* (attribute modification).

■ The *Payment* was associated with the *Sale* (relationship formed).

■ The *Sale* was associated with the *Store*, to add it to the historical log of completed sales (relationship formed).

A collaboration diagram will be constructed to satisfy the post-conditions of *makePayment*. As stressed in the GRASP patterns chapter, each choice of message implies the assignment of a responsibility, and the GRASP patterns will be used to choose and justify the messages.

## 19.7.1 Choosing the Controller Class

Our first choice involves handling the responsibility for the system operation message *makePayment*. Based on the Controller GRASP pattern, as for *enterItem*, we will continue to use *POST* as a controller. It is common to use the same controller throughout a use case.

## 19.7.2   Creating the Payment

One of the contract post-conditions states:

■   A *Payment* was created (instance creation)

This is a creation responsibility, so the Creator GRASP pattern should be applied.

Who records, aggregates, most closely uses, or contains a *Payment*? There is some appeal in stating that a *POST* logically records a *Payment*, so it is a candidate. Additionally, it is reasonable to think that a *Sale* will closely use a *Payment*; thus, it may be a candidate.

Another way to find a creator is to use the Expert pattern in terms of who is the Expert with respect to initializing data—the amount tendered in this case. The *POST* is the controller which receives the system operation *makePayment(amountTendered)* message, so it will initially have the amount tendered. Consequently the *POST* is again a candidate.

In summary, there are two candidates:

■   *POST*

■   *Sale*

Consider some of the implications of these choices in terms of the High Cohesion and Low Coupling GRASP patterns. If the *Sale* is chosen to create the *Payment*, the work (or responsibilities) of the *POST* is lighter—leading to a simpler *POST* definition. Also, the *POST* does not need to know about the existence of a *Payment* instance because it can be recorded indirectly via the *Sale*—leading to lower coupling in the *POST*. This leads to the collaboration diagram shown in Figure 19.10.

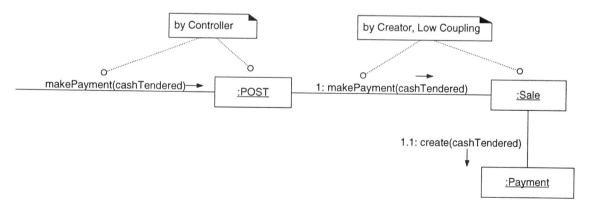

**Figure 19.10** POST--makePayment collaboration diagram.

This collaboration diagram satisfies the post-conditions of the contract: the *Payment* has been created, associated with the *Sale*, and its *amountTendered* has been set.

## 19.7.3 Logging the Sale

Once complete, the requirements state that the sale should be placed in an historical log. As always, Expert should be the first pattern considered unless it is a controller or creation problem (which it is not), and the responsibility should be stated:

Who is responsible for knowing all the logged sales, and doing the logging?

It is reasonable for a *Store* to know all the logged sales, since they are strongly related to its finances. Other alternatives include classic accounting concepts, such as a *SalesLedger*. Using a *SalesLedger* object makes sense as the design grows and the *Store* becomes incohesive (see Figure 19.11).

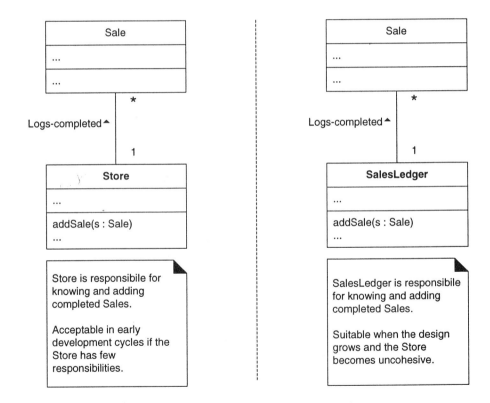

**Figure 19.11** Who should be responsible for knowing the completed sales?

Note also that the post-conditions of the contract indicate relating the *Sale* with the *Store*. This is an example where the post-conditions may not be what we want to actually achieve in the design. Perhaps we didn't think of a *SalesLedger* early, but now that we have, we choose to use it instead of a *Store*. If this were the case, *SalesLedger* would ideally be added to the conceptual model as well. This kind of discovery and change during the design phase is to be expected. Fortunately, iterative development provides a life-cycle for continual change.

In this case, we will stick with the original plan of using the *Store*.

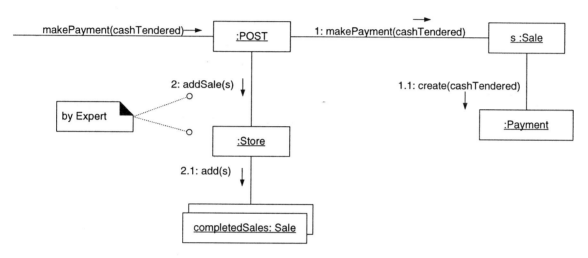

**Figure 19.12** Logging a completed sale.

## 19.7.4 Calculating the Balance

The responsibilities section states that the balance has been calculated; it will presumably be printed on a receipt and displayed on a monitor.

Because of the Model-View Separation principle, we should not concern ourselves with how the balance will be displayed, but it is necessary to ensure that it is known. Note that no class currently knows the balance, so we need to create a design of object interactions, using a collaboration diagram, that satisfies this requirement.

As always, Expert should be the first pattern considered unless it is a controller or creation problem (which it is not), and the responsibility should be stated:

Who is responsible for knowing the balance?

To calculate the balance, the sale total and payment cash tendered are required. Therefore, *Sale* and *Payment* are partial Experts on solving this problem.

If the *Payment* is primarily responsible for knowing the balance, it would need visibility to the *Sale*, in order to ask the *Sale* for its total. Since it does not currently know about the *Sale*, this approach would increase the overall coupling in the design—it would not support the Low Coupling pattern.

In contrast, if the *Sale* is primarily responsible for knowing the balance, it needs visibility to the *Payment*, in order to ask it for its cash tendered. Since the *Sale* already has visibility to the *Payment*—as its creator—this approach does not increase the overall coupling, and is therefore a preferable design.

Consequently, the collaboration diagram in Figure 19.13 provides a solution for knowing the balance.

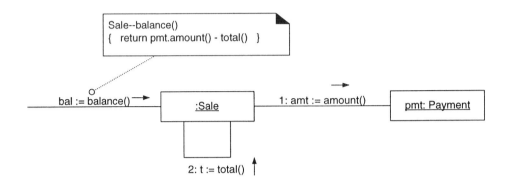

**Figure 19.13** Sale--balance collaboration diagram.

# 19.8    Collaboration Diagram: startUp

## 19.8.1    When Create the startUp Collaboration Diagram?

Most, if not all, systems have a *Start Up* use case, and some initial system operation related to the starting up of the application. Although this *startUp* system operation is the earliest one to execute, delay the development of a collaboration diagram for it until after all other system operations have been considered. This ensures that significant information has been discovered concerning what initialization activities are required to support the later system operation interaction diagrams.

Create the *startUp* collaboration diagram last.

## 19.8.2    How Applications Start Up

The *startUp* operation abstractly represents the initialization phase of execution when an application is launched. In order to understand how to design a collaboration diagram for this operation, it is helpful to understand the contexts in which initialization can occur. How an application starts and initializes is dependent upon the programming language and operating system.

In all cases, a common design idiom is to ultimately create an **initial domain object**, which is the first problem domain object created. In its initialization method (for example, a Java constructor) this object is then responsible for the creation of other problem domain objects and for their initialization.

The place where this initial domain object is created is dependent upon the object-oriented programming language and operating system. For example, in a Java applet its launch may cause the attributes (instance variables) to be instantiated. One of these attributes may be the initial domain object, such as a *Store* which creates some other objects, such as a *POST*.

```
public class POSTApplet extends Applet
{
public void init()
{
   post = store.getPOST();
}

// Store is the initial domain object.
// The Store constructor creates
// other domain objects.
private Store store = new Store();

private POST post;
private Sale sale;
}
```

## 19.8.3   Interpretation of the startUp System Operation

The preceding discussion of the different ways in which an application starts illustrates that the *startUp* system operation is a language independent abstraction. During the design phase there is variation in where the initial object is created, and whether or not it takes control of the process. The initial domain object does not usually take control if there is a graphical user interface, otherwise it often does.

The collaboration diagrams for the *startUp* operation represent what happens when the initial problem domain object is created, and optionally what happens if it takes control. It does not include any prior or subsequent activity in the graphical user interface layer of objects, if one exists.

---

Hence, the *startUp* operation may be reinterpreted as:

1. In one collaboration diagram, send a *create()* message to create the initial domain object.

2. (optional) If the initial object is taking control of the process, in a second collaboration diagram send a *run* message (or something equivalent) to the initial object.

---

## 19.8.4    The Point-of-Sale Application startUp Operation

The *startUp* system operation occurs when a manager powers on the point-of-sale system and the software loads. Assume there is a graphical user interface, and that an object in the presentation layer (for example, a Java applet instance) will be responsible for creating the initial problem domain object.[1] Also, assume that the initial object is *not* responsible for taking control of the process; control will remain in the applet after the initial domain object is created. Therefore, the collaboration diagram for the *startUp* operation may be reinterpreted solely as a *create()* message sent to create the initial object.

## 19.8.5    Choosing the Initial Domain Object

What should the class of the initial domain object be?

Choose as an initial domain object:

■   A class representing the entire logical information system.

■   A class representing the overall business or organization.

Choosing between these alternatives may be influenced by High Cohesion and Low Coupling considerations.

Therefore, for the point-of-sale application, reasonable choices for the initial object include:

| | |
|---|---|
| Entire logical information system | *POST, RetailInformationSystem* |
| Overall business or organization | *Store* |

In this application, the *Store* is chosen as the initial object.

## 19.8.6    Persistent Objects: ProductSpecification

In a realistic application the *ProductSpecification* instances will reside in a persistent storage medium, such as relational or object database. During the *startUp* operation, if there are only a few of these objects, they may all be loaded

---

[1]. Realistically, it probably would not be a Java applet, but an applet as an example provides a simple, widely known standard.

into the computer's direct memory. However, if there are many, loading them all would consume too much memory or time. Alternately—and more likely—individual instances will be loaded on-demand into memory as they are required.

The design of how to dynamically on-demand load objects from a database into memory is simple if an object database is used, but difficult for a relational database. This problem is deferred for now and makes a simplifying assumption that all the *ProductSpecification* instances can be "magically" created in memory by the *ProductCatalog* object.

Chapter 38 explores the question of persistent objects and how to load them into memory.

## 19.8.7 *Store--create() Collaboration Diagram*

Here is the *startUp* contract:

Contract

| | |
|---|---|
| Name: | startUp() |
| Responsibilities: | initialize the system. |
| Type: | System |
| Cross References: | |
| Notes: | |
| Exceptions: | |
| Output: | |
| Preconditions: | |
| Post-conditions: | |

- A *Store, POST, ProductCatalog* and *ProductSpecifications* have been created (*instance creation*)

- *ProductCatalog* was associated with *ProductSpecifications* (*association formed*)

- *Store* was associated with *ProductCatalog* (*association formed*)

- *Store* was associated with *POST* (*association formed*)

- *POST* was associated with *ProductCatalog* (*association formed*)

As discussed, this will be interpreted as what happens as a result of the creation of the initial object—the *Store*—when a *create* message is sent.

Figure 19.14 shows a collaboration diagram which satisfies these post-conditions. The *Store* was chosen to create the *ProductCatalog* and *POST* by the Creator pattern. *ProductCatalog* was likewise chosen to create the *ProductSpecifications*.

Observe that the creation of all the *ProductSpecification* instances and their addition to a container happens in a repeating section, indicated by the '*' following the sequence numbers.

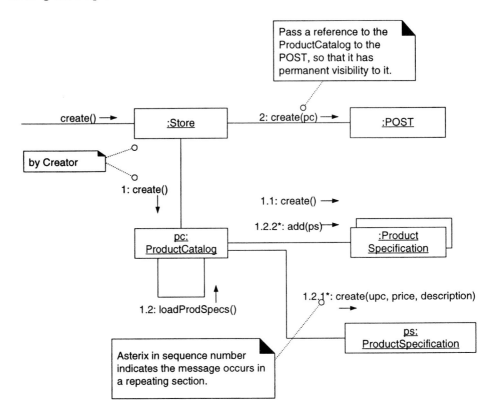

**Figure 19.14** Creation of the initial domain object and subsequent objects.

An interesting deviation between analysis and design is illustrated in the fact that the *Store* only creates *one POST* object. Analytically, a real store may house *many* real point-of-sale terminals. However, we are now considering a software design, not real life. The *Store* in the collaboration diagram is not a real store; it is a software object. The *POST* in the diagram is not a real terminal; it is a software object. In our current requirements, our software *Store* only needs to create a single instance of a software *POST*.

The multiplicity between classes of objects in the analysis and design phase may not be the same.

## 19.9    Connecting the Presentation Layer to the Domain Layer

As has been discussed, if a graphical user interface is involved, such as a Java applet (which is part of the application coordinator and presentation layer), then the applet will be responsible for initiating the creation of the initial domain object, as illustrated in Figure 19.15. First the applet creates the initial domain object (a *Store* instance), which in turn creates a *POST* instance. Then the applet requests a reference to the *POST* instance from the *Store*, and stores the reference in an attribute, so that the applet may directly send messages to it.

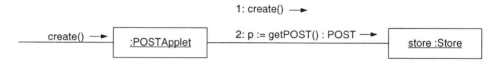

**Figure 19.15** Connecting the presentation and domain layers.

Once the applet has a connection to the *POST* instance, it can forward system event messages to it, such as the *enterItem* and *endSale* message (see Figure 19.16).

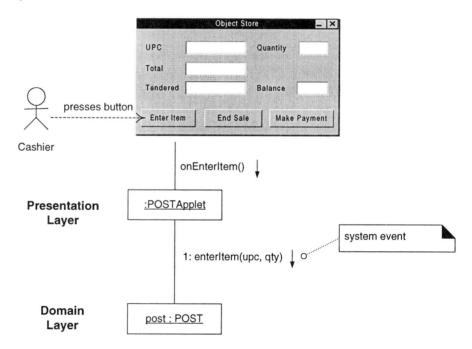

**Figure 19.16** Connecting the presentation and domain layers.

In the case of the *enterItem* message, the window needs to show the running total after each entry. As illustrated in Figure 19.17, after the *POSTApplet* forwards the *enterItem* message to the *POST* object, it:

1. Gets a reference to the *Sale* (if it did not already have one).

2. Stores the *Sale* reference in an attribute.

3. Sends a *total* message to the *Sale* in order to get the information needed to display the running total on the window.

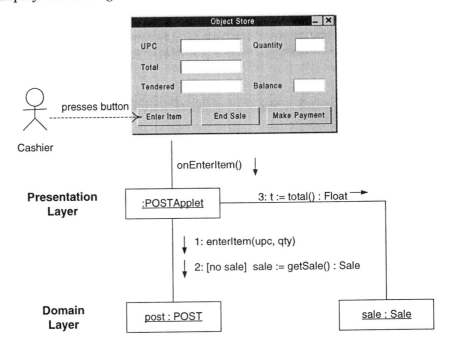

**Figure 19.17** Connecting the presentation and domain layers.

Notice in these collaboration diagrams that the Java applet (*POSTApplet*), which is part of the presentation layer, is not responsible for handling the logic of the application. It forwards requests for work (the system operations) to the domain layer, via the *POST*. This leads to the following design principle:

---

### Presentation and Domain Layer Responsibilities

The presentation layer should not have any domain logic responsibilities. It should only be responsible for presentation (interface) tasks, such as updating widgets.

The presentation layer should forward requests for all domain-oriented tasks on to the domain layer, which is responsible for handling them.

---

# 19.10   Summary

Designing the message interactions and assigning responsibilities is the heart of object-oriented design. These choices have can have a profound impact on the extensibility, clarity and maintainability of an object-oriented software system, plus on the degree and quality of reusable components. There are principles by which the choices of responsibility assignment can be made; the GRASP patterns summarize some of the most general and common used by object-oriented designers.

This chapter has explored the application of the GRASP patterns to create well-designed classes and a system of interacting objects.

**20**

# DETERMINING VISIBILITY

---

### Objectives

- Identify four kinds of visibility.
- Design to establish visibility.
- Illustrate kinds of visibility in the UML notation.

---

## 20.1    Introduction

Visibility is the ability of one object to see or have reference to another. This chapter explores design issues related to visibility.

## 20.2    Visibility Between Objects

The collaboration diagrams created for the system events (*enterItem*, and so on) illustrate messages between objects. For a sender object to send a message to a receiver object, the sender must be visible to the receiver—the sender must have some kind of reference or pointer to the receiver object.

For example, the *specification* message sent from a *POST* to a *ProductCatalog* implies the *ProductCatalog* instance is visible to the *POST* instance, as shown in Figure 20.1.

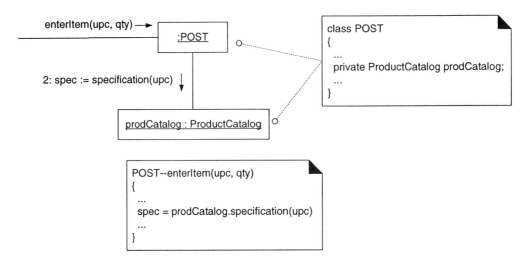

**Figure 20.1** Visibility from the POST to ProductCatalog is required.[1]

When creating a design of interacting objects, it is necessary to ensure that the necessary visibility is present in order to support message interaction.

The UML has special notation for illustrating visibility; this chapter explores various kinds of visibility and their depiction.

## 20.3   Visibility

In common usage, **visibility** is the ability of an object to "see" or have a reference to another object. More generally, it is related to the issue of scope: Is one resource (such as an instance) within the scope of another? There are four common ways that visibility can be achieved from object $A$ to object $B$:

1.  *Attribute visibility*—B is an attribute of A.

2.  *Parameter visibility*—B is a parameter of a method of A.

3.  *Locally declared visibility*—B is declared as a local object in a method of A.

4.  *Global visibility*—B is in some way globally visible.

---

1. In this and subsequent code examples, language simplifications may be made for the sake of brevity and clarity.

The motivation to consider visibility is the following:

> For an object A to send a message to an object B, B must be visible to A.

For example, to create a collaboration diagram in which a message is sent from a *POST* instance to a *ProductCatalog* instance, the *POST* must have visibility to the *ProductCatalog*. A typical visibility solution is that a reference to the *ProductCatalog* instance is maintained as an attribute of the *POST*.

## 20.3.1   Attribute Visibility

**Attribute visibility** from A to B exists when B is an attribute of A. It is a relatively permanent visibility because it persists as long as A and B exist. This is a very common form of visibility in object-oriented systems.

To illustrate, in a Java class definition for *POST*, a *POST* instance may have attribute visibility to a *ProductCatalog*, since it is an attribute (Java instance variable) of the *POST*.

```
public class POST
{
...
private ProductCatalog prodCatalog;
...
}
```

This visibility is required because in the *enterItem* collaboration diagram shown in Figure 20.2, a *POST* needs to send the *specification* message to a *ProductCatalog*:

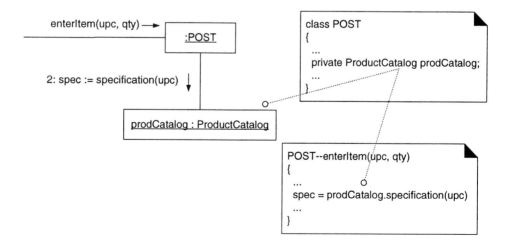

**Figure 20.2** Attribute visibility.

## 20.3.2  Parameter Visibility

**Parameter visibility** from A to B exists when B is passed as a parameter to a method of A. It is a relatively temporary visibility because it persists only within the scope of the method. After attribute visibility, it is the second most common form of visibility in object-oriented systems.

To illustrate, when the *makeLineItem* message is sent to a *Sale* instance, a *ProductSpecification* instance is passed as a parameter. Within the scope of the *makeLineItem* method, the *Sale* has parameter visibility to a *ProductSpecification* (see Figure 20.3).

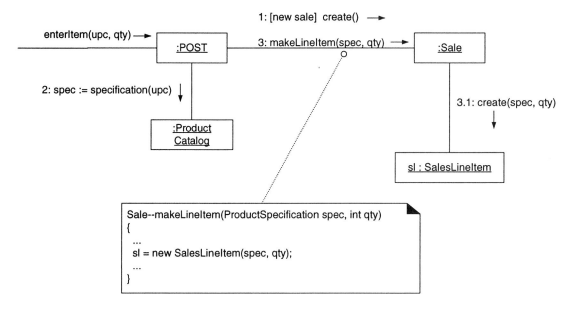

**Figure 20.3**  Parameter visibility

It is common to transform parameter visibility into attribute visibility. For example, when the *Sale* creates a new *SalesLineItem*, it passes a *ProductSpecification* in to its initializing method (in C++ or Java this would be its **constructor**). Within the initializing method, the parameter is assigned to an attribute, thus establishing attribute visibility (Figure 20.4).

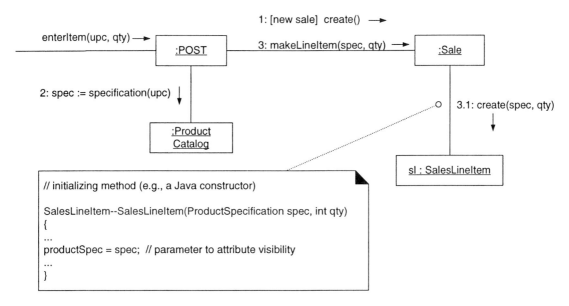

**Figure 20.4** Parameter to attribute visibility.

## 20.3.3 Locally Declared Visibility

**Locally declared visibility** from A to B exists when B is declared as a local object within a method of A. It is a relatively temporary visibility because it persists only within the scope of the method. After parameter visibility, it is the third most common form of visibility in object-oriented systems. Two common means by which this form of visibility is achieved are:

**1.** Create a new local instance and assign it to a local variable.

**2.** Assign the return object from a method invocation to a local variable.

A variation on (2) is when the method does not explicitly declare a variable, but one implicitly exists as the result of a return object from a method invocation.

As with parameter visibility, it is common to transform locally declared visibility into attribute visibility.

An example of the second variation can be found in the *enterItem* method of class *POST* (Figure 20.5).

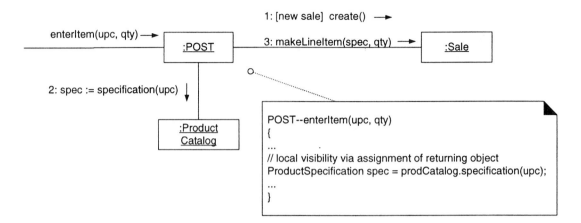

**Figure 20.5** Local visibility.

## 20.3.4 Global Visibility

**Global visibility** from A to B exists when B is global to A. It is a relatively permanent visibility because it persists as long as A and B exist. It is least common form of visibility in object-oriented systems.

The most obvious—but least desirable—way to achieve global visibility is to assign an instance to a global variable.

The preferred method to achieve global visibility is to use the **Singleton** pattern [GHJV95], which is discussed in Chapter 35.

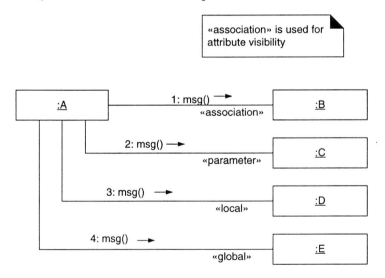

**Figure 20.6** Implementation stereotypes for visibility.

## 20.4    Illustrating Visibility in the UML

The UML includes a notation to illustrate the implementation of the various kinds of visibility in a collaboration diagram (Figure 20.6).These adornments are optional and not normally called for; they are useful when clarification is needed.

# DESIGN CLASS DIAGRAMS

---

### Objectives

- Create design class diagrams.

- Identify the classes, methods, and associations to show in a design class diagram.

---

## 21.1   Introduction

With the completion of interaction diagrams for the current development cycle of the point-of-sale application, it is possible to identify the specification for the software classes (and interfaces) which participate in the software solution, and annotate them with design details, such as methods.

The UML has notation for showing design details in static structure—or class—diagrams; in this chapter we explore it and create design class diagrams.

## 21.2   Activities and Dependencies

The definition of design class diagrams occurs within the design phase of a development cycle. Their creation is dependent upon the prior creation of:

- Interaction diagrams—from this, the designer identifies the software classes that participate in the solution, plus the methods of classes.

- Conceptual model—from this, the designer adds detail to the class definitions.

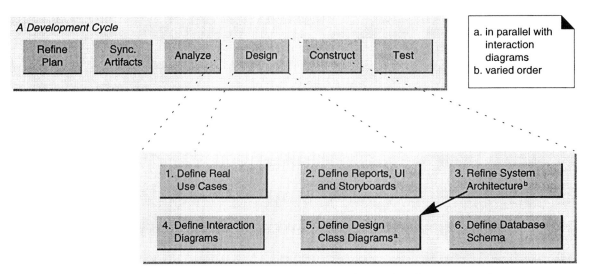

Design phase activities within a development cycle.

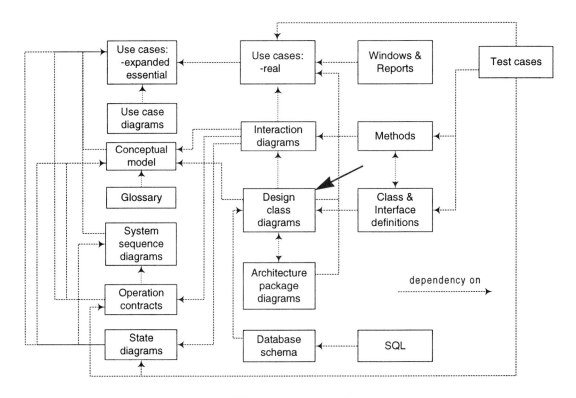

Build phase artifact dependencies.

## 21.3    When to Create Design Class Diagrams

Although this presentation of design class diagrams *follows* the creation of interaction diagrams, in practice they are usually created in parallel. Many classes, method names and relationships may be sketched out very early in the design phase by applying responsibility assignment patterns, prior to the drawing of interaction diagrams. They may be used as an alternative, more graphical notation over CRC cards in order to record responsibilities and collaborators.

## 21.4    Example Design Class Diagram

The design class diagram in Figure 21.1 illustrates a partial software definition of the *POST* and *Sale* classes.

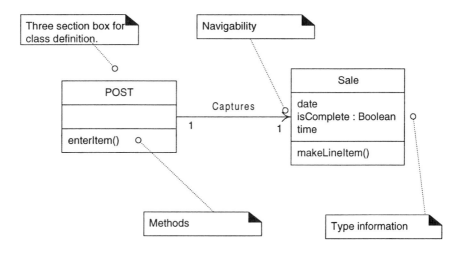

**Figure 21.1** Sample design class diagram.

In addition to basic associations and attributes, the diagram is extended to illustrate, for example, the methods of each class, attribute type information, and attribute visibility and navigation between objects.

## 21.5    Design Class Diagrams

A **design class diagram** illustrates the specifications for software classes and interfaces (for example, Java interfaces) in an application. Typical information it includes is as follows:

■  classes, associations and attributes

- interfaces, with their operations and constants

- methods

- attribute type information

- navigability

- dependencies

In contrast with a conceptual model, a design class diagram shows definitions for software entities rather than real-world concepts. The UML does not specifically define an element called "design class diagram", but uses the more generic term "class diagram". I have chosen to include the term "design" in "design class diagram" to emphasis that this is a design view on software entities, rather than an analytical view on domain concepts.

# 21.6    How to Make a Design Class Diagram

Apply the following strategy to create a design class diagram:

---

To make a design class diagram:

1. Identify all the classes participating in the software solution. Do this by analyzing the interaction diagrams.

2. Draw them in a class diagram.

3. Duplicate the attributes from the associated concepts in the conceptual model.

4. Add method names by analyzing the interaction diagrams.

5. Add type information to the attributes and methods.

6. Add the associations necessary to support the required attribute visibility.

7. Add navigability arrows to the associations to indicate the direction of attribute visibility.

8. Add dependency relationship lines to indicate non-attribute visibility.

---

## 21.7    Conceptual Model versus Design Class Diagrams

In the conceptual model, a *Sale* does *not* represent a software definition; rather, it is an abstraction of a real-world concept that we are interested in making a statement about. In contrast, design class diagrams express—for the software application—the definition of classes as software components. In these diagrams, a *Sale* represents a software class (see Figure 21.2).

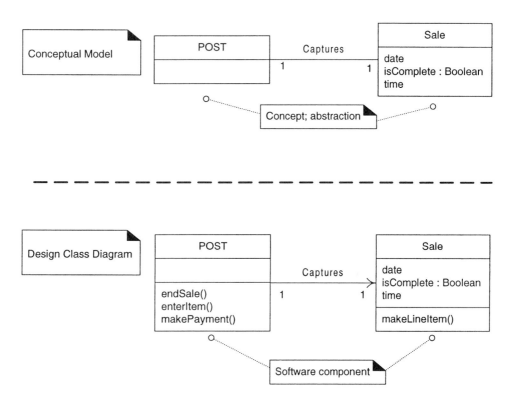

**Figure 21.2** Conceptual model versus design class diagram.

## 21.8    Creating the Point-of-Sale Design Class Diagrams

### 21.8.1    *Identify Software Classes and Illustrate Them*

The first step in the creation of design class diagrams as part of the solution model is to identify those classes that participate in the software solution. These can be found by scanning all the interaction diagrams and listing the classes mentioned. For the POST application, these are:

POST                    Sale

ProductCatalog          ProductSpecification

Store                   SalesLineItem

Payment

The next step is to draw a class diagram for these classes and include the attributes previously identified in the conceptual model (see Figure 21.3).

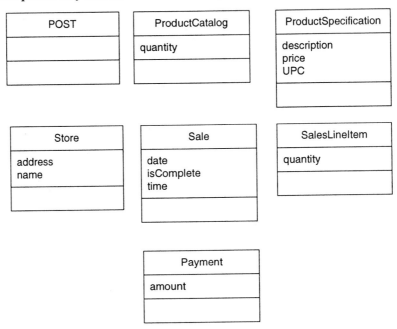

**Figure 21.3** Software classes in the application.

Note that many of the concepts in the conceptual model, such as *Cashier, Manager,* and *Item*, are not present in the design. There is no need—for the current development cycle—to represent them in software. However, in later cycles, as new requirements and use cases are tackled, they may enter into the design.

## 21.8.2   Add Method Names

The methods of each class can be identified by analyzing the collaboration diagrams. For example, if the message *makeLineItem* is sent to an instance of class *Sale*, then class *Sale* must define a *makeLineItem* method (see Figure 21.4).

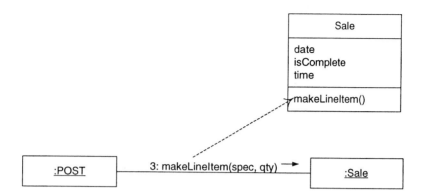

**Figure 21.4** Method names from collaboration diagrams.

In general, the set of all messages sent to a class X across all collaboration diagrams indicates the majority of methods that class X must define.

Inspection of all the collaboration diagrams for the point-of-sale application yields the allocation of methods shown in Figure 21.5.

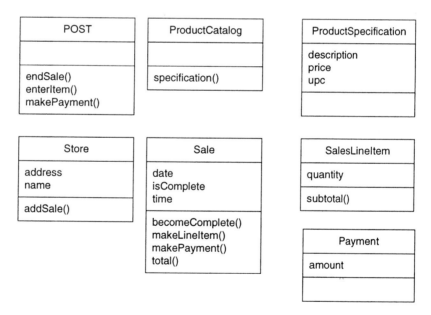

**Figure 21.5** Methods in the application.

## 21.8.3   Method Names: Issues

The following special issues must be considered with respect to method names:

- Interpretation of the *create()* message
- Depiction of accessing methods
- Interpretation of messages to multiobjects
- Language dependent syntax

## 21.8.4   Method Names—create

The *create* message is the UML language independent form to indicate instantiation and initialization. When translating the design to an object-oriented programming language it must be expressed in terms of its idioms for instantiation and initialization. There is no actual *create* method in C++, Java, or Smalltalk. For example, in C++ it implies automatic allocation, or free store allocation with the *new* operator, followed by a constructor call. In Java, it implies the invocation of the *new* operator, followed by a constructor call.

Because of its multiple interpretations, and also because initialization is a very common activity, it is common to omit creation-related methods and constructors from the design class diagram.

## 21.8.5   Method Names—Accessing Methods

**Accessing methods** are those which retrieve (accessor method) or set (mutator method) attributes. It is a common idiom to have an accessor and mutator for each attribute, and to declare all attribute private (to enforce encapsulation). These methods are usually excluded from depiction in the class diagram because of the high noise-to-value ratio they generate; for N attributes there are 2N uninteresting methods.

For example, the *ProductSpecification's price* (or *getPrice*) method is not shown, although present, because *price* is a simple accessor method.

## 21.8.6   Method Names—Multiobjects

A message to a multiobject is interpreted as a message to the container/collection object itself

For example, the following *find* message to the multiobject is meant be interpreted as a message to the container/collection object, such as to a Java *Hashtable,* a C++ *map* or a Smalltalk *Dictionary* (see Figure 21.6).

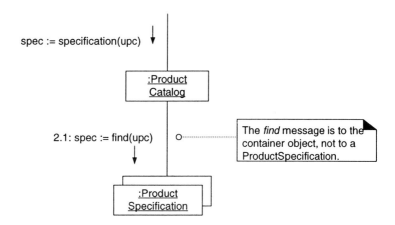

**Figure 21.6** Message to a multiobject.

Therefore, the *find* method is not part of the *ProductSpecification* class; rather, it is part of the *Hashtable* or *Dictionary* class definition. Consequently, it is incorrect to add *find* as a method to the *ProductSpecification* class.

These container/collection classes (such as java.util.Vector and java.util.Hashtable) are predefined library classes, and it is not usually useful to show these classes explicitly in the design class diagram, since they add noise, but little new information.

## 21.8.7   Method Names—Language Dependent Syntax

Some languages, such as Smalltalk, have a syntactic form for methods that is different than the basic UML format of *methodName(parameterList)*. It is recommended that the basic UML format be used, even if the planned implementation language uses a different syntax. The translation should ideally take place during the code generation time, instead of during the creation of the class diagrams. However, the UML does allow other syntax for method specification, such as Smalltalk syntax.

## 21.8.8   Adding More Type Information

The type of the attributes, method parameters, and method return values may all optionally be shown. The question as to whether to show this information or not should be considered in the following context:

The design class diagram should be created by considering the audience.

■ If it is being created in a CASE tool with automatic code generation, full and exhaustive details are necessary.

■ If it is being created for software developers to read, exhaustive detail may adversely effect the noise-to-value ratio.

For example, is it necessary to show all the parameters and their type information? It depends on how obvious the information is to the intended audience.

The point-of-sale design class diagram in Figure 21.7 shows exhaustive type information.

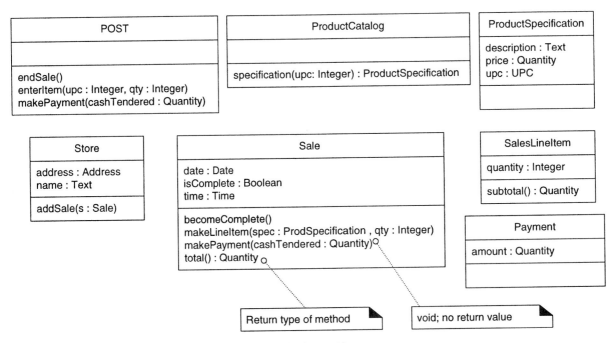

**Figure 21.7** Adding type information.

## 21.8.9   Adding Associations and Navigability

Each end of an association is called a role, and in the design-oriented class diagrams the role may be decorated with a navigability arrow. **Navigability** is a property of the role which indicates that it is possible to navigate uni-directionally across the association from objects of the source to target class. Navigability implies visibility; usually attribute visibility. An example is shown in Figure 21.8

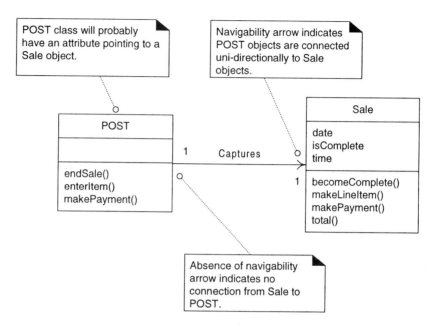

**Figure 21.8** Showing navigability, or attribute visibility.

The usual interpretation of an association with a navigability arrow is attribute visibility from the source to target class. During implementation in an object-oriented programming language it is usually translated as the source class having an attribute that refers to an instance of the target class. For instance, the *POST* class will define an attribute that references a *Sale* instance.

> Most, if not all, associations in design-oriented class diagrams should be adorned with the necessary navigability arrows.

In a design class diagram, associations are chosen by a spartan software-oriented need-to-know criterion—what associations are required in order to satisfy the visibility and ongoing memory needs indicated by the interaction diagrams? This is in contrast with associations in the conceptual model, which may be justified by the intention to enhance comprehension of the problem domain. Once again we see a distinction between the goals of the design class diagrams and the conceptual model: one is analytical, the other a description of software components.

The required visibility and associations between classes are indicated by the interaction diagrams. Here are common situations suggesting a need to define an association with a navigability adornment from A to B:

■ *A* sends a message to *B*.

■ *A* creates an instance *B*.

■ *A* needs to maintain a connection to *B*.

For example, from the collaboration diagram in Figure 21.9 starting with the *create* message to a *Store*, and from the larger context of the other collaboration diagrams, it is discernible that the *Store* should probably have an ongoing connection to the *POST* and *ProductCatalog* instances that it created. It is also reasonable that the *ProductCatalog* needs an ongoing connection to the collection of *ProductSpecifications* it created. In fact, the creator of another object very typically requires an ongoing connection to it.

The implied connections will therefore be present as associations in the class diagram.

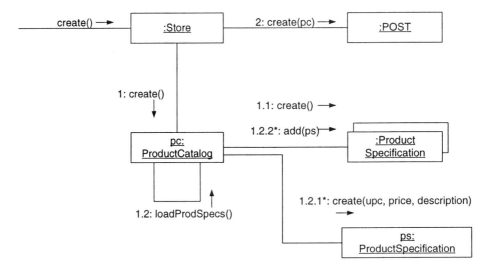

**Figure 21.9** Navigability is identified from collaboration diagrams.

Based on the above criterion for associations and navigability, analysis of all the collaboration diagrams generated for the point-of-sale application will yield a class diagram (seen in Figure 21.10) with the following associations. (Exhaustive type information is hidden for the sake of clarity.)

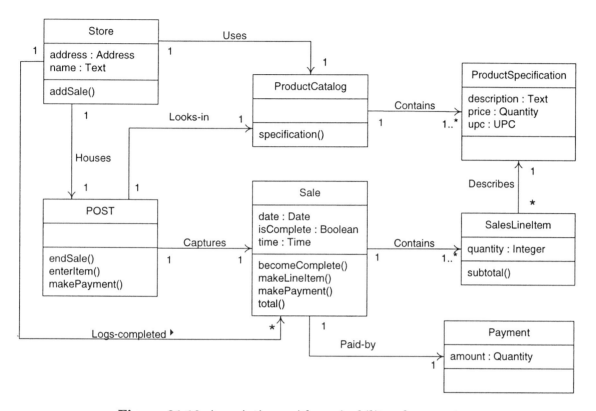

**Figure 21.10** Associations with navigability adornments.

Note that this is not exactly the same set of associations that was generated for the class diagrams in the Investigation Model. For instance, there was no *Looks-in* association between *POST* and *ProductCatalog* in the conceptual model—it was not discovered as an important lasting relationship at that time. But during the creation of the collaboration diagrams it was decided that a *POST* software object should have a lasting connection to a software *ProductCatalog* in order to look up *ProductSpecifications*.

## 21.8.10  Adding Dependency Relationships

The UML includes a general **dependency relationship** which indicates that one element (of any kind, including classes, use cases, and so on) has knowledge of another element. It is illustrated with a dashed arrowed line. In class diagrams the dependency relationship is useful to depict non-attribute visibility between classes; in other words, parameter, global, or locally declared visibility. In contrast, plain attribute visibility is shown with a regular association line and a navigability arrow.

For example, the *POST* software object receives a return object of type *ProductSpecification* from the specification message it sent to a *ProductCatalog*. Thus *POST* has a short-term locally declared visibility to *ProductSpecifications*. And *Sale* receives a *ProductSpecification* as a parameter in the *makeLineItem* message; it has parameter visibility to one. These non-attribute visibilities may be illustrated with the dashed arrowed line indicating a dependency relationship (Figure 21.11). (There is no significance in the curving of the dependency lines; it was graphically convenient in this example.)

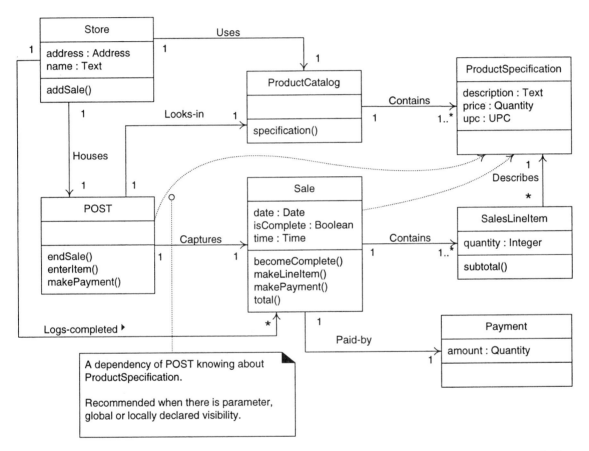

**Figure 21.11** Dependency relationships indicating non-attribute visibility.

## 21.9 Notation for Member Details

The UML provides a rich notation to describe features of class and interface members, such as visibility, initial values, and so on. Attributes are assumed to be private by default. An example is shown in Figure 21.12.

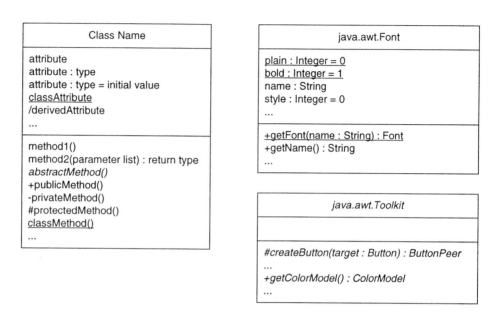

**Figure 21.12** Class member details notation.

The current iteration of the point-of-sale design class diagram (Figure 21.13) does not have many interesting member details; all attributes are private and all methods public.

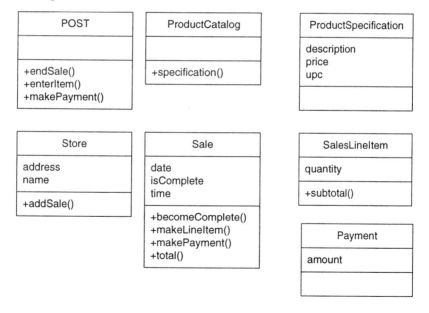

**Figure 21.13** Member details in the point-of-sale class diagram.

## 21.10   Sample Models

Design class diagrams compose the Class Model—the model of software classes and interfaces.

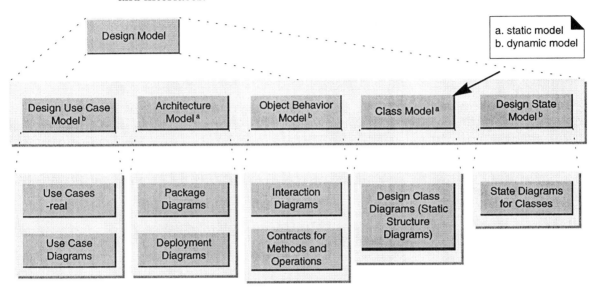

**Figure 21.14** The Design Model.

## 21.11   Summary

A design class diagram for the point-of-sale-terminal application has now been created as part of the Design Model shown in Figure 21.14. It illustrates the definition of the classes as software components. These diagrams are succinct and very informative—desirable qualities in a notation. Because of these qualities, when working on an existing object-oriented system, or designing a new one, developers tend to turn to these diagrams more often than any other.

# ISSUES IN SYSTEM DESIGN

---

## Objectives

- Design a system architecture in terms of layers and partitions.

- Illustrate the architectural design using UML package diagrams.

- Apply the Facade, Model-View Separation and Publish-Subscribe patterns, and event notification to support various architectural goals.

---

## 22.1   Introduction

The preceding case study has emphasized problem domain objects (such as *Sale*), since it defines the core concepts and behavior of a system. However, a system is composed of multiple subsystems, of which the domain objects are but one. A typical information system has to connect to a user interface and a persistent storage mechanism.

This chapter briefly explores the larger architecture of a system, communication and coupling between subsystems, and the UML notation—package diagrams—by which subsystems can be illustrated.

Information systems with a user interface (including application software such as word processors) are the most common category of application, so discussion starts with an exploration of common architectural issues related to information systems. Many of the concepts are applicable to other types of applications.

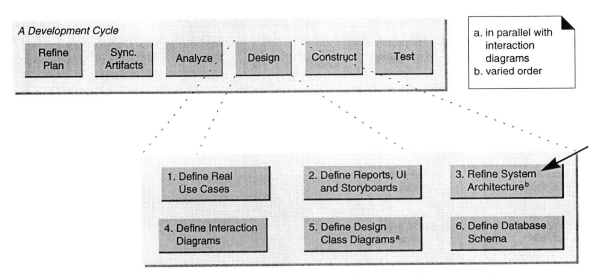

Design phase activities within a development cycle.

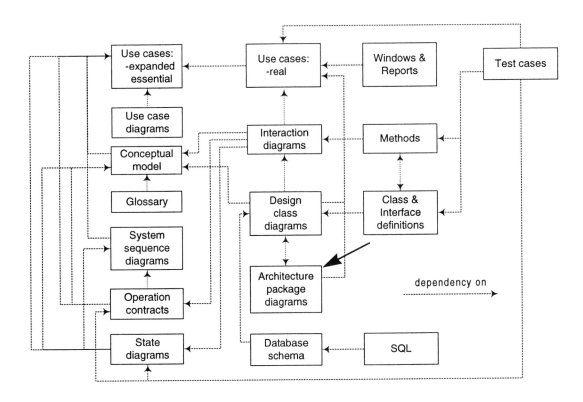

Build phase artifact dependencies.

## 22.2   Classic Three-Tier Architecture

One common architecture for information systems that includes a user interface and persistent storage of data is known as the **three-tier architecture** [Gartner95], shown in Figure 22.1. A classic description of the vertical tiers is:

1.  **Presentation**—windows, reports, and so on.

2.  **Application Logic**—tasks and rules that govern the process.

3.  **Storage**—persistent storage mechanism.

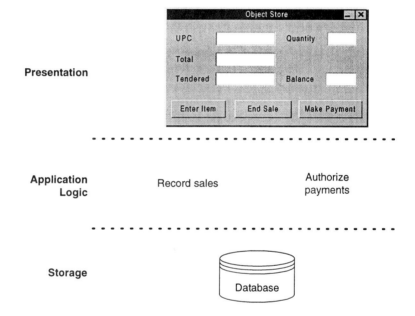

**Figure 22.1** Classic view of a three-tier architecture.

The singular quality of a three-tier architecture is the separation of the application logic into a distinct logical middle tier of software. The presentation tier is relatively free of application processing; windows forward task requests to the middle tier. The middle tier communicates with the back-end storage layer.

This architecture is in contrast to a **two-tier** design, in which, for example, application logic is placed within window definitions, which read and write directly to a database; there is no middle tier that separates out the application logic. A disadvantage of a two-tier design is the inability to represent application logic in separate components, which inhibits software reuse. It is also not possible to distribute application logic to separate computer.

# 22.3 Multi-Tiered Object-Oriented Architectures

A recommended multi-tiered architecture for object-oriented information systems includes the separation of responsibilities implied by the classic three-tier architecture. These responsibilities are assigned to software objects.

## 22.3.1 Decomposing the Application Logic Tier

In an object-oriented design, the application logic tier is decomposed into finer layers. This architecture, organized in terms of software classes, is shown in Figure 22.2. The application logic layer is itself composed of the following layers:

- **Domain Objects**—Classes representing domain concepts, such as a sale.
- **Services**—Service objects for functions such as database interaction, reporting, communications, security, and so on.

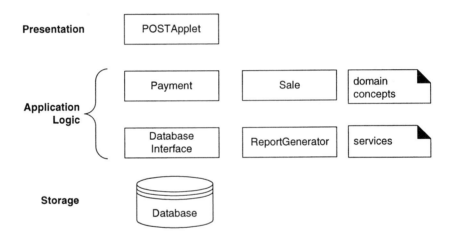

**Figure 22.2** Decomposition of application logic tier into finer layers.

## 22.3.2 Beyond Three Tiers—Multi-Tiered Architectures

When the architecture is viewed in terms of the finer decomposition illustrated in Figure 22.2, one may dispense with the appellation "three-tiered architecture" and instead speak of **multi-tiered architectures**; the middle application logic tier is implicit.

It is possible to add additional tiers and further decompose the existing ones. For instance, the *Services* tier may be divided into high-level and low-level services (for example, report generation versus file input/output).

## 22.3.3 Deployment

A *logical* three-tier architecture may be *physically* deployed in various configurations; these include:

1.  Presentation and application logic tiers on a client computer, storage on server.

2.  Presentation on client computer, application logic on an application server, and storage on a separate data server.

With the increased use of languages and technologies which easily support distributed computing, such as Java, deployment of subsystems will likewise be increasingly distributed.

## 22.3.4 Motivation for a Multi-Tiered Architecture

Motivations for a multi-tiered architecture include:

■  Isolation of application logic into separate components which can be reused in other systems.

■  Distribution of tiers on different physical computing nodes, and/or different processes. This can improve performance and increase coordination and shared information in a client-server system.

■  Allocation of developers to construct specific tiers, such as a team working solely on the presentation layer. This supports specialized expertise in terms of development skills, and the ability to run parallel team development efforts.

# 22.4 Showing Architecture with UML Packages

The UML provides the **package** mechanism for the purpose of illustrating groups of elements or subsystems. A package is a set of model elements of any kind, such as classes, use cases, collaboration diagrams or other packages (nested packages). An entire system may be considered within the scope of a single top level package—the *System* package. A package defines a nested name space, so elements with the same name may be duplicated within different packages.

## 22.4.1 UML Package Notation

Graphically, a package is shown as a tabbed folder (Figure 22.3). Subordinate packages may be shown within it. The package name is within the tab if the package depicts its elements, otherwise it is centered within the folder itself.

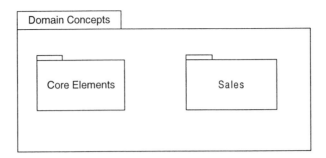

**Figure 22.3** Packages in the UML.

## 22.4.2 Architecture Package Diagrams

To illustrate system architecture with the UML notation, packages can be used. An alternate view to Figure 22.2, using UML package diagrams to represent logical groupings, is shown in Figure 22.4. Such a diagram may be called an **architecture package diagram**.

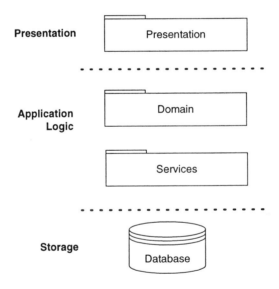

**Figure 22.4** Architectural units expressed in terms of UML packages.

## 22.4.3 Example Packages and Dependencies

Figure 22.5 illustrates a more detailed breakdown of common packages in the architecture of an information system, plus dependencies between packages.

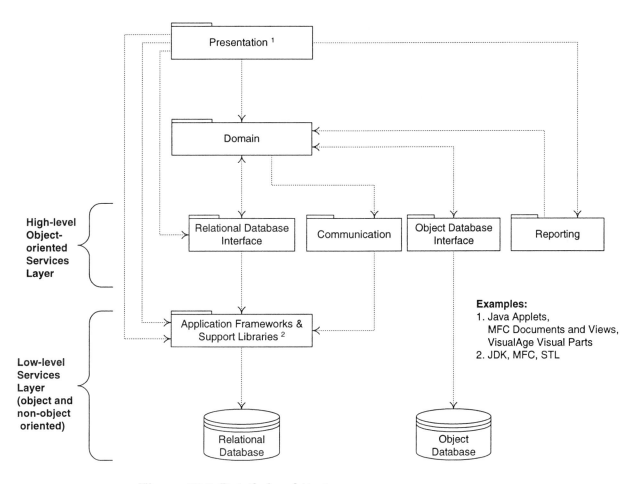

**Figure 22.5** Detailed architecture.

## Package comments

- The Relational and Object-Database Interface packages provide mechanisms for communicating with databases. An object database interface will be provided by the object database vendor. However, it is necessary to either custom develop a relational database interface, or buy a third-party product that performs this function.

- High-level object-oriented service packages are services such as reporting, database interfaces, security, and inter-process communications developed using object technology; they are usually written by the application developers. In contrast, low-level services provide basic functions such as window and file manipulation, and are usually provided as standard language libraries or purchased from a third-party vendor.

- Application Frameworks and Support Libraries typically include support for creating windows, defining application coordinators, accessing databases and files, inter-process communication, and so on.

### Dependency comments

- The dependency relationships (dashed arrowed line) indicates if a package has knowledge of (coupling) to another package. *Lack* of dependency from package A to B implies the components of package A have *no* references to any classes, components, interfaces, methods, or services of package B.

- Note that the domain package has no dependency (coupling) to the presentation layers. This illustrates the principle of *Model-View Separation* discussed ahead.

# 22.5    Identifying Packages

Group elements into a package by this guideline:

> Group elements that provide a common service (or family of related services), with relatively high coupling and collaboration, into a package.
>
> At some level of abstraction the package will be viewed as highly cohesive—it has strongly related responsibilities.
>
> In contrast, the coupling and collaboration between elements of different packages will be relatively low.

# 22.6    Layers and Partitions

A multi-tiered architecture can be characterized as composed of layers and partitions (see Figure 22.6).

The **layers** of an architecture represent the vertical tiers, while **partitions** represent a horizontal division of relatively parallel subsystems of a layer. For example, the *Services* layer may be divided into partitions such as *Security* and *Reporting*.

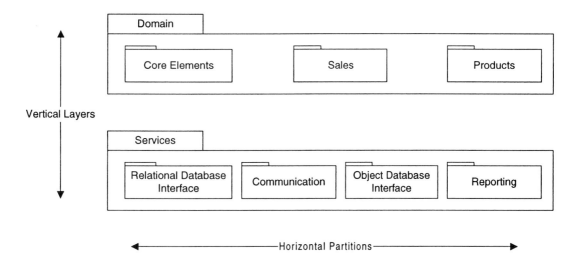

**Figure 22.6** Layers and partitions.

## 22.6.1 "Relaxed" Layered Architecture

The layers in most multi-tiered object-oriented architectures are *not* coupled in the same limited sense as a network protocol based on the OSI 7-Layer Model. In the protocol model, there is restriction that elements of Layer N only access the services of the immediate lower Layer N-1. Although such a limitation is possible, it is more common that the architecture is a "relaxed layered" or "transparent layered" architecture [BMRSS96], in which elements of a layer communicate with several other layers. Figure 22.5 illustrates a typical coupling between layers and partitions. For example, it is very common for the presentation (or application coordination) layer to be coupled to both the Domain and Services layer.

# 22.7    Visibility Between Package Classes

How should package components be related? Visibility to classes in different packages typically conform to the following pattern:

- **Access into the Domain packages**—other packages, typically the presentation package, have visibility into *many* of the classes representing domain concepts.

- **Access into the Service packages**—other packages, typically the Domain and Presentation packages, have visibility into only *one* or a very few classes in each particular Service package (usually a **Facade** class—see discussion ahead).

■ **Access into the Presentation packages**—no other packages have direct visibility to the Presentation layer. Communication is indirect, if at all (using the **Observer** pattern—see discussion ahead).

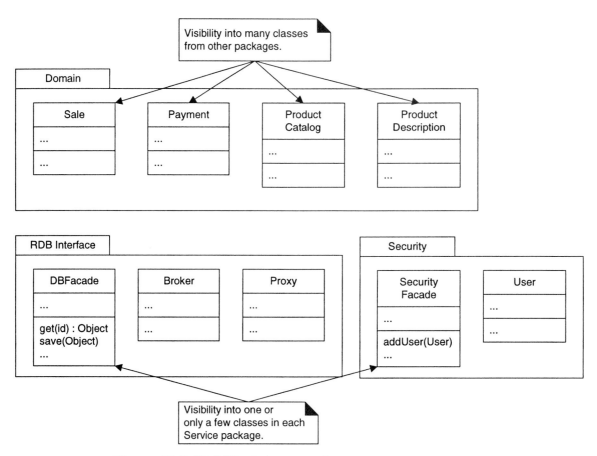

**Figure 22.7** Visibility between packages.

# 22.8    Service Packages Interface—The Facade Pattern

How should components interface with the classes in a Service package, such as the *RelationalDatabaseInterface* package, which provides services to transform between objects and rows in tables? When a class is defined that provides a common interface to a group of other components or a disparate set of interfaces, it is called a **Facade** [GHJV95]. The disparate elements may be the classes in a package, a set of functions, a framework, or a subsystem (local or remote).

---

**Facade**

*Context / Problem*

A common, unified interface to a disparate set of interfaces—such as to a subsystem—is required. What to do?

*Solution*

Define a single class that unifies the interface and give it responsibility for collaborating with the subsystem.

---

The Facade pattern is often used to provide a public interface to a Service package. For example, if a *RelationalDatabaseInterface* package exists with many internal classes, one class, such as *DBFacade*, may be defined that provides the common public interface into the services of the package (Figure 22.7). Classes in other packages send messages only to an instance of *DBFacade*, and have no coupling to other classes in the package. *DBFacade* collaborates with the other (private) classes of the package to provide services. This design supports low coupling.

# 22.9 No Direct Visibility to Windows—The Model-View Separation Pattern

What kind of visibility should other packages have to the Presentation layer? How should non-window classes communicate with windows? It is usually desirable that there is no direct coupling from other components to window objects because the windows are related to a particular application, while (ideally) the non-windowing components may be reused in new applications or attached to a new interface. The principle is the Model-View Separation pattern.

In this context, **model** is a synonym for the domain layer of objects. **View** is a synonym for presentation objects, such as windows, applets and reports.

The **Model-View Separation** pattern[1] (or **Domain-Presentation Separation**, if you will) states that model (domain) objects should not have *direct* knowledge of or be directly coupled to view (presentation) objects.

---

1. Fully described as a pattern in [BMRSS96] by the name *Model-View-Controller*. In reality, the *Controller* (low-level input handler) portion of the pattern is an anachronism, since controller responsibilities are normally included within views, and provided by the operating system; controllers were included years ago in Smalltalk-80 before modern operating system and graphical windowing services were available. "Model-View Separation" better describes the intent and modern architecture.

There should not be any statements in the methods of a model class that send messages directly to a view object; a model class should have no knowledge or code related to user interfaces.

A model class will not have any direct visibility to a view class. However, as will be seen, indirect visibility is acceptable.

A further recommendation of this pattern is that the domain (view) classes encapsulate the information and behavior related to application logic.

The window (view) classes are relatively thin; they are responsible for input and output, but do not maintain data or directly provide application functionality.

---

### Model-View Separation

*Context / Problem*

It is desirable to de-couple domain (model) objects from windows (views), to support increased reuse of domain objects, and minimize the impact of changes in the interface upon the domain objects. What to do?

*Solution*

Define the domain (model) classes so that they do not have direct coupling or visibility to the window (view) classes, and so that application data and functionality is maintained in domain classes, not window classes.

---

For example, suppose that (in Java) a *POSTApplet* object exists which displays information from a *Sale* object, and sends system event messages to a *POST* object.

The *POSTApplet* may have visibility to and send messages to domain objects, such as a *POST* (the controller for the system events) and *Sale*.

But the *POST* and *Sale* objects will be ignorant of the existence of the window; there are no statements in the *POST* and *Sale* methods related to windowing or display logic.

Therefore, it is not suitable for the *POST* to send a *displayMessage* message to the window, as in Figure 22.8.

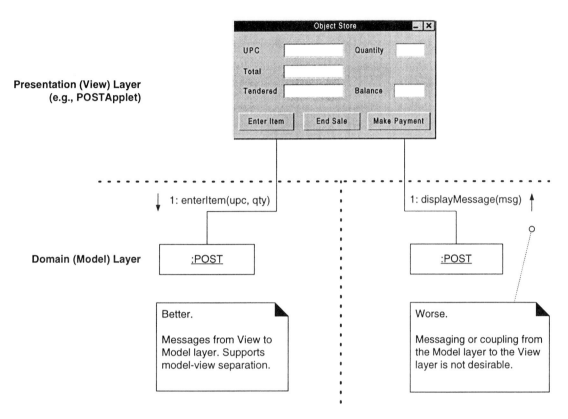

**Figure 22.8** Conformance to versus violation of Model-View Separation.

In short, domain layer objects have no direct communication with the presentation layer.

In contrast, it is acceptable for views to have visibility to models; for example, a *POSTApplet* object may send messages to the *POST*.

## 22.9.1   Motivation for Model-View Separation

The motivation for Model-View Separation includes:

- To support cohesive model definitions that focus on the domain processes, rather than on computer interfaces.

- To allow separate development of the model and user interface layers.

- To minimize the impact of requirements changes in the interface upon the domain layer.

- To allow new views to be easily connected to an existing domain layer, without affecting the domain layer.

- To allow multiple simultaneous views on the same model object, such as both a tabular and business chart view of sales information.

- To allow execution of the model layer independent of the user interface layer, such as in a message-processing or batch-mode system.

- To allow easy porting of the model layer to another user interface framework.

## 22.9.2 Model-View Separation and Indirect Communication

How can windows obtain information to display? Usually, it is sufficient for them to send messages to domain objects, querying for information which they then display in widgets—a **polling** or **pull-from-above** model of display updates.

However, a polling model is sometimes insufficient—domain objects need to (indirectly) communicate with windows to cause a real-time ongoing display update as the state of information in the domain objects changes. Typical situations of this case include:

- Monitoring applications, such as telecommunications network management.

- Simulation applications which require visualization, such as aerodynamics modeling.

In these situations, a **push-from-below** model of display update is required. Because of the restriction of the Model-View Separation pattern, this leads to the need for *indirect* communication from other objects to windows—pushing up notification to update from below, albeit indirectly.

# 22.10 Indirect Communication in a System

The Model-View Separation pattern provides one of many examples in which it is necessary to provide indirect communication between elements within a system. A message between a sender and receiver object in common object-oriented languages requires that the sender has direct visibility to the receiver. Consequently, other mechanisms besides direct messaging are required if it is desirable to de-couple the send and receiver, or support for a broadcast or multicast of a "signal" is needed.

This section explores variations of indirect communication, and how they support architectural goals, such as low coupling and Model-View Separation.

## 22.10.1 The Publish-Subscribe Pattern

The solution to the indirect communication required from domain objects to windows is the **Observer** or **Publish-Subscribe** Pattern—a technique discussed in both [GHJV95] as **Observer** and in [BMRSS96] as **Publisher-Subscriber**.

---

**Publish-Subscribe**

*Context / Problem*

A change in state (an event) occurs within a Publisher of the event and other objects are dependent on or interested in this event (Subscribers to the event). However, the Publisher should not have direct knowledge of its Subscribers. What to do?

*Solution*

Define an event notification system so that the Publisher can indirectly notify Subscribers.

---

For example, an *EventManager* class can be defined which maintains mappings between events and subscribers (it is both a *Pure Fabrication* and an *Indirection* in the GRASP pattern sense). An event is published by the publisher sending a *signalEvent* message to the *EventManager*. When published, the *EventManager* finds all subscribers that are interested in the event, and they are notified, ideally via a parameterized message (or *callback* object) that they provided upon subscription (Figure 22.9). The event is represented as a simple string; more likely it will be an instance of an *Event* class. In a home-grown event system, there will typically be a single instance of the *EventManager* class, globally accessed using the Singleton pattern (discussed later).

The *EventManager* design is a simple, language independent illustration of the concepts; language-specific facilities should be used when available. For example, Java specifies a delegation event model that supports the goals of publish-subscribe. Subscriber objects implement an *EventListener* interface and subscribe to events by registering with event source objects (the publishers). The source objects maintain a list of all registered listeners, and notify them when an event of interest occurs. Coupling is reduced by defining subscribers in terms of a Java interface rather than a class.

A classic design of Publish-Subscribe has the Publisher object maintain direct visibility to its collection of Subscribers who are interested in notification of Publisher changes. This has the disadvantage of impacting the coupling and implementation of Publishers. Alternatively, the use of an indirect *EventManager* class which manages subscribers has the advantage of minimizing publisher coupling and responsibilities, but may suffer from performance problems, since it is a bottleneck for all events.

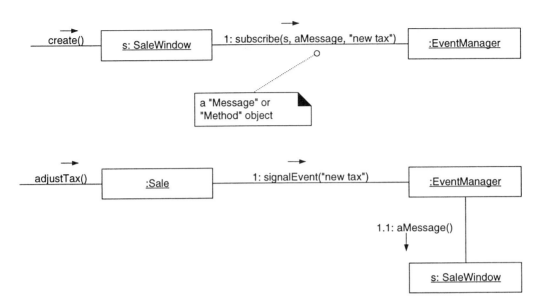

**Figure 22.9** Publish-Subscribe with event notification.

## 22.10.2 Callbacks

The design illustrated in Figure 22.9 requires passing a parameterized message and potential receiver to the *EventManager*. The message and receiver can be encapsulated in a *Callback* class.[1] Then the *EventManager* is passed a *Callback* instance, which it executes on signalling of an event by sending the *Callback* an *execute* message.[2]

The use of *Callback* objects has the advantage of hiding the details of the receiver and message, and simplifying the responsibilities of the user of the *Callback*.

## 22.10.3 Event Notification Systems

The Publish-Subscribe architecture provides a general purpose mechanism for event notification and indirect communication in a system. This opens up a new approach to the design of object-oriented systems—an event notification-based

---

1. For example, using the Java Reflection API or with a Java inner class instance.

2. In Java, there are variations of this design that do not require an explicit *Callback* class. This is possible with interfaces and anonymous inner classes, and also with the delegation event model.

design. Its distinguishing qualities are:

- Direct coupling between senders and receivers is not required.

- A single event can be broadcast to any number of subscribers.

- The reaction to an event can be generalized in *Callback* objects.

- It is relatively easy to provide concurrency by executing each *Callback* on its own thread.

Besides the advantages of reduced coupling, broadcasting and simple concurrency, in some situations an event notification-based system is more efficient when long chains of messages can be collapsed down to one level of indirection.

Finally, a system design which relies heavily on asynchronous event notification and broadcasting to subscribers increasingly takes on the flavor of a state-machine design. State modeling of objects is explored in a subsequent chapter.

# 22.11  Application Coordinators

An **application coordinator** is a class that is responsible for mediating between the interface (for example, windows) and the domain layer. It has the following basic responsibilities:

- Map information between domain objects and interface. For example, consolidate and transform information from one or more domain objects.

- Respond to events from the interface.

- Open windows that display information from domain objects.

- Manage transactions, such as performing commit and rollback.

If the architecture is designed to support multiple views or windows that display the same information, then application coordinators additionally support the following multi-view responsibilities:

- Support the ability to have multiple windows ("dependent windows") simultaneous display information from one application coordinator instance.

- Notify dependent windows when information changes and the windows need to refresh (repaint) with new information.

Some application frameworks include support for some form of application coordinator. For example, in MFC application coordinators are *Documents* in the Document-View architecture; they are subclasses of class *CDocument*.[1]

To give a concrete example of the relationship between various components with

---

1. In Smalltalk VisualWorks, an *ApplicationModel* fulfills the role of an application coordinator. In Visual Smalltalk, it is a *ViewManager* or *ApplicationCoordinator*.

the MFC Document-View architecture, consider Figure 22.10. The attribute visibility is illustrated on the links of the collaboration diagram. Note that—in support of Model-View Separation—the domain objects *POST* and *Sale* have no visibility to the *SaleDocument* or *SaleView.*

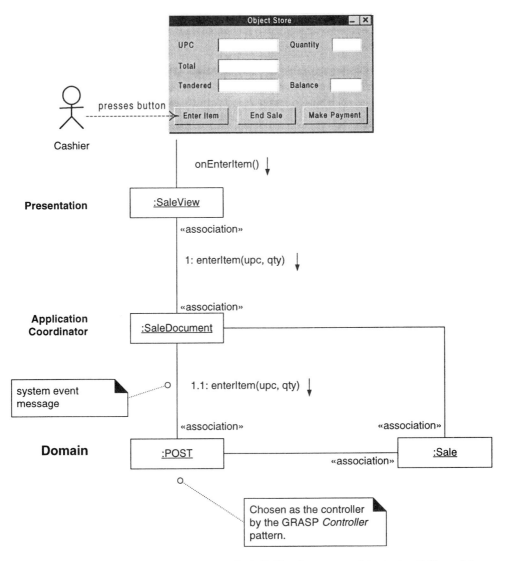

**Figure 22.10** Collaboration and visibility between objects in different layers in the Microsoft Foundation Class Document-View architecture.

The *SaleDocument* (the application coordinator) has visibility to the *POST* as the chosen controller (in the GRASP pattern sense) for system operation messages, and has visibility to the *Sale* for which information is being displayed in the *SaleView* window. The *SaleDocument* established attribute visibility to the *Sale* by requesting it from the *POST*—the creator of the *Sale.*

Consider the following sample flow of control:

1. The cashier presses a button on the window.

2. The event is forwarded as the *onEnterItem* message to the *SaleView* instance, which represents the displayed window.

3. The *SaleView* forwards the event as the *enterItem* message the *SaleDocument*.

The *SaleDocument* forwards the *enterItem* message (the system event message) to the *POST* controller in the domain layer.

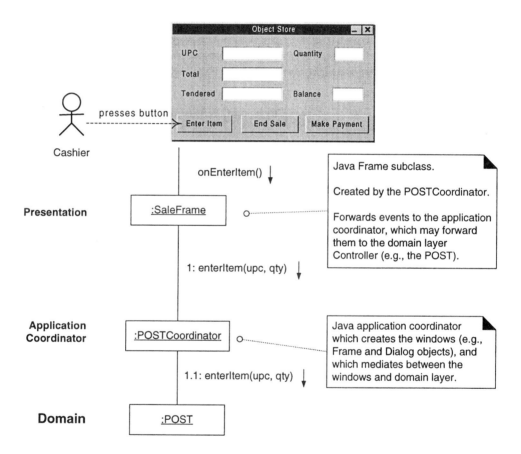

**Figure 22.11** Adding an application coordinator to a Java application.

## 22.11.1 *Application Coordinators and Window Objects*

In the absence of explicit framework support for application coordinators, it is common for the window or view class itself to take on some of the responsibilities of the coordinator. For example, the Java JDK does not inherently provide separate application coordination from presentation. If a Java applet is used, it typically fulfills both presentation and application coordination responsibilities.

### 22.11.2 Home-Grown Application Coordinators

Even in the absence of framework support for application coordinators, it is possible to add them to perform transaction management, notify multiple dependent windows, and map information.

For instance, a regular Java application (not an applet) can be designed so that a *POSTCoordinator* class, representing the application coordinator, mediates between windows (for example, a *Frame*) and the domain layer (Figure 22.11).

If prior architectural support for application coordinators is not provided, such as is the case with Java, be cautious in their addition—they are an incongruous element in that environment.

## 22.12 Storage and Persistence

If an object database is used to store domain layer objects, there is relatively little effort required on the part of the developers in order to interact with the database; the database supplier provides an interface. However, if a non-object database (for example, a relational database) is used, then a subsystem (Figure 22.12) is required that maps between objects and rows in tables. The design of such a subsystem is explored in Chapter 38.

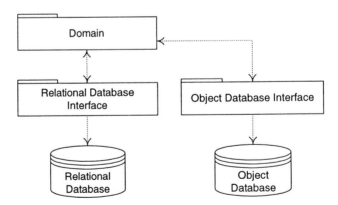

**Figure 22.12** Persistence subsystems.

## 22.13   Sample Models

Architecture package diagrams compose part of the Architecture Model—the model of layers and system subsystems, and the deployment of components to processors.

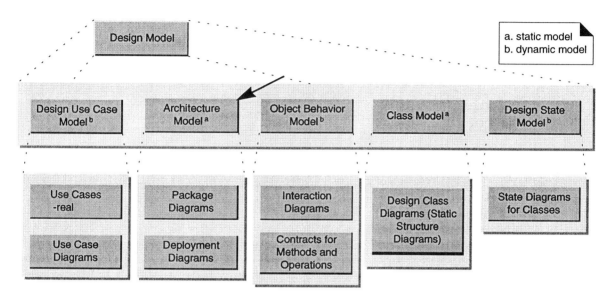

**Figure 22.13**  The Design Model.

# PART IV CONSTRUCT PHASE (1)

# MAPPING DESIGNS TO CODE

## Objectives

- Map design artifacts to code in an object-oriented language.

## 23.1    Introduction

With the completion of design class diagrams for the current development cycle of the point-of-sale application, there is sufficient detail to generate code for the domain layer of objects.

The UML artifacts created during the design phase—the collaboration diagrams and design class diagrams—will be used as input to the code generation process.

## 23.2    Programming and the Development Process

To reduce risk and increase the likelihood of developing a suitable application, development should be based on a significant amount of analysis and design modeling before coding begins.[1] This is not to suggest that there is no room to prototype or design while programming; modern development tools provide an excellent environment to quickly explore alternate approaches, and some (or even lots) design-by-coding is usually worthwhile.

---

1. "Software" is harder than it sounds. Modification and the exploration of alternatives is more difficult and expensive during the programming phase than during analysis and design.

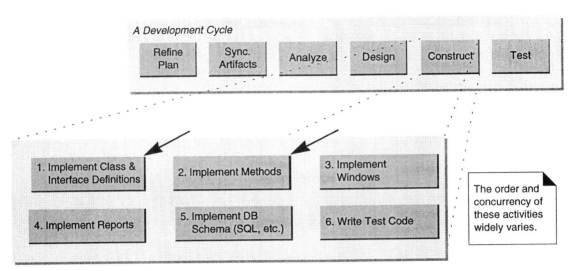

Construct phase activities within a development cycle.

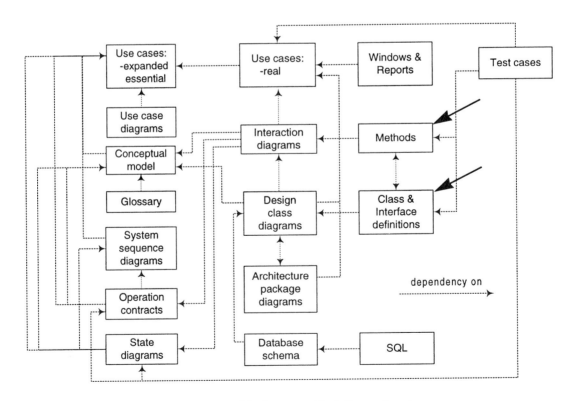

Build phase artifact dependencies.

However, the core of the application, such as the basic conceptual model, architectural layers, major allocations of responsibilities, and major object interactions are best determined in a formal investigation and design process rather than by a "rush to code." Rushing to code creates systems that are harder to understand, extend and maintain, and does not support a successfully repeatable process.

That said, oftentimes it is best to break from the design phase to do some exploratory programming in order to discover a workable design, and then return to the formal design phase.

The creation of code in an object-oriented programming language—such as Java or Smalltalk—is not part of object-oriented analysis and design; it is an end goal. The artifacts created in the design phase provide a significant degree of the information necessary in order to generate the code, and as will be seen, it is a relatively straightforward translation process.

A strength of object-oriented analysis and design and object-oriented programming—when used with a development process like the one suggested—is that it provides a complete end-to-end roadmap from requirements through to code. The various artifacts feed into later artifacts in a traceable and useful manner, ultimately culminating in a running application. This is not to suggest that the road will be smooth, or can simply be mechanically followed—there are too many variables. But having a roadmap provides a starting point for experimentation and discussion.

## 23.2.1 Creativity and Change During the Construct Phase

A significant amount of decision making and creative work was accomplished during the analysis and design phases. It will be seen during the following discussion that the generation of the code—in this example—is a relatively mechanical translation process.

However, in general, the programming phase is not a trivial code generation step—quite the opposite. Realistically, the results generated during design are an incomplete first step; during programming and testing myriad changes will be made and detailed problems will be uncovered and resolved.

Done well, the design artifacts will provide a resilient core that scales up with elegance and robustness to meet the new problems encountered during programming.

Consequently, expect and plan for change and deviation from design during the construction and testing phase.

## 23.2.2 Code Changes and the Iterative Process

A strength of an iterative and incremental development process is that the results of a prior cycle can feed into the beginning of the next cycle. Thus subsequent analysis and design results are continually being refined and informed from prior implementation work. For example, when the code in cycle N deviates from the design of cycle N (which it inevitably will), the final design based on the implementation can be input into the analysis and design models of cycle N+1.

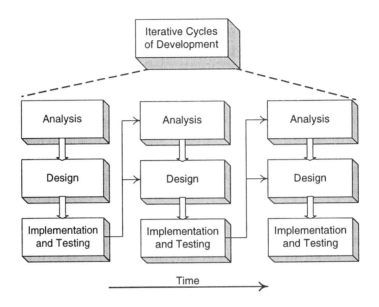

**Figure 23.1** Implementation in a development cycle influences later design.

That is why an early activity within a development cycle is to synchronize the artifacts; the diagrams of cycle N will not match the final code of cycle N, and they need to be synchronized before being extended with new analysis and design results.

### 23.2.3 Code Changes, CASE Tools and Reverse Engineering

It is desirable for the diagrams generated in the design phase to be semi-automatically updated to reflect changes in the subsequent coding phase. Ideally this should be done with a computer-aided software engineering (CASE) tool that can read source code (such as Java) and automatically generate, for example, class and collaboration diagrams. This is an aspect of **reverse engineering**—the activity of generating logical models from executable source code.

## 23.3  Mapping Designs to Code

Implementation in an object-oriented programming language requires writing source code for:

- class definitions
- method definitions

The following sections discuss their generation in Java (as a typical case); the next chapter illustrates a full implementation.

# 23.4 Creating Class Definitions from Design Class Diagrams

At the very least, design class diagrams depict the class name, superclasses, method signatures, and simple attributes of a class. This is sufficient to create a basic class definition in an object-oriented programming language. Later discussion will explore the addition of interface and name space information, among other details.

## 23.4.1 Defining a Class with Methods and Simple Attributes

From the design class diagram, a mapping to the basic attribute definitions (simple Java instance variables) and method signatures for the Java definition of *SalesLineItem* is straightforward, as shown in Figure 23.2.

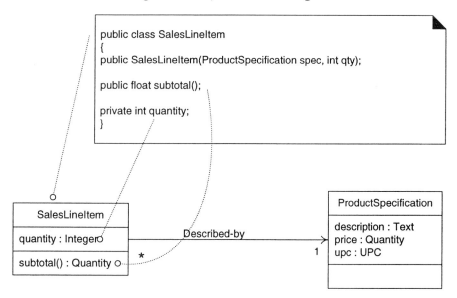

**Figure 23.2** SalesLineItem in Java.

Note the addition of the Java constructor *SalesLineItem(...)*. It is derived from the fact that a *create(spec, qty)* message is sent to a *SalesLineItem* in the *enterItem* collaboration diagram. This indicates, in Java, that a constructor supporting these parameters is required. The *create* method is often excluded from the class diagram because of its commonality and multiple interpretations, depending on the target language.

Observe also that the return type for the *subtotal* method was changed from *Quantity* to a simple *float*. Assume that in the initial coding work, the developer does not want to take the time to implement a *Quantity* class, and will defer that.

## 23.4.2 Adding Reference Attributes

A **reference attribute** is an attribute that refers to another complex object, not to a primitive type such as a String, Number, and so on.

> The reference attributes of a class are suggested by the associations and navigability in a class diagram.

For example, a *SalesLineItem* has an association to a *ProductSpecification*, and with navigability to it. It is common to interpret this as a reference attribute in class *SalesLineItem* that refers to a *ProductSpecification* instance (see Figure 23.3).

In Java, this means that an instance variable referring to a *ProductSpecification* instance is suggested.

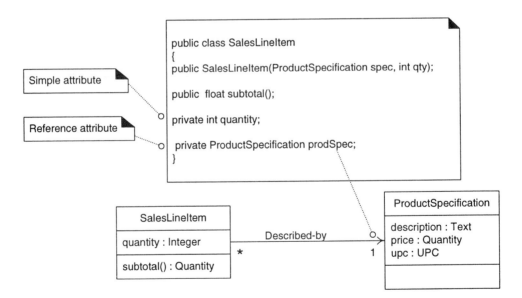

**Figure 23.3** Adding reference attributes.

> Note that the reference attributes of a class are often implied, not explicit, in a design class diagram.

For example, although we have added an instance variable to the Java definition of *SalesLineItem* to point to a *ProductSpecification*, it is not explicitly declared as an attribute in the attribute section of the class box. There is a *suggested* attribute visibility—indicated by the association and navigability—which is explicitly defined as an attribute during the code generation phase.

## 23.4.3   Reference Attributes and Role Names

The next iteration will explore the concept of role names in static structure diagrams. Each end of an association is called a role. Briefly, a **role name** is a name that identifies the role and often provides some semantic context as to the nature of the role.

If a role name is present in a class diagram, use it as the basis for the name of the reference attribute during code generation, as shown in Figure 23.4.

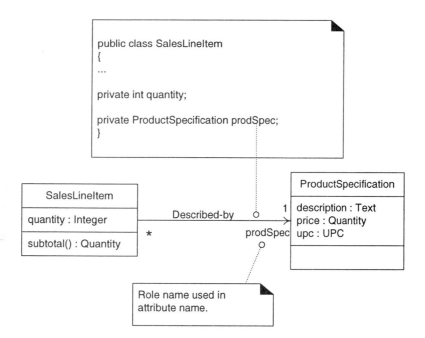

**Figure 23.4** Role names may be used to generate instance variable names.

# 23.5    Creating Methods from Collaboration Diagrams

A collaboration diagram shows the messages that are sent in response to a method invocation. The sequence of these messages translates to a series of statements in the method definition.

The *enterItem* collaboration diagram in Figure 23.5 will be used to illustrate the Java definition of the *enterItem* method.

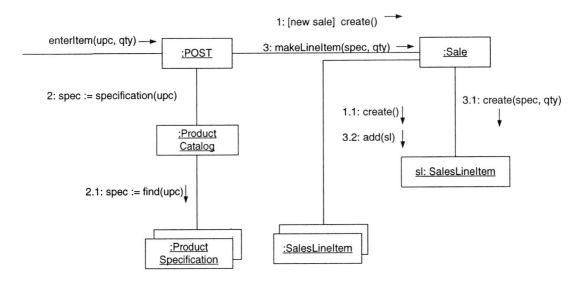

**Figure 23.5** The enterItem collaboration diagram.

In this example, the *POST* class will be used. A Java definition is shown in Figure 23.6.

## 23.5.1    The POST--enterItem Method

The *enterItem* message is sent to a *POST* instance, therefore, the *enterItem* method is defined in class *POST*.

```
public void enterItem(int upc, int qty)
```

**Message 1:** According to the collaboration diagram, in response to the *enterItem* message, the first statement is to conditionally create a new *Sale*[1].

```
if ( isNewSale() ) { sale = new Sale(); }
```

---

1. For brevity, the use of accessing methods is ignored, although it is generally recommended.

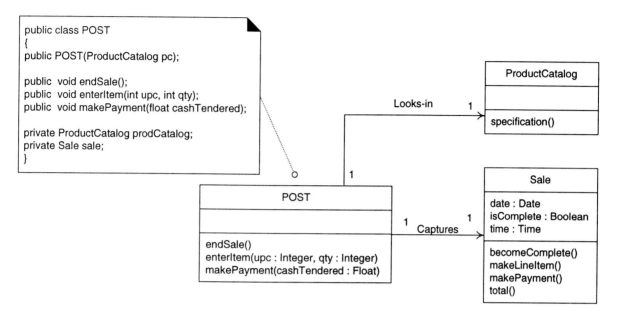

**Figure 23.6** The POST class.

**Message 2:** Second, we send a *specification* message to the *ProductCatalog* to retrieve a *ProductSpecification*.

```
ProductSpecification spec =
            prodCatalog.specification(upc);
```

**Message 3:** Third, we send the *makeLineItem* message to the *Sale*.

```
sale.makeLineItem(spec, qty);
```

In summary, each sequenced message within a method, as shown on the collaboration diagram, is mapped to a statement in the Java method.

The complete *enterItem* method and its relationship to the collaboration diagram is shown in Figure 23.7

## 23.5.2 The POST--isNewSale Method

The *POST--enterItem* method definition introduced a new method to the *POST* class: *isNewSale*. This is a small example of how, during the coding phase, changes from the design will appear. It is possible that this method could have been discovered during the earlier solution phase, but the point is that changes will inevitably arise while programming.

As a first attempt, this helper method will perform a test based on whether or not the *sale* instance variable is *null*.

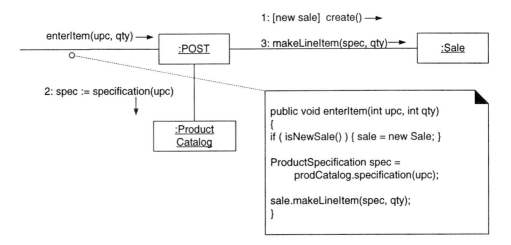

**Figure 23.7** The enterItem method.

Thus,

```
private boolean isNewSale()
{
   return ( sale == null );
}
```

Why not simply hard-code this test into the *enterItem* method? The reason is that it relies on a design decision about the representation of information. In general, expressions that are dependent on representation decisions are best wrapped in helper methods so that if the representation changes, the change impact is minimized. Furthermore, to a reader of the code, the *isNewSale* test is more informative in terms of the semantic intent. Consider the relative semantic clarity of the following alternate expressions:

```
if ( isNewSale() ) ...

     // versus

if ( sale == null ) ...
```

On reflection, you will realize that this test is not adequate in the general case. For example, what if one sale has completed, and a second sale is about to begin. In that case, the *sale* attribute will not be *null*; it will point to the last sale. Consequently, some additional test is required to determine if it is a new sale. To solve this problem, assume that if the current sale is in the *complete* state, then a new sale can begin. If it turns out in a later iteration that this is an inappropriate business rule, a change can be easily made.

Therefore,

```
private boolean isNewSale()
{
    return ( sale == null ) || ( sale.isComplete() );
}
```

This late-breaking change to the meaning of "a new sale" again illustrates the advantage of encapsulating its test within a helper method; a change is only required within this method.

## 23.6    Updating Class Definitions

Based on these coding decisions, one new method needs to be added to the *POST* class definition: *isNewSale*. The design class diagram depicting the *POST* class should be updated to reflect this code change. If using a CASE tool with reverse engineering capabilities, it may be a simple task to regenerate the diagrams based on the state of the code. Otherwise, manual maintenance is required. Maintaining the diagrams is valuable, but since manual maintenance is seldom done effectively and is expensive, this is a strong justification to invest in a CASE tool which can reverse-engineer the generation of UML diagrams.

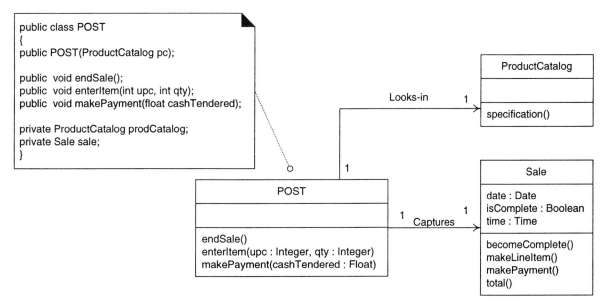

**Figure 23.8** Updated POST class definition.

# 23.7    Container/Collection Classes in Code

It is often necessary for an object to maintain visibility to a group of other objects; the need for this is usually evident from the multiplicity value in a class diagram—it may be greater than one. For example, a *Sale* must maintain visibility to a group of *SalesLineItem* instances, as shown in Figure 23.9.

In object-oriented programming languages these relationships are often implemented with the introduction of a intermediate container or collection. The one-side class defines a reference attribute pointing to a container/collection instance, which contains instances of the many-side class.

For example, the Java JDK contains container classes such as *Hashtable* and *Vector*. Using *Vector*, the *Sale* class can define an attribute that maintains an ordered list of *SalesLineItem* instances.

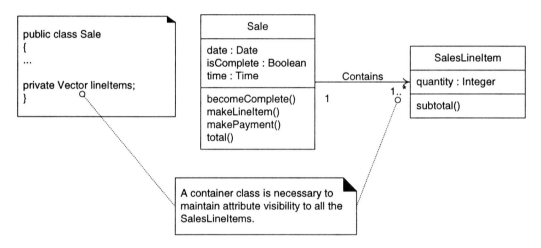

**Figure 23.9** Adding a container.

The choice of container class is influenced by the requirements; key-based lookup requires the use of a *Hashtable*, a growing ordered list requires a *Vector*, and so on.

# 23.8    Exceptions and Error Handling

Error handling has been ignored so far in the development of a solution. This was intentional in order to focus on the basic questions of responsibility assignment and object-oriented design. However, in real application development, it is wise to consider error handling during the design phase. For example, the contracts can be annotated with a brief discussion of typical error situations and the general plan of response.

The UML does not have a special notation to illustrate exceptions. Rather, the message notation of collaboration diagrams is used to illustrate exceptions. A collaboration diagram may start with a message representing a thrown exception.

# 23.9    Defining the Sale--makeLineItem Method

As a final example, the *makeLineItem* method of class *Sale* can also be written by inspecting the *enterItem* collaboration diagram. An abridged version of the collaboration diagram, with the accompanying Java method, is shown in Figure 23.10.

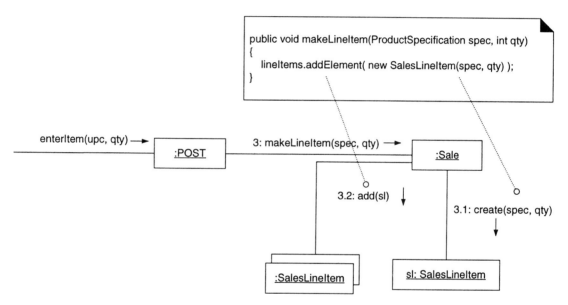

**Figure 23.10** Sale--makeLineItem method.

There is another example of code deviating from the collaboration diagram in this method: the generic *add* message has been translated into the Java-specific *addElement* message. It is also possible to use language or library specific messages in the collaboration diagrams, such as *addElement*.

# 23.10   Order of Implementation

Classes need to be implemented (and ideally, fully unit tested) from least coupled to most coupled (see Figure 23.11). For example, possible first classes to implement are either *Payment* or *ProductSpecification*. Next are classes only dependent on the prior implementations—*ProductCatalog* or *SalesLineItem*.

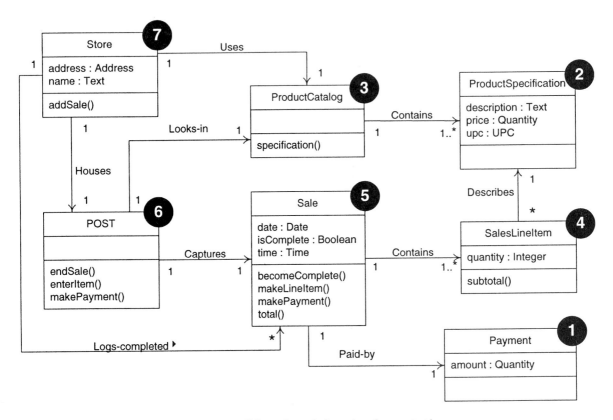

**Figure 23.11** Possible order of class implementation

# 23.11 Summary of Mapping Designs to Code

The translation process from design-oriented class diagrams to class definitions, and from collaboration diagrams to methods is relatively straightforward. There is still lots of room for decision making, design changes and exploration during the programming phase, but the overall architecture and major decisions have ideally been completed prior to the coding phase.

# PROGRAM SOLUTION IN JAVA

## 24.1    Introduction to the Program Solution

This chapter presents sample domain object layer program solution in Java to development cycle one of the point-of-sale application. The code generation is largely derived from the design class diagrams and collaboration diagrams defined in the design phase, based on the principles of mapping designs to code as explored in the previous chapter.

> The main point of this listing is that there is a relatively straightforward translation from design artifacts to a foundation of code. The code defines a simple test case; it is not meant to illustrate a robust, fully developed Java program with synchronization, exception handling, and so on.

### Class Payment

```
package post;

public class Payment
{
private float amount;

public Payment( float cashTendered )
{
   this.amount = cashTendered;
}
public float getAmount() { return amount; }
}
```

### Class ProductCatalog

```
package post;
```

```java
import java.util.*;

public class ProductCatalog
{
private Hashtable productSpecifications
   = new Hashtable();

public ProductCatalog()
{
   ProductSpecification ps =
       new ProductSpecification( 100, 1, "product 1" );
   productSpecifications.put( new Integer( 100 ), ps );
   ps = new ProductSpecification(200,1,"product 2");
   productSpecifications.put( new Integer( 200 ), ps );
}

public ProductSpecification getSpecification
   ( int upc )
{
   return (ProductSpecification)
       productSpecifications.get( new Integer( upc ) );
}
}
```

## Class POST

```java
package post;
import java.util.*;

class POST
{
private ProductCatalog productCatalog;
private Sale sale;

public POST( ProductCatalog catalog )
{
   productCatalog = catalog;
}

public void endSale()
{
   sale.becomeComplete();
}

public void enterItem( int upc, int quantity )
{
   if( isNewSale() )
   {
       sale = new Sale();
   }
   ProductSpecification spec =
```

```
        productCatalog.specification( upc );
   sale.makeLineItem( spec, quantity );
}

public void makePayment( float cashTendered )
{
   sale.makePayment( cashTendered );
}

private boolean isNewSale()
{
   return ( sale == null ) || ( sale.isComplete() );
}
}
```

## Class ProductSpecification

```
package post;

public class ProductSpecification
{
private int    upc         = 0;
private float  price       = 0;
private String description = "";

public ProductSpecification
   ( int upc, float price, String description )
   {
       this.upc         = upc;
       this.price       = price;
       this.description = description;
   }

public int getUPC() { return upc;}

public float getPrice() { return price; }

public String getDescription() { return description; }
}
```

## Class Sale

```
package post;
import java.util.*;

class Sale
{
private Vector lineItems = new Vector();
private Date date = new Date();
private boolean isComplete = false;
```

```
private Payment payment;

public float getBalance()
   {
       return payment.getAmount() - total();
   }

public void becomeComplete() { isComplete = true; }

public boolean isComplete() { return isComplete; }

public void makeLineItem
   ( ProductSpecification spec, int quantity )
   {
       lineItems.addElement(
           new SaleLineItem( spec, quantity ) );
   }

public float total()
   {
       float total = 0;
       Enumeratione = lineItems.elements();
       while( e.hasMoreElements() )
           {
           total += ( (SaleLineItem)
               e.nextElement() ).subtotal();
       }
   return total;
   }

public void makePayment( float cashTendered )
   {
       payment = new Payment( cashTendered );
   }
}
```

## Class SaleLineItem

```
package post;

class SaleLineItem
{
private intquantity;
privateProductSpecificationproductSpec;

public SaleLineItem
   (ProductSpecification spec, int quantity )
{
   this.productSpec = spec;
   this.quantity = quantity;
}
```

```java
public float subtotal()
{
  return quantity * productSpec.getPrice();
}
}
```

## Class Store

```java
package post;

class Store
{
private ProductCatalog productCatalog
  = new ProductCatalog();
private POST post = new POST( productCatalog );

public POST getPOST() { return post; }
}
```

# PART V ANALYZE PHASE (2)

# CHOOSING DEVELOPMENT CYCLE 2 REQUIREMENTS

## 25.1 Development Cycle Two Requirements

In the second development cycle of the point-of-sale application we revisit the *Buy Items* and *Start Up* use cases, but add more functionality to them, so that they approach the final complete use case. It is common to take the same use case repeatedly over several development cycles and extend it to ultimately handle all the functionality required.

The first cycle made many simplifications so that the problem was not overly complex. Once again—for the same reason—a relatively small amount of additional functionality will be considered.

> The additional functionality is that cash, credit, and check payments will be supported.

In a development project this would not be the undisputed choice of additional functionality for cycle two—another possibility is automatic updating of inventory, or a completely different use case. However, this choice is rich with valuable learning opportunities.

## 25.2 Assumptions and Simplifications

The following assumptions and simplifications are made for the two use cases under consideration.

**Buy Items**

No inventory maintenance.

It is a stand-alone store, not part of a larger organization.

Manual entry of UPCs; no bar code reader.

No tax calculations.

No coupons.

No special pricing policies.

Cashier does not have to log in.

There is no record maintained of the individual customers and their buying habits.

There is no control of the cash drawer.

Name and address of store and date and time of sale, are shown on the receipt.

Cashier ID and POST ID are not shown on receipt.

All completed sales are recorded in an historical log.

Only one payment, of one type, is used for a sale.

All payments are made in full; no partial or installment payments.


**Buy Items**

Check and credit payments are authorized.

A different credit authorization service is used for each credit type (Visa, MasterCard, and so on.).

The same check authorization service is used for all checks.

The point-of-sale terminal is responsible for communicating with the credit authorization service; the credit card reader is a dumb device that only sends the card information to the terminal.

Communication with an external service is via a modem. A phone number must be dialed each time.

Credit authorization services are usually provided by a bank.

Check and credit payments are for the exact amount of the sale total.

**Start up**     Assume date and time are correct.

Minimal initialization required to support the *Buying Items* use case.

No initializing information is stored in a database.

# RELATING MULTIPLE USE CASES

## 26.1 Introduction

The processes related to the different forms of payment in the point-of-sale application may be expressed as separate use cases, and related to others.

The goal is to create an updated use case diagram which shows these additional use cases, and their relationship.

The UML has special notation for illustrating use case relationships; this chapter explores it and illustrates a new use case diagram for the system.

## 26.2 When to Create Separate Use Cases

In the previous use case exploration, the different payment processes were written in subsections of the *Buy Items* use case. Alternatively, they could have been split into separate use cases. When should a major step or branching activity in a use case be written as a subsection branch versus a discrete use case?

Write major steps or branching activities of a use case as separate use cases when:

■ They are duplicated in other use cases.

■ They are complex and long, and separating them helps factor the use cases into manageable comprehensible units.

In the point-of-sale application, the different payment methods are branching activities that may additionally be present in other use cases such as *Exchange Items* or *Contribute to a Lay-away Plan*. Therefore, it is justifiable to treat them as separate use cases and named as follows:

■ *Pay by Cash, Pay by Credit, Pay by Check*

## 26.3    Use Case Diagrams with *uses* Relationships

If one use case initiates or includes the behavior of another use case, it is said to *use* the second use case and they are said to be in a *uses* relationship

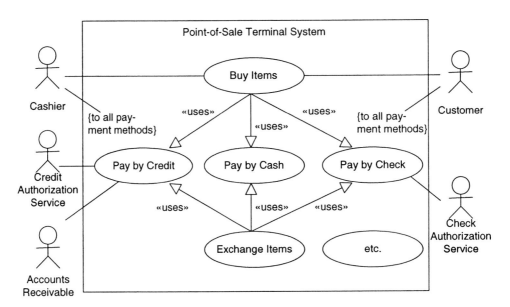

**Figure 26.1** Relating use cases with a *uses* relationship.

## 26.3.1  Example

For example, suppose that the different payment processes in the *Buy Items* process are described in the separate use cases *Pay by Cash*, *Pay By Credit* and *Pay by Check*. The *Buy Items* use case will initiate one of these others, and therefore is in a *uses* relationship to them.

In the UML the *uses* relationship is illustrated (as shown in Figure 26.1) with a generalization line (a solid line with a hollow arrow) adorned with a «uses» label.

# 26.4  Use Case Documents with *uses* Relationships

When use cases are in a *uses* relationship, the use case documents need to express the association in prose. The use case that uses the behavior of another should indicate the connection with the *initiate* keyword in the use case text, as follows:

**Use Case: Buy Items**

...

Customer chooses payment method:

a. If cash payment, **initiate** *Pay by Cash*.

b. If credit payment, **initiate** *Pay by Credit*.

c. If check payment, **initiate** *Pay by Check*.

...

## 26.4.1  Example

For example, if the different payment processes in the *Buy Items* process are described in the separate use cases *Pay by Cash*, *Pay By Credit* and *Pay by Check*, then the *Buy Items* use case will initiate one of these others, and therefore is in a *uses* relationship to them.

With this approach, the payment methods are no longer expressed in subsections of the *Buy Items* use case, they are separate use cases. Note that an additional *Related Use Cases* section may be added that summarizes related use cases—helpful if the use case is large and it is not obvious what others are involved.

## 26.4.2   Buying Items

| | |
|---|---|
| Use case: | **Buy Items** |
| Actors: | Customer (initiator), Cashier |
| Overview: | A Customer arrives at a checkout with items to purchase. The Cashier records the purchase items and collects a payment. On completion, the Customer leaves with the items. |

**Typical Course of Events**

| Actor Action | System Response |
|---|---|
| 1. This use case begins when a Customer arrives at the POST checkout with items to purchase. | |
| 2. The Cashier records each item.<br><br>If there is more than one of the same item, the Cashier can enter the quantity as well. | 3. Determines the item price and adds the item information to the running sales transaction.<br><br>The description and price of the current item are displayed. |
| 4. On completion of item entry, the Cashier indicates to the POST that the sale is complete. | 5. Calculates and displays the sale total. |
| 6. The Cashier tells the Customer the total. | |
| 7. **Customer chooses payment type:**<br><br>a. **If cash payment, initiate** *Pay by Cash.*<br><br>b. **If credit payment, initiate** *Pay by Credit.*<br><br>c. **If check payment, initiate** *Pay by Check.* | |
| | 8. Logs the completed sale. |
| | 9. Prints a receipt. |

**Typical Course of Events**

| Actor Action | System Response |
|---|---|
| **10.** The Cashier gives the receipt to the Customer. | |
| **11.** The Customer leaves with the items purchased. | |

**Alternative Courses**

- Section 2: Invalid item identifier entered. Display error.

- Section 7: Customer could not pay. Cancel sales transaction.

**Related Use Cases**

- uses *Pay by Cash*

- uses *Pay by Credit*

- uses *Pay by Check*

## 26.4.3   Pay by Cash

| | |
|---|---|
| Use case: | **Pay by Cash** |
| Actors: | Customer (initiator), Cashier |
| Overview: | A Customer pays for a sale by cash at a point-of-sale terminal. |

**Typical Course of Events**

| Actor Action | System Response |
|---|---|
| **1.** This use case begins when a Customer chooses to pay by cash, after being informed of the sale total. | |
| **2.** The Customer gives a cash payment—the "cash tendered"—possibly greater than the sale total. | |

**Typical Course of Events**

| Actor Action | System Response |
|---|---|
| **3.** The Cashier records the cash tendered. | **4.** Shows the balance due back to the Customer. |
| **5.** The Cashier deposits the cash received and extracts the balance owing. | |
| The Cashier gives the balance owing to the Customer. | |

**Alternative Courses**

- Section 2: Customer does not have sufficient cash. May cancel sale or initiate another payment method.

- Section 3: Cash drawer does not contain sufficient cash to pay balance. Cashier requests additional cash from supervisor or asks Customer for different payment method.

## 26.4.4  Pay by Credit

| | |
|---|---|
| Use case: | Pay by Credit—essential form |
| Actors: | Customer (initiator), Cashier, Credit Authorization Service, Accounts Receivable |
| Overview: | A Customer pays for a sale by credit at a point-of-sale terminal. The payment is validated by an external credit authorization service, and is posted to an accounts receivable system. |

**Typical Course of Events**

| Actor Action | System Response |
|---|---|
| 1. This use case begins when a Customer chooses to pay by credit, after being informed of the sale total. | |
| 2. The Customer communicates their credit information for the credit payment. | 3. Generates a credit payment request and sends it to an external Credit Authorization Service. |
| 4. Credit Authorization Service authorizes the payment. | 5. Receives a credit approval reply from the Credit Authorization Service (CAS). |
| | 6. Posts (records) the credit payment and approval reply information to the Accounts Receivable system. (The CAS owes money to the Store, hence A/R must track it.) |
| | 7. Displays authorization success message. |

**Alternative Courses**

■ Section 4: Credit request denied by Credit Authorization Service. Suggest different payment method.

## 26.4.5  Pay by Check

| | |
|---|---|
| Use case: | Pay by Check—essential form |
| Actors: | Customer (initiator), Cashier, Check Authorization Service |
| Overview: | A Customer pays for a sale by check at a point-of-sale terminal. The payment is validated by an external check authorization service. |

**Typical Course of Events**

| Actor Action | System Response |
|---|---|
| 1. This use case begins when a Customer chooses to pay by check, after being informed of the sale total. | |
| 2. The Customer writes a check and identifies self. | |
| 3. Cashier records identification information and requests check payment authorization. | 4. Generates a check payment request and sends it to an external Check Authorization Service. |
| 5. Check Authorization Service authorizes the payment. | 6. Receives a check approval reply from the Check Authorization Service. |
| | 7. Displays authorization success message. |

**Alternative Courses**

■ Section 5: Check request denied by Check Authorization Service. Suggest different payment method.

# EXTENDING THE CONCEPTUAL MODEL

## Objectives

- Identify new concepts for the second development cycle.

## 27.1 New Concepts in the Point-of-Sale System

As in development cycle one, the conceptual model may be incrementally developed by considering the current use cases for this cycle. First go through the *Concept Category List*, and then apply noun phrase identification from the use cases (with the usual admonition that the latter method requires caution and judgment). As discussed in earlier chapters, a very effective approach to developing a robust and rich conceptual model is to study the work of other authors on this subject, especially those that use a case study approach, such as [Fowler96]. The myriad subtle modeling issues they explore are beyond the scope of this work.

Our basic strategies will not result in the most useful conceptual model. In this chapter we generate a draft model, simply identifying initial concepts. The subsequent chapters fill in details in terms of other concepts, attributes and associations in order to develop a better model.

### 27.1.1 Concepts Category List

The following table only shows new concepts in the point-of-sale system problem.

| Category | Examples |
|---|---|
| physical or tangible objects | *CreditCard, Check* |
| specifications, designs or descriptions of things | |
| places | |
| transactions | *CashPayment, CreditPayment, CheckPayment* |
| transaction line items | |
| roles of people | |
| containers of other things | |
| things in a container | |
| other computer or electro-mechanical systems external to our system | *CreditAuthorizationService, CheckAuthorizationService* |
| abstract noun concepts | |
| organizations | *CreditAuthorizationService, CheckAuthorizationService* |
| events | |
| rules and policies | |
| catalogs | |
| records of finance, work, contracts, legal matters | *AccountsReceivable* |
| financial instruments and services | |
| manuals, books | |

## 27.1.2 Noun Phrase Identification from the Use Cases

To reiterate, noun phrase identification cannot be mechanically applied in order to identify relevant concepts to include in a conceptual model. Judgement must be applied and suitable abstractions developed, since natural language is ambiguous and relevant concepts are not always explicit or clear in existing text. However, it is a practical technique in conceptual modeling since it is very straightforward.

Ideally, use the *real* use cases—rather than the essential use cases—for concept identification, because the real use cases contain more concrete and detailed specifications.

## Pay by Cash

No new concepts, since it was treated in iteration one. However, the name of the payment may be refined as *CashPayment*.

## Pay by Credit

1. This use case begins when a Customer chooses to pay by credit, after being informed of the sale total.

2. The Customer swipes their **credit card** through a card reader in order to complete the **credit payment**.

3. Generates a **credit payment request** and sends it to an external **Credit Authorization Service** via a modem attached to the POST. Requires dialing the service, sending out a request record, and waiting for a reply record.

4. Receives a **credit approval reply** from the Credit Authorization Service (CAS). The reply is encoded in a reply record and received via the modem.

5. Posts (records) the credit payment and approval reply information to the **Accounts Receivable** system. (The CAS owes money to the Store, hence A/R must track it.)

6. Displays authorization success message.

## Pay by Check

1. This use case begins when a Customer chooses to pay by check, after being informed of the sale total.

2. The Customer writes a **check**, and gives it and their **drivers license** to the Cashier.

3. Cashier writes the **drivers license number** on the check, types it into the *DL Number* text field on the window and presses the *Check Authorization* button to requests check payment authorization.

4. Generates a **check payment request** and sends it to an external **Check Authorization Service** via a **modem** attached to the POST. Requires dialing the service, sending out a request record, and waiting for a reply record.

5. Receives a **check approval reply** from the Check Authorization Service. The reply is encoded in a reply record and received via the modem.

6. Displays authorization success message.

## 27.1.3 Authorization Service Transactions

Noun phrase identification in the use cases reveals concepts such as *CreditPaymentRequest* and *CreditApprovalReply*. These may in fact be viewed as kinds of transactions with external services, and in general it is useful to identify such transactions because activity and processes tend to revolve around them.

These transactions do not have to represent computer records or bits travelling over a line. They represent the abstraction of the transaction independent of its means of execution. For example, a credit payment request may be executed by people talking on the phone, by two computers sending records or messages to each other, and so on.

## 27.1.4 POST Conceptual Model—Draft One

Based on concept identification using the checklist and noun identification, the early draft conceptual model is shown in Figure 27.1. It is not as useful or complete as desirable, so we will explore additional modeling issues in subsequent chapters.

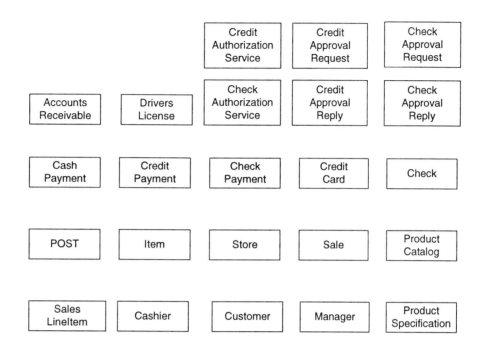

**Figure 27.1** Draft conceptual model for point-of-sale terminal domain.

# GENERALIZATION

## 28.1    Generalization

The concepts *CashPayment*, *CreditPayment,* and *CheckPayment* are all very similar. In this situation, it is possible (and useful[1]) to organize them (as in Figure 28.1) into a **generalization-specialization type hierarchy** (or simply **type hierarchy**) in which the **supertype** *Payment* represents a more general concept, and the **subtypes** more specialized ones.

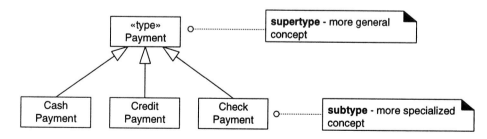

**Figure 28.1**  Generalization-specialization hierarchy.

---

1. Later in the chapter we investigate reasons to define type hierarchies.

**Generalization** is the activity of identifying commonality among concepts and defining supertype (general concept) and subtype (specialized concept) relationships. It is a way to construct taxonomic classifications among concepts which are then illustrated in type hierarchies.

Identifying super and subtypes is of value in a conceptual model because their presence allows us to understand concepts in more general, refined and abstract terms. It leads to economy of expression, improved comprehension and a reduction in repeated information. And although we are focusing now on a conceptual model and not a software implementation, the later implementation of super and subtypes as classes that use inheritance yields better software.

Thus:

> Identify domain supertypes and subtypes relevant to the current investigation, and illustrate them in the conceptual model.

## 28.1.1 UML Notation

In the UML, the generalization relationship between elements is indicated with a large hollow triangle pointing to the more general element from the more specialized one. Either a separate target or shared target arrow style may be used.

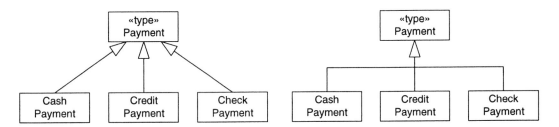

**Figure 28.2** Type hierarchy with separate and shared arrow notations.

## 28.2 Defining Super and Subtypes

Since it is valuable to identify super and subtypes, it is useful to very clearly and precisely understand generalization, supertypes and subtypes in terms of type definition and type sets[1]. This following sections explore these.

---

1. That is, a type's intension and extension. This discussion was inspired by [MO95].

## 28.2.1 Generalization and Type Definition

What is the relationship of a supertype to subtype?

> A supertype definition is more general or encompassing than a subtype definition.

For example, consider the supertype *Payment* and its subtypes (*CashPayment*, and so on). Assume the definition of *Payment* is that it represents the transaction of transferring money (not necessarily cash) for a purchase from one party to another, and that all payments have an amount of money transferred. The model corresponding to this is shown in Figure 28.3.

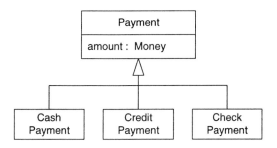

**Figure 28.3** Payment type hierarchy.

A *CreditPayment* is a transfer of money via a credit institution which needs to be authorized. My definition of *Payment* encompasses and is more general than my definition of *CreditPayment*.

## 28.2.2 Generalization and Type Sets

Subtypes and supertypes are related in terms of set membership.

> All the members of a subtype set are members of their supertype set.

For example, in terms of set membership, all instances of the set of *CreditPayment* are also members of the set of *Payment*. In a Venn diagram, this is shown as in Figure 28.4.

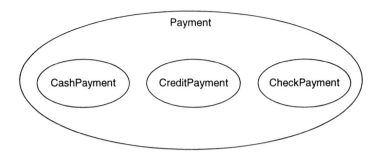

**Figure 28.4** Venn diagram of set relationships.

## 28.2.3 Subtype Definition Conformance

When a type hierarchy is created, statements about supertypes that apply to subtypes are made. For example, Figure 28.5 states that all *Payments* have an *amount* and are associated with a *Sale*.

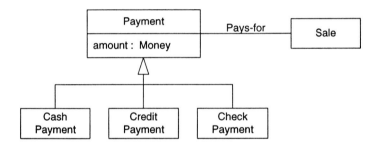

**Figure 28.5** Subtype conformance.

All *Payment* subtypes must conform to having an amount and paying for a *Sale*. In general, this rule of conformance to a supertype definition is the *100% Rule*:

---

### 100% Rule

100% of the supertype's definition should be applicable to the subtype. The subtype must conform to 100% of the supertype's:

- attributes
- associations

---

## 28.2.4  Subtype Set Conformance

A subtype should be a member of the set of the supertype. *CreditPayment* should be a member of the set of *Payments*.

Informally, this expresses the notion that the subtype *is a kind of* supertype. *CreditPayment is a kind of Payment*. More tersely, *is-a-kind-of* is called *is-a*.

This kind of conformance is the *Is-a Rule*:

---

**Is-a Rule**

All the members of a subtype set must be members of their supertype set.

In natural language this can usually be informally tested by forming the statement

*Subtype **is a** Supertype*

---

For instance, the statement *CreditPayment is a Payment* makes sense, and conveys the notion of set membership conformance.

## 28.2.5  What is a Correct Subtype?

From the above discussion, apply the following tests[1] to define a correct subtype when constructing a conceptual model:

---

A potential subtype should conform to the:

■  100% Rule (definition conformance)

■  Is-a Rule (set membership conformance)

---

# 28.3  When to Define a Subtype

Rules to ensure that a subtype is correct have been examined (the 100% and Is-a Rules). However, *when* should we even bother to define a subtype? First, a definition: A **type partition** is a division of a type into disjoint subtypes [MO95].

---

1. These rule names have been chosen for their mnemonic support rather than precision.

> The question may be restated as, "when is it useful to show a type partition?"

For example, in the point-of-sale domain, *Customer* may be correctly partitioned (or subtyped) into *MaleCustomer* and *FemaleCustomer*. But is it relevant or useful to show this in our model (Figure 28.6)?

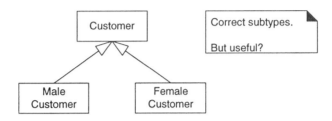

**Figure 28.6** Legal type partition, but is it useful in our domain?

This partition is not useful for our domain; the next section explains why.

## 28.3.1  Motivations to Partition a Type into Subtypes

The following are strong motivations to partition a type into subtypes.

> Create a subtype of a supertype when either:
> 1.  The subtype has additional attributes of interest.
> 2.  The subtype has additional associations of interest.
> 3.  The subtype concept is operated upon, handled, reacted to or manipulated differently than the supertype or other subtypes, in ways that are of interest.
> 4.  The subtype concept represents an animate thing (for example, animal, robot) that behaves differently than the supertype or other subtypes, in ways that are of interest.

Based on the above criteria, it is not compelling to partition *Customer* into *Male-Customer* and *FemaleCustomer* because they have no additional attributes or associations, are not operated upon (treated) differently, and do not behave differently in ways that are of interest[1].

---

1.  Men and women do exhibit different shopping habits. However, these are not relevant to our current use case requirements—the criterion that bounds our investigation.

Here are some examples of type partitions from the domain of payments and other areas, using these criteria:

| Subtype Motivation | Examples |
|---|---|
| The subtype has additional attributes of interest. | Payments—not applicable.<br><br>Library—*Book*, subtype of *LoanableResource*, has an *ISBN* attribute. |
| The subtype has additional associations of interest. | Payments—*CreditPayment*, subtype of *Payment*, is associated with a *CreditCard*.<br><br>Library—*Video*, subtype of *LoanableResource*, is associated with *Director*. |
| The subtype concept is operated upon, handled, reacted to, or manipulated differently than the supertype or other subtypes, in ways that are of interest. | Payments—*CreditPayment*, subtype of *Payment*, is handled differently than other kinds of payments in how it is authorized.<br><br>Library—*Software*, subtype of *LoanableResource*, requires a deposit before it may be loaned. |
| The subtype concept represents an animate thing (for example, animal, robot) that behaves differently than the supertype or other subtypes, in ways that are of interest. | Payments—not applicable.<br><br>Library—not applicable.<br><br>Market Research—*MaleHuman*, subtype of *Human*, behaves differently than *FemaleHuman* with respect to shopping habits. |

# 28.4 When to Define a Supertype

Generalization into a common supertype is usually motivated when commonality is identified among potential subtypes.

The following are motivations to generalize and define a supertype.

---

Create a supertype in a generalization relationship to subtypes when:

- The potential subtypes represent variations on a similar concept.

- The subtypes will conform to the 100% and Is-a rules.

- All subtypes have the same attribute which can be factored out and expressed in the supertype.

- All subtypes have the same association which can be factored out and related to the supertype.

---

The following sections illustrate these points.

# 28.5 Point-of-Sale Type Hierarchies

## 28.5.1 Payment Types

Based on the above criteria for partitioning the *Payment* type, it is useful to create a type hierarchy of various kinds of payments. The motivation for the supertype and subtypes is shown in Figure 28.7.

## 28.5.2 Authorization Service Types

Credit and check authorization services are variations on a similar concept, and have common attributes of interest. This leads to the type hierarchy in Figure 28.8.

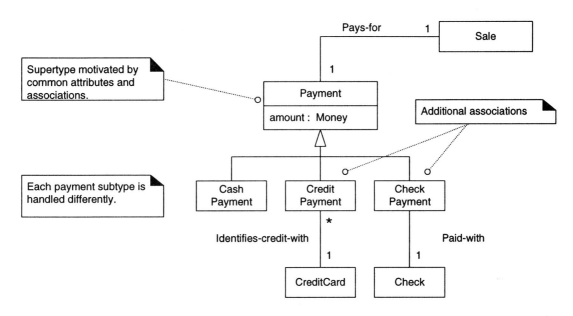

**Figure 28.7** Justifying *Payment* subtypes.

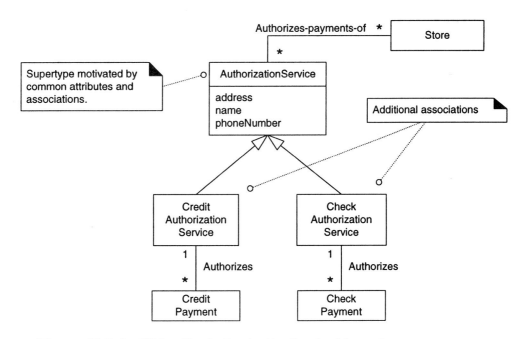

**Figure 28.8** Justifying the AuthorizationService hierarchy.

## 28.5.3   Authorization Transaction Types

Modeling the various kinds of authorization service transactions (requests and replies) presents an interesting case. In general, transactions with external services are useful to show in a conceptual model because activity and processes tend to revolve around them. They are important concepts.

Should the modeler illustrate *every* variation of external service transaction? It depends. As mentioned, conceptual models are not necessarily correct or wrong, but rather more or less useful. It is useful, because each transaction type is related to differently concepts, processes, and business rules.[1]

A second interesting question is the degree of generalization that is useful to show in the model. For arguments sake, let us assume that every transaction has a date and time. These common attributes, plus the desire to create an ultimate generalization for this family of related concepts, justifies the creation of *PaymentAuthorizationTransaction*.

But is it useful to generalize a reply into a *CreditPaymentAuthorizationReply* and *CheckPaymentAuthorizationReply*, as shown in Figure 28.9, or is it sufficient to show less generalization, as depicted in Figure 28.10?

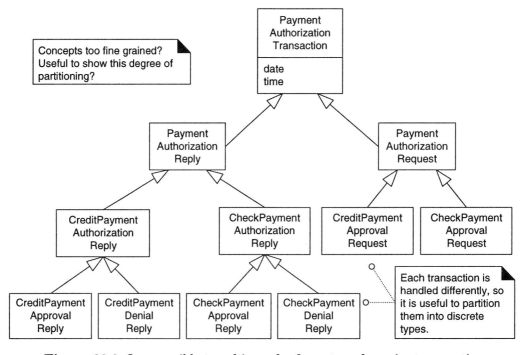

**Figure 28.9** One possible type hierarchy for external service transactions.

---

1. In telecommunications conceptual models, it is similarly useful to identify each kind of exchange or switch message.

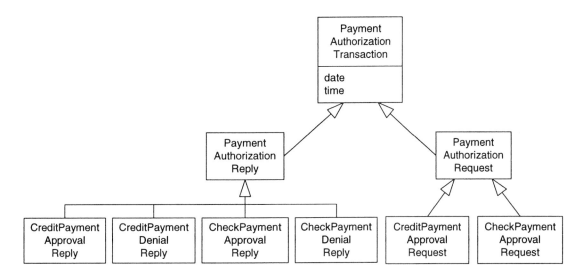

**Figure 28.10** An alternate transaction type hierarchy.

The type hierarchy shown in Figure 28.10 is sufficiently useful in terms of generalization, because the additional generalizations do not add obvious value. The hierarchy of Figure 28.9 expresses a finer granularity of generalization that does not significantly enhance our understanding of the concepts and business rules, but it does make the model more complex—and added complexity is undesirable unless it confers others benefits.

# 28.6    Abstract Types

This section defines the term abstract type. It is useful to identify abstract types in a conceptual model because they constrain what types it is possible to have concrete instances of, thus clarifying the rules of the problem domain.

> If every member of a type T must also be a member of a subtype, then type T is called an **abstract type**.

For example, assume that every *Payment* instance must more specifically be an instance of the subtype *CreditPayment, CashPayment,* or *CheckPayment*. This is illustrated in the Venn diagram Figure 28.11 (b). Since every *Payment* member is also a member of a subtype, *Payment* is an abstract type by definition.

In contrast, if there can exist *Payment* instances which are not members of a subtype, it is not an abstract type, as illustrated in Figure 28.11 (a).

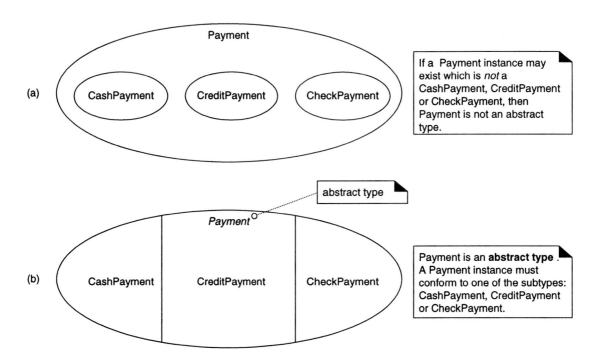

**Figure 28.11** Abstract types.

In the point-of-sale domain, every *Payment* is really a member of a subtype. Figure 28.11 (b) is the correct depiction of payments, and therefore *Payment* is an abstract type.

## 28.6.1 Abstract Type Notation in the UML

UML provides a notation to indicate abstract types—the type name is italicized.

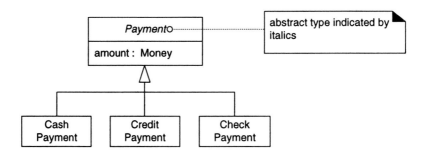

Identify abstract types and illustrate them with an italicized name in the conceptual model.

### 28.6.2   Abstract Classes and Methods

If an abstract type is implemented in software as a class during the design phase, it will usually be represented by an **abstract class**, meaning that no instances may be created for the class. An **abstract method** is one that is declared in an abstract class, but not implemented; in the UML it is also notated with italics.

# 28.7   Modeling Changing States

Assume that a payment can either be in an unauthorized or authorized state, and it is meaningful to show this in the conceptual model (it may not really be, but assume so for discussion). As shown in Figure 28.12, one approach to modeling this is to define subtypes of *Payment*: *UnauthorizedPayment* and *Authorized-Payment*. However, note that a payment does not stay in one of these states; it typically transitions from unauthorized to authorized. This leads to the following guideline:

---

Do not model the states of a concept X as subtypes of X. Rather:

1.  Define a state hierarchy and associate the states with X, or

2.  Ignore showing the states of a concept in the conceptual model; show the states in state diagrams instead.

---

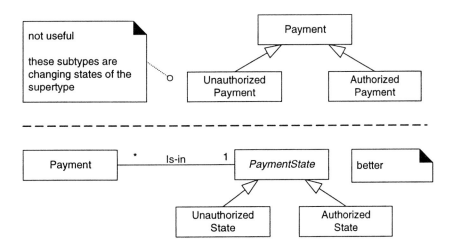

**Figure 28.12** Modeling changing states.

# 28.8    Class Hierarchies and Inheritance

This deliberation of type hierarchies has not mentioned *inheritance*, because the discussion is focused on a conceptual model of things in the world, not of software artifacts. A class is a software implementation of a concept or type, and in an object-oriented programming language a subclass **inherits** the attribute and operation definitions of its superclasses by the creation of **class hierarchies**. **Inheritance** is a software mechanism to implement subtype conformance to supertype definitions. Therefore inheritance has no real part to play in the discussion of a conceptual model, although it most definitely does when we transition to the design phase.

The type hierarchies generate here may or may not be reflected in our solution. For example, the hierarchy of authorization service transaction types may be collapsed or expanded into alternate software class hierarchies, depending upon language features and other factors. For instance, C++ templatized classes could be used to reduce the number of classes.

# PACKAGES: ORGANIZING ELEMENTS

---

### Objectives

■ Organize elements into packages.

---

## 29.1    Introduction

The conceptual model for development cycle two of the point-of-sale application is approaching an unwieldy size; it illustrates the need to partition model elements into smaller subsets.

The benefit of organizing elements into packages is that it chunks detailed elements into larger abstractions—supporting a higher-level view and viewing a model in simple groupings.

In this chapter we examine the use of packages to partition the conceptual model.

### 29.1.1   Layers and Partitions

As discussed earlier, the overall system architecture may be viewed as composed of vertical layers and horizontal partitions. The packages of the conceptual model, if carried through to design, may be considered *partitions* of the domain objects layer.

## 29.2    UML Package Notation

Graphically, a package is shown as a tabbed folder (Figure 29.1). Subordinate packages may be shown within it. The package name is within the tab if the package depicts its elements, otherwise it is centered within the folder itself.

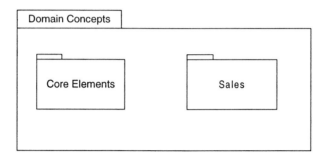

**Figure 29.1**  A UML package.

### 29.2.1    Ownership and References

An element, such as a type or class, is *owned* by the package within which it is defined, but may be *referenced* in other packages. In that case the element name is qualified by the package name using the pathname format *PackageName::ElementName* (see Figure 29.2). A type or class shown in a foreign package may be modified with new associations, but must otherwise remain unchanged.

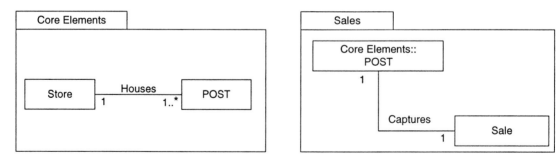

**Figure 29.2**  A referenced type in a package.

### 29.2.2    Package Dependencies

If a model element is in some way dependent on another, the dependency may be shown with a dependency relationship, depicted with an arrowed line. A package dependency indicates that elements of the dependent package in some way know about or are coupled to elements in the target package.

For example, if a package references an element owned by another, a dependency exists. Thus, the *Sales* package has a dependency on the *Core Elements* package (Figure 29.3).

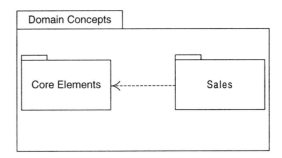

**Figure 29.3** A package dependency.

### 29.2.3 *Package Indication without Package Diagram*

At times it is inconvenient to draw a package diagram, but still desirable to indicate the package that the elements are a member of.

In this situation, include a constraint note (dog-eared note) on the diagram, as illustrated in Figure 29.4.

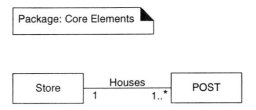

**Figure 29.4** Illustrating package ownership with a constraint.

## 29.3   How to Partition the Conceptual Model

This section emphasizes partitioning the conceptual model; while Chapter 22 discusses organizing the software architecture into packages.

How should the types in a conceptual model be organized within packages?

Apply the following general guidelines:

> To partition the conceptual model into packages, place elements together that:
>
> ■ are in the same subject area—closely related by concept or purpose
>
> ■ are in a type hierarchy together
>
> ■ participate in the same use cases
>
> ■ are strongly associated.

It is useful that all elements related to the conceptual model be rooted in a package called *Domain Concepts*, and that widely shared, common, core concepts be defined in a packaged named something like *Core Elements* or *Common Concepts*, in the absence of any other meaningful package within which to place them.

## 29.4    Point-of-Sale Conceptual Model Packages

Based on the above criteria, the package organization for the point-of-sale domain is shown in Figure 29.5.

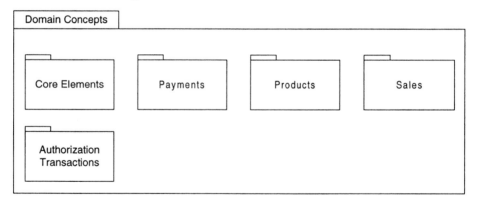

**Figure 29.5** Domain concept packages.

The package diagrams of Figure 29.6 and Figure 29.7 illustrate the ownership of individual types. In the next chapters the details of the associations and attributes will be examined.

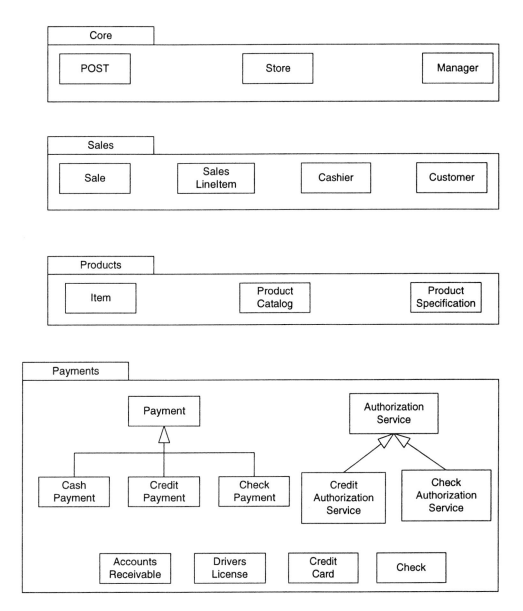

**Figure 29.6** Domain packages.

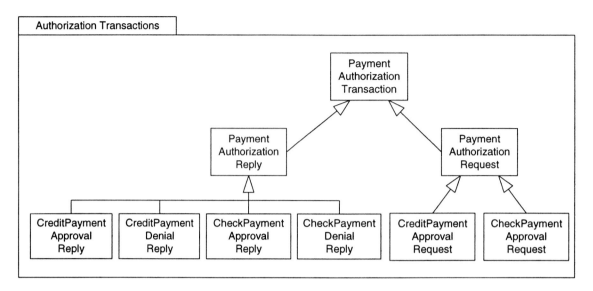

**Figure 29.7** More domain packages.

# POLISHING THE CONCEPTUAL MODEL

---

### Objectives

- Add associative types to the conceptual model.
- Add aggregation relationships.
- Choose how to model roles.

---

## 30.1 Introduction

This chapter explores additional useful ideas and notation available for conceptual modeling and applies them to refine aspects of the point-of-sale model. The subsequent chapter consolidates the results.

## 30.2 Associative Types

The following domain requirements set the stage for associative types:

- Authorization services assign a merchant ID to each store for identification during communications.

- A payment authorization request from the store to an authorization service requires the inclusion of the merchant ID that identifies the store to the service.

- Furthermore, a store has a different merchant ID for each service.

Where in the conceptual model should the merchant ID attribute reside?

Placing the *merchantID* in the *Store* is incorrect because a *Store* can have more than one value for *merchantID*. The same is true with placing it in the *AuthorizationService* (see Figure 30.1).

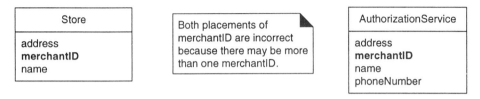

**Figure 30.1** Inappropriate use of an attribute.

This leads to the following modeling principle:

> In a conceptual model, if a type T can simultaneously have many values for the same kind of attribute A, do not place attribute A in T. Place attribute A in another type that is associated with T.
>
> For example:
>
> ■ A *Person* may have many phone numbers. Place phone number in another type, such as *PhoneNumber*, or *ContactInformation*, and associate many of these to *Person*.

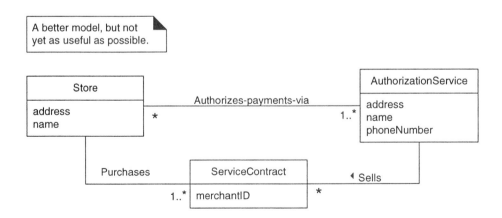

**Figure 30.2** First attempt at modeling the merchantID problem.

The above principle suggests that something like the model in Figure 30.2 is required. In the business world, what concept formally records the information related to the services that a service provides to a customer?—a *Contract* or *Account*.

The fact that both the *Store* and *AuthorizationService* are related to the *Service-Contract* is a clue that it is dependent on the relationship between the two. The *merchantID* may be thought of as an attribute related to the association between the *Store* and *AuthorizationService*.

This leads to the notion of an **associative type** in which we can add features to the assocation itself.

*ServiceContract* may be modeled as an associative type related to the association between *Store* and *AuthorizationService*.

In the UML, this is illustrated with a dashed line from the association to the associative type (Figure 30.3).

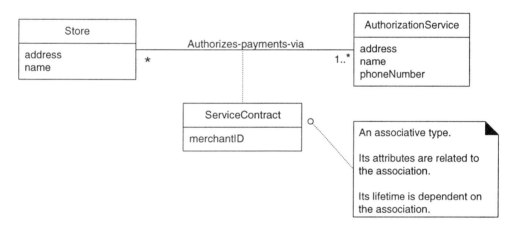

**Figure 30.3** An associative type.

Figure 30.3 visually communicates the idea that a *ServiceContract* and its attributes are related to the association between a *Store* and *AuthorizationService*, and that the lifetime of the *ServiceContract* is dependent on the relationship.

## 30.2.1 Guidelines

Guidelines for adding associative types include the following.

Clues that an associative type might be useful in a conceptual model:

- An attribute is related to an association.

- Instances of the associative type have a life-time dependency on the association.

- There is a many-to-many association between two concepts, and information associated with the assocation itself.

- Only one instance of the associative type exists between two objects participating in the association.

The presence of a many-to-many association is a common clue that a useful associative type is lurking in the background somewhere; when you see one, consider an associative type.

Here are some other examples of associative types:

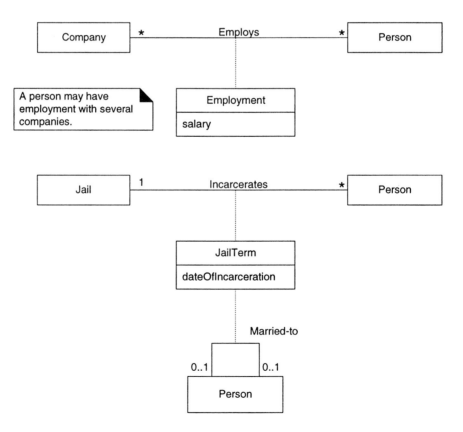

**Figure 30.4** Associative types.

# 30.3    Aggregation and Composition

**Aggregation** is a kind of association used to model whole-part relationships between things. The whole is generally called the **composite**, but the parts have no standard name—*part* or *component* is common.

For instance, physical assemblies are organized in aggregation relationships, such as a *Hand* aggregates *Fingers*.

## 30.3.1    Aggregation in the UML

Aggregation is shown in the UML with a hollow or filled diamond symbol at the composite end of a whole-part association (Figure 30.5).

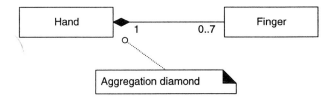

**Figure 30.5** Aggregation notation.

Aggregation is a property of an association role.[1]

The association name is often excluded in aggregation relationships since it is typically thought of as *Has-part*. However, one may be used to provide more semantic detail.

## 30.3.2    Composite Aggregation—Filled Diamond

**Composite aggregation** or **composition** means that the multiplicity at the composite end may be at most one, and is signified with a filled diamond. It implies that the composite solely owns the part, and that they are in a tree structure parts hierarchy; it is the most common form of aggregation shown in models.

For example, a finger is a part of at most one hand (we hope!), thus the aggregation diamond is filled to indicate composite aggregation (Figure 30.6).

---

1. Recall that each end of an association is a role, and that a role has various properties, such as multiplicity, name, navigability and isAggregate.

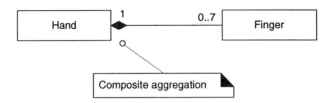

**Figure 30.6** Composite aggregation.

## 30.3.3 Shared Aggregation—Hollow Diamond

**Shared aggregation** means that the multiplicity at the composite end may be more than one, and is signified with a hollow diamond. It implies that the part may be in many composite instances. Shared aggregation seldom (if ever) exists in physical aggregates, but rather in nonphysical concepts.

For instance, a UML package may be considered to aggregate its elements. But an element may be referenced in more than one package (it is owned by one, and referenced in others), an example of shared aggregation (see Figure 30.7).

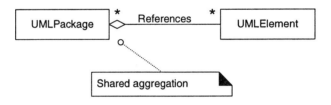

**Figure 30.7** Shared aggregation.

## 30.3.4 How to Identify Aggregation

In some cases the presence of aggregation is obvious—usually in physical assemblies. But sometimes it is not clear.

On aggregation: If in doubt, leave it out.

Here are some guidelines that suggest when to show aggregation:

> Consider showing aggregation when:
>
> - The lifetime of the part is bound within the lifetime of the composite—there is a create-delete dependency of the part on the whole.
>
> - There is an obvious whole-part physical or logical assembly.
>
> - Some properties of the composite propagate to the parts, such as its location.
>
> - Operations applied to the composite propagate to the parts, such as destruction, movement, recording.

Other than something being an obvious assembly of parts, the next most useful clue is the presence of a create-delete dependency of the part on the whole.

## 30.3.5 Benefit of Showing Aggregation

Identifying and illustrating aggregation is not profoundly important; it is quite feasible to exclude it from a conceptual model. Discover and show aggregation because it has the following benefits, most of which relate to the software solution phase rather than the conceptual modeling phase, which is why its exclusion from the conceptual model is not very significant.

- It clarifies the domain constraints regarding the eligible existence of the part independent of the whole. In composite aggregation, the part may not exist outside of the lifetime of the whole.

    - During the solution phase, this has an impact on the create-delete dependencies between the whole and part software classes.

- It assists in the identification of a creator (the composite) using the GRASP Creator pattern.

- Operations—such as copy or delete—applied to the whole should often propagate to the parts.

- Identifying a whole in relation to a part supports encapsulation. The GRASP Don't Talk to Strangers pattern is used to hide the parts within the whole.

## 30.3.6 Aggregation in the Point-of-Sale Model

In the point-of-sale domain, the *SalesLineItems* may be considered a part of a composite *Sale*; in general transaction line items are viewed as parts of an aggregate transaction (see Figure 30.8). In addition to conformance to that pattern, there is a create-delete dependency of the line items on the Sale—their life-time is bound within the lifetime of the Sale.

By similar justification, the *ProductCatalog* is an aggregate of *ProductSpecifica-tions.*

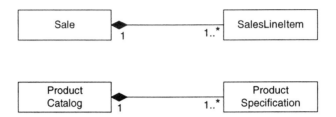

**Figure 30.8** Aggregation in the point-of-sale application.

No other relationship is a compelling combination that suggests whole-part semantics and a create-delete dependency, and "if in doubt, leave it out."

# 30.4   Association Role Names

Each end of an association is a role, which has various properties, such as:

■   name

■   multiplicity

A role name identifies an end of an association and ideally describes the role played by objects in the association.

Figure 30.9 shows role name examples.

An explicit role name is not required—it is useful when the role of the object is not clear. It usually starts with a lowercase letter. If not explicitly present, assume that the default role name is equal to the related type name, though starting with a lowercase letter.

As mentioned previously in Chapter 30, roles used in design class diagrams may be interpreted as the basis for an attribute name during code generation.

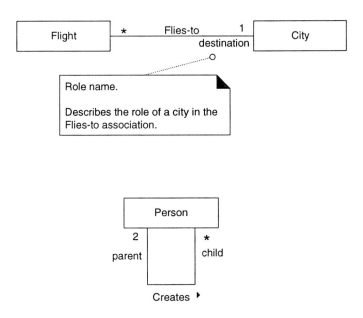

**Figure 30.9** Role names.

## 30.5 Roles As Concepts versus Roles in Associations

In a conceptual model a real-world role—especially a human role—may be modeled in a number of ways, such as a discrete concept, or expressed as a role in an association[1].

For example, the role of cashier and manager may be expressed in at least the two ways illustrated in Figure 30.10.

The first approach may be called "roles in associations;" the second "roles as concepts". Both approaches have advantages.

Roles in associations are appealing because they are a relatively accurate way to express the notion that the same instance of a person takes on multiple (and dynamically changing) roles in various associations. I, a person, simultaneously or in sequence may take on the role of teacher, object technologist, parent, and so on.

---

1. For simplicity, other excellent solutions such as those discussed in [Fowler96] are ignored.

On the other hand, roles as concepts provides ease and flexibility in adding unique attributes, associations and additional semantics. Furthermore, the implementation of roles as separate classes is easier because of limitations of current popular object-oriented programming languages—it is not convenient to dynamically mutate an instance of one class into another, or dynamically add behavior and attributes as the role of a person changes.[1]

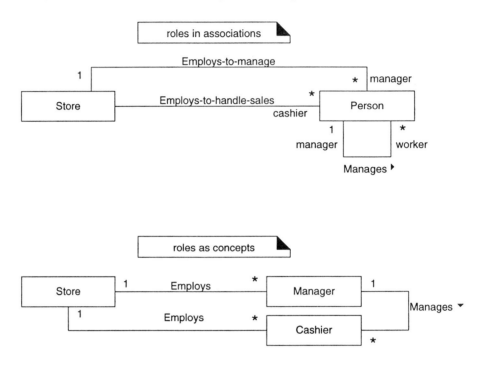

**Figure 30.10** Two ways to model human roles.

# 30.6    Derived Elements

A derived element can be determined from others. Attributes and associations are the most common derived elements.

For example, a *Sale total* can be derived from *SalesLineItem* and *ProductSpecification* information (Figure 30.11). In the UML it is shown with a "/" preceding the element name.

---

1. What is needed is a popular language that supports dynamically changing and multiple roles. Agent-based Java technology has a good chance of filling this need.

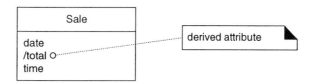

**Figure 30.11** Derived attribute.

When should derived elements be shown?

> Avoid showing derived elements in a diagram, since they add complexity without new information. However, add a derived element when it is prominent in the terminology of the domain, and excluding it impairs comprehension.

As another example, a *SalesLineItem quantity* is actually derivable from the number of instances of *Items* associated with the line item (Figure 30.12).

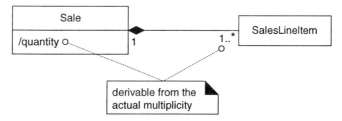

**Figure 30.12** Derived attribute related to multiplicity.

# 30.7    Qualified Associations

A **qualifier** may be used in an association; it distinguishes the set of objects at the far end of the association based upon the qualifier value. An association with a qualifier is a **qualified association**.

For example, *ProductSpecifications* may be distinguished in a *ProductCatalog* by their universal product code (UPC), as illustrated in Figure 30.13 (b). As contrasted in Figure 30.13 (a) versus (b), qualification reduces the multiplicity at the far end from the qualifier, usually down from many to one. Depicting a qualifier in a conceptual model communicates how, in the domain, things of one type are distinguished in relation to another type. They should not, in the conceptual model, be used to express design decisions about lookup keys, although that is suitable in later design diagrams.

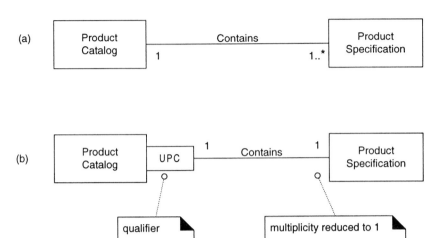

**Figure 30.13** Qualified association.

Qualifiers do not usually added compelling useful new information, and one can fall into the trap of "design-think." However, used judiciously, they can sharpen understanding about the domain. The qualified associations between *Product-Catalog* and *ProductSpecification* provides a reasonable example of a value-added qualifier.

# 30.8   Recursive or Reflexive Associations

A concept may have an association to itself; this is known as a **recursive association** or **reflexive association**[1].

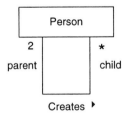

**Figure 30.14** Recursive association.

1. [MO95] constrains the definition of reflexive associations further.

# CONCEPTUAL MODEL— SUMMARY

---

### Objectives

■ Consolidate the previous conceptual modeling chapter information and illustrate the results in the point-of-sale model.

---

## 31.1    Introduction

This chapter consolidates and illustrates the ideas and UML notation introduced in the previous four chapters. The results are presented in a complete conceptual model for the second development cycle of the point-of-sale application.

A conceptual model is not strictly correct or wrong, but more or less useful. Consequently, there are decisions expressed in this model that can reasonably be disputed or changed; this is especially true of the choice of associations. However, this model provides a useful description of the concepts and their important relationships—certainly useful enough to form the basis for later investigation and solution phase work. Subsequent work will invariably expose flaws and omissions in the current model; this is to be expected. As improvements are found, the model is updated.

## 31.2    Domain Concepts Package

The motivation for top level domain package in Figure 31.1 was explored in Chapter 29. Package dependencies are not shown.

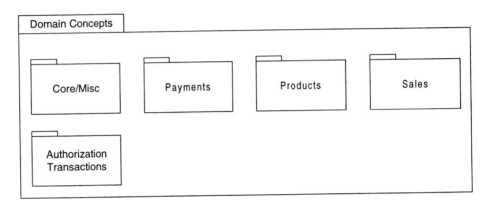

**Figure 31.1** Top domain concepts package.

## 31.3    Core/Misc Package

A Core/Misc package (Figure 31.2) is useful to own widely shared concepts or those without an obvious home. In later references, the package name will be abbreviated to *Core*.

There are no new concepts or associations particular to iteration two in this package.

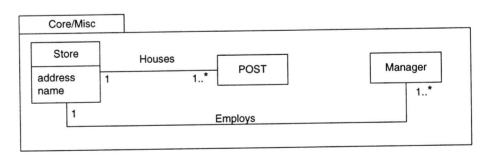

**Figure 31.2** Core package.

# 31.4   Payments

As in iteration one, new associations are primarily motivated by a need-to-know criterion. For example, there is a need to remember the relationship between a *CreditPayment* and a *CreditCard*. In contrast, some associations are added more for comprehension, such as *DriversLicense Identifies Customer* (see Figure 31.3)

Note that *PaymentAuthorizationReply* is expressed as an associative class. A reply arises out of the association between a payment and its authorization service.

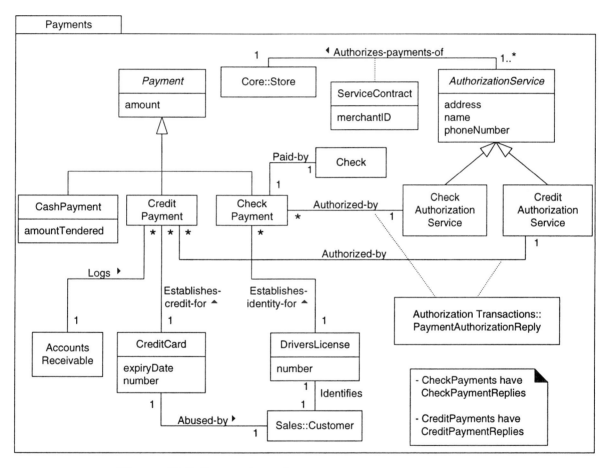

**Figure 31.3** Payments package.

# 31.5   Products

With the exception of composite aggregation, there are no new concepts or associations particular to iteration two in this package (Figure 31.4).

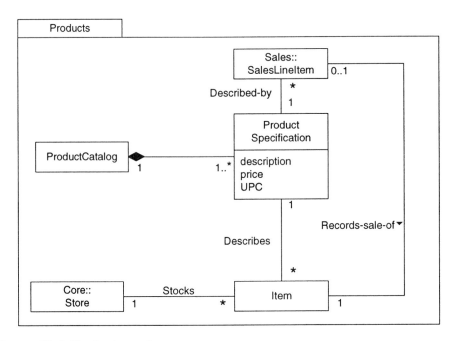

**Figure 31.4** Products package.

# 31.6   Sales

With the exception of composite aggregation and derived attributes, there are no new concepts or associations particular to iteration two in this package (Figure 31.5).

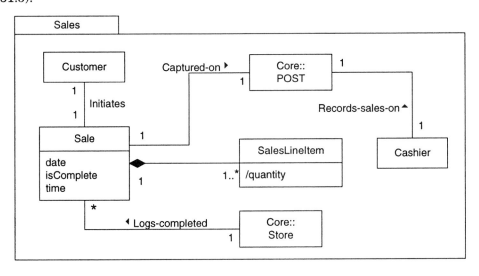

**Figure 31.5** Sales package.

# 31.7    Authorization Transactions

Although providing meaningful names for associations is recommended, in some circumstances it may not be compelling, especially if the purpose of the association is considered obvious to the audience. A case in point is the associations between payments and their transactions. Their names have been left unspecified because I assume the audience reading the type diagram in Figure 31.6 will understand that the transactions are for the payment; adding the names merely makes the diagram more busy.

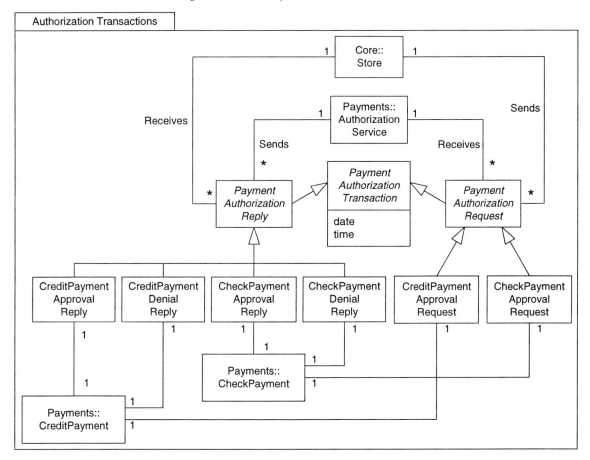

**Figure 31.6** Authorization transaction package.

Is this diagram too detailed, showing too many specializations? It depends. The real criteria is usefulness. Although it is not incorrect, does it add any value in improving understanding of the domain? The answer should influence how many specializations to illustrate in a conceptual model.

# SYSTEM BEHAVIOR

## 32.1    System Sequence Diagrams

In the second development cycle, the system sequence diagrams (SSDs) must support the payment type branching that occurs. Group common sequences into separate SSDs, as illustrated in the following examples.

### 32.1.1  Common Beginning of Buying Items

The SSD for the beginning portion of the use case includes the *enterItem* and *endSale* system events; it is common regardless of the payment method.

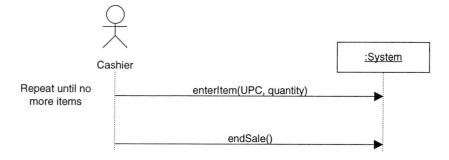

**Figure 32.1** SSD common beginning.

## 32.1.2   Credit Payment

This SSD starts off after a common beginning, when a credit payment is used.

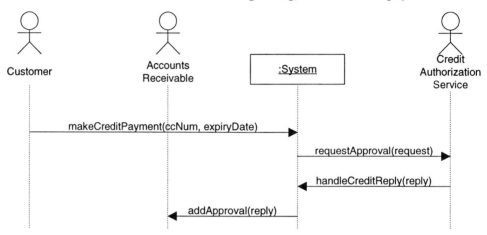

**Figure 32.2**  Credit payment SSD.

## 32.1.3   Check Payment

This SSD starts off after a  common beginning, when a check payment is used.

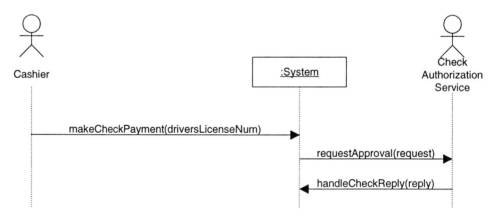

**Figure 32.3**  Check payment SSD.

# 32.2    New System Events

In this development cycle, the new system events for our point-of-sale terminal system are:

- makeCreditPayment
- handleCreditReply
- makeCheckPayment
- handleCheckReply

### 32.2.1 Renaming MakePayment

In the first iteration, the system event and operation for the cash payment was *MakePayment*. Now that the payments are of different types, it will be renamed to:

- makeCashPayment

# 32.3 Contracts

A system operation is defined for each system event.

```
            System
  ────────────────────────
  endSale()
  enterItem()
  handleCheckReply()
  handleCreditReply()
  makeCashPayment()
  makeCheckPayment()
  makeCreditPayment()
```

Contracts need to be written for the new system operations. These are a best guess at the state changes that should occur in response to a system event, but should be considered tentative—during the design phase it is likely that they will be found to be useful but incomplete.

The following sections present the system operation contracts for the point-of-sale application.

|  |  |
|---|---|
| | **Contract** |
| **Name:** | **makeCreditPayment**<br>(ccNum : number,<br>expiryDate : date) |
| **Responsibilities:** | Create and request authorization for a credit payment. |
| **Type or Class:** | System (type) |
| **Cross References:** | |
| **Notes:** | The request has to be transformed into a flat record. |

**Output:**          A credit payment request was sent to a credit authorization service.

**Pre-conditions:**    The current sale is complete.

**Post-conditions:**

- A *CreditPayment pmt* was created.

- *pmt* was associated with the current *Sale*.

- A *CreditCard cc* was created; *cc*.number = ccNum, cc.expiryDate = expiryDate.

- *cc* was associated with *pmt*.

- A *CreditPaymentRequest cpr* was created.

- *pmt* was associated with *cpr*.

- *cpr* was associated with the *CreditAuthorizationService*.

<br>

### Contract

**Name:**          **handleCreditReply**
(reply : CreditPaymentReply)

**Responsibilities:**    Respond to authorization reply from the credit authorization service. If approved, complete the sale, and record the payment in accounts receivable.

**Type or Class:**    System (type)

**Cross References:**

**Notes:**          *reply* is actually a record that needs to be transformed into a *CreditPaymentApprovalReply* or *CreditPaymentDenialReply*.

**Output:**          If approved, credit payment approval reply sent to accounts receivable.

**Pre-conditions:**    The credit payment request was sent to the credit authorization service.

**Post-conditions:**

- If reply represented approval:
    - A *CreditPaymentApprovalReply approval* was created.
    - *approval* was associated with *AccountsReceivable*.
    - The *Sale* was associated with the *Store*, to add it to the historical log of completed sales.
- Else if reply represented denial:
    - A *CreditPaymenDenialReply denial* was created.

### Contract

| | |
|---|---|
| **Name:** | makeCheckPayment<br>(driversLicenceNum :number) |
| **Responsibilities:** | Create and request authorization for a check payment. |
| **Type or Class:** | System (type) |
| **Cross References:** | |
| **Notes:** | The request has to be transformed into a flat record. |
| **Output:** | |
| **Pre-conditions:** | The current sale is complete. |
| **Post-conditions:** | |

- A *CheckPayment pmt* was created.
- *pmt* was associated with the current *Sale*.
- A *DriversLicense dl* was created, and *dl*.number = driversLicenseNum.
- *dl* was associated with *pmt*.
- A *CheckPaymentRequest cpr* was created.
- *pmt* was associated with *cpr*.
- *cpr* was associated with the *CheckAuthorizationService*.

## Contract

| | |
|---|---|
| **Name:** | handleCheckReply |
| | (reply : CheckPaymentReply) |
| **Responsibilities:** | Respond to authorization reply from the check authorization service. If approved, complete the sale. |
| **Type or Class:** | System (type) |
| **Cross References:** | |
| **Notes:** | *reply* is actually a record that needs to be transformed into a *CheckPaymentApprovalReply* or *CheckPayment-DenialReply*. |
| **Output:** | |
| **Pre-conditions:** | The check payment request was sent to the check authorization service. |
| **Post-conditions:** | |

- If reply represented approval:

    □ A *ChecktPaymentApprovalReply approval* was created.

    □ The *Sale* was associated with the *Store*, to add it to the historical log of completed sales

- Else if reply represented denial:

    □ A *CheckPaymenDenialReply denial* was created.

# MODELING BEHAVIOR IN STATE DIAGRAMS

---

### Objectives

■   Create state diagrams for concepts and use cases.

## 33.1    Introduction

The UML includes a state diagram notation to illustrate the events and states of objects. The most important notational features are shown, but there are others not covered in this introduction. The use of state diagrams is emphasized for showing system events in use cases, but they may additionally be applied to any type.

## 33.2    Events, States, and Transitions

An **event** is a significant or noteworthy occurrence. For example:

■   a telephone receiver is taken off the hook.

A **state** is the condition of an object at a moment in time—the time between events. For example:

■   a telephone is in the state of being "idle" after the receiver is placed on the hook and until it is taken off the hook.

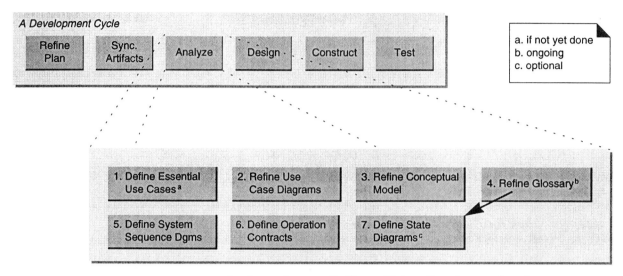

Analyze phase activities within a development cycle.

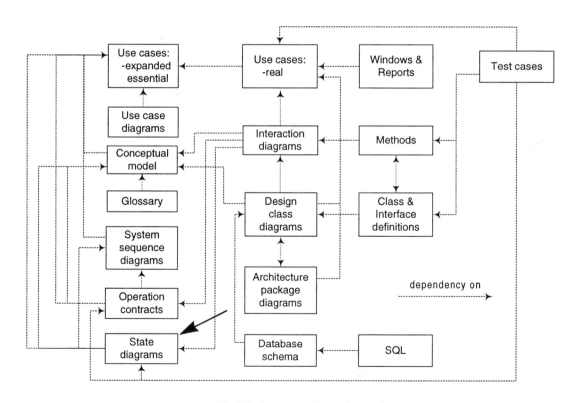

Build phase artifact dependencies.

A **transition** is a relationship between two states that indicates that when an event occurs, the object moves from the prior state to the subsequent state. For example:

- when the event "off hook" occurs, transition the telephone from the "idle" to "active" state."

## 33.3    State Diagrams

A UML state diagram, as in Figure 33.1, illustrates the interesting events and states of an object, and the behavior of an object in reaction to an event. Transitions are shown as arrows, labeled with their event. States are shown in rounded rectangles. It is common to include an initial pseudo-state which automatically transitions to another state when the instance is created.

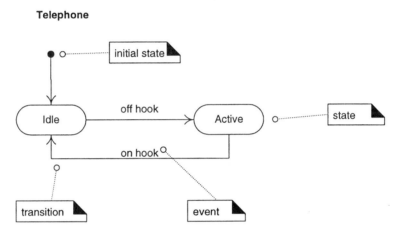

**Figure 33.1** State diagram for a telephone.

A state diagram shows the life-cycle of an object; what events it experience, its transitions, and the states it is in between these events. It need not illustrate every possible event; if an event arises that is not represented in the diagram, the event is ignored as far as the state diagram is concerned. Therefore, we can create a state diagram which describes the life-cycle of an object at arbitrarily simple or complex levels of detail, depending on our needs.

### 33.3.1  Subject of a State Diagram

A state diagram may be applied to a variety of UML elements, including:

- software classes

- types (concepts)

- use cases

Since the entire "system" may be represented by a type, concept, or a set of systems in a problem domain that includes distributed systems, it too may have its own state diagram.

## 33.4  Use Case State Diagrams

A useful application of state diagrams is to describe the legal sequence of external system events that are recognized and handled by a system in the context of a use case. For example:

    ❑ During the *Buy Items* use case in the point-of-sale application, it is not legal to perform the *makeCreditPayment* operation until the *endSale* event has happened.

    ❑ During the *Process Document* use case in a word processor, it is not legal to perform the File-Save operation until the File-New or File-Open event has happened.

A state diagram that depicts the overall system events and their sequence within a use case is a kind of **use case state diagram**.The use case state diagram in Figure 33.2 shows a simplified version of the system events for the *Buy Items* use case in the point-of-sale application. It illustrates that it is not legal to generate a *makePayment* event if an *endSale* event has not previously caused the system to transition to the *WaitingForPayment* state.

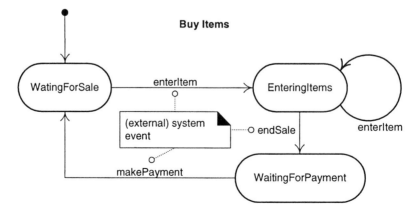

**Figure 33.2**  Use case state diagram for *Buy Items*.

## 33.4.1 Utility of Use Case State Diagrams

The number of system events and their legal order for the *Buy Items* use case is (so far) relatively trivial, thus the use of a state diagram to show legal sequence may not seem compelling. But for a complex use case with myriad system events—such as when using a word processor—a state diagram that illustrates the legal order of external events is helpful.

Here's how: during the design and implementation phases, it is necessary to create and implement a design that ensures no out-of-sequence events occur, otherwise an error condition is possible. For example, the POST should not be allowed to receive a payment unless a sale is complete; code must be written to guarantee that.

Given a set of use case state diagrams, a designer can methodically develop a design that ensures correct system event order. Possible design solutions include:

- hard-coded conditional tests for out-of-order events

- use of the *State* pattern (discussed in a subsequent chapter)

- disabling widgets in active windows to disallow illegal events (a desirable approach)

- a state machine interpreter that runs a state table representing use case state diagram

In a domain with many system events, the conciseness and thoroughness of use case state diagrams helps a designer ensure that nothing is missed.

## 33.5 System State Diagrams

A variation of a use case state diagram is a **system state diagram**, which illustrates, for one system, all the transitions for system events across all the use cases. It is a union of all the use case state diagrams, and is useful as long as the total number of system events is small enough to keep it comprehensible.

## 33.6    Use Case State Diagrams for the Point-of-Sale Application

### 33.6.1    Buy Items

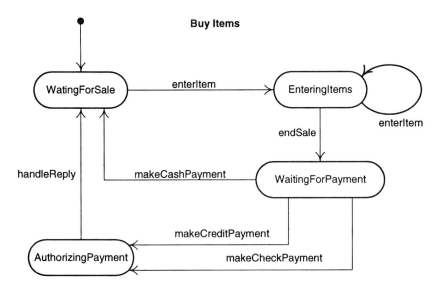

### 33.6.2    Start Up

The state diagram for the *Start Up* use case is not interesting, and so is excluded. In practice, use case state diagrams are not necessary if there is no significant system event ordering.

## 33.7    Types That Need State Diagrams

In addition to state diagrams for use cases or the overall system, they may be created for virtually any type or class.

### 33.7.1    State-Independent and State-dependent Types

If an object always responds the same way to an event, then it is considered **state-independent** (or modeless) with respect to that event. For example, if an object receives a message, and the responding method always does the same thing—the method will typically have no conditional logic. The object is state-independent with respect to that message. If, for all events of interest, a type always reacts the same way, it is a **state-independent type**. In contrast, **state-dependent types** react differently to events depending on their state.

> Create state diagrams for state-dependent types with complex behavior.

In general, business information systems have a minority of interesting state-dependent types. In contrast, process control and telecommunication domains often have many state-dependent objects.

## 33.7.2 Common state-dependent Types and Classes

Following is a list of common classes or types which are usually state-dependent, and for which it may be useful to create a state diagram:

- **Use cases (processes)**.
  - Viewed as a type, the *Buy Items* use case reacts differently to the *endSale* event depending if a sale is underway or not.

- **Systems**. A type representing the overall application or system.
  - The *"point-of-sale system."*

- **Windows**.
  - Edit-Paste action is only valid if there is something in the "clipboard" to paste.

- **Application Coordinators.**
  - "Applets" in Java
  - "Documents" in the Microsoft MFC C++ Document-View application framework.
  - "ApplicationModels" in the Smalltalk VisualWorks application framework.
  - "Visual Parts" in VisualAge Smalltalk.

- **Controllers**. A non-window, non-application-manager class that is responsible for handling system events, as explained by the Controller GRASP pattern.
  - The *POST* class, which handles the *enterItem* and *endSale* system events.

- **Transactions**. The way a transaction reacts to an event is often dependent on its current state within its overall life-cycle.
  - If a *Sale* received a *makeLineItem* message after the *endSale* event, is should either raise an error condition or be ignored.

- **Devices**.
  - ◻ POST, TV, lightbulb, modem: they all react differently to a particular event depending upon their current state.
- **Mutators**. Types that change their type or role.
  - ◻ A Person changing roles from being a civilian to a veteran.

## 33.8    Other State Diagrams for the Point-of-Sale Application

Of the previous suggestions for types that may be state-dependent, controllers (in the GRASP sense) are a common candidate. For example, the controller so far used in the application has been the *POST* class. Note that the *POST* class, as illustrated in Figure 33.3, has a conditional test within the *EnterItem* method to determine if it is a new sale, creating a *Sale* instance if it is.

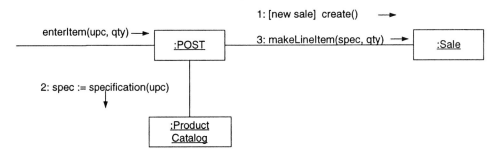

**Figure 33.3** The *enterItem* method has a conditional step, suggesting POST is state-dependent.

A *POST* instance reacts differently to the *EnterItem* message (which arises as a result of the *EnterItem* system event), depending on its state. A state diagram which illustrates this is shown in Figure 33.4.

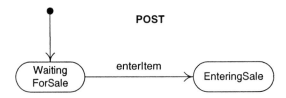

**Figure 33.4** POST state diagram.

# 33.9    Illustrating External and Interval Events

## 33.9.1    Event Types

It is useful to categorize events as follows:

- **External event**—also known as a system event, is caused by something (for example, an actor) outside our system boundary. System sequence diagrams illustrate external events. Noteworthy external events precipitate the invocation of system operations to respond to them.

  ❏ When a cashier presses the "enter item" button on a point-of-sale terminal, an external event has occurred.

- **Internal event**—caused by something inside our system boundary. In terms of software, an internal event arises when an operation is invoked via a message or signal that was sent from another internal object. The messages in collaboration diagrams suggest internal events.

  ❏ When a *Sale* receives a *makeLineItem* message, an internal event has occurred.

- **Temporal event**—caused by the occurrence of a specific date and time or passage of time. In terms of software, a temporal event is driven by a real-time or simulated-time clock.

  ❏ Suppose that after an *endSale* operation occurs, a *makePayment* operation must occur within five minutes, otherwise the current sale is automatically purged.

## 33.9.2    State Diagrams for Internal Events

A state diagram can show *internal* events which typically represent messages received from other objects. Since collaboration diagrams also show messages and their reactions (in terms of other messages), why use a state diagram to illustrate internal events and object design? The object-oriented design paradigm is that of objects that collaborates via messages to fulfill tasks; the UML collaboration diagram directly illustrates that paradigm. It is somewhat incongruous to use a state diagram to show a design of object messaging and interaction.[1]

Consequently, I have reservations about recommending the use of state diagrams that show internal events for the purpose of creative object-oriented

---

1. A reader of object-oriented analysis and design literature will encounter periodical and textbook examples of complex state diagrams that are devoted to *internal* events and the object's reaction to them. Essentially, their creators have replaced the paradigm of object interaction and collaboration via messages with the paradigm of objects as state machines, and have used state diagrams to design the behavior of objects, rather than using collaboration diagrams. Abstractly, the two views are equivalent.

design.[1] However, they may be useful to summarize the results of a design, after it is complete.

In contrast, as the previous discussion on use case state diagrams explained, a state diagram for *external* events can be a helpful and succinct tool.

> Prefer using state diagrams to illustrate external and temporal events, and the reaction to them, rather than using them to design object behavior based on internal events.

# 33.10   Additional State Diagram Notation

The UML notation for state diagrams contains a rich set of features that are not exploited in this introduction. Three significant features are:

- transition actions
- transition guard conditions
- nested states

## 33.10.1  Transition Actions and Guards

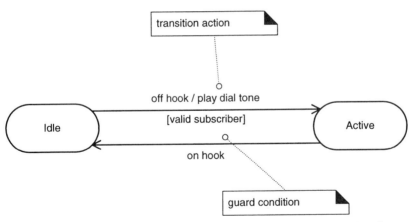

A transition can cause an action to fire. In a software implementation, this may represent the invocation of a method of the class of the state diagram.

---

1. One reasonable use of state diagrams to show object design based on internal events is when code is to be produced with a code generator that is driven by the state diagrams, or when a state machine interpreter will be used to run the software system.

A transition may also have a conditional guard—or boolean test. The transition is only taken if the test passes.

## 33.10.2 Nested States

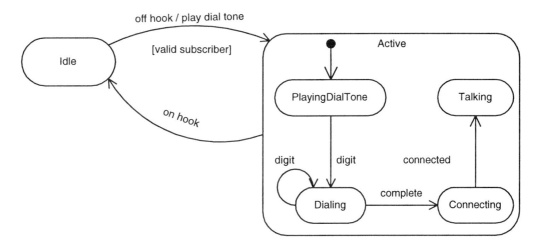

A state allows nesting to contain substates; a substate inherits the transitions of its superstate (the enclosing state). This is a key contribution of the Harel state diagram notation that UML is based on, as it leads to succinct state diagrams. Substates may be graphically shown by nesting them in a superstate box.

For example, when a transition to the *Active* state occurs, creation and transition into the *PlayingDialTone* substate occurs. No matter what substate the object is in, if the *on hook* event related to the *Active* superstate occurs, a transition to the *Idle* state occurs.

# PART VI DESIGN PHASE (2)

# GRASP: MORE PATTERNS FOR ASSIGNING RESPONSIBILITIES

---

## Objectives

■ Learn to apply the remaining GRASP patterns.

---

## 34.1 GRASP: General Responsibility Assignment Software Patterns

Previously, we explored the application of the first five GRASP patterns:

■ Expert, Creator, High Cohesion, Low Coupling, Controller

The final four GRASP patterns are:

■ Polymorphism

■ Pure Fabrication

■ Indirection

■ Don't Talk to Strangers

This chapter introduces the remaining patterns, which represent very fundamental principles by which responsibilities are assigned to objects. The next chapter introduces other useful patterns, and following that they will be applied to the development of the second iteration of the point-of-sale-terminal application.

# 34.2  Polymorphism

**Solution**  When related alternatives or behaviors vary by type (class), assign responsibility for the behavior—using polymorphic operations—to the types for which the behavior varies.[1]

*Corollary*: Do not test for the type of an object and use conditional logic to perform varying alternatives based on type.

**Problem**  How to handle alternatives based on type? How to create pluggable software components?

*Alternatives based on type.* Conditional variation is a fundamental theme in programs. If a program is designed using if-then-else or case statement conditional logic, then if a new variation arises, it requires modification of the case logic. This approach makes it difficult to easily extend a program with new variations because changes tend to be required in several places—wherever the conditional logic exists.

*Pluggable software components.* Viewing components in client-server relationships, how can one replace one server component with another, without effecting the client?

**Example**  In the point-of-sale application, who should be responsible for authorizing different kinds of payments?

Since the behavior of authorizing varies by the kind of payment—cash,[2] credit or check, by Polymorphism we should assign the responsibility for authorizing to each payment type, implemented with a polymorphic *authorize* operation, (see Figure 34.1). The implementation of each *authorize* operation will be different: *CreditPayments* will communicate with a credit authorization service, and so on.

---

1. **Polymorphism** has several related meanings. In this context it means "giving the same name to services in different objects" [Coad95] when the services are similar or related. The different object types are usually related in a hierarchy with a common superclass, but this is not strictly necessary (especially in dynamic binding languages, such as Smalltalk, or languages that support interfaces, such as Java).

2. Some point-of-sale terminals have a device that authorizes paper currency by determining if it is counterfeit or not. This is relatively common in certain European countries, for example.

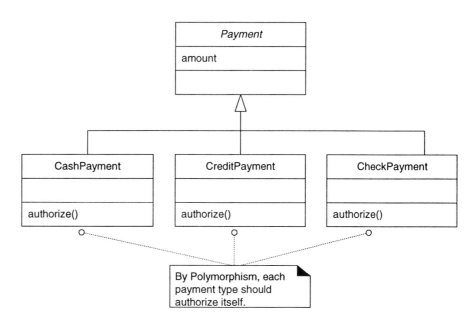

**Figure 34.1** Polymorphism in payment authorization.

**Discussion**  Like Expert, the use of Polymorphism is in the spirit of the pattern "Do it Myself" [Coad95]. Instead of externally operating upon a payment to authorize it, a payment authorizes itself—this is quintessentially object-oriented.

If Expert can be characterized as the most important basic *tactical* pattern, Polymorphism is the most important basic *strategic* pattern in object-oriented design. Polymorphism is a fundamental principle on which is founded the overall strategies, or plans of attack, in designing how a system is organized to handle work. A design based on assigning responsibilities by Polymorphism can be easily extended to handle new variations. For example, adding a new *DebitPayment* class with its own polymorphic *authorize* operation will have minor impact on the existing design with respect to how authorization is handled.

Viewing the objects in client-server relationships, the client objects need little or no modification when a new type of server object is introduced, as long as the new server supports the polymorphic operations that the client expects.

**Benefits** ■ Future extensions required for unanticipated new variations are easy to add.

**Also Known As;**  "Do it Myself," "Choosing Message," "Don't Ask 'What Kind?'"
**Similar To**

# 34.3    Pure Fabrication

**Solution**      Assign a highly cohesive set of responsibilities to an artificial class that does not represent anything in the problem domain—something made up, in order to support high cohesion, low coupling, and reuse.

Such a class is a *fabrication* of the imagination. Ideally, the responsibilities assigned to this fabrication support high cohesion and low coupling, so that the design of the fabrication is very clean, or *pure*—hence a pure fabrication.

Finally, a pure fabrication implies making something up, which we do when we're desperate!

**Problem**      Who, when you are desperate, and do not want to violate High Cohesion and Low Coupling?

Object-oriented designs are characterized by implementing as software classes representations of concepts in the real-world problem domain; for example a *Sale* and *Customer* class. However, there are many situations in which assigning responsibilities only to domain classes leads to problems in terms of poor cohesion or coupling, or low reuse potential.

**Example**      For example, suppose that support is needed to save *Sale* instances in a relational database. By Expert, there is some justification to assign this responsibility to the *Sale* class itself. But consider the following implications:

■ The task requires a relatively large number of supporting database-oriented operations, none related to the concept of sale-ness, so the *Sale* class becomes incohesive.

■ The *Sale* class has to be coupled to the relational database interface (usually provided by the development tool vendor), so its coupling goes up. And the coupling is not even to another domain object, but to an idiosyncratic database interface.

■ Saving objects in a relational database is a very general task for which many classes need support. Placing these responsibilities in the *Sale* class suggests there is going to be poor reuse or lots of duplication in other classes that do the same thing.

Thus, even though *Sale* is a logical candidate by virtue of Expert to save itself in a database, it leads to a design with low cohesion, high coupling, and low reuse potential—exactly the kind of desperate situation that calls for making something up.

A reasonable solution is to create a new class that is solely responsible for saving objects in some kind of persistent storage medium, such as a relational database; call it the *PersistentStorageBroker*.[1] This class is a Pure Fabrication—a figment of the imagination.

It solves the following design problems:

- The Sale remains well designed, with high cohesion and low coupling.

- The *PersistentStorageBroker* class is itself relatively cohesive, having the sole purpose of storing objects in a persistent storage medium.

- The *PersistentStorageBroker* class is a very generic and reusable object.

Creating a pure fabrication in this example is exactly the situation in which their use is called for—eliminating a bad design with poor cohesion and coupling with a good design in which there is greater potential for reuse.

Note that, as with all the GRASP patterns, the emphasis is on where responsibilities should be placed. In this example the responsibilities are shifted from the *Sale* class to a Pure Fabrication.

**Discussion**  A Pure Fabrication should be designed with a high potential for reuse in mind by ensuring their responsibilities are small and cohesive. These classes tend to have a *fine-grained* set of responsibilities.

A Pure Fabrication is usually partitioned based on related functionality, and so is a kind of function-centric object.

A Pure Fabrication is usually considered part of the High-level Object-oriented Services Layer in an architecture.

Many existing object-oriented design patterns are examples of Pure Fabrications: Adapter, Observer, Visitor, and so on [GHJV95].

**Benefits**  ■  High Cohesion is supported because responsibilities are factored into a fine-grain class that only focuses on a very specific set of related tasks.

■  Reuse potential may increase because of the presence of fine-grain Pure Fabrication classes whose responsibilities have applicability in other applications.

**Potential Problems**  The spirit of good object-oriented designs that are object-centric rather than function-centric may be lost, as Pure Fabrications are usually partitioned based on related functionality; in other words, making classes for sets of functions. If

---

1. In a real persistence framework, more than a single pure fabrication class is ultimately necessary to create a reasonable design.

abused, the creation of Pure Fabrications will lead to a function or process-oriented design that is implemented in an object-oriented language.

**Related Patterns**
- Low Coupling

- High Cohesion

- A Pure Fabrication usually takes on responsibilities from the domain class that would be assigned those responsibilities based on the Expert pattern.

- Many existing object-oriented design patterns are examples of Pure Fabrications: Adapter, Observer, Visitor and so on [GHJV95].

# 34.4    Indirection

**Solution**    Assign the responsibility to an intermediate object to mediate between other components or services so that they are not directly coupled.

The intermediary creates an *indirection* between the other components or services.

**Problem**    Who, to avoid direct coupling? How to de-couple objects so that Low Coupling is supported and reuse potential remains high?

**Examples**    **PersistentStorageBroker**

The Pure Fabrication example of de-coupling the *Sale* from the relational database services through the introduction of a *PersistentStorageBroker* class is also an example of assigning responsibilities to support Indirection. The *PersistentStorageBroker* acts as a intermediary between the *Sale* and database.

### Modem

Assume that:

- A point-of-sale terminal application needs to manipulate a modem in order to transmit credit payment requests.

- The operating system provides a low-level function call API for doing so.

- A class called *CreditAuthorizationService* is responsible for talking to the modem.

If the *CreditAuthorizationService* invokes the low-level API function calls directly, it is highly coupled to the idiosyncratic API of the particular operating system. If the class needs to be ported to another operating system (for use in the same or a different application), then it will require modification.

Add an intermediate *Modem* class between the *CreditAuthorizationService* and the modem API. It is responsible for translating abstract modem requests to the API and creates an Indirection between the *CreditAuthorizationService* and the modem API. (A class like *Modem* that represents and interfaces with an electro-mechanical device is also known as a **device proxy**).

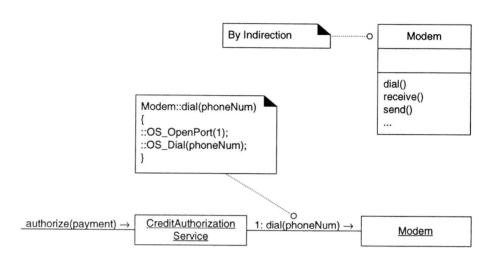

## 34.4.1   Publish-Subscribe or Observer

The Publish-Subscribe or Observer pattern [GHJV95] also provides an example of the Indirection pattern. Objects subscribe to interest in events with an *Event-Manager*; other objects publish events to the *EventManager*, which notifies the subscribers. Through the indirection of the *EventManager*, publishers and subscribers are de-coupled.

**Discussion**   "Most problems in computer science can be solved by another level of indirection" is an old adage with particular relevance to object-oriented designs. [1]

Just as many existing design patterns are specializations of Pure Fabrication, many are also specializations of Indirection. Adapter, Facade, and Observer are examples [GHJV95]. In addition, many Pure Fabrications are generated because of Indirection. The motivation for Indirection is usually Low Coupling; an intermediary is added in order to de-couple other components or services.

---

1. If any adage is old in computer science! I have forgotten the source (Parnas?).

**Benefits** ■ Low coupling

**Related Patterns** ■ Low Coupling

■ Mediator [GHJV95]

■ Many Indirection intermediaries are Pure Fabrications.

# 34.5   Don't Talk to Strangers

**Solution**   Assign the responsibility to a client's direct object to collaborate with an indirect object, so that the client does not need to know about the indirect object.

The pattern—also known as the Law of Demeter [Sakkinen88]—places constraints on what objects you should send messages to within a method. It states that within a method, messages should only be sent to the following objects:

**1.**   The *this* object (or *self*).

**2.**   A parameter of the method.

**3.**   An attribute of *self*.

**4.**   An element of a collection which is an attribute of *self*.

**5.**   An object created within the method.

The intent is to avoid coupling a client to knowledge of indirect objects and the internal representations of direct objects. Direct objects are a client's 'familiars', indirect objects are 'strangers,' and a client should only talk to familiars, not to strangers.

Fulfilling these constraints implies that direct objects may require new operations to act as intermediary operations so that a client can avoid "talking to strangers."

**Problem**   Who, to avoid knowing about the structure of indirect objects?

If an object has knowledge of the internal connections and structure of other objects, then it suffers from high coupling. If a client object has to use a service or obtain information from an indirect object, how can it do so without being coupled to knowledge of the internal structure of its direct server or indirect objects?

**Example**   In a point-of-sale application, assume that a *POST* instance has an attribute referring to a *Sale*, which has an attribute referring to a *Payment*.

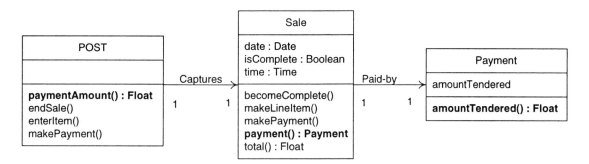

**Figure 34.2** Partial design class diagram.

Furthermore, assume that:

- *POST* instances support the *paymentAmount* operation, which returns the current amount tendered for the payment.

- *Sale* instances support the *payment* operation, which returns the *Payment* instance associated with the *Sale*.

One approach to return the payment amount is:

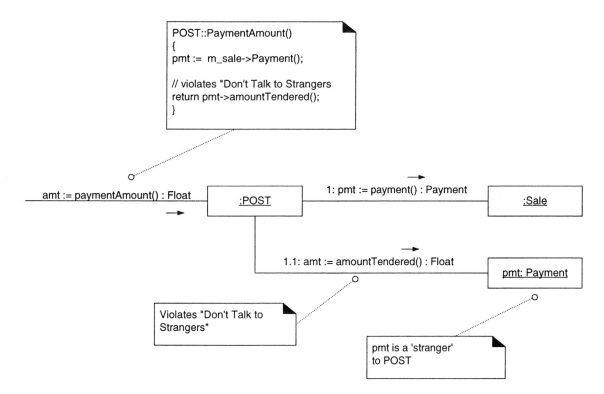

**Figure 34.3** Violating "Don't Talk to Strangers"

The solution in Figure 34.3 is a violation of the Don't Talk to Strangers principle because the *POST* instance is sending a message to an indirect object—the *Payment* is not one of the five candidate 'familiars.'

The solution, as the pattern suggests, is to add the responsibility to the direct object—the *Sale* in this case—to return the payment amount to the *POST*. This is known as **promoting the interface**, which is the general solution to support this principle. Therefore, a *paymentAmount* operation is added to *Sale* so that the *POST* does not have to talk to a stranger (see Figure 34.4).

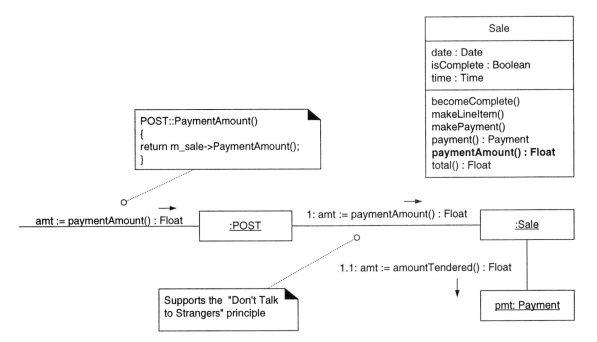

**Figure 34.4** Supporting "Don't Talk to Strangers"

**Discussion**    Don't Talk to Strangers is about avoiding gaining temporary visibility to indirect objects—objects that are known by other objects, but not by the client. The disadvantage of gaining visibility to strangers is that the solution is then coupled to knowledge of the internal structure of other objects. This leads to high coupling, which makes the design less robust and more likely to require a change if the indirect structural relationships change.

For example, assume that the solution in Figure 34.3 is used and then the class definition of *Sale* is changed so that it no longer maintains a reference to a *Payment*. In that case, the *POST-paymentAmount* method is invalidated and requires maintenance. In this small example it does not appear to be an onerous problem, but in a system with many hundreds—if not thousands—of classes that are being simultaneously developed by many software developers, it is a problem. Designing a solution which is dependent on knowledge of indirect structural relationships makes a system fragile.

In contrast to the solution in Figure 34.3, if the solution in Figure 34.4 is used, then the *POST* methods are not affected by any change in the internal representations and connections of the *Sale*. All that the *POST* knows is that a *Sale* can answer its payment total, but has no knowledge of how it is achieved.

Violating this principle is especially common in Smalltalk, where public methods to access the private structural connections of an object are pervasive. Code that looks similar to the following is common:

```
myBadMethodToGetPrice
    "hop along from X to A to B to C to D,
    to return the price of D"

    myDirectX getA getB getC getD getprice
```

This code is hopping along structural connections from one object to the next. Consider how fragile this code is; it is highly coupled to knowledge of many indirect structural relationships.

## 34.5.1   *Breaking the Law*

The first thing to know about software laws is that they were meant to be broken. So although Don't Talk to Strangers (the Law of Demeter) is sound advice, there are situations where it is reasonable to ignore it. One common reasonable situation in which it is violated is when there is some kind of "broker" or "object server" (usually a Pure Fabrication) that is responsible for returning other objects based upon lookup by a key value. It is considered acceptable to get visibility to an object *X* via a broker, and then send messages to *X* directly, even though this violates Don't Talk to Strangers.

**Benefits** ■ Low Coupling

**Related Patterns** ■ Low Coupling, Indirection, Chain of Responsibility [GHJV95]

# DESIGNING WITH MORE PATTERNS

Objectives

- Apply GRASP and Gang-of-Four patterns in the design of the point-of-sale application.

## 35.1    Introduction

This chapter explores the creation of collaboration diagrams for the second iteration of the point-of-sale application. The emphasis is to show how to apply all the GRASP patterns, plus useful patterns that have been published by others. It attempts to illustrate that object-oriented design and the assignment of responsibilities can be explained and learned based on the application of patterns—a vocabulary of principles and idioms that can be combined to design objects.

To reiterate, the assignment of responsibilities to objects, and object collaboration design, is the essence of object-oriented design. Most of the previous analysis work was done to support the current object-oriented design phase.

Although the contracts for the system operations are not explicitly mentioned here, the post-conditions they specify are fulfilled by the following object collaborations. In practice, contracts are reviewed as the design is developed.

### 35.1.1    The Gang of Four Patterns

The additional patterns presented in this chapter are drawn from "Design Patterns" [GHJV95], a seminal work that presents twenty-three patterns useful during the object-oriented design phase. Since the book was written by four authors, these patterns have become known as the "Gang of Four"—or "GoF"—patterns.[1]

This chapter provides an introduction to some of the GoF patterns; other chapters present additional ones, including Template Method and Observer.. A thorough study of the "Design Patterns" text is recommended.

## 35.2   State (GoF)

As discussed in the previous chapter on state diagrams, the *POST* class reacts differently to the *EnterItem* message, depending on its state. The collaboration and state diagrams in Figure 35.1 and Figure 35.2 illustrate this.

Instead of using a conditional test, an alternate technique is the GoF State pattern. In general, the State pattern can be used to eliminate conditional tests that are caused by state dependencies.

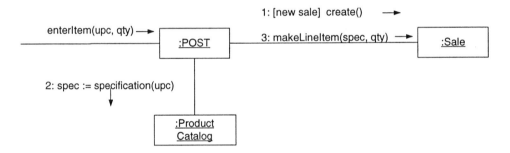

**Figure 35.1** Partial enterItem collaboration diagram showing mode-dependent reaction.

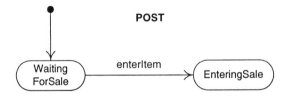

**Figure 35.2** State diagram for *POST*.

---

1. With a tangential reference to Chinese politics.

---

**State**

*Context / Problem*

An object's behavior is dependent on its state. Conditional logic is undesirable because of complexity, scalability, or duplication.

*Solution*

1.  Create a class for each state that influences the behavior of the state-dependent object (the "context" object).

2.  Based on Polymorphism, assign methods to each state class to handle the behavior of the context object.

3.  When a state-dependent message is received by the context object, forward it to the state object.

---

As shown in Figure 35.3, a hierarchy of classes representing the states of the *POST* class is defined. Each includes an *enterItem* method since its behavior is state dependent. A *POST* instance has attribute visibility to its current *POST-State* instance

As illustrated in Figure 35.4, when the *EnterItem* message is received by the *POST* instance, it is forwarded on to its state, which handles it by Polymorphism.

Note that the context object is passed along to the state object; this gives it parameter visibility back to the context so that messages may be sent to it, such as a message to change its state.

---

Notation Comment

In Figure 35.4, observe that the *enterItem* message is shown sent to an instance of the superclass *POSTState*, even though in actuality it is an instance of one of the subclasses.

For each subclass polymorphic case, a new collaboration diagram is drawn, starting with the polymorphic message.

Use this style when showing a polymorphic message.

---

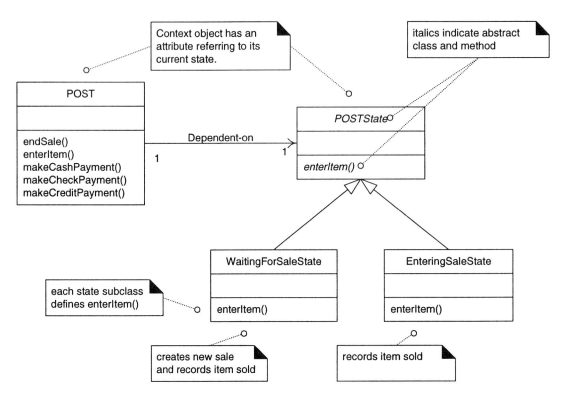

**Figure 35.3** State classes used in the State pattern.

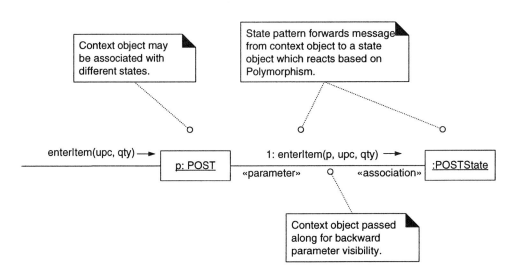

**Figure 35.4** State pattern starts with context object forwarding message to its associated state object.

Figure 35.5 and Figure 35.6 start with the *enterItem* message sent to an instance of *WaitingForSaleState* and *EnteringSaleState,* respectively.

In Figure 35.5 the *enterItem* method first initiates the creation of a new sale before recording the item sold. Additionally—and this is an common part of the State pattern—the current state assigns a new state to the context object.

In this example, a new state instance is created, but it is also common to use the GoF **Singleton** pattern, described ahead, to assign a Singleton state instance rather than create one. Another related pattern that can be used for the State objects is the GoF **Flyweight** pattern, which is similar to Singleton. The Flyweight pattern is useful when you can share an instance among many objects because the instance holds no state, but only possesses behavior. For example, the *POSTState* instances do not maintain any information; the context object is passed in as a parameter when needed. In this case, only one instance of each concrete class (*WaitingForSaleState*, and so on) is needed in the system.

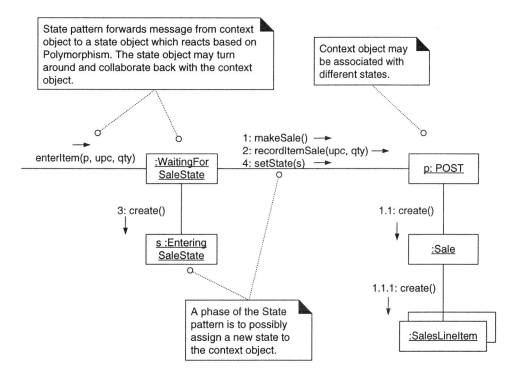

**Figure 35.5** One polymorphic case of the state pattern: WaitingForSaleState.

Figure 35.6 shows the polymorphic case of *enterItem* for the *EnteringSaleState*. In this case it is not necessary to create a new sale, but only to record the item sold. Notice that there is no change of state this time; a state method is not required to cause a state change.

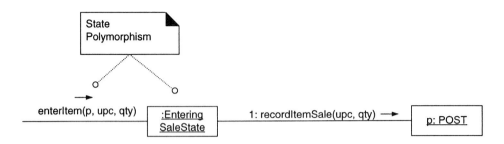

**Figure 35.6** A second polymorphic case of the state pattern: EnteringSaleState.

Finally, the common recordItemSale collaboration diagram is shown in Figure 35.7.

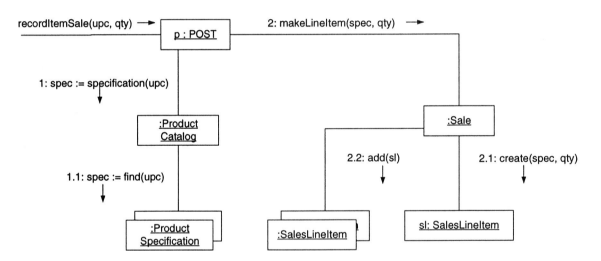

**Figure 35.7** The RecordItemSale method of class POST.

## 35.2.1 State—Conclusion

The State pattern is useful when an object's behavior is dependent on its state. It eliminates conditional logic in the methods of the context object and provides an elegant mechanism for extending the context object's behavior without modifying it.

If there are many states in a system, the State pattern may not be suitable because of class explosion. Another alternative is to define a state machine interpreter that runs against a set of state transition rules.

# 35.3    Polymorphism (GRASP)

As discussed in the previous GRASP patterns chapter, it is very much in the spirit of object-oriented design for a payment to authorize itself—the "Do it Myself" pattern [Coad95]. Additionally, since there are multiple payment types, the Polymorphism pattern is called for, so that each payment type authorizes itself.

Thus, as shown in Figure 35.8, each *Payment* subclass has its own *Authorize* method.

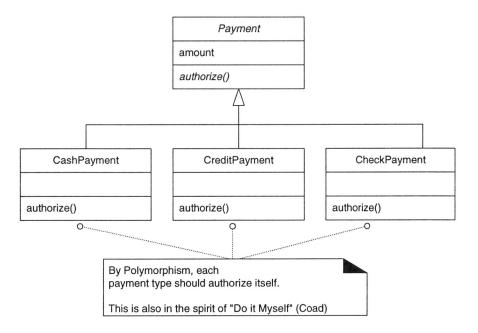

**Figure 35.8** Payment hierarchy with multiple Authorize methods.

For example, as illustrated in Figure 35.9 and Figure 35.10, a *Sale* instantiates a *CreditPayment* or *CheckPayment* and asks it to authorize itself.

Also note creation of the *CreditCard*, *DriversLicense* and *Check* software objects. One's first impulse might be to record the data they hold simply in their related payment classes, and eliminate such fine-grained classes. However, it is usually a more profitable strategy to use them; they often end up providing useful behavior and being very reusable. For example, the *CreditCard* is a natural Expert on telling you its credit company type (Visa, MasterCard, and so on and so on). This behavior will turn out to be necessary for our application.

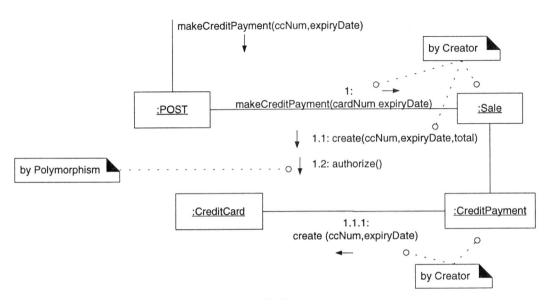

**Figure 35.9** Creating a CreditPayment

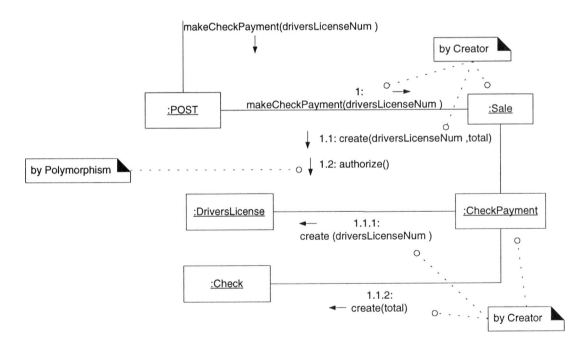

**Figure 35.10** Creating a CheckPayment

# 35.4    Singleton (GoF)

When a *CreditPayment* receives an *Authorize* message, it needs to send a message to the *Store* to find which credit authorization service to communicate with (Bank of Foo for Visa, Bank of Bar for MasterCard, and so on). Why ask the *Store*? It is a natural information Expert on its authorization services.

But there is a visibility problem: The newly created *CreditPayment* does not have access to the *Store* instance. One solution is pass the *Store* on down (as a parameter) from the *POST* (which has attribute visibility to it), and assign it to an attribute of the *CreditPayment* so it also has attribute visibility to it. This is acceptable but slightly inconvenient; an alternative is the Singleton pattern.

Occasionally, it is desirable to support global visibility or a single access point to a single instance of a class rather than some other form of visibility. It turns out this is true for the *Store* instance.

---

**Singleton**

*Context / Problem*

Exactly one instance of a class is allowed—it is a "singleton". Objects need a single point of access.

*Solution*

Define a class method or non-member function (in C++) that returns the singleton.

---

For example, as shown in Figure 35.11, suppose that the Singleton pattern is needed for a *Store*. One solution is to define a class attribute *instance* in the *Store* class that will refer to a *Store* instance, and a class method *Instance()* that returns the class attribute.[1]

Note that class members in UML are indicated with a "$".

With this interface, as shown in Figure 35.12, the *CreditPayment* asks the *Store* **class** for visibility to its single instance, and then asks the instance for a *CreditAuthorizationService*, based on a *CreditCard*.

Since visibility to classes is (relatively) global in scope, any object can directly invoke the class method that returns the singleton.

---

1. Static data and methods in Java terms.

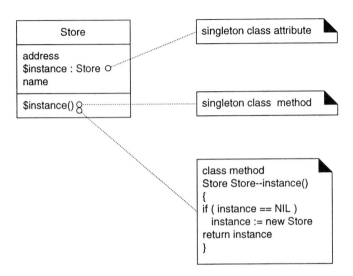

**Figure 35.11** Singleton support in the Store class.

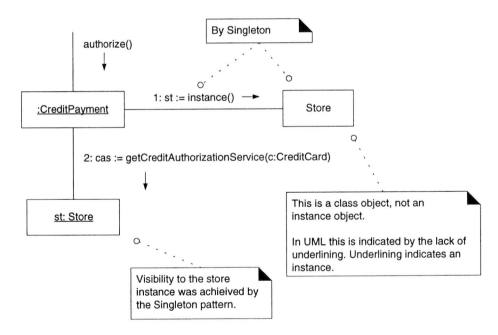

**Figure 35.12** Using the Singleton pattern.

## 35.4.1 Sample Code

In an object-oriented programming language, use of the Singleton pattern requires sending a message to the class to get visibility to the instance, which can then be sent messages.

| C++ | `Store::instance()->getCAS(aCard);` |
|-----------|-------------------------------------|
| Java | `Store.instance().getCAS(aCard);` |
| Smalltalk | `Store instance getCAS: aCard.` |

## 35.4.2 UML Shorthand for Singleton

A UML notation that implies—but does not explicitly show—the singleton access is to stereotype the instance with «singleton».

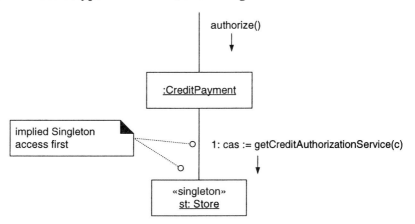

## 35.4.3 Implementation

- If thread safety is required, the Singleton method needs some kind of guard.
- Alternative access points:
    - a class method in a "utility" class
    - (C++) a non-member function

415

## 35.5     Remote Proxy and Proxy (GoF)

The previous section alluded to the need to access an instance of *CreditAuthorizationService* without really explaining why. The system must communicate with an external service. In this situation, the GoF pattern Remote Proxy suggests making a local software class that represents the external service and giving it responsibility for communicating with the real service. Therefore, a local *CreditAuthorizationService* object could be used to talk to the outside world.

---

**Remote Proxy**

*Context / Problem*

The system must communicate with a component in another address space. Who should be responsible?

*Solution*

Make a local software class that represents the external component and give it responsibility for communicating with the real component.

---

Remote Proxy is a special case of the general GoF Proxy pattern, which suggests using a surrogate for a component (object, server, device driver, DLL, and so on) in certain contexts.

---

**Proxy**

*Context / Problem*

Direct access to a component is not desired or possible. What to do?

*Solution*

Define a surrogate software class that represents the component and give it responsibility for communicating with the real component.

---

In our system, we need to find which authorization service to use, and then based on Remote Proxy, ask it to communicate with the real service.

As illustrated in Figure 35.13, since a *Store* is a natural Expert on knowing its services, the payment asks it for one. Since the service is keyed by the type of credit company, the *CreditCard* is passed along and queried for its type (the *CreditCard* is an Expert on telling its type). Then the appropriate service can be retrieved.

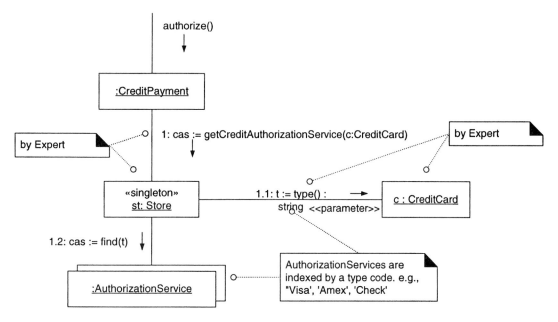

**Figure 35.13** Finding a service.

Once the correct Remote Proxy is found, it is given the responsibility for completing the authorization, as shown in Figure 35.14.

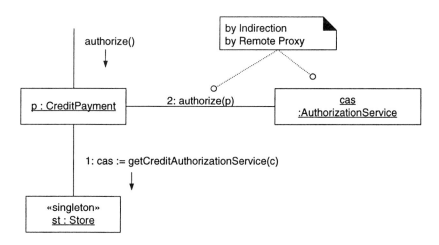

**Figure 35.14** Using the Remote Proxy.

The *CreditAuthorizationService* Remote Proxy needs to send off a request message and receive a reply, which it does in Figure 35.15.

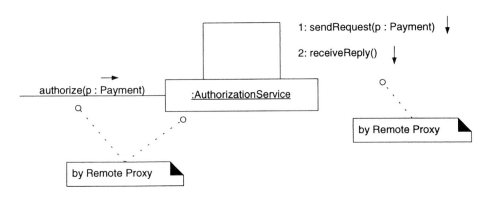

**Figure 35.15** Remote Proxy actions.

## 35.5.1 *Issues*

- The reader may have noticed that this design violates the Don't Talk to Strangers principle when the *CreditPayment* gets visibility to the *CreditAuthorizationService* and sends it the *Authorize* message. When an object is a registry for other kinds of objects (like *Store* is for *CreditAuthorizationServices*), it is common to violate this principle. Alternatively, the *Store* could be given an *Authorize(aPayment)* interface to support Don't Talk to Strangers.

- Remote Proxy is but one of several kinds of proxies. Please see [GHJV95] and [BMRSS96] for details.

- Remote Proxy is a simple approach to communication handling. For other pattern-based approaches, see [BMRSS96].

# 35.6    Facade and Device Proxy (GoF)

## 35.6.1 *Wrapping*

Our system must use a modem to dial into the external service. Suppose that the underlying operating system provides a function-based interface for using a modem (for example, *OS_DIAL(...)* ). These non-object-oriented functions can be wrapped within a class that groups them together, providing an object and method interface to the functions. In general, this is known as **wrapping**, and can be applied to create an object-oriented interface to any non-object-oriented one.

For example, a *Modem* class can be defined that wraps the calls.

## 35.6.2   Facade

When a class is defined that provides a common interface to a disparate set or interfaces, such as the *Modem* class, it is called a Facade—one of the GoF patterns. The disparate interfaces may be to a set of functions, a framework, a group of other classes, or a subsystem (local or remote).

---

**Facade**

*Context / Problem*

A common, unified interface to a disparate set of interfaces—such as to a subsystem—is required. What to do?

*Solution*

Define a single class that unifies the interface and give it responsibility for collaborating with the subsystem.

---

## 35.6.3   Device Proxy

In addition to being a Facade, a *Modem* is also a kind of Proxy for the real physical modem—a Device Proxy.

---

**Device Proxy**

Context/Problem

Interaction with an electro-mechanical device is required. What to do?

*Solution*

Define a class that represents the device and give it responsibility for interacting with it.

---

## 35.6.4   Indirection

Observe that Facade, Remote Proxy, and Device Proxy, like many patterns, are a variation on the very basic Indirection GRASP pattern.

## 35.6.5 Marshalling and Serialization

A common idiom in object-oriented design when communicating with the out-side world via a non-object-oriented communication mechanism is to create objects representing the in- and outbound messages, and transforming them between objects and strings. The transformation of an object into a string repre-sentation is called **serialization**, which some languages (such as Java) have built-in support for. Sending what we think of as an object-oriented message with parameters out over a non-object-oriented communication medium (for example, a socket) usually requires transforming the message and parameters (via serialization) into a stream of bytes suitable for transmission and for the receiving server. This process is known as **marshalling**. Our responsibility for serialization and marshalling depends on the language and communication mechanism. If using Java and its Remote Method Invocation (RMI) mechanism, we are only responsible for ensuring that the serialization produces a suitable string layout for parameters. In the absence of a built-in distributed communi-cation mechanism such as RMI, it is common for the Remote Proxy to be respon-sible for marshalling and **unmarshalling** (transforming returning strings into commands and objects).

## 35.6.6 Using the Remote and Device Proxies

In conclusion, the *Modem* class is both a Device Proxy and a Facade. The *Autho-rizationService* Remote Proxy creates an object representing the out-going mes-sage, serializes it into a string, and then collaborates with the *Modem* to send it off. This is shown in Figure 35.16.

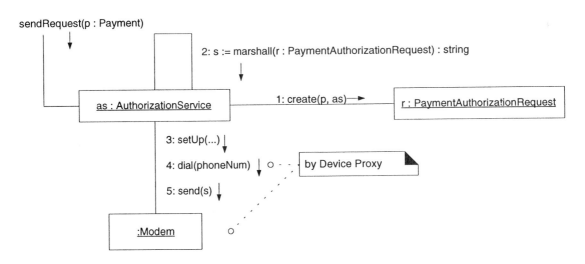

**Figure 35.16** Using a Device Proxy.

# 35.7 Command (GoF)

After the *AuthorizationService* sends off the request, it sends itself a *receiveReply* message and waits for an in-coming message.[1]

When received, this string-format message is unmarshalled into a *CreditPaymentApprovalReply* or a *CreditPaymentDenialReply* instance, depending on the approval code.

How should execution proceed? The GoF Command pattern suggests that each of these reply objects represents a kind of command or action request, and each should execute itself, based on the Polymorphism pattern.

---

**Command**

*Context / Problem*

A variety of requests, or commands, can be received by an object or system. Reduce the receiver's responsibility in handling the commands, increase the ease with which new commands may be added, and provide a foundation for logging, queuing, and undoing commands.

*Solution*

For each command, define a class that represents it and give it responsibility for executing itself.

---

As shown in Figure 35.17, each reply has its own Command class, with a polymorphic *execute* method.

When a reply is unmarshalled into a *CreditPaymentApprovalReply* or a *CreditPaymentDenialReply* instance, it is sent an *execute* message, as illustrated in Figure 35.18.

Note that Figure 35.18 only shows the creation of the abstract superclass *PaymentAuthorizationReply*, even though an instance of a subclass is actually created.

Each polymorphic *execute* case is shown in a new collaboration diagram, such as in Figure 35.19 and Figure 35.20.

---

1. An asynchronous wait on a thread is also likely, but outside the scope of our investigation.

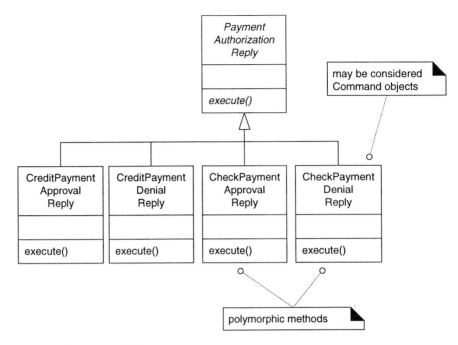

**Figure 35.17** Command classes.

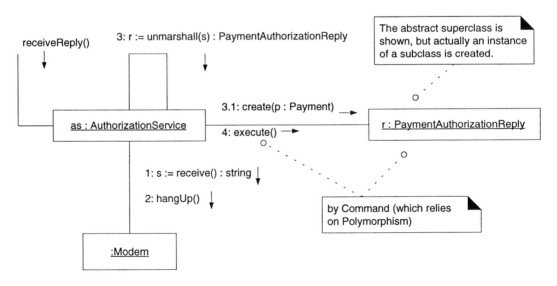

**Figure 35.18** Applying the Command pattern.

## 35.7.1 CreditPaymentApprovalReply—execute

By Command and Polymorphism, the *CreditPaymentApprovalReply* receives an *execute* message. In the approval case, the reply must log the reply in the external accounts receivable system. As shown in Figure 35.19, it does so by using the patterns Singleton, Don't Talk to Strangers, and Remote Proxy.[1]

Finally, the payment state must be changed to authorized. (Note that the reply was given attribute visibility to the payment when the reply was created.)

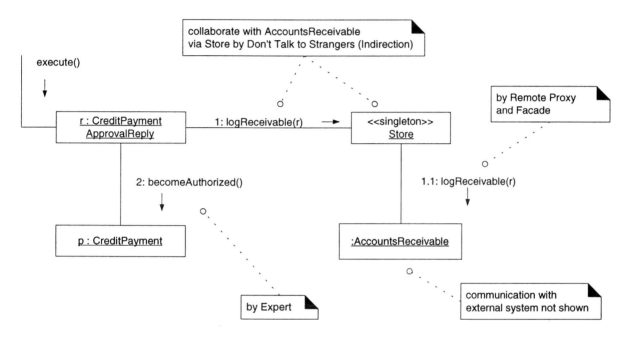

**Figure 35.19** CreditPaymentApprovalReply Execute.

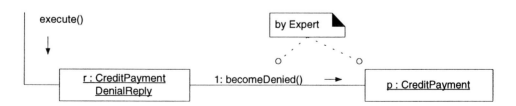

**Figure 35.20** CreditPaymentDenialReply Execute.

---

1. Observe the abstraction possible in communicating designs when pattern names are used.

### *CreditPaymentDenialReply--execute*

By Command and Polymorphism, the *CreditPaymentDenialReply* also receives an *execute* message. In the denial case, the reply must change the state of the payment to denied (see Figure 35.20).

# 35.8 Conclusion

Several new GoF patterns have been explored, and the GRASP patterns have been applied.

The main lesson to draw from this exposition is that the assignment of responsibilities during object-oriented design can be done based on the use of patterns. These provide an explainable set of idioms by which well-designed object-oriented systems can be built.

# PART VII SPECIAL TOPICS

# OTHER UML NOTATION

## 36.1    Introduction

This chapter provides a brief survey of some UML notation not yet emphasized. Please read the annotations within the diagrams for elaboration.

## 36.2    General Notation

### 36.2.1    Notes and Constraints

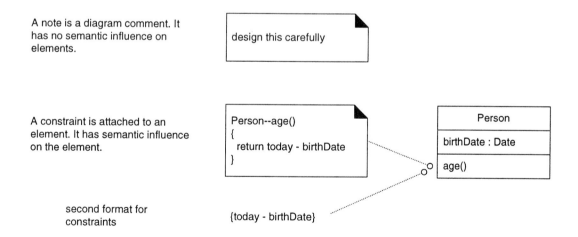

**Figure 36.1** Notes and constraints.

## 36.2.2   Dependency

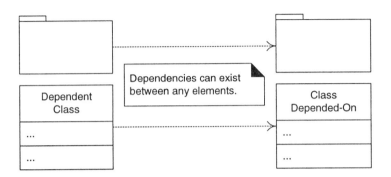

**Figure 36.2**  Dependencies.

## 36.2.3   Stereotypes and Property Specifications

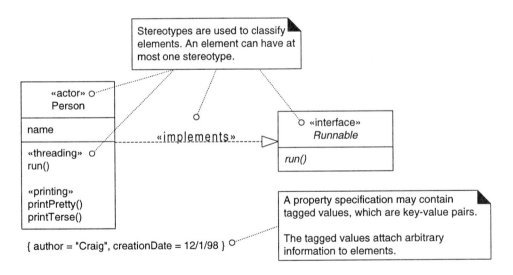

**Figure 36.3**  Stereotypes and properties.

# 36.3    Interfaces

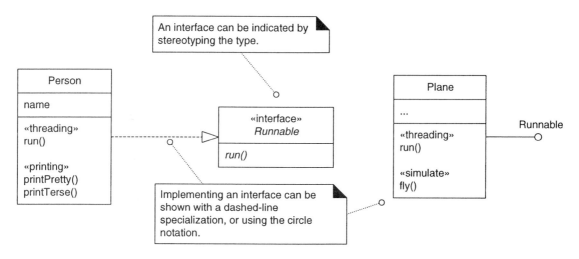

**Figure 36.4** Interfaces.

# 36.4    Implementation Diagrams

## 36.4.1    *Component Diagrams*

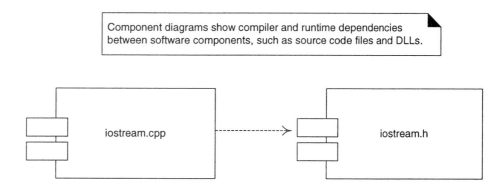

**Figure 36.5** Software components.

## 36.4.2  Deployment Diagrams

Deployment diagrams show the distribution of processes and components to processing nodes.

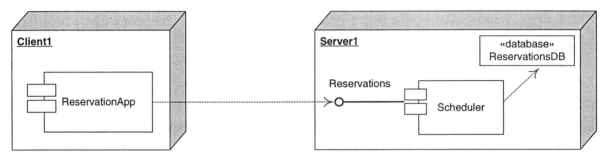

**Figure 36.6**  A deployment diagram.

# 36.5    Asynchronous Messages in Collaboration Diagrams

The UML includes notation to show asynchronous messages, and new threads of control. For example, in Java a *Plane* instance which implements the *Runnable* interface (the *run* method) can create a *Thread* and send it an (asynchronous) *start* message. A *run* message will then be sent back to the *Plane* instance. The *run* method is the body of the thread, and the *Plane* is an "active object" running on its own thread.

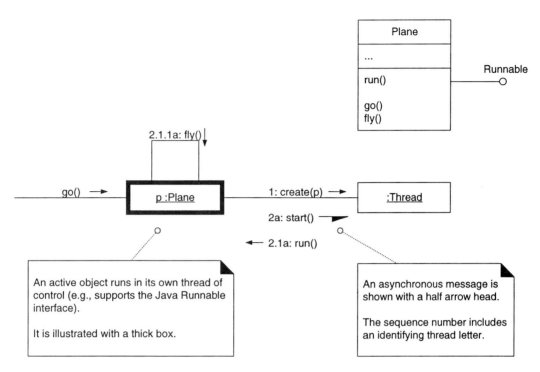

**Figure 36.7** Concurrency and asynchronous messages.

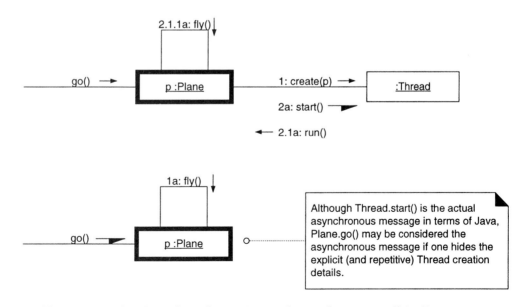

**Figure 36.8** Implicit thread creation and asynchronous call in Java.

## 36.6    Package Interfaces

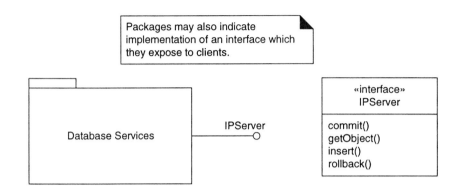

Packages may also indicate implementation of an interface which they expose to clients.

**Figure 36.9** Interface of a package.

# DEVELOPMENT PROCESS ISSUES

---

### Objectives

- Follow a development process that is iterative, incremental, and use case driven.

- Organize work in terms of development cycles.

- Schedule a development cycle within a time-box.

- Organize parallel team development along architectural lines.

- Express non-evident technical requirements as system development cases, and schedule them.

---

## 37.1   Introduction

This chapter explores some basic issues related to the development of systems. It expands on topics introduced earlier, and at a few points repeats and then elaborates ideas that were presented in earlier chapters. The topic of software development processes is large; it includes not only the basic steps in a a project, but also project management and myriad related issues. This chapter touches only on a few highlights.

## 37.2    Why Bother?

It is common to hear horror stories of software project failures that involve liter-ally billions of dollars—tax systems, defence systems and so on. The bottom line is that software development is a risky business. One study showed that 31% of software projects are never completed, that 53% cost almost 200% of their origi-nal estimate, and estimated that American companies and government agencies spent 81 billion dollars for cancelled software projects in 1995 [Standish94]. The status quo is not working.

Following a development process and performing object-oriented analysis and design take time, and thus money. Why bother? Why not jump straight to pro-gramming? Reasons include:

1.  As the statistics above illustrate, software projects are a risky business, so a primary motivation is to reduce risk—to increase the likelihood of creating a successful system. Carefully understanding the requirements and making a formal design are strategies to reduce risk.

2.  It is useful to create a process that can be repeated and duplicated by indi-viduals and especially teams. Development that relies on individual heroic efforts is not sustainable.

3.  It is cheaper and easier to make changes during analysis and design activi-ties than during the construction phase—software is "harder" than it sounds.

4.  By modeling systems and abstracting to find essential details, the otherwise overwhelming complexity can be broken down and managed; complexity overload is avoided.

5.  It is desirable to create systems that are robust, maintainable and support increased software reuse. These goals are not usually met without careful consideration and design prior to programming.

These goals are all supported by the skillful application of analysis and design. Unfortunately, many organizations have been penny wise and pound foolish when it comes to committing resources to formal analysis and design activities, typically opting for a rush to code.

## 37.3    Guiding Principles of a Successful Process

The following principles are part of a recommended development process [Booch96]:

■   iterative and incremental

■   use case driven

■   early emphasis on defining the architecture ("architecture-centric")

# 37.4   Iterative and Incremental Development

## 37.4.1   *Disadvantages of a Waterfall Life-cycle*

The singular characteristic of a waterfall life-cycle of development is that it involves a *single* pass of analysis, design, and construction; one does *all* the analysis, then *all* the design, then the coding, and finally, all the testing. Some of its flaws include:

- front-loading of tackling complexity—complexity overload

- delayed feedback

- specifications frozen early, while business environment changes

## 37.4.2   *An Iterative Life-cycle*

In contrast to the waterfall life-cycle, an iterative life-cycle is based on successive refinement of a system through *multiple* cycles of analysis, design and construction, as shown in Figure 37.1.

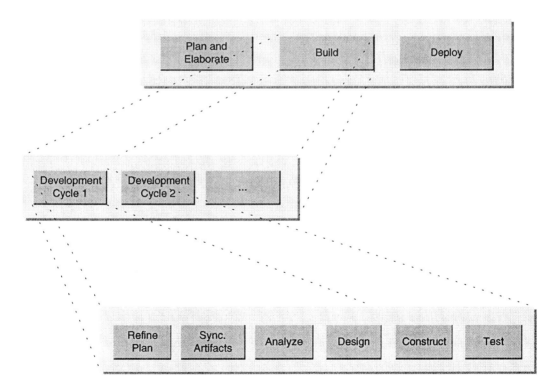

**Figure 37.1**  Iterative life-cycle.

Each cycle tackles a relatively small set of requirements and the system grows incrementally as each cycle is completed. Hence this process is characterized as iterative and incremental; it includes the following benefits:

- The complexity is never overwhelming, because only manageable units of complexity are tackled in a cycle. Avoids "analysis paralysis" and "design paralysis."

- Early feedback is generated, because implementation occurs rapidly for a small subset of the system. This feedback can inform and enhance the analysis of subsequent cycles. This feedback may be to the developers from the results of their own implementation and testing phase, or to them from the user community working with a released version of the system.

- The development team can gradually reapply their growing maturity with their tools—they are not required to apply all the best (and most complex) language/tool features from the beginning, or alternatively, only apply unskillful techniques to portion of the system.

- Requirements can be adjusted to match changing business needs, as the project proceeds.

Iterative development does not mean to hack away for awhile, reach a milestone, and then hack some more. A more precise definition of **iterative development** is that it is a *planned* process of revisiting an area repeatedly, each time enhancing the system. It is a formally planned and scheduled process, not haphazard.

It is possible to perform multiple iterative development cycles upon the same requirements, in which the system (or subsystem) is refined and tuned, or upon new requirements—the more common case.

The definition of **incremental development** is to add functionality to a system during several release cycles; each release contains more functionality. An incremental release is composed of multiple iterative development cycles, not just one. Having relatively frequent (every six or twelve months) incremental releases includes the following benefits:

- Early overall integration and system testing.

- Early feedback to the developer from the end-user community using the released system.

- Feedback to the client and end-user community about the skill and reliability of the development team.

- Assuming the released version is successful, generates early trust and satisfaction among the user community.

The main disadvantage of iterative and incremental development is raised expectations by the client and management. Since this process allows early demonstrations, the client and management will be inclined to think the system is "nearly done"—the "user interface is working = finished system" problem. Vigorous expectations management and lots of tone-setting communication is

436

needed on the part of the development team to try and alleviate this otherwise inevitable reaction.

# 37.5    Use Case Driven Development

The development process should be influenced by and organized around use cases. For example:

- Requirements are organized by and phrased in use cases.

- Estimates are influenced directly and indirectly by use cases, such as the number of use cases, their complexity, required support services, and so on.

- Schedules are organized by iterative cycles which are based on use case fulfillment.

- The choice of what requirements to fulfill in a particular iterative cycle are drawn from use cases.

    - For instance, in iteration 1 we will handle use case A, in iteration 2 a simplified version of use case B, and in iteration 3 the rest of B, and all of C and D.

- The activities within a development cycle are focused on fulfilling the use case(s) under consideration in that cycle.

- Concepts and software classes can be identified from consideration of use cases.

- Test cases are written to validate that the use cases are fulfilled.

# 37.6    Early Emphasis on Architecture

In this context, **architecture** refers to the high-level structure of subsystems and components, and their interfaces, connections, and interactions. It consists of a set of frameworks, subsystems, classes, responsibility assignments, and object collaborations that satisfy the system functions.

A successful process encourages *early* generation of an overall system architecture—it is architecture-centric. This means that the early development cycles emphasize research and development of a well-designed architectural framework, and there is an ongoing and overarching vision of a cohesive architecture throughout the project. The design is not haphazardly cobbled together.

A well-designed architecture has the following ideal qualities:

- layered architectural subsystems
- low inter-subsystem coupling
- easy to understand
- robust, resilient, and scales up well
- high degree of reusable components
- driven by the most important and risky use cases
- well-defined interfaces to the system and subsystems

During early development, the focus should be on layers and subsystems with the highest degree of risk and uncertainty. This may be the domain layer, or some of the high-level services layers. However, an emphasis on architecture additionally implies that some attention to most of the layers and subsystems in the architecture be considered early on. This includes their components, interfaces and interactions with other layers.

# 37.7   Phases of Development

## 37.7.1   Production Releases

At the macro level, a development project is composed of one or more incremental production releases—a release which goes into use. For commercial software this means a version which is sold; for in-house software this means it is in operational use.

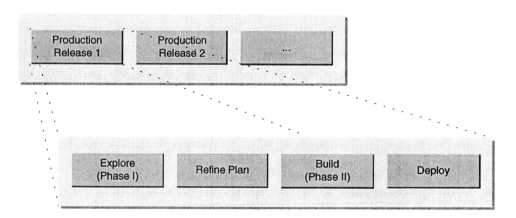

**Figure 37.2** Incremental product development.

Each incremental production release involves the following phases:

1. **Explore**—define requirements and build the system through several development cycles to the point where a believable plan can be created.

2. **Refine Plan**—modify the schedule, budget, and so on, based on the results of exploration.

3. **Build**—the major phase of completing the development.

4. **Deploy**—move the system into production use.

## 37.7.2  Major Development Steps

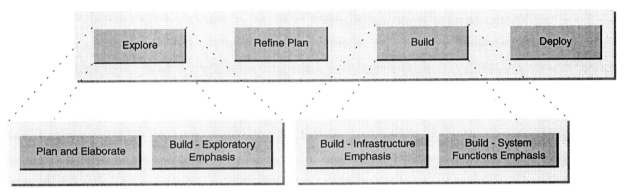

**Figure 37.3** Major steps in development.

Within a single production release, the purpose of the Explore phase (also known as Phase I) is to understand the requirements and then explore building a system to the point that a credible estimate and schedule can be generated.[1] Within the Explore phase the two major phases are:

1. **Plan and Elaborate**—the initial requirements gathering and definition, planning, and elaboration of the problem.

2. **Build - Exploratory Emphasis**—one to three months of development cycles in which some high ranking use cases and architecture work is completed.

The purpose of the major Build phase (also known as Phase II) is to develop the complete system. The development cycles within this phase may be loosely grouped as follows:

1. **Build - Infrastructure Emphasis**—the early development cycles which emphasize establishing and refining the overall technical architecture, such

---

1. Estimates and schedules created without any exploratory development cycles to concretely measure the size and difficulty of the problem, and the speed of the development team, are essentially fictions.

as frameworks, layers and subsystems. This phase *does* include fulfilling domain use cases (for example, *Buy Items*), but much of the effort is devoted to creating the architectural foundation to support their fulfillment.[1]

2. **Build - System Functions Emphasis**—the remaining cycles which emphasize completing the application functions, during which little infrastructure work remains.

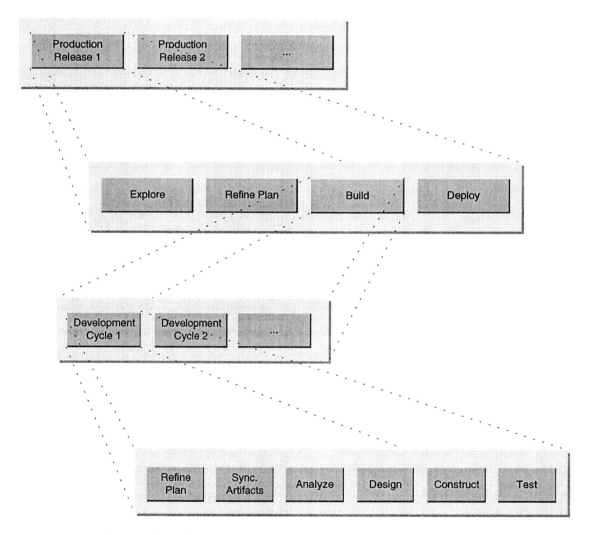

**Figure 37.4** Iterative development cycles.

---

1. The time to develop the infrastructure and complete this phase is often seriously underestimated.

## 37.7.3  Production Release versus Development Cycles

A common misunderstanding in iterative development is to equate a production release and a development cycle.

For example, to have a single six month development cycle, and then release a production system at the end of that six month period, is not an ideal iterative development approach.

Rather, if it is necessary to deliver (release) a production system every six months, the time should be broken up into (for example) six one-month development cycles—six cycles of analyze-design-implement-test.

Thus a production release is composed of *multiple* development cycles, as illustrated in Figure 37.4.

## 37.7.4  The Plan and Elaborate Phase

The Plan and Elaborate phase of a project (shown in Figure 37.5) includes the initial conception, investigation of alternatives, planning, specification of requirements and so on.

Artifacts generated in this phase may include:

- *Plan*—schedule, resources, budget, and so on.

- *Preliminary Investigation Report*—motivation, alternatives, business needs, and so on.

- *Requirements Specification*—declarative statement of requirements.

- *Glossary*—a dictionary of terms (concept names, and so on) and any associated information, such as constraints and rules.

- *Prototype*—a prototype system created to aid understanding of the problem, high risk problems, and requirements.

- *Use Cases*—prose descriptions of domain processes.

- *Use Case Diagrams*—illustration of all use cases and their relationships.

- *Draft Conceptual Model*—a rough preliminary conceptual model as an aid in understanding the vocabulary of the domain, especially as it relates to the use cases and requirement specification.

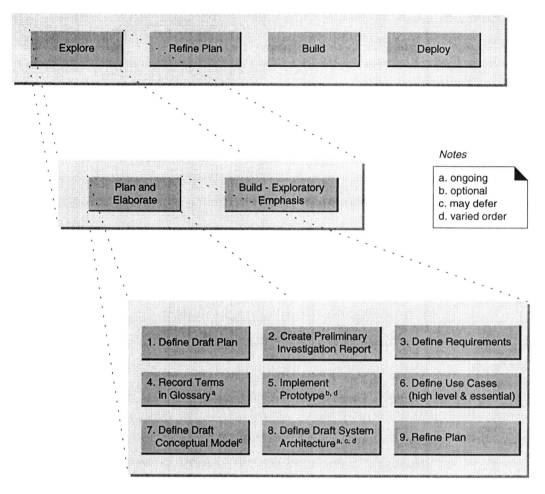

**Figure 37.5** Plan and Elaborate phase of development.

## 37.7.5 The Build-Exploratory Emphasis Phase

The Build-Exploratory Emphasis phase shown in Figure 37.6 involves one to three months of development cycles. High ranking use cases which significantly effect the architecture are tackled. The purpose is to explore enough to acquire information from which to develop a reliable schedule and estimate for the project.

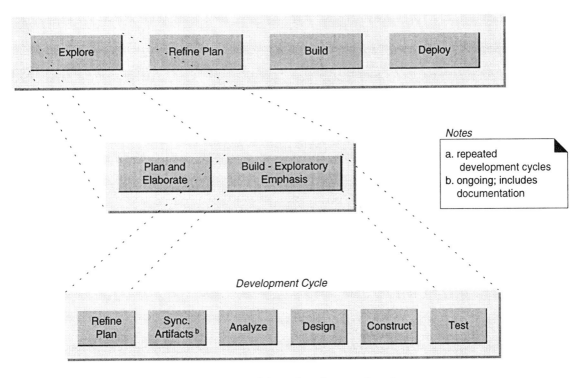

Figure 37.6 Activities within a development cycle.

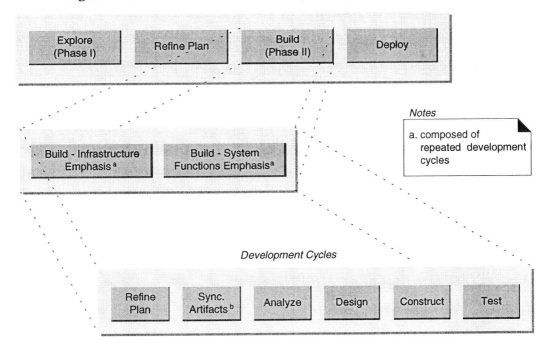

Figure 37.7 The Build phase is composed of repeated development cycles.

## 37.7.6   The Major Build Phase

The primary Build phase (Figure 37.7) is composed on multiple development cycles, which may be broadly grouped into those which emphasize creating the infrastructure, and those which emphasize fulfilling the system functions. The boundary between these groupings in not sharp; during infrastructure-oriented development cycles one or more teams will be working on system functions, and vice versa. The purpose of this demarcation is to emphasize that in many projects that is significant early effort devoted to laying the foundation, which consumes considerable resources.

## 37.7.7   The Deploy Phase

The Deploy phase (Figure 37.8) involves the deployment of the system into production use. For commercial software this means sold to and used by customers; for in-house software this means it is in operational use. The activities in this phase vary widely; for major commercial software systems it may include extraordinary tasks such as acceptance testing by thousands of users and the establishment of large support centers. A discussion of deployment is outside the scope of this chapter.

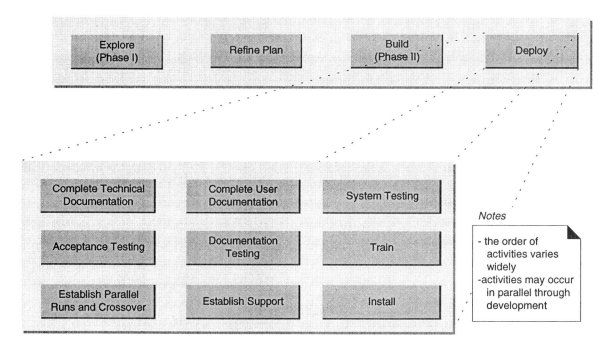

**Figure 37.8** The Deployment phase.

## 37.7.8 The Analyze Phase of a Development Cycle

The Analyze phase (shown in Figure 37.9) of a development cycle emphasizes an investigation of the problem and requirements analysis. It has been explored in detail in earlier chapters.

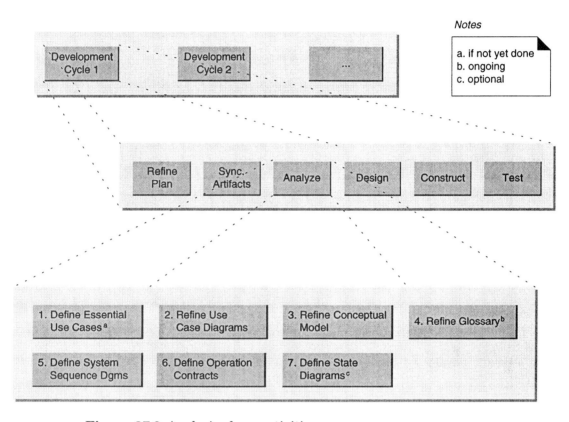

**Figure 37.9** Analysis phase activities.

## 37.7.9 The Design Phase of a Development Cycle

The Design phase of a development cycle emphasizes defining a logical solution (Figure 37.10). It has been explored in detail in earlier chapters.

## 37.7.10 The Construct Phase of a Development Cycle

The Construct phase involves implementation of the design in software and hardware (Figure 37.11).

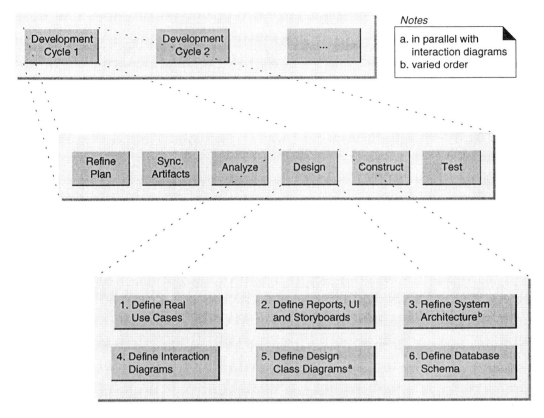

**Figure 37.10** Design phase activities.

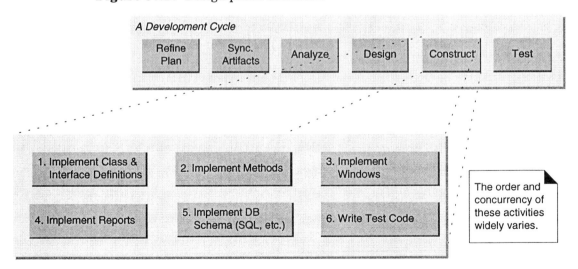

**Figure 37.11** Construct phase activities.

## 37.7.11 The Test Phase

Although the Test phase is shown as a final step within a development cycle, it is also recommended as an ongoing activity during the Construct phase. Not all the testing suggested in Figure 37.12 is suitable during each development cycle. For example, integration testing of the entire system may happen less frequently than each development cycle.

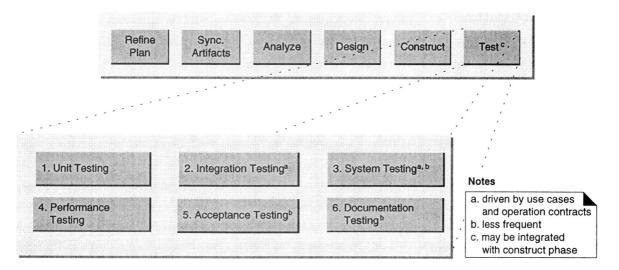

**Figure 37.12** Test phase activities.

# 37.8    Length of Development Cycles

Any less, and it is difficult to complete a meaningful set of requirements and coordinate activities; any more, and there is risk of complexity overload and insufficient early feedback.

> A development cycle should last between two weeks and two months.

All things being equal, two to four week cycles work out well. Factors which cause a cycle to lengthen towards two months include:

- Early development cycles in which the infrastructure and basic services are being developed, and there is a high degree of exploratory research. And be warned: There is often a significant underestimate of the amount of time needed to complete the infrastructure.

- Introduction of new technology or methods.

- Lack of access to subject domain experts.

- Significant distributed or concurrent process and communication work.

- Novice staff (in object technology, the problem domain or iterative development).

- Parallel development teams.

- Physically distributed parallel development teams.[1]

- Large teams.

## 37.8.1 *Time-boxing a Development Cycle*

A useful strategy within each development cycle is to bound it within a time-box—a rigidly fixed time, such as four weeks. All work must be accomplished in that time frame.

Three factors that can be adjusted within a development effort are time, scope and labor. In a time-box approach time is frozen, so that only scope and labor can be adjusted. As illustrated in *The Mythical Man-Month* [Brooks75], "nine women don't make a baby in one month;" adding people to a project in crisis usually exacerbates rather than relieves a problem. Therefore, scope is the main factor that is adjusted to meet the constraints of the time-box; if short of time, defer functionality to a later development cycle.

> The choice of what requirements to fulfill within a time-box should be made by the development team—they are the ones who have to deliver the results.

# 37.9 Development Cycle Issues

## 37.9.1 *Parallel Development Teams and Cycles*

A large project is usually broken into parallel development efforts, where multiple teams work in parallel (see Figure 37.13).

One way to organize the teams is along architectural lines: by layers and subsystem. Another organizational structure is by feature set, which may very well correspond to architectural organization. For example:

---

1. Having a team on another floor of the same building has almost as much impact as if it were in a completely separate geographical location.

- Domain layer team (or domain subsystem team)

- User interface team

- Internationalization team

- High-level service layer team (persistence team, reporting team, and so on)

These teams can work in parallel development cycles, all completing a cycle on the same date.

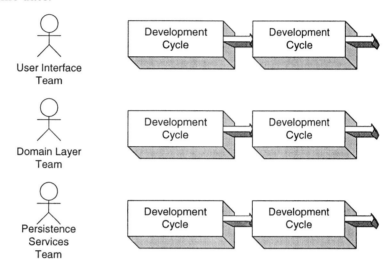

**Figure 37.13** Parallel development teams.

With very complex layers in which progress is invariably slow at first (for example, persistence services), it makes sense to increase the length of the development cycle (Figure 37.14). Thus, teams may be working on different cycle lengths. All cycle lengths should be a multiple of the shortest cycle length.

## 37.9.2  Non-Evident Requirements and Technical Architecture

Some requirements may be implicit—not explicitly evident in the requirements specifications and use cases. This is especially true of the work to design an overall technical architecture and high-level services, such as persistence.

There is a significant amount of work required to design and implement the overall technical architecture of a system, such as the architectural layers, physical deployment, distributed computing, and so on. This work needs to be identified and scheduled; the next section suggests how.

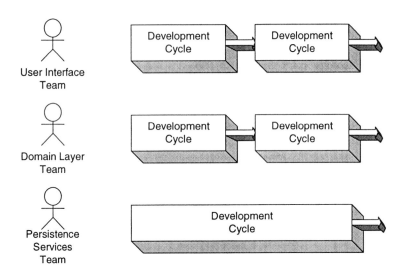

**Figure 37.14** Varying length development cycles.

## 37.9.3   System Development Cases

In order to clarify non-evident technical architecture requirements, create **system development cases**—a kind of use case which describes the design work and functional goals of the development activity.[1] These system development cases can then be scheduled like other domain-oriented use cases.

Example system development cases include:

■   Design architectural layers and subsystems

■   Develop a persistence service

In fact, all activities related to the development and maintenance of software may themselves be considered system development cases and modeled in the same way as regular domain process use cases, with system development case diagrams, *uses* relationships, and so on (see Figure 37.15).

Consequently, a system development case, like a use case, can be identified and allocated to development cycles.

---

1. These are related to processes, procedures, and activity blocks in Jacobson's development case model [Jacobson92].

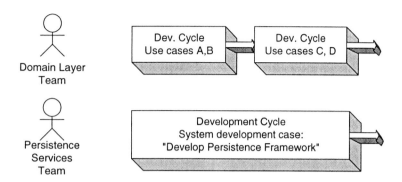

**Figure 37.15** Assigning a system development case to a development cycle.

## 37.9.4 Parallel Development Dependencies

When there is more than one team on the project, dependencies exist across the teams, such as:

- User interface layer relies on the domain layer.

- Domain layer relies on services layers, such as persistence.

- The testing team (if one exists) is dependent on something being finished and stable enough to test.

The problem in this situation is that one team wants to use the output from another, but it is not complete. Strategies for dealing with these dependencies include:

- *Stubbing*—calls to incomplete services are implemented as do-nothing or do-minimal stubs. As the services are completed, the stubs are replaced.

- *Staggered development cycles.* Some teams work on a development cycle that is related to the finished work of a previous development cycle of another team. It is especially convenient for the user interface team to work with the results of a prior domain layer team development cycle (Figure 37.16).

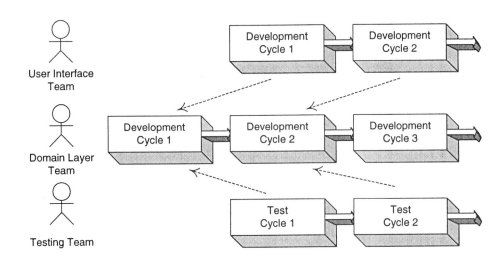

**Figure 37.16** Staggered dependent development and test cycles.

## 37.10  Scheduling Development of Architectural Layers

Typical layers in a system include the domain, database access (persistence), high-level services, and user interface.There is no right answer as to which layers to focus on in early development, but here are some issues to consider:

- Typically, the user interface is the visible realization of the system. It is what the non-developers (managers, clients) see and viscerally think of as the system. People are visual oriented. Usually, an appealing user interface will provide client satisfaction, even when there is no significant functionality to go with it. Therefore, getting an early start on an alluring user interface is helpful. The downside is that clients, seeing the interface, think the system is nearly complete, when in fact it is hardly begun.

- Within a development cycle, if there is one team developing both the domain and services layer, start with the domain layer. Complete the domain layer to the point of fulfilling all system functions related to the use cases for the current iteration. Define the supporting high-level services layer (such as persistence or reporting) as do-nothing stubs. Finally, implement these stubbed services.

- Add persistence (database) support early, but not immediately.

  - Developing persistence services and database support can consume an inordinate amount of resources. Tackling it too early tends to divert attention from a well-designed domain layer. Unfortunately, with current technology, tackling it too late tends to instigate significant retrofitting or design modifications because of the interplay in terms of metadata, database schema, class hierarchy design, transaction management and so on.

❑   When persistence services are developed, create the minimal database schema and persistence framework necessary for persistence in the current iteration. Along with fulfillment of the domain processes, incrementally improve the persistence services over multiple development cycles.

# FRAMEWORKS, PATTERNS, AND PERSISTENCE

## Objectives

- Define what a framework is.

- Apply the most fundamental framework GoF pattern: Template Method.

- Apply other patterns uses in persistent frameworks, such as Complex Object Instantiation.

- Apply other GoF patterns, especially Virtual Proxy.

## 38.1    Introduction

Most applications require storing and retrieving information in a persistent storage mechanism, such as a relational database. This chapter explores the object-oriented design of a framework for persistent objects that need to saved in a persistent store.

The intention is not to show the design of an industrial-strength framework for persistence, but rather to use the problem of persistence frameworks as a vehicle for explaining general framework design issues, and some critical issues in persistence services. It is also a demonstration of how to use the UML to communicate a design.

Not all design issues are discussed in the text; the illustrations contain comments which elaborate in ways that would otherwise be awkward to express.

# 38.2    The Problem: Persistent Objects

Suppose that in the point-of-sale application a large number of *ProductSpecification* instances reside in some persistent storage mechanism—such as a database—and they must be brought into local memory during application use.

Most applications require storing data in and retrieving data from a persistent storage mechanism, such as a relational or object database. **Persistent objects** are those which require persistent storage, such as *ProductSpecification* instances.

The subject of this chapter is how to design persistent object services, both because it is a common problem and because it is a useful vehicle to learn more patterns and object-oriented design principles.

## 38.2.1    *Storage Mechanisms and Persistent Objects*

**Object Databases**. If an object database is used to store and retrieve objects, no additional custom or third-party persistence services are required. This is one of several attractions for their use.

**Relational Databases**. Because of the prevalence of relational databases, their use is often required, rather than the more convenient object databases. If this is the case, a number of problems arise due to the mismatch between record-oriented and object-oriented representations of data; these problems will be explored later. Special object-relational services are required with relational databases.

**Other**. In addition to relational databases, it is sometimes desirable to store objects in other storage mechanisms, such as flat files, hierarchical databases, and so on. As with relational databases, a representation mismatch exists between objects and the non-object-oriented ways they are stored in these mechanisms. As with relational databases, special services are required to make them work with objects.

# 38.3    The Solution: A Persistence Framework

A **persistence framework** is a reusable—and usually extendable—set of classes that provide services for persistent objects. A persistence framework is usually written to work with relational databases, or a common record-oriented data services API such as Microsoft's ODBC. Typically, a persistence framework has to translate objects to records and save them in a database, and translate records to objects when retrieving from a database (Figure 38.1).

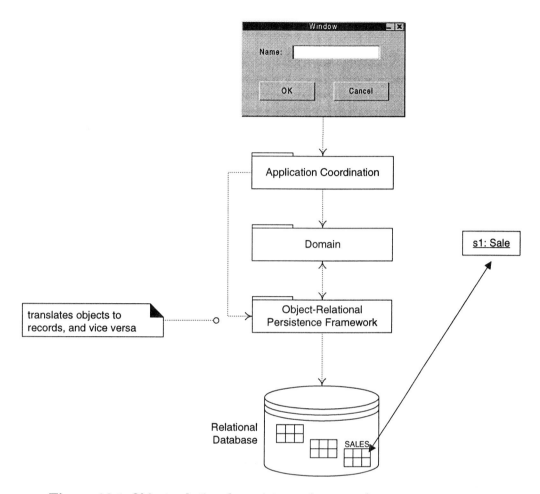

**Figure 38.1** Object-relational persistence framework.

If an object database is used, no persistence framework is needed. However, if another storage mechanism is used, a persistence framework is highly desirable; for example, it is useful for relational databases and flat files. This chapter examines the design of a persistence framework and the patterns that can be applied.

# 38.4 What is a Framework?

At the risk of oversimplification, a framework is an extendable subsystem for a set of related services, such as:

■ Graphical user interface frameworks (for example, Microsoft Foundation Classes, Smalltalk-80 Model-View-Controller).

■ Persistence frameworks (that is, services to make persistent objects).

The persistence framework example in this chapter will concretely illustrate what a framework is. In general, a **framework**:

■ Is a cohesive set of classes that collaborate to provide services for the core, unvarying part of a logical subsystem.

■ Contains concrete (and especially) abstract classes that define interfaces to conform to, object interactions to participate in, and other invariants.

■ Usually (but not necessarily) requires the framework user to define subclasses of existing framework classes in order to make use of, customize, and extend the framework services.

■ Has abstract classes that may contain both abstract and concrete methods.

■ Relies on the **Hollywood Principle**— *"Don't call us, we'll call you."* This means that the user-defined classes (for example, new subclasses) will receive messages from the predefined framework classes. These are usually handled by implementing superclass abstract methods.

The following persistence framework example will demonstrate these principles.

## 38.4.1   *Frameworks are Very Reusable*

Frameworks provide a very high degree of reuse—much more so than individual classes. Consequently, if an organization is interested (and who isn't?) in significantly increasing their degree of software reuse, then it is critical to emphasize the creation of frameworks.

## 38.5   Requirements for the Persistence Framework

We desire a persistence framework, one that provides services for persistent objects. Let's call it PFW (Persistence FrameWork). PFW is a simplified framework; a full-blown industrial strength persistence framework is outside the scope of this introduction, although areas that need development or alternative design will be mentioned.

In particular, the framework should provide these functions:

■ Store and retrieve objects in a persistent storage mechanism.

■ *Commit* and *rollback* transactions.

The design should support these qualities:

- Be extendable to support any kind of storage mechanism, such as relational databases, flat files, and so on.

- Require minimal modification to existing code.

- Be easy to use (as a programmer).

- Very transparent—exist in the background without intrusion.

# 38.6    PersistentObject Superclass?

A common partial design solution to providing persistence for objects is to create an abstract utility superclass *PersistentObject* that all persistence objects inherit from (see Figure 38.2). Such a class usually defines attributes for persistence, such as a unique object identifier, and methods for saving to a database.

This is not wrong, but suffers from the weakness of strongly coupling the existing class to the *PersistentObject* class; domain classes end up inheriting from a utility class.

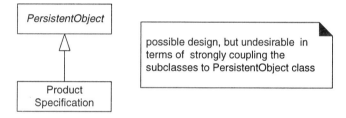

**Figure 38.2**  Problems with a PersistentObject superclass.

The PFW design will explore ways to avoid a *PersistentObject* superclass, and discuss the trade-offs imposed by various object-oriented languages.

# 38.7    Key Ideas

The following key ideas will be explored in subsequent sections:

- **Mapping**. There must be some mapping between a class and its persistent store (for example, a table in a database), and between object attributes and the fields (columns) in a record.

- **Object Identity**. In order to easily relate records to objects, and to ensure there are no inappropriate duplicates, records and objects have a unique object identifier.

- **Database Brokers**. A Pure Fabrication database broker is responsible for materialization and dematerialization.

- **Materialization and dematerialization**. Materialization is the act of transforming a non-object representation of data (for example, records) from a persistent store into objects. Dematerialization is the opposite activity (also known as passivation).

- **Caches**. Database brokers cache materialized objects.

- **Lazy on-demand materialization**. Not all objects are materialized at once; a particular instance is only materialized on-demand, when needed.

- **Smart References**. Lazy on-demand materialization is implemented using a smart reference known as a virtual proxy.

- **Complex objects**. How to represent and materialize objects that have complex structures, such as connections to many other objects.

- **Transaction State of Object**. It is useful to know the state of objects in terms of their relationship to the current transaction. For example, it is useful to know which objects have been modified (are *dirty*), so that it is possible to determine if they need to be saved back to their persistent store.

- **Transaction Operations**. Commit and rollback operations.

- **Searching**. Finding and materialization objects based on some criteria.

## 38.8    Mapping—Pattern *Representing Objects as Tables*

How to map an object to a file or relational database schema?

The **Representing Objects as Tables** pattern [Brown96] proposes defining a table (if an RDB is used) for each persistent object class. Object attributes containing primitive data types (number, string, boolean, and so on) map to columns.

If an object only has attributes of primitive data types, the mapping is straightforward. But as we will see, matters are not that simple, since objects may have attributes that refer to other complex objects, while the relational model requires that values be atomic (First Normal Form)

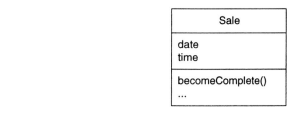

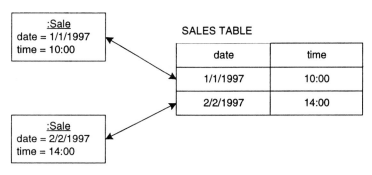

**Figure 38.3**  Mapping objects and tables.

# 38.9    Object Identify—*Object Identifier* Pattern

It is desirable to have a consistent way to relate objects to records, and be able to ensure that repeated materialization of a record does not result in duplicate objects.[1]

The **Object Identifier** pattern [Brown96] proposes assigning an **object identifier** (OID) to each record and object (or proxy of an object).

An OID is usually an alpha-numeric value; it is unique to a specific object. An excellent choice for OID is the thirty-two-character-long Universally Unique Identifier[2] (UUID), each one guaranteed unique on planet Earth, for any date and time. In recognition that our planet does not represent the universe, they have been renamed in Microsoft's terminology as a *Globally* Unique Identifier, or GUID, and the Microsoft Windows API provides a function for their automatic generation.

Every RDB table will have an OID as primary key, and each object will (directly or indirectly) also have an OID.

If every object is associated with an OID, and every table has an OID primary key, every object can be uniquely mapped to some row in some table.

---

1. Duplication problems are explored later.

2. Based on an algorithm from the Open Software Foundation.

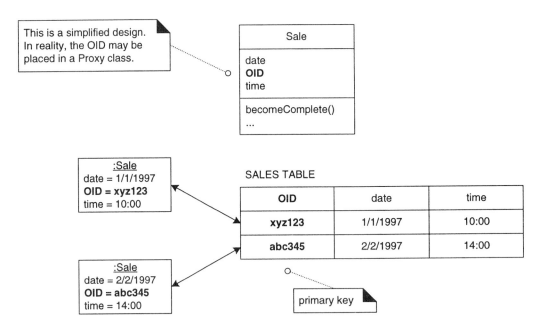

**Figure 38.4** Object identifiers link objects and records.

This is a simplified view of the design. In reality, the OID may not actually be placed in the persistent object—although that is possible. Instead, it may be placed in a Proxy object, as discussed later. The design is influenced by the choice of language.

# 38.10   Brokers—*Database Broker* Pattern

Who should be responsible for materialization and dematerialization of objects (for example, a *ProductSpecification*) from a persistent store? The Expert pattern suggests that the persistent object class (*ProductSpecification*) should be, but this has a number of defects, including:

- Coupling of the persistent object class to persistent storage knowledge (violation of Low Coupling).

- Complex responsibilities in a new and unrelated area to what the object was previously responsible for (violation of High Cohesion).

The solution, as usual when coupling is high, is the Indirection pattern—add something in between, usually a Pure Fabrication.

The **Database Broker** pattern [Brown96] proposes making a class that is responsible for materialization, dematerialization, and object caching. A different broker class may be defined for each persistent object class.[1] A Database Broker is a Pure Fabrication that supports High Cohesion and Low Coupling via Indirection. Figure 38.5 illustrates that each persistent object may have its own broker class, and that there may be different kinds of brokers for different storage mechanisms.

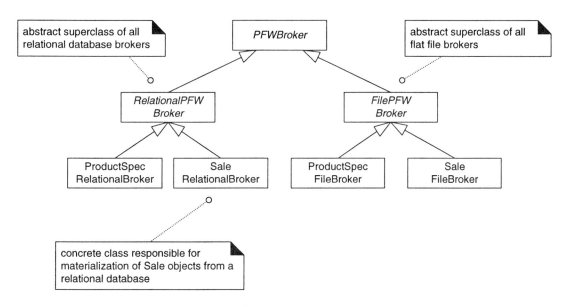

**Figure 38.5** Database Broker hierarchy.

# 38.11  Framework Design—*Template Method* Pattern

The next section describes some of the essential design features of the Database Brokers, which are a central part of the persistence framework. These design features are based on the **Template Method** GoF pattern [GHJV95].

This pattern is at the heart of framework design. The idea is to define a method (the Template Method) in a superclass that defines the skeleton of an algorithm, with its varying and unvarying parts. The Template Method invokes other methods, some of which are operations which may be overridden in a subclass.

Thus, subclasses can override the varying methods in order to add their own unique behavior at points of variability.

The Template Method pattern illustrates the Hollywood Principle—"Don't call us, we'll call you." In Figure 38.6 class *ConcreteClass* overrides *primitiveOperation*. It will be called automatically when the inherited *templateMethod* is invoked.

---

1. An alternative based on meta-data and parameterized instances is mentioned later on.

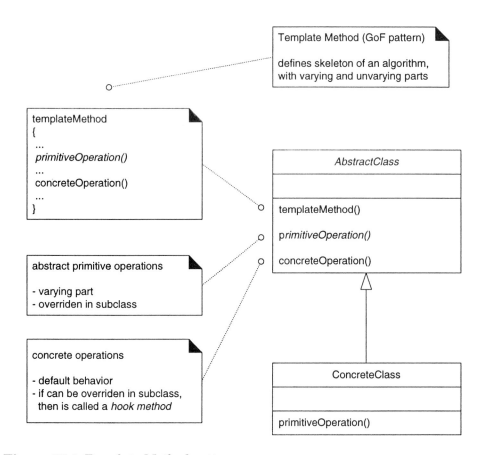

**Figure 38.6** Template Method pattern.

# 38.12 Materialization—*Template Method* Pattern

In the PFW framework, objects can be retrieved by invoking the *objectWith(anOID)* method defined in class *PFWBroker*. This method may in turn invoke the *materializeWith(anOID)* to materialize the object. As illustrated in Figure 38.7, materialization logic typically involves creating an instance of the appropriate class, and moving data from the record into the attributes of the new instance. For example, the *time* field of a row in the *SALES* table can be copied to the *time* attribute of the associated *Sale* instance.

The Database Broker class hierarchy is an essential part of the PFW framework; new subclasses may be added by the application programmer to customize it for new kinds of persistent storage mechanisms or for new particular tables or files within an existing storage mechanism.

For example, it is possible to add a new subclass of *PFWBroker* such as *FilePF-WBroker* for object materialization from flat files. And within the *RelationalPF-*

*WBroker*, it is possible to add materialization for new classes, such as the a *SaleRelationalBroker*.

As illustrated in Figure 38.7, the extendible design is based upon the Template Method pattern.[1]

The most important public method in *PFWBroker* is *objectWith(anOID)*, a template method which takes an OID as a parameter, and returns the object for that OID. If the object was previously materialized and is currently in a cache, it is simply returned. But if it was not in a cache, then it is materialized with the *materializeWith(anOID)* method, which is a "primitive operation" of the *objectWith* template method. New subclasses may be added which materialize in varying ways.

Note the characteristic nature of the *objectWith* template method. It defines varying and unvarying parts of the framework. The pattern of cache look up and materialization is unvarying, but the particulars of how materialization occurs can vary, and is left as a primitive operation for subclasses to define.

Similarly, *currentRecordAsObject* is a primitive operation for the template method *RelationalPFWBroker::materializeWith*. Each concrete broker for each class/table pair defines how to transform the current database record that has been read into an object. Within this example, the transformation appears fairly trivial; later we will see more complex materialization logic.

The *PFWBroker* hierarchy demonstrates the following three classic framework design features:

1. The use of template methods in predefined abstract superclasses.

2. The addition of programmer defined subclasses.

3. The definition of "primitive operation" methods in the subclasses to complete the inherited template methods.

---

1. Later, an alternate solution based on metadata will be discussed.

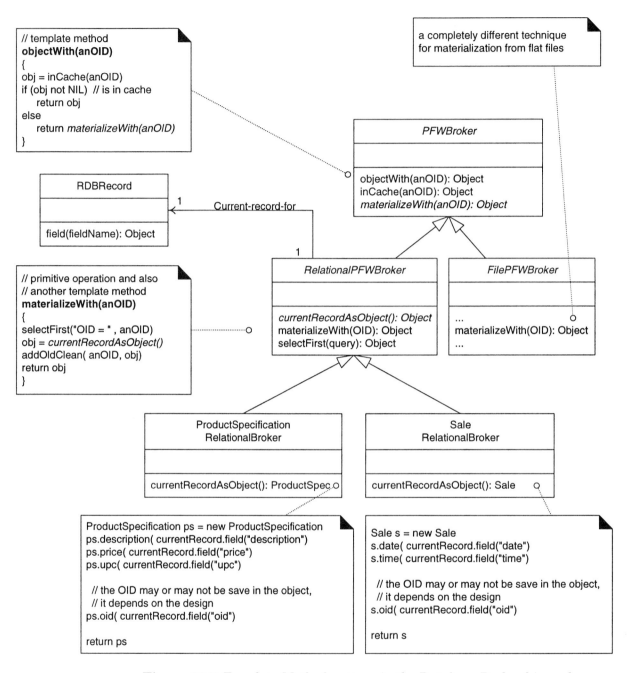

**Figure 38.7** Template Method pattern in the Database Broker hierarchy.

# 38.13   Cached Objects—*Cache Management* Pattern

It is desirable to maintain materialized objects in a local cache in order to improve performance (materialization is relatively slow) and to support transaction management operations such as a commit (see Figure 38.8).

The **Cache Management** pattern [Brown96] proposes making the Database Brokers responsible for maintaining its cache. If a different broker is used for each class of persistent object, each broker can maintain its own cache.

When objects are materialized, they are placed in the cache, with their OID as the key. Subsequent requests to the broker for an object will cause the broker to first search the cache, thus avoiding unnecessary materialization.

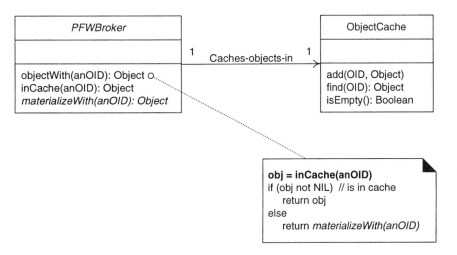

**Figure 38.8** Brokers maintain a cache of materialized objects.

## 38.13.1  Caches for Transaction Management

A variation on the single cache is to maintain objects in different caches depending on their state in the context of the current transaction (see Figure 38.9). In this approach, up to six caches are maintained by the broker.[1] This provides the basis for determining how to commit and rollback from transactions.

---

1. For most applications less than six are required because the transaction rules are the same for several caches. For example, the New Clean and New Dirty caches are treated the same for both a commit (insert in database) and rollback (flush). Further, an alternative to multiple caches based on state objects is discussed later.

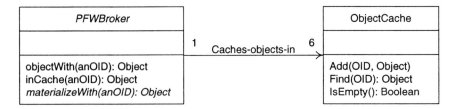

**Figure 38.9** Multiple caches for the broker.

The six caches are:

1. **New Clean Cache**. New objects, unmodified.

2. **Old Clean Cache**. Old objects materialized from a database, unmodified.

3. **New Dirty Cache**. New objects, modified.

4. **Old Dirty Cache**. Old objects materialized from a database, modified.

5. **New Delete Cache**. New objects, to be deleted.

6. **Old Delete Cache**. Old objects materialized from a database, to be deleted.

How objects move into these different caches, and the reasoning that is applied to them with commit and rollback operations is discussed in later sections.

# 38.14  Smart References—*Virtual Proxy, Bridge* Patterns

As will soon be explored in greater detail, it is sometimes desirable to defer the materialization of an object until it is absolutely required. This is known as **lazy** or **on-demand materialization**. On-demand materialization can be implemented using the Virtual Proxy GoF pattern—one of many variations of the Proxy pattern [GHJV95] (Remote Proxy and Device Proxy were examined in an earlier chapter).

A **Virtual Proxy** is a smart reference proxy for another object (the *real subject*) that materializes the real subject when it is first referenced; therefore, it implements on-demand materialization. It is a lightweight object that stands for a "real" object that may or may not be materialized. A Virtual Proxy is considered a smart reference because it is treated by a client as a regular reference to the real subject.

A Virtual Proxy is a special case of the Indirection pattern. As shown in Figure 38.10, a client object has a reference to the Virtual Proxy object rather than to the real subject, but the client treats the Virtual Proxy as though it were the real subject. The Virtual Proxy implements the same interface that the real subject does, so the client object essential views the Virtual Proxy as being the real subject.

A Virtual Proxy is also a specialization of another GoF pattern: Bridge (also known as Handle-Body) [GHJV95]. The **Bridge** pattern is itself a special case of the Indirection pattern in which an intermediate object (the *Handle*) receives requests from a client and forwards them on to another object (the *Body*) to fulfill. The Handle object is usually very lightweight in terms of its responsibilities; in general, it just forwards requests to its Body. The Bridge pattern allows the designer to de-couple implementation from interface.

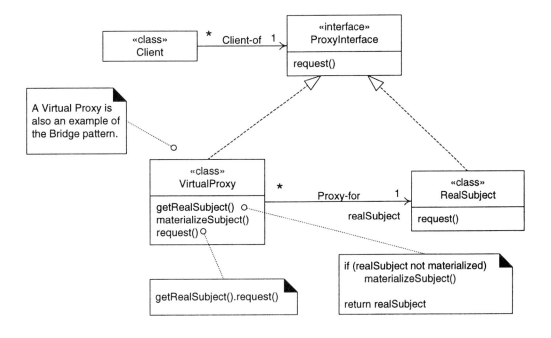

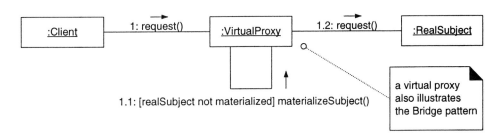

**Figure 38.10** Virtual Proxy and Bridge.

A concrete example of the Virtual Proxy pattern with *SalesLineItem* and *ProductSpecification* is shown in Figure 38.11. This design is based on the assumption that proxies know the OID of their real subject, and when materialization is required, the OID is used to help identify and retrieve the real subject.

Note that the *SalesLineItem* has attribute visibility to a *ProductSpecificationProxy* instance. The *ProductSpecification* for this *SalesLineItem* may not yet be materialized in memory. When the *SalesLineItem* sends a *description* message to the proxy, it materializes the real *ProductSpecification*, using the OID of the real *ProductSpecification* to identify the real subject.

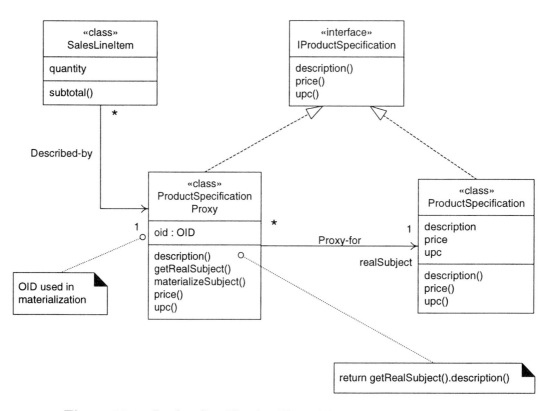

**Figure 38.11** ProductSpecification Virtual Proxy.

## 38.14.1 Generalized Virtual Proxy

Since all Virtual Proxy classes need to perform on-demand materialization, need to know their real subject, and can know the OID of their real subject, it is possible to create a generalized abstract superclass *VirtualProxy* with these responsibilities. Concrete subclasses only need to add support for the particular real subject interface they must implement. This design is illustrated in Figure 38.12.

## 38.14.2 No Common PersistentObject Superclass Required

Note that in this design it is not necessary to maintain the OID in the domain object itself (for example, *ProductSpecification*). This obviates the need for domain objects to inherit from a common superclass such as *PersistentObject* (see Figure 38.13).

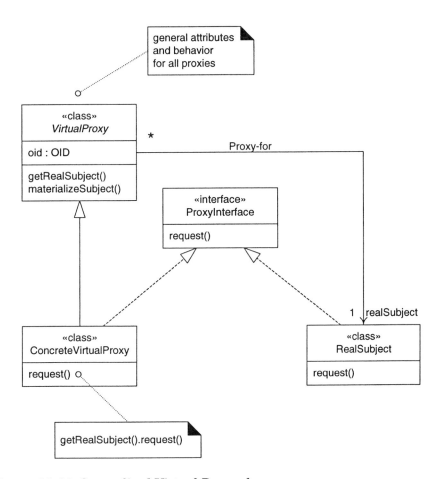

**Figure 38.12** Generalized Virtual Proxy class.

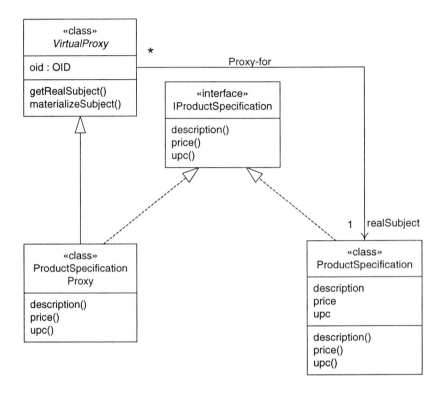

**Figure 38.13** ProductSpecificationProxy class.

## 38.14.3 Implementation of Virtual Proxy

The implementation of a Virtual Proxy varies by language. The details are outside the scope of this chapter, but here follows a synopsis:

| Language | Virtual Proxy Implementation |
|---|---|
| C++ | Define a templatized smart pointer class. The abstract *VirtualProxy* class and *ConcreteVirtualProxy* classes are not defined, but their behavior is fulfilled by the smart pointer. No *ProxyInterface* definition is needed. |

| Language | Virtual Proxy Implementation |
|----------|------------------------------|
| Java | The *VirtualProxy* class is implemented. *ConcreteVirtual-Proxy* classes are implemented. *ProxyInterface* interfaces are defined. |
| Smalltalk | 1. The *VirtualProxy* class is implemented. *ConcreteVirtualProxy* classes are implemented. No *ProxyInterfaces* are needed due to the dynamic binding of Smalltalk.<br><br>2. Define a Virtual Morphing Proxy (or Ghost Proxy) which uses *#doesNotUnderstand:* and *#become:* to morph into the real subject. The abstract *VirtualProxy* class and *ConcreteVirtualProxy* classes are not defined. No *ProxyInterface* definition is needed. |

## 38.15   Virtual Proxies and Database Brokers

Now some of the central pieces are in place to flesh out the details of the persistence framework. A Virtual Proxy can collaborate with a Database Broker in order to materialize an object, based on the OID maintained by the proxy (see Figure 38.14).

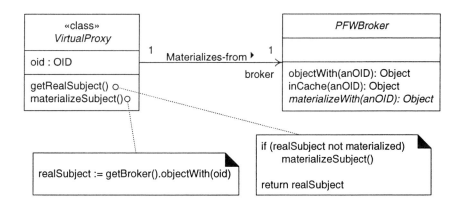

**Figure 38.14** Collaboration between Virtual Proxy and Database Broker.

### 38.15.1  Connecting Proxy and Broker—Factory Method Pattern

How does a concrete Virtual Proxy know which particular concrete Database Broker to use? The answer is to apply the Factory Method GoF pattern [GHJV95]. The **Factory Method** pattern (shown in Figure 38.15) is a special case of the Template Method pattern in which the primitive operation (the Factory Method) is responsible for creating an instance. The Factory Method pattern, in addition to its more general Template Method pattern, is very common in framework design. The *createBroker* Factory Method uses the Singleton pattern to return a Database Broker, since it is desirable to only have one instance of each broker.

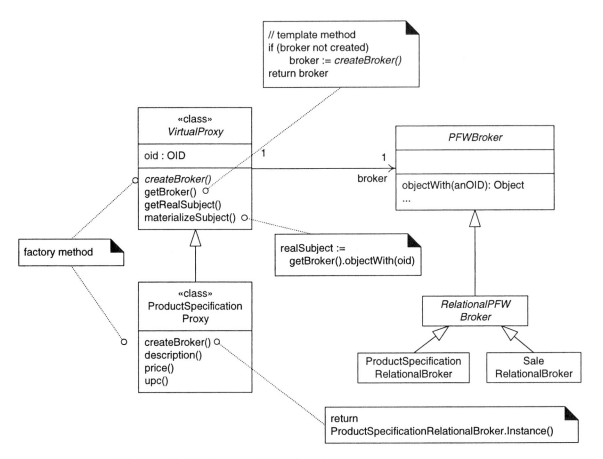

**Figure 38.15** Factory Method pattern.

It is now possible to see a repeated theme in framework design: the *PFWBroker* and *VirtualProxy* classes are both part of the framework, and they share some qualities common to frameworks. For example:

- Abstract superclasses which may be subclasses by the framework user.

- Define template methods whose primitive operations are defined in a subclass by the framework user.

## 38.15.2 Making Everything a Proxy

When virtual proxies are used, it is useful if *all* reference to objects are via the proxy objects instead of direct references.This means that:

- All attribute definitions are to proxy objects or to interfaces, rather than the direct objects.

- All parameters are to proxy objects or to interfaces.

For example, if C++ is being used and proxies are implemented with templatized smart pointers, then all data members and parameter declarations are for smart pointers, not for persistent objects. In the case of C++, this approach can also be used to support automatic memory management; the brokers can manage memory.

If Java is being used, all instance field and parameter declarations will be to interfaces (which is desirable in any event because of its flexibility).

This consistent use of proxies ensures that on-demand materialization and transaction operations will occur correctly.

# 38.16   How to Represent Relationships in Tables

The next major section discusses how to materialize complex objects—those with connections to other objects as opposed to only maintaining simple primitive attributes. In preparation for that discussion, it is necessary to consider the ways that object relationships may be defined in a persistent store. Relational tables will be used in this discussion, although schemes are available for other storage mechanisms.

How to represent object relationships in a relational database table? The answer is given in the **Representing Object Relationships as Tables** pattern [Brown96] which proposes the following:

- **One-to-one** associations.
    - ❏ Place an OID foreign key in one or both tables representing the objects in relationship.
    - ❏ Or, create an associative table that records the OIDs of each object in relationship.
- **One-to-many** associations, such as a collection.
    - ❏ Create an associative table that records the OIDs of each object in relationship.
- **Many-to-many** associations.
    - ❏ Create an associative table that records the OIDs of each object in relationship.

For simplicity in this discussion, an associative table will always be used.

# 38.17   The *Complex Object Instantiation* Pattern

## 38.17.1   Problem: Materializing a Composition Hierarchy

The use of Virtual Proxy and Database Broker objects provides the means to achieve on-demand materialization. But why bother? The reason is that objects may contain many connections to other objects, forming a composition hierarchy. For example, suppose that *Sale*, *SalesLineItem* and *ProductSpecification* objects are all persistent. What does it mean to materialize a *Sale*? Does it mean that just the *Sale* it materialized, or does it mean that the *Sale*, and its *SalesLineItems*, and their associated *ProductSpecifications* are materialized? If one is materializing a root object with a deep composition hierarchy, it is possible that dozens or hundreds of related objects may also need materialization. Materialization of an entire composition hierarchy is both slow and space-inefficient.

## 38.17.2   Solution: On-demand Materialization

Consequently, the solution is the **Complex Object Instantiation** pattern [Brown96] which proposes to defer instantiation (materialization) of objects depending on access patterns and performance requirements. The extreme case of this pattern—taken in this chapter for simplicity—is 100% on-demand materialization: defer the materialization of every object until called for. In many applications a middle ground solution in which a composition hierarchy is materialized one or two levels deep may be more appropriate. With a different broker for each persistent object, it is possible on a broker-by-broker basis to decide the degree of materialization for each persistent object and its associated objects.

## 38.17.3   Example: Materializing a SalesLineItem

To understand how complex object instantiation works in the context of the PFW framework, the case of materializing a *SalesLineItem* instance will be examined. Assume that the *SalesLineItem* and its related information are stored in relational tables, as illustrated in Figure 38.16.

SALESLINEITEMS

| OID | quantity |
|-----|----------|
| sli1 | 1 |
| sli2 | 2 |

PRODUCTSPEC

| OID | description | price | upc |
|-----|-------------|-------|-----|
| p1 | tofu | 1.50 | 111 |
| p2 | tempeh | 2.25 | 222 |

SALESLINEITEMS-TO-PRODUCTSPEC

| SLI-OID | PS-OID |
|---------|--------|
| sli1 | p1 |
| sli2 | p2 |

**Figure 38.16** Tables for the SalesLineItem and its related information.

Also, assume that we know that the OID of the *SalesLineItem* is *"sli1"*.[1] Consider what happens if the following code is executed:

```
// create the proxy
SalesLineItemProxy anSLI =
          new SalesLineItemProxy("sli1");

// cause materialization of objects
int total = anSLI.subtotal();
```

The collaborations are illustrated starting in Figure 38.17. Note that the simple statement *anSLI.subtotal()* causes a significant behind-the-scenes materialization of objects. A critical step is found within the *currentRecordAsObject* method of *SalesLineItemRelationalBroker*. After the *SalesLineitem* instance is created, the OID of the associated *ProductSpecification* is determined by reading from the associative table.[2] Instead of materializing the *ProductSpecification*, a *ProductSpecificationProxy* is created and associated with the *SalesLineItem*.

---

1. Determining the OID of the initialize object to materialize will be discussed later.

2. A pseudo-SQL is used to indicate reading from another table. Details of how to read from a table vary widely.

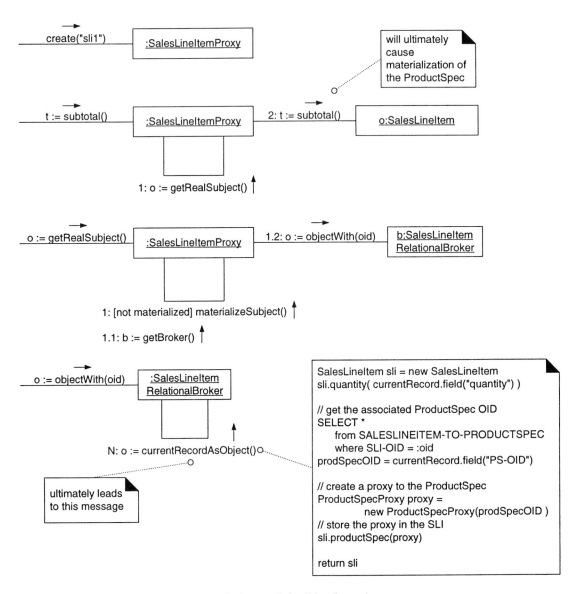

**Figure 38.17** Materializing a SalesLineItem instance.

Thus, the *SalesLineItem* references a proxy, not the real *ProductSpecification*. The real one won't be materialized until the *price* message is sent to it, as illustrated in Figure 38.18.

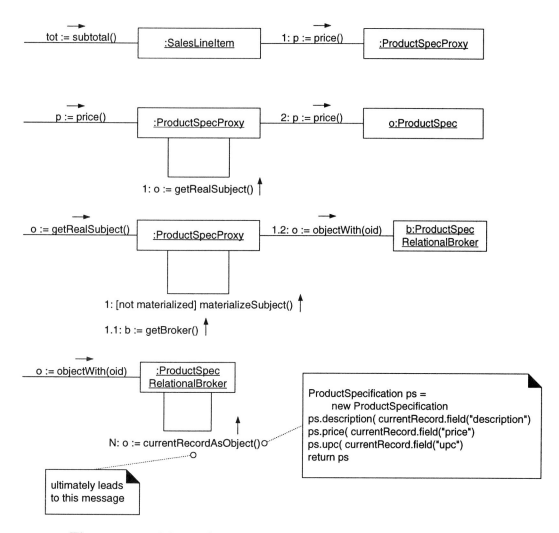

**Figure 38.18** Materializing a ProductSpecification instance.

## 38.18 Transaction Operations

Ultimately, a transaction is usually committed to a database. When a *commit* operation is invoked, objects are treated differently, depending on the their transaction state. For example, if an old object has been materialized from a database, but has not been modified, it is not necessary to write it back to the database. On the other hand, if it was modified, its associated database record must be updated.

## 38.18.1 Transaction State of Objects

Possible relevant transaction states are:

1. **New Clean**. New objects, unmodified.

2. **Old Clean**. Old objects materialized from a database, unmodified.

3. **New Dirty**. New objects, modified.

4. **Old Dirty**. Old objects materialized from a database, modified.

5. **New Delete**. New objects, to be deleted.

6. **Old Delete**. Old objects materialized from a database, to be deleted.

As previously discussed, a Database Broker will maintain separate caches for each of these states, and ensure that an object is in the appropriate cache.

When an object is first materialized, its broker places it in the Old Clean cache. When it is modified, it is moved into the Old Dirty cache. New objects start in the New Clean cache, and may move to the New Dirty cache when modified. If an object is marked to be deleted, it is moved into its respective Delete cache.

## 38.18.2 Getting Dirty

An object becomes *dirty* if any of its attributes are modified. The common way to signal getting dirty is within the mutator (setter) methods. For example:

```
// class ProductSpecification
void price(float p)
{
  price = p;
  BrokerServer.instance().dirty(this);
}
```

A Singleton Facade Pure Fabrication *BrokerServer* can be notified that a particular object is dirty. The *BrokerServer* will find the appropriate Database Broker for this class of object, and notify it that the object is dirty. The Database Broker will then move the object into a dirty cache. If it was a materialized object, it will be moved into the Old Dirty Cache. If it was a new object not yet in the database, it will be move to the New Dirty Cache.

Why send messages to a *BrokerServer* Facade object, as opposed to anything else? The reason is that it keeps the coupling of the domain objects to a minimum. They only know about one class that is part of the persistence framework—the *BrokerServer*. This supports Low Coupling, thus minimizing the impact of changes.

## 38.18.3  Getting Deleted

If an object is to be deleted it is necessary to explicitly record the fact, so that the database can be appropriate modified after a *commit* operation. As with the *dirty* signal, this can be done with a message to the *BrokerServer*. For example:

```
// class ProductCatalog
void removeProductSpec(ProductSpec p)
{
   // remove p from the collection of ProductSpecs
   productSpecs.remove(p);

   // inform the broker that p is to be deleted from the DB
   BrokerServer.instance().delete(p);
}
```

A Singleton Facade *BrokerServer* can be notified that a particular object is dirty. The *BrokerServer* will find the appropriate Database Broker for this class of object, and notify it that the object is dirty. The Database Broker will then move the object into a dirty cache. If it was a materialized object, it will be moved into the Old Dirty Cache. If it was a new object not yet in the database, it will be move to the New Dirty Cache.

## 38.18.4  The Commit Operation

When it is decided to commit the transaction, a *commit* message is sent to the *BrokerServer* Facade. Although any object may send this message, it is common for an Application Coordinator to have this responsibility.

```
BrokerServer.instance().commit();
```

The *BrokerServer--commit* method simply sends a *commit* message to each broker.

```
void BrokerServer.commit()
{
   for each broker b
           b.commit()
}
```

Within the time of a transaction, objects may be modified, created and deleted. Assuming that objects are in their appropriate transaction state cache (Old Dirty, and so on) here are the rules of what a commit should do:

■ New Clean Cache.

◻ insert in database

◻ move to Old Clean Cache.

■ Old Clean Cache.

◻ ignore; they haven't changed

- New Dirty Cache.
    - ◻ insert in database
    - ◻ move to Old Clean Cache.
- Old Dirty Cache.
    - ◻ update in database
    - ◻ move to Old Clean Cache.
- New Deleted Cache.
    - ◻ remove from cache
- Old Deleted Cache.
    - ◻ removed from database
    - ◻ remove from cache

## 38.18.5 The Rollback Operation

When it is decided to rollback the transaction, a *rollback* message is sent to the *BrokerServer* Facade. Although any object may send this message, it is common for an Application Coordinator to have this responsibility.

```
BrokerServer.instance().rollback();
```

The *BrokerServer--rollback* method simply sends a *rollback* message to each broker.

Here are the rules of what a commit should do:

- Old Clean Cache
    - ◻ ignore; they haven't changed
- All other caches
    - ◻ remove from cache

One of the advantages of consistently using a Virtual Proxy to an object rather than a direct reference is the effect in the case of a rollback. After the caches are flushed, all the Virtual Proxies will refer to unmaterialized objects rather than to modified objects in local memory. The next reference to a Virtual Proxy will cause the old object to be re-materialized from the persistent store; any changes to the object evaporated when the cache was flushed.

# 38.19   Searching for Objects in the Persistent Store

How is a record retrieved from a persistent store? The solution is dependent on the tools, libraries and operating environment. For example, in Microsoft operating system environments, one can use the DAO services within MFC. Further details are outside of the scope of this discussion.

Within the framework, the *RelationalPFWBroker--selectFirst(query)* method was defined to provide the service of finding the first record (row in a table) that met the query criteria. Its implementation varies depending on operating environment.

A Database Broker needs to provide two search patterns when retrieving records from a persistent store:

1.   Search by OID (the most common search criterion).

2.   Search by arbitrary criteria, such as a domain primary key (for example, Social Security Number).

When using a persistence framework there is the problem of *priming the pump*—by what criteria should the root object in a composition hierarchy be retrieved? Non-root objects in a composition hierarchy may be materialized using Virtual Proxies and searching by their OID as the lookup key. However, the OID of the root object will not normally be known. For example, consider materializing a *Sale* instance, its associated *SalesLineItems,* and their associated ProductSpecifications. Assuming the *Sale* was materialized and had references to Virtual Proxies for all its *SalesLineItems,* then the line items will be on-demand materialized based upon the OID values in the proxies. Similarly, if a *SalesLineItem* was materialized and had a reference to a Virtual Proxy for its ProductSpecification, then it too may be materialized by its OID value. However, if the OID of the root *Sale* object in this composition hierarchy is not known; how do we prime the pump and get this first *Sale* instance into memory?

This problem leads to the need for domain-oriented search capabilities, such as searching for *Sales* by their date and time, or some other appropriate primary key. For example, in the case of the *Sale*, the *SaleRelationalBroker* class may additionally provide a public method to materialize by date and time, as illustrated in Figure 38.19.

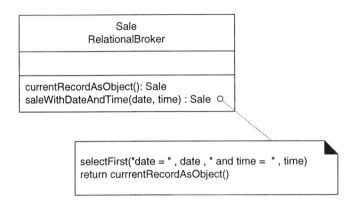

**Figure 38.19** Domain-oriented search capabilities.

# 38.20   Alternate Designs

## 38.20.1 *Metadata and Parameterized Brokers*

In contrast to creating a separate concrete Database Broker for each persistent object class, it is possible to define metadata (data about data) regarding the class and table mapping, the attribute and field name mapping, and so on. The metadata may be maintained in a *PersistentStoreMetadata* object. With this approach it is not necessary to create a large hierarchy of brokers. It is possible, for example, that the *RelationalPFWBroker* be a concrete class that is instantiated and parameterized with metadata for each persistent object class. No subclasses of *RelationalPFWBroker* would be necessary.

The metadata approach is more robust and flexible than the subclassing approach taken in the existing PFW framework, and is recommended for applications involving many persistent object classes and a rapidly changing schema. Since it is more complex to explain and implement, it will not be explored in detail. Please see the Reflection pattern in [BMRSS96] for a deeper discussion.

## 38.20.2 *Query Objects*

In contrast to the simple string queries illustrated in this discussion (for example, "OID = 123"), it is possible to create a *Query* class whose instances are parameterized with boolean expressions. The advantage of this scheme is the ability to abstract from any particular data manipulation language (say, SQL) and to manipulate and reason with queries (for example, compiling them into some more efficient form).

### 38.20.3 Changing Brokers and In-memory Database Brokers

It is both possible and desirable to create an In-Memory Broker that does not actually store objects in an external persistent store when a *commit* is signaled. This is useful during early development and testing, to avoid the performance impact of using a real broker, and the complexity of its complete implementation.

Because clients of all subclasses of *PFWBroker* use only a few general public methods, such as *objectWith(anOID)*, it is possible to unplug one broker and plug in another without any effect on the client objects. Thus, a developer can use an In-Memory Broker (Figure 38.20) for some period of time, and then later switch to a relational or flat file broker. This switch can be made by changing the *createBroker* Factory Method in the Virtual Proxy which specifies which broker to use.

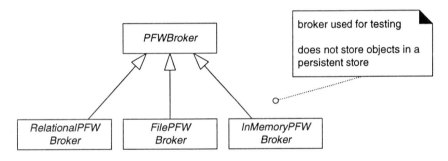

**Figure 38.20** In-memory Broker.

### 38.20.4 Transaction States versus Multiple Caches

Placing an object in one of the broker caches, such as the *OldClean* or *OldDirty* cache, is a way to remember the transaction state of the object. For a broker, it is an efficient mechanism. However, an alternate design is possible in which each object has an associated *TransactionState* object which indicates if it is old-and-clean, old-and-dirty, or so on. All objects can be in one cache, and the transaction state of the object is known via the associated state object rather than its cache membership.

Where should the *TransactionState* relationship be remembered? Because it is desirable not to add persistence knowledge directly in the domain object definitions, the recommended choices are:

■ If a common *PersistentObject* superclass is used, the state is an attribute defined in that class.

■ In a *Map* (*Dictionary* or *Hashtable*) maintained by the Broker. The *Map* key is the object, the associated *Map* value is the *TransactionState* of the object.

■ As an attribute of the *VirtualProxy*. The complication with this design is if there are multiple proxies related to the same real object, all proxies must remain synchronized.

In addition, each *TransactionState* class may possibly define a method that specifies what to do on a commit or rollback. And since the state objects probably do not maintain any information, they may also be singletons—only one instance of each class is needed in the application.

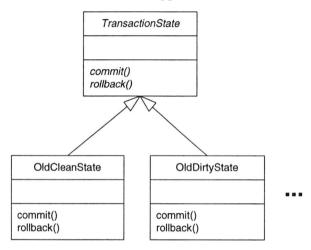

**Figure 38.21** Transaction states of persistent objects.

# 38.21  Unresolved Issues

This has been a very brief introduction to the problems and design solutions in a persistence framework. Many important issues have been glossed over, including:

■ Dematerializing objects. Briefly, concrete brokers must define an objectAsRecord method that transforms an object into a record. Dematerializing composition hierarchies requires collaboration between multiple brokers and the maintenance of associative tables (if a relational database is used).

■ Backpointers. A persistence framework sometimes tempts the designer to add pointers backwards to other objects which the object would not otherwise require.

■ Materialization and dematerialization of collections.

■ Error handling when a database operation fails.

■ Multiuser access and locking strategies.

■ Security—controlling access to the database.

# APPENDIX A. RECOM-MENDED READINGS

## General Object-Oriented Analysis and Design

Booch, G., 1994. *Object-Oriented Analysis and Design*. Redwood City, CA.: Benjamin/Cummings.

Coad, P. 1995. *Object Models: Stategies, Patterns and Applications*. Englewood Cliffs, NJ.: Prentice-Hall.

Coleman, D., *et al*. 1994. *Object-Oriented Development: The Fusion Method*. Englewood Cliffs, NJ.: Prentice-Hall.

Jacobson, I., *et al*. 1992. *Object-Oriented Software Engineering: A Use Case Driven Approach*. Reading, MA.: Addison-Wesley.

Rumbaugh, J., *et al*. 1991. *Object-Oriented Modelling and Design*. Englewood Cliffs, NJ.: Prentice-Hall.

## Conceptual Modeling

Fowler, M. 1996. *Analysis Patterns: Reusable Object Models*. Reading, MA.: Addison-Wesley.

Hay, D. 1996. *Data Model Patterns: Conventions of Thought*. NY, NY.: Dorset House.

Martin, J., and Odell, J. 1995. *Object-Oriented Methods: A Foundation*. Englewood Cliffs, NJ.: Prentice-Hall.

## Object-Oriented Design

Riel, A. 1996. *Object-Oriented Design Heuristics*. Reading, MA.: Addison-Wesley.

Wirfs-Brock, R., Wilkerson, B. and Wiener, L. 1990. *Designing Object-Oriented Software*. Englewood Cliffs, NJ.: Prentice-Hall.

## Patterns

Buschmann, F., Meunier, R., Rohnert, H., Sommerlad, P.,and Stal, M. 1996. *A System of Patterns*. West Sussex, England: Wiley.

Coad, P. 1995. *Object Models: Stategies, Patterns and Applications*. Englewood Cliffs, NJ.: Prentice-Hall.

Fowler, M. 1996. *Analysis Patterns: Reusable Object Models*. Reading, MA.: Addison-Wesley.

Gamma, E., Helm, R., Johnson, R., and Vlissides, J. 1995. *Design Patterns: Elements of Reusable Object-Oriented Software*. Reading, MA.: Addison-Wesley.

Riel, A. 1996. *Object-Oriented Design Heuristics*. Reading, MA.: Addison-Wesley.

various editors. *Pattern Languages of Program Design*. All volumes. Reading, MA.: Addison-Wesley.

## Requirements Analysis

Gause, D., and Weinberg, G. 1989. *Exploring Requirements*. NY, NY.: Dorset House.

Jacobson, I., *et al*. 1992. *Object-Oriented Software Engineering: A Use Case Driven Approach*. Reading, MA.: Addison-Wesley.

## The Unified Modeling Language

Booch, G., Jacobson, I., and Rumbaugh, J. 1997. The UML specification documents. Santa Clara, CA.: Rational Software Corp. Available at www.rational.com.

# APPENDIX B. SAMPLE DEVELOPMENT ACTIVITIES AND MODELS

# Sample Development Activities

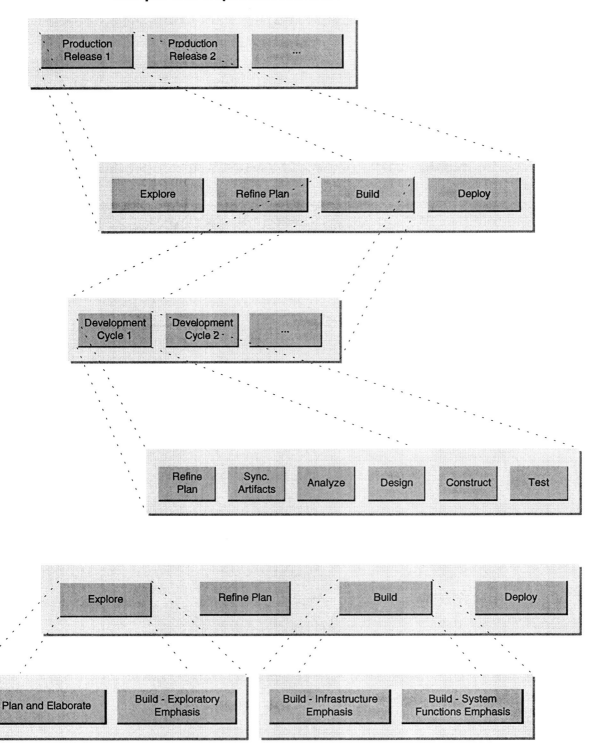

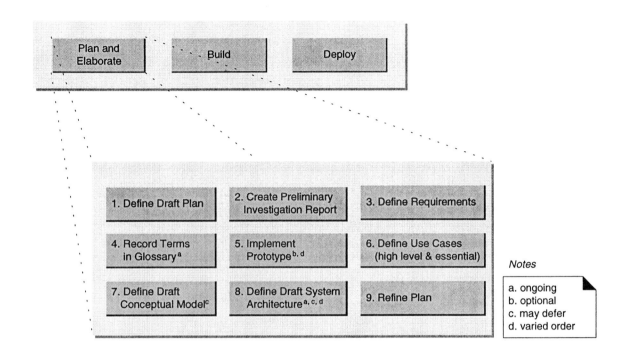

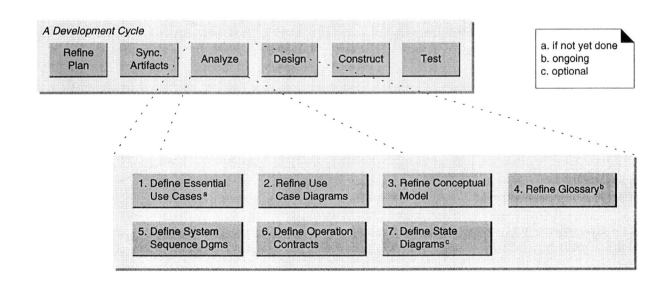

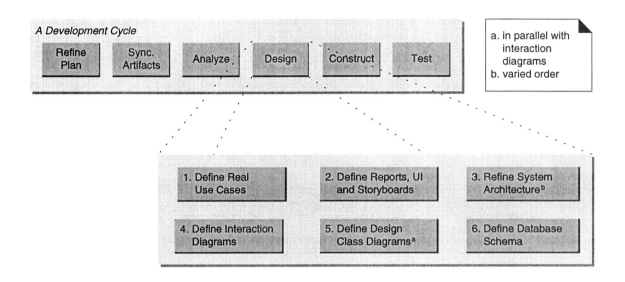

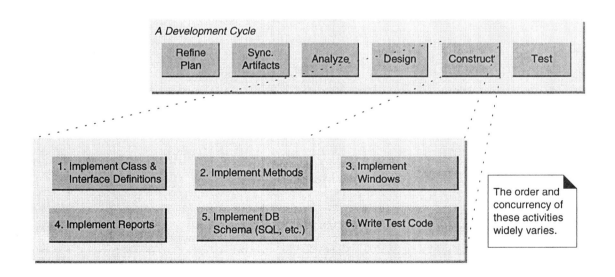

# Sample Models

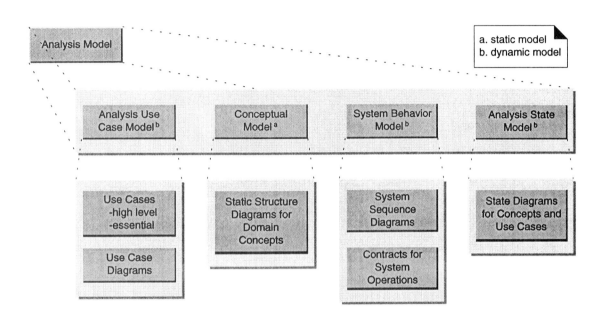

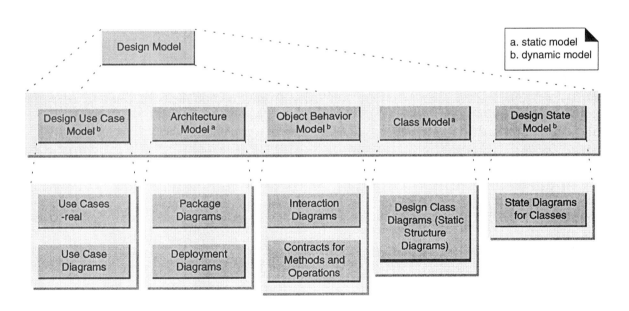

# BIBLIOGRAPHY

**Abbot83**   Abbott, R. 1983. Program Design by Informal English Descriptions. *Communications of the ACM* vol. 26(11).

**AIS77**   Alexander, C., Ishikawa, S., and Silverstein, M. 1977. *A Pattern Language—Towns-Building-Construction.* Oxford University Press.

**BC89**   Beck, K., and Cunningham, W. 1989. A Laboratory for Object-oriented Thinking. *Proceedings of OOPSLA 89.* SIGPLAN Notices, Vol. 24, No. 10.

**Beck94**   Beck, K. 1994. Patterns and Software Development. *Dr. Dobbs Journal.* Feb 1994.

**BJR97**   Booch, G., Jacobson, I., and Rumbaugh, J. 1997. The UML specification documents. Santa Clara, CA.: Rational Software Corp. See documents at www.rational.com.

**BMRSS96**   Buschmann, F., Meunier, R., Rohnert, H., Sommerlad, P.,and Stal, M. 1996. *A System of Patterns.* West Sussex, England: Wiley.

**Booch94**   Booch, G., 1994. *Object-Oriented Analysis and Design.* Redwood City, CA.: Benjamin/Cummings.

**Booch96**   Booch, G., 1996. *Object Solutions: Managing the Object-Oriented Project.* Menlo Park, CA.: Addison-Wesley.

**Brooks75**   Brooks, F., 1975. *The Mythical Man-Month.* Reading, MA.: Addison-Wesley.

**Brown96**   Brown, K., and Whitenack, B. 1996. Crossing Chasms. *Pattern Languages of Program Design* vol. 2. Reading, MA.: Addison-Wesley.

**Coad95**   Coad, P. 1995. *Object Models: Stategies, Patterns and Applications.* Englewood Cliffs, NJ.: Prentice-Hall.

**Coleman94**    Coleman, D., *et al.* 1994. *Object-Oriented Development: The Fusion Method.* Englewood Cliffs, NJ.: Prentice-Hall.

**Constantine97**    Constantine, L. 1997. The Case for Essential Use Cases. *Object Magazine* May 1997. NY, NY: SIGS Publications.

**Coplien95**    Coplien, J. 1995. *The History of Patterns.* See http://c2.com/cgi/wiki?HistoryOf-Patterns.

**Fowler96**    Fowler, M. 1996. *Analysis Patterns: Reusable Object Models.* Reading, MA.: Addison-Wesley.

**Gartner95**    Schulte, R., 1995. *Three-Tier Computing Architectures and Beyond.* Published Report. GartnerGroup.

**GHJV95**    Gamma, E., Helm, R., Johnson, R., and Vlissides, J. 1995. *Design Patterns.* Reading, MA.: Addison-Wesley.

**GW89**    Gause, D., and Weinberg, G. 1989. *Exploring Requirements.* NY, NY.: Dorset House.

**Jacobson92**    Jacobson, I., *et al.* 1992. *Object-Oriented Software Engineering: A Use Case Driven Approach.* Reading, MA.: Addison-Wesley.

**MO95**    Martin, J., and Odell, J. 1995. *Object-Oriented Methods: A Foundation.* Englewood Cliffs, NJ.: Prentice-Hall.

**Rumbaugh91**    Rumbaugh, J., *et al.* 1991. *Object-Oriented Modelling and Design.* Englewood Cliffs, NJ.: Prentice-Hall.

**Rumbaugh97**    Rumbaugh, J. 1997. Models Through the Development Process. *Journal of Object-Oriented Programming* May 1997. NY, NY: SIGS Publications.

**Sakkinen88**    Sakkinen, M. 1998. Comments on "the Law of Demeter" and C++. *SIGPLAN Notices* vol 23(12).

**Standish94**    anonymous. 1994. *Charting the Seas of Information Technology: Chaos.* Published Report. The Standish Group

**Wirfs-Brock93**    Wirfs-Brock, R. 1993. Designing Scenarios: Making the Case for a Use Case Framework. *Smalltalk Report* Nov-Dec 1993. NY, NY: SIGS Publications.

# GLOSSARY

**abstract class**  A class that can be used only as a superclass of some other class; no objects of an abstract class may be created except as instances of a subclass. An abstract class is typically used to define a common interface for a number of subclasses.

**abstract type**  A type such that all objects conforming to it must also conform to one of its subtypes.

**abstraction**  The act of concentrating the essential or general qualities of similar things. Also, the resulting essential characteristics of a thing.

**active object**  An object with its own thread of control.

**aggregation**  A property of an association representing a whole-part relationship and (usually) life-time containment.

**analysis**  An investigation of a domain that results in models describing its static and dynamic characteristics. It emphasizes questions of "what," rather than "how."

**architecture**  A description of the organization and structure of a system. Many different levels of architectures are involved in developing software systems, from physical hardware architecture to the logical architecture of an application framework.

**association**  A description of a related set of links between objects of two types.

**attribute**  A named characteristic or property of a type.

**class**  In the UML, "a description of a set of objects that share the same attributes, operations, methods, relationships, and semantics" [BJR97]. In this book, often used as a synonym for a UML "implemention class"—the software mechanism used to define and implement the attributes and methods for a particular type.

**class attribute**  A characteristic or property that is the same for all instances of a class. This information is usually stored in the class definition.

**class hierarchy**  A description of the inheritance relations between classes.

**class method**  A method that defines the behavior of the class itself, as opposed to the behavior of its instances.

**classification**  Classification defines a relation between a type and its instances. The classification mapping identifies the extension of a type.

**collaboration**  Two or more objects that participate in a client/server relationship in order to provide a service.

**component**  A discrete software module with an interface.

**composition**  The identification of a type in which each instance is comprised of other objects.

**concept**  A category of ideas or things. In this book, used to designate real-world things rather than software entities. A concept's intension is a description of its attributes, operations and semantics. A concept's extension is the set of instances or example objects that are members of the concept. Often defined as a synonym for type.

**concrete class**  A class that can have instances.

**concrete type**  A type that can have instances.

**conformance**  A relation between types such that if type X conforms to type Y, then values of type X are also members of type Y and satisfy the definition of type Y.

**constraint**  A restriction or condition on an element.

**constructor**  A special method called whenever an instance of a class is created in C++ or Java. The constructor often performs initialization actions.

**container class**  A class designed to hold and manipulate a collection of objects.

**contract**  Defines the responsibilities and post-conditions that apply to the use of an operation or method. Also used to refer to the set of all conditions related to an interface.

**coupling**  A dependency between elements (usually types, class, and subsystems), typically resulting from collaboration between the elements to provide a service.

**delegation**  The notion that an object can issue a message to another object in response to a message. The first object therefore delegates the responsibility to the second object.

**derivation**  The process of defining a new class by reference to an existing class and then adding attributes and methods The existing class is the superclass; the new class is referred to as the subclass or derived class.

**design**    A process that uses the products of analysis to produce a specification for implementing a system. A logical description of how a system will work.

**domain**    A formal boundary that defines a particular subject or area of interest.

**encapsulation**    A mechanism used to hide the data, internal structure, and implementation details of an object. All interaction with an object is through a public interface of operations.

**event**    A noteworthy occurrence.

**extension**    The set of objects to which a concept applies. The objects in the extension are the examples or instances of the concept.

**framework**    A set of collaborating abstract and concrete classes that may be used as a template to solve a related family of problems. It is usually extended via subclassing for application-specific behavior.

**functional decomposition**    The process of refining a problem solution by repeatedly decomposing a problem into smaller and smaller functional steps.

**generalization**    The activity of identifying commonality among concepts and defining supertype (general concept) and subtype (specialized concept) relationships. It is a way to construct taxonomic classifications among concepts which are then illustrated in type hierarchies. Subtypes conform to supertypes in terms of intension and extension.

**inheritance**    A feature of object-oriented programming languages by which classes may be specialized from more general superclasses. Attributes and method definitions from superclasses are automatically acquired by the subclass.

**instance**    An individual member of a type or class.

**instance method**    A method whose scope is an instance. Invoked by sending a message to an instance.

**instance variable**    As used in Java and Smalltalk, an attribute of an instance.

**instantiation**    The creation of an instance of a type or class.

**intension**    The definition of a concept.

**interface**    A set of signatures of public operations.

**link**    A connection between two objects; an instance of an association.

| | |
|---|---|
| **message** | The mechanism by which objects communicate; usually a request to execute a method. |
| **metamodel** | A model that defines other models. The UML metamodel defines the element types of the UML, such as Type and Operation. |
| **method** | In the UML, the specific implementation or algorithm of an operation for a class. Informally, the software procedure that can be executed in response to a message. |
| **model** | A description of static and/or dynamic characteristics of a subject area, portrayed through a number of views (usually diagrammatic or textual). |
| **multiplicity** | The number of objects permitted to participate in an association. |
| **object** | In the UML, a instance of a class that encapsulates state and behavior. More informally, an example of a thing. |
| **object identity** | The feature that the existence of an object is independent of any values associated with the object. |
| **object-oriented analysis** | The investigation of a problem domain or system in terms of domain concepts, such as object types, associations, and state changes. |
| **object-oriented design** | The specification of a logical software solution in terms of software objects, such as their classes, attributes, methods, and collaborations. |
| **object-oriented programming language** | A programming language that supports the concepts of encapsulation, inheritance, and polymorphism. |
| **OID** | Object Identifier. |
| **operation** | In the UML, "a service that can requested from an object to effect behavior" [BJR97]. An operation has a signature, specified by its name and parameters, and it is invoked via a message. A method is an implementation of an operation with a specific algorithm. |
| **pattern** | A pattern is a named description of a problem, solution, when to apply the solution, and how to apply the solution in new contexts. |
| **persistence** | The enduring storage of the state of an object. |
| **persistent object** | An object that can survive the process or thread that created it. A persistent object exists until it is explicitly deleted. |
| **polymorphic operation** | The same operation implemented differently by two or more types. |

| | |
|---|---|
| **polymorphism** | The concept that two or more types of objects can respond to the same message in different ways, using polymorphic operations. Also, the ability to define polymorphic operations. |
| **post-condition** | A constraint that must hold true after the completion of an operation. |
| **pre-condition** | A constraint that must hold true before an operation is requested. |
| **private** | A scoping mechanism used to restrict access to class members so that other objects cannot see them. Normally applied to all attributes, and to some methods. |
| **public** | A scoping mechanism used to make members accessible to other objects. Normally applied to some methods, but not to attributes, since public attributes violates encapsulation. |
| **pure data values** | Data types for which unique instance identity is not meaningful, such as numbers, booleans, and strings. In the UML, also known as DataTypes. |
| **qualified association** | An association whose membership is partitioned by the value of a qualifier. |
| **receiver** | The object to which a message is sent. |
| **recursive association** | An association where the source and the destination are the same object type. |
| **requirements specifications** | A document describing what a software system does—its functions and attributes. Usually written from a user's point of view. |
| **responsibility** | A service or group of services provided by a type; a responsibility embodies one or more of the purposes or obligations of a type. |
| **role** | A named end of an association to indicate its purpose. |
| **state** | The condition of an object between events. |
| **state transition** | A change of state for an object; something that can be signaled by an event. |
| **state diagram** | A form of finite state machine used to describe the dynamic behavior of a type. |
| **subclass** | A specialization of another class (the superclass). A subclass inherits the attributes and methods of the superclass. |
| **subtype** | A specialization of another type (the supertype) that conforms to the intension and extension of the supertype. |
| **superclass** | A class from which another class inherits attributes and methods. |

**supertype** In a generalization-specialization relation, the more general type; an object that has subtypes.

**transition** A relationship between states that is traversed if the specified event occurs and the guard condition met.

**type** In the UML, a description of a set of like objects with attributes and operations, but which may not include any methods. Some authors define type and concept as synonyms.

**use case** A narrative, textual description of the sequence of events and actions that occur when a user participates in a dialog with a system during a meaningful process.

**visibility** The ability to see or have reference to an object.

# INDEX

## A

abstract class  347
abstract method  347
abstract type  345
    UML notation  346
abstract use case  53
actor  52
    initiator  52
    participating  53
aggregation  198, 359
    composite  359
    shared  360
analysis  6
analysis and design
    definition  6
analysis and design models  29–32
analysis model  31
application coordinator  287
architecture  437
architecture package diagram  276
artifact  30
    relationships  31
association  105
    adding  105–118
    criteria for useful  106
    emphasize need-to-know  115
    finding with list  107
    guidelines  110
    high-priority ones  109
    level of detail  109
    link  173
    multiple between types  112
    multiplicity  110
    naming  111
    navigability  264
    qualified  365
    recursive  366
    reflexive  366
    role names  362
    UML notation  106
associative type  357
asynchronous message
    UML notation  430
attribute  120
    adding  119–130
    and quantities  125
    derived  128, 364
    no foreign keys  123

    non-primitive types  124
    pure data value  121, 122
    simple  121
    UML notation  120
    valid types  120

## B

behavior
    system  137, 147
bloated controller  210
Bridge  469
business process reengineering  57

## C

callback  286
class  102
    abstract  347
    UML notation  257
class definition
    from design class diagram  299
class diagram
    design  257
class hierarchy  348
code
    creating  295–308
    Java solution  309–313
cohesion  203
    low  210
collaboration diagram  9, 12, 169
    and other artifacts  218
    collections  181
    conditional messages  180
    creating  172, 217–245
    example  170
    instance creation  177
    instances  173
    iteration  176
    links  173
    message sequencing  179
    message syntax  175
    message to class object  182
    messages  174
    multiobject  181
    mutually exclusive conditionals  180
    notation  167–183
    parameters  174

# P

package 275
  dependencies 350
  ownership 350
  reference 350
  UML notation 275, 350
package diagram 276
  creating 349–354
partition 349
pattern 4, 189
  Bridge 469
  Command 214, 421
  Controller 206
  Creator 197
  Device Proxy 400, 418
  Do It Myself 196, 394
  Don't Talk to Strangers 401
  Expert 193
  Facade 418
  Factory Method 473
  GRASP 190
  High Cohesion 203
  Indirection 399
  Law of Demeter 401
  Low Coupling 200
  Model-View Separation 224, 281
  names 190
  Polymorphism 394
  Pure Fabrication 396
  Remote Proxy 415
  Singleton 413
  State 158
  Template Method 463
  Virtual Proxy 468
pattern-Publish-Subscribe 285
patterns
  Gang of Four 405
persistence framework 456
  alternate designs 484
  design 455–486
  key ideas 459
  materialization 464
  pattern-Cache Management 467
  pattern-Database Broker 462
  pattern-Object Identifier 461
  pattern-Representing Objects as Tables 460
  representing relationships in tables 475
  requirements 458
  searching for objects 483
  transaction operations 479
persistent objects 456
point-of-sale case study
  introduction 35–38
Polymorphism 394
  application 411
polymorphism 394
postcondition
  a metaphor 151
primary use case 58

property specification
  UML notation 428
Proxy
  Device Proxy 400
  Remote Proxy 415
  Virtual Proxy 468
Publish-Subscribe 285
pure data value 121, 122
Pure Fabrication 396

# Q

qualified association 365
qualifier 365

# R

real use case 59, 163
recursive association 366
reference attribute 300
reflexive association 366
Remote Proxy 415
requirements 41
  creating 39–46
requirements analysis 8
responsibilities
  and interaction diagrams 188
  and methods 187
  GRASP patterns 190
  patterns 189
responsibility 187
  doing 187
  knowing 188
responsibility assignment 9
  importance 5
reverse engineering 298
role 110
  versus concept 363
role name 301

# S

scheduling
  by use case ranking 76
  use case versions 77
secondary use case 58
sequence diagram 137, 169
simple attribute 121
Singleton 413
  UML shorthand notation 415
software development process 17
specialization 335
state 379
  modeling 347
state diagram 381
  creating 379–389
  example 384
  for use case 382

# _Sample UML and Related Notation_

## Use Cases

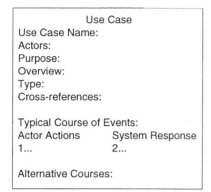

Use Case
Use Case Name:
Actors:
Purpose:
Overview:
Type:
Cross-references:

Typical Course of Events:
Actor Actions     System Response
1...                    2...

Alternative Courses:

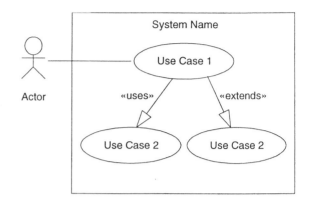

System Name

Actor

Use Case 1

«uses»          «extends»

Use Case 2     Use Case 2

## Static Structure Diagrams

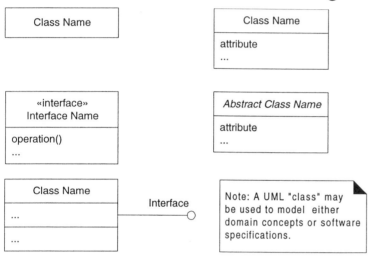

Class Name

Class Name

attribute
...

Software Specification Class Name

attribute
attribute : type
attribute : type = initial value
classAttribute
/derivedAttribute
...

method1()
method2(parameter : Type) : return type
abstractMethod()
+publicMethod()
-privateMethod()
#protectedMethod()
classMethod()
...

«interface»
Interface Name

operation()
...

Abstract Class Name

attribute
...

Class Name

...

...

Interface

Note: A UML "class" may
be used to model either
domain concepts or software
specifications.

**Associations:**

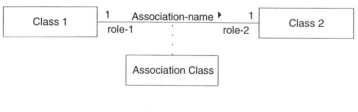

Class 1      1   Association-name ▸   1   Class 2
                role-1              role-2

Association Class

**Multiplicity:**

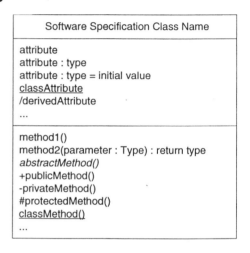

*          Class        zero or more;
                         "many"

1..*       Class        one or more

1..40      Class        one to forty

5          Class        exactly five

3, 5, 8    Class        exactly three,
                        five or eight

**Generalization:**

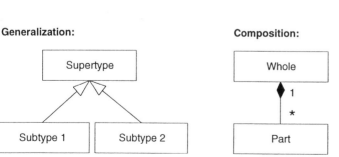

Supertype

Subtype 1     Subtype 2

**Composition:**

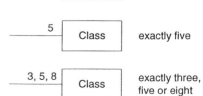

Whole

1
*

Part